CRISTIAN BOARIU

DAILY WITH GOD

"For our heart shall rejoice in Him,
because we have trusted in His holy name."
Psalm 33:21

CRISTIAN BOARIU

DAILY WITH GOD

365 DEVOTIONS *for everyday* LIVING

TOTAL PUBLISHING HOUSE

This book is a product of Cristi Boariu Ministries, a mission that seeks to evangelize exclusively through text, audio, and video messages. It is self-funded by selling Christian materials, which is why we are grateful if you are willing to share with others the resources that have edified you spiritually, using our website: www.cristiboariu.com

CIP description of the National Library of Romania

BOARIU, CRISTIAN
Daily with God : 365 Devotions for Every Day / Cristian Boariu. - Bucharest: Total Publishing House, 2024
ISBN 978-606-9643-75-4

2

Translated from Romanian by Tabita Măgduț

Editor: Monica Nae
Cover graphics: Denis Felvinczi
DTP: Adrian Gligorașcu

Total Publishing House
www.totalpublishing.ro
ISBN 978-606-9643-75-4

With heartfelt gratitude, I extend my deepest thanks to:

God, whose grace, love, and guidance illuminate my path and sustain me through every season of life.

My beloved wife, Crina, whose unwavering love, support, and partnership bring immeasurable joy and strength to my journey.

My precious children, Grace, Elisa, Ianis, Lucas, Salome, Marcus, Matias, and Amias, whose laughter, curiosity, and love fill our home with warmth and purpose.

My parents, Beniamin and Aurica, for their unconditional love, wisdom, and sacrifices that have shaped my character and nurtured my faith.

My parents-in-law, Lidia and Petru, for their kindness, acceptance, and the blessings of family they have bestowed upon us.

My pastor, Cornel Raducanu, whose faithful leadership, wisdom, and counsel inspire and challenge me to grow deeper in my relationship with God.

My church family, whose fellowship, prayers, and support create a nurturing community where I can grow in faith and serve alongside fellow believers.

May the gratitude expressed on these pages reflect the depth of my appreciation for each of you and the profound impact you have had on my life.

PREFACE

Dear Reader,

It is with deep gratitude and joy that I present to you this collection of 365 spiritual devotions. As I reflect on the journey that has led to the creation of this book, I am filled with awe at the faithfulness of God and the countless ways He has revealed Himself to me.

Each devotion in this book is a testament to the richness of the spiritual life and the transformative power of encountering God's presence daily. Through moments of prayer, reflection, and meditation on Scripture, I have sought to capture the essence of our shared journey of faith.

In crafting these devotions, my heart's desire has been to provide you, dear reader, with a source of inspiration, encouragement, and guidance for your own spiritual walk. Whether you are seeking solace in times of trial, guidance in moments of decision, or simply a deeper connection with the Divine, my hope is that you will find something meaningful within these pages.

I invite you to embark on this journey with me, as we explore the depths of God's love, grace, and truth together. May each devotion serve as a stepping stone on your path to spiritual growth and a reminder of the abundant blessings that await those who seek God wholeheartedly.

May this book be a companion to you in your daily walk with the Lord, guiding you closer to His heart and renewing your spirit each day. As you delve into these pages, may you be refreshed, inspired, and transformed by the power of God's Word and His presence in your life.

With heartfelt blessings,

Cristian Boariu

JANUARY 1

NO EXCUSES

You have a new chance! A new beginning! A new year in which you can achieve something great!

Yet, there is something that can hinder you. Do you know what it is?

Excuses.

In the following lines, I want to list ten commonly encountered excuses and some solutions for them.

1. "I am too tired!"

Set your priorities in such a way to see if what exhausts you is worth the effort.

2. "I don't have enough time!"

Classify your daily tasks (both material and spiritual) into two categories: urgent and important. Start with the important ones.

Remember that we always are available for what we love. Therefore, the problem is often not the clock but the heart.

3. "It's not worth getting involved!"

Do not underestimate your involvement. Each of us has a specific contribution to teamwork in our families, at work, and at church.

4. "I don't know how to do it!"

No one was born an expert. Everything is learned. The issue is not with the hands but with the mind. The hand executes what the brain commands. If the brain is willing to learn, our external body parts will put into practice all the accumulated knowledge.

Humbly ask questions! Seek clarification! It's not bad not to know; it's bad not to want to learn.

5. "I'm not prepared enough!"

We all make mistakes in the learning process. But it's better to make mistakes while working than to make the biggest mistake: do nothing. Experience is gained through discipline and continuous effort.

6. "It can be done without me!"

If it can be done without you at work, it can be done without you on payday. If it can be done without you in ministry, it can be done without you on the reward day.

7. "I don't feel motivated enough!"

Rejoice in the small steps you have taken so far.

8. "I don't have the necessary resources!"

Be creative! See what you have at hand. Humanity has come this far for 6,000 years because someone did what they could with what they had.

9. "I'll do it later!"

Everything you postpone for another day might remain undone.

10. "I'm not paid enough!"

Your compensation depends on your involvement. Do you want to earn more at work? Look for solutions, not excuses.

Do you want to earn more in eternal life?

"But this I say: He who sows sparingly will also reap sparingly, and he who sows bountifully will also reap bountifully." – 2 Corinthians 9:6

For this year, I hope that you do not use these excuses. Be a resolute, hard-working, disciplined, and passionate person in the ministry to which you are called, regardless of the field of that work. You can only reach the top by helping others get there. However, you can influence others only by becoming a role model for them.

The year ahead has much to offer to those who roll up their sleeves and get to work, but almost nothing to give to those who seek excuses...

I wish you success in your work!

Say NO to excuses!

January 2

THEY ALL RETURNED…

"Let your gentleness be known to all men. The Lord is at hand." – Philippians 4:5

Tim Kimmel tells the story of a woman who was a role model through her life. I will relay it in a few lines without adding further comments.

"In 1921, Lewis Lawes became the chief of the Sing Sing prison guard. At that time, no other prison regime was as tough as Sing Sing's. But when Lawes retired 20 years later, the prison had become a humanitarian institution. Those who studied the system credited Lawes with the change, but when asked about the secret of the transformation, he said, 'It's all due to my wonderful wife, Kathryn, who is buried beyond the prison walls!'

Kathryn Lawes was a young mother with three small children when her husband began working at the prison.

Everyone warned her from the start that she should never go inside the prison walls, but nothing stopped Kathryn!

When the first basketball game inside the prison took place, she walked into the gym with her three children and sat down in the stands next to the inmates. Her conviction was, 'My husband and I intend to take care of these people, and I believe they will take care of me too! I have nothing to fear!' She continued to get to know them and their records.

Once, she discovered that one of the convicted murderers was blind, so she paid him a visit. Holding his hand, she asked, 'Do you read Braille?'

'What is Braille?' he replied.

Kathryn taught him how to read. Years later, his transformed heart would cry for her.

At one point, Kathryn found a deaf-mute in prison. She went to school to learn sign language. Many people said that Kathryn Lawes was the embodiment of Jesus in Sing Sing prison from 1921 to 1937.

One day, Kathryn was killed in a car accident. The next morning, Lewis Lawes did not come to work, so his deputy took his place.

Almost instantly, the prisoners seemed to know that something was wrong. The next day, her lifeless body rested at home in a coffin, three-quarters of a mile from the prison.

When the guard took his morning walk, he was shocked to see a large crowd, consisting of the toughest and most insensitive murderers, gathered like a herd of animals at the main gate. Approaching, he noticed tears of pain and sadness on the faces of the inmates. He knew how much they loved Kathryn!

Then he turned to them and said, 'Okay, guys, you can go. But be careful and come back tonight!' Then he opened the gate, and a crowd of murderers walked out, without any guards, for three-quarters of a mile, lining up in front of the coffin to pay a final tribute to Kathryn Lawes. And they all came back that evening! All of them!"

January 3

CHOICES

"And if it seems evil to you to serve the Lord, choose for yourselves this day whom you will serve, whether the gods which your fathers served that were on the other side of the River, or the gods of the Amorites, in whose land you dwell. But as for me and my house, we will serve the Lord." — Joshua 24:15

Each of us is born the same, but the trajectory of our lives differs based on the choices we make. Our choices are determined by our values and principles.

If my core values are material things, every day I will make choices that bring me more of these things. If my values are spiritual, my choices will consequently focus on what God has entrusted me to do.

Each decision will influence your future because choices define habits. Ultimately, life is composed of habits. You cannot directly decide your future, but your habits will decide your future.

At the same time, our choices are influenced by external factors such as friends, family, the news we read, our ideals about life, etc. Therefore, I must be careful with these external factors because they will determine whether I make wrong or right choices.

If we could turn back time, wouldn't we change some of our past choices? However, we are masters only of today's choices.

Therefore, Joshua said, "Choose today!"

Because tomorrow you will be what you choose today.

Next year, you will be what you choose this year.

And in eternity, you will be what you choose during your lifetime...

JANUARY 4

THE BEE AND THE FLY

"Dead flies putrefy the perfumer's ointment, and cause it to give off a foul odor; so does a little folly to one respected for wisdom and honor." – Ecclesiastes 10:1

A bee will never engage in a conversation with a fly with the goal of convincing it that honey is better than garbage.

We must learn something very important from this, namely, that you cannot tell a person what to look for and where to go as long as their inner nature is not changed.

As long as a thief is not convinced in his heart that stealing is a sin, he will not stop looking for the next victim. The problem is not the stolen CD player, but the corrupt character.

It is useless to tell a habitual gossiper that they`ve got the wrong person or that their gossip is not true. The problem is not that he got the wrong person to gossip about, but the character of the gossiper himself. The problem of a broken bucket is not with the water it carries, but with the hole it has.

Sometimes we should focus on the pollen entrusted to us instead of engaging in endless debates with flies.

Jesus did not endlessly try to convert the Pharisees and scribes. He did not perform miracles in front of Herod. And He did not lecture Pilate.

Some people are not receptive to our words and endless knocks on their doors. If a person does not sincerely desire change, there is absolutely no chance of conversion.

Focus on the honey you need to produce daily. Focus on a strong faith in Jesus, on the sneakers that need to be taken to the orphan, and on the bag of potatoes that needs to reach a widow.

Let those who deal with garbage keep on getting dirty.

I have not seen a fly coming out of a dumpster with the scent of roses on its wings.

Whoever wants to produce honey should stop going to the gatherings where flies are the keynote speakers.

January 5

BOSS OR LEADER?

I had to go somewhere the other day, and I told one of my children: "Lucas, you are in charge of the house and your little siblings until I come back!"

"So, Dad, you mean I am the boss?" he asked with a genuine smile on his face.

His question made me think. At his age, I'm not surprised by it. However, I am surprised by those who say they are mature and yet they want a certain position without any of its responsibilities. They want to be the first without washing the feet of others. They want to give orders but do not want to serve. They want to be in charge but do not want to sacrifice.

Do not forget that you are not a boss of the church but a leader; one whom God has placed there for a time. A boss gives others as an example to be followed, but a leader sets an example himself.

"Not as being lords over those entrusted to you, but being examples to the flock." – 1 Peter 5:3

Do not forget that you are not a boss in your family but a leader. The boss bangs his fist on the table, but the leader is ready, if necessary, to change the baby`s diaper.

Do not forget that you are not a boss at work.

A boss does whatever he wants. A leader listens to the opinions of the entire team and makes the necessary decisions by considering the people he leads.

A boss criticizes and discourages. A leader provides motivating and constructive criticism.

A boss leads with tyranny, threats, and constraints. A leader leads with love and kindness.

A boss demands results without providing the necessary resources. A leader inspires and provides everything the team needs to achieve the necessary performance.

Be a leader wherever God has placed you! There are enough bosses...

JANUARY 6

TODAY...

Today, I think about Maria and all the children with butterfly disease. With her face all burnt, she lives in a foster home, and her father is the only one still coming to see her...

Today, I think about a 48-year-old mother who passed away a few days ago. Three out of her seven children are still single... How many orphans weep during these holidays?

Today, I think about the lady who asked me several times last year for morphine. She does not want a ski vacation in Austria nor a vacation in Dubai, just some morphine... Do you understand what I`m saying? Morphine! To relieve her excruciating pain.

Today, I think about Andriy, who died on the front lines in Ukraine a few days ago. His wife had a heart attack when she received the news. Two children were left orphaned...

Today, I think about Ukrainian and Russian soldiers who are fighting for the greed of a godless man. I think about the tens of thousands of parents who, at the end of 2022, did not wish for fireworks or firecrackers but rather for their children to enter through their house door one more time...

Today, I think about spouses betrayed by infidelity. About the children who, in 2022, were divided between parents in the courtrooms of Romania, along with the washing machine and the ironing machine. What kind of joy can the tears of betrayal still bring?

Today, I think about the elderly who calculate their pension money carefully, to make ends meet for the electricity bill. They stare at the phone that rings less and less to ask them how they`ve been...

Today, I think about the people in prisons. About the regrets of those who lost not an iPhone but their freedom.

Today, I think about the thousands of gifts distributed to poor children. We all do good deeds on Christmas. But how do we tell them that their next gifts will come only a year from now?

Today, I think about Anastasia. She wrote to her mother who left for England, asking her to come home... One in three Romanian children does not have his parents living with him...

Who are you thinking about?

January 7

BAGGAGE CONTROL

When we go to the airport, both we and the baggage we want to take with us are scanned. Why? Does security have something personal against us? Not at all. However, safety rules are very clear and prohibit the transport of certain objects on board the aircraft.

For those who have walked with God, the end of life promises a final flight. A flight to God's paradise. And for that flight, a thorough check is made on us and the baggage we carry.

"Pursue peace with all people, and holiness, without which no one will see the Lord." – Hebrews 12:14

Certain qualities are checked for this flight. Peace and holiness are not optional but mandatory. Boarding the aircraft heading to heaven will be denied to those who always sought to sow hatred among others and always spread words that destroyed relationships, as well as for those who could not forgive. The promise of paradise is conditioned by holiness, by avoiding sin, and by living a righteous life.

At the final check, immorality, greed, and idol worshipping are prohibited.

"For this you know, that no fornicator, unclean person, nor covetous man, who is an idolater, has any inheritance in the kingdom of Christ and God." – Ephesians 5:5

Do not play with such things! Any attitude on this list will result in boarding denial!

"Now the works of the flesh are evident, which are: adultery, fornication, uncleanness, lewdness, idolatry, sorcery, hatred, contentions, jealousies, outbursts of wrath, selfish ambitions, dissensions, heresies, envy, murders, drunkenness, revelries, and the like; of which I tell you beforehand, just as I also told you in time past, that those who practice such things will not inherit the kingdom of God." – Galatians 5:19-21

Is there any other similar state of sin in which you consciously and continuously live?

Bow down on your knees, ask God for forgiveness, and start a new life!

The preparation for the flight is done now, not at the time of departure.

January 8

LOVE THAT DELAYS

"Now Jesus loved Martha and her sister and Lazarus. So when He heard that he was sick, He stayed two more days in the place where He was." – John 11:5-6

When something serious happens to a dear friend and we truly care about him, isn't it true that we rush to help him?

During His time on this earth, Jesus had a few people closer to Him – people to whom He felt more attached. Among them were Martha, Mary, and Lazarus.

When illness unexpectedly came into their home, they sent for Jesus. They had this assurance that He could solve their problem.

Everyone imagined that Jesus would come immediately, that He would run to get there as soon as possible – before the disease worsened and while Lazarus still breathed. However, there is something interesting in this narrative, namely, the conjunction "so" which means "therefore," "consequently". Freely translated, the verse says this:

As a result of the fact that Jesus loved Martha and Mary, when He heard that Lazarus was sick, He stayed two more days in the place where He was...

What does that mean? Can delaying sometimes be the consequence of love? Can you love a God who delays when you cry out to Him? A God who says, "Wait!" when you are in agony?

I noticed two reasons for this delay. The first is implicit. The delay can be the test of faith. The wait is the test of our patience. The delayed response is the test of our faithfulness.

If you truly love Me, trust in Me. I don't delay just to set you ablaze. Nor to disappoint you or to mock you. I delay in order to test you, to see if you truly love Me when I do what I want and not what you want!

The second reason for the delayed love is clearly stated by Jesus:

"When Jesus heard that, He said, 'This sickness is not unto death, but for the glory of God, that the Son of God may be glorified through it.'" – John 11:4

Jesus means to say here that He delays so that the miracle may be greater. *You have seen healings before, but this time I have something more precious for you:*

a resurrection! And this resurrection's ultimate purpose is not to amaze you but to glorify My Father!

We should all ask ourselves: Can we be faithful even when prayers do not have the answer we have hoped for? Can we remain in love with the Sovereign God even when the answer is, "Wait!"? Can we stay dependent on a love that does not always come in time but allows itself to be delayed?

Let's not forget the essential:

Even when it seems to us that He is delayed, Jesus comes on time...

JANUARY 9

MY STRENGTH

It was the summer of 1974 when brother Nicolae Moldoveanu[1] was called once again by the secret services (Securitate) to be interrogated. As usual, he was threatened and subjected to all kinds of pressures aimed at stopping him from the spiritual work he was doing with so much passion.

In those moments, he thought again of the Lord Jesus` words which say that those who will serve Him will be persecuted. Therefore, instead of complaining about suffering, Nicolae Moldoveanu chose once again to trust in the One who can alleviate all suffering!

When he returned home from the secret services, he was inspired to write a song. I wish that through these verses, God speaks to you and gives you the strength to endure any suffering:

My strength, my strength is You, O Spirit of life!
Through You, I have and will have a greater victory.
My strength, my strength! Through You, I have and will have
A greater victory.

Let us take inspiration from the unwavering faith of Nicolae Moldoveanu. Despite the immense trials and tribulations, his steadfast trust in God and his decision to glorify Him through music serve as a beacon of hope and resilience. May we also find solace and strength in our faith, turning to God in moments of distress, and letting His eternal love be our guiding light through all of life's adversities.

---

[1] Nicolae Moldoveanu was born on February 3, 1922, Movileni commune, Tecuci county, currently Galați. He died on July 12, 2007 in Sibiu. He was a Romanian Christian composer, poet and writer.

JANUARY 10

GEORGE HARLEY

In 1926, George Harley founded a medical mission in an ethnic group in Liberia, 8,000 miles away from his home and family. The locals were receptive and helped him build a clinic and a chapel. Harley treated more than ten thousand patients per year. In the first five years, however, no person from the tribe visited his chapel.

Shortly after he arrived with his wife, she gave birth to their first child, Robert. When he was almost five years old, Robert fell ill with tropical fever. Although his father, being a doctor, tried all the treatments he knew, the fever raged, and soon the disease took the boy's life. The parents were overwhelmed with grief.

After building a coffin and placing Robert in it, Harley headed to a meadow to find a place to dig a grave. One of the village elders saw him and offered to help carry the coffin. After they covered the grave with dirt, Harley could no longer bear the pain and began to cry uncontrollably.

The old man looked at him for a while, amazed by Harley's reaction. Then, suddenly, he jumped up and ran back on the trail through the jungle, shouting, "The white man, the white man cries just like us!"

That evening, while Harley and his wife were inside their cabin, filled with sadness, they heard a knock on the door. There stood the chief and almost every other man, woman, and child from the village. They returned again the following Sunday and filled the chapel. They wanted to hear about Jesus. Everything changed when the villagers saw the tears of the missionary.

Everything changes when we know that Jesus came among us and sought us. He looked like us, wept like us, was hungry and thirsty like us. Therefore, He understands our needs and pains.

Perhaps it's time for us to do as those native people... Seek not just the physical healing but also the spiritual healing.

Let us fill the churches. Hospitals are already full...

JANUARY 11

LOVE TRIUMPHED

Richard Wurmbrand[2] recounts an incident that should make us all ponder deeply:

"In the Târgu-Ocna prison[3], there was a very young prisoner named Matchevici. He had been imprisoned at the age of 18. Due to torture, he had become seriously ill with tuberculosis.

His family somehow learned about his very grave health condition and, with great difficulty, sent him a hundred vials of streptomycin, which could have made the difference between life and death.

The officer in charge of the prison policy called Matchevici and showed him the package, saying, 'Here is the medicine that can save your life, but officially, you are not allowed to receive anything from your family. Personally, I would like to help you. You are young. I don't want you to die in prison. Help me, so I can help you in return. Give me information about the other prisoners so that I can justify to my superiors why I gave you the medicine.'

Matchevici replied: 'I don't want to stay alive and be ashamed when I look in the mirror, seeing the face of a traitor. I cannot accept that. I prefer to die.'

The security officer shook his hand and said, 'Congratulations, I expected no less from you. Some prisoners, claiming to be communists, denounce you and play both sides. We don't trust them. These traitors inform us about your actions. If you provide information on them, you can save your life.'

Matchevici responded just as promptly as the first time, 'I am a disciple of Jesus, the One from whom I learned to love my enemies. Those who betray us do us a lot of harm indeed, but I cannot respond in kind. I cannot give you any information about them. I feel sorry for them and pray for their souls. I regret, but I do not wish to have any connection with the communists.'

Matchevici returned from the conversation with the political officer and died in the same cell where I was. I saw him die, glorifying God. Love triumphed even over the natural thirst for life."[4]

---

[2] Richard Wurmbrand was born on March 24, 1909, in Bucharest, Romania. He died on February 17, 2001, in Torrance, California, USA. He was a Romanian Christian minister, author, and founder of the Voice of the Martyrs.

[3] Târgu-Ocna prison: A notorious prison in Romania, used during the communist regime to detain and persecute political prisoners, including many Christians and intellectuals. It was known for its harsh conditions and the severe treatment of inmates.

[4] Richard Wurmbrand, *Tortured for Christ*, Living Sacrifice Book Company, 1998.

January 12

THE LIGHT IN THE DARKNESS

"Unto the upright there arises light in the darkness; He is gracious, and full of compassion, and righteous." – Psalm 112:4

Navigating the sea of this world is not without dangers. Perils are at every step, avoiding rocks is a constant challenge, and avoiding a shipwreck is not easy at all.

However, the psalmist gives us an extraordinary hope: for the one who lives according to God's will, a light will appear in the critical moments of life. A ray of sunshine. Guidance. A lighthouse in the night.

You may say today that you can handle it alone, that the storm will not catch up with you. You think you will manage difficult situations on your own, just as you did in good times, right?

A middle school classmate wrote to me today that, because of the cancer she has been battling against for 2 years, she became paralyzed a few days ago and can no longer move her legs at all.

A mother asked me yesterday, during counseling, to pray for her son who cannot stand to see her praying in the house anymore.

A father called me a few days ago to ask me to support his family in prayer. Their house feels empty since his wife passed away.

Light is not always the solution we desire or the salvation we expect, the way out of our bad circumstance...

Light can be the power to endure the darkness of illness. The patience to overcome a son's disobedience. The hope that when loved ones pass away, God remains.

We are surrounded by a dense fog at every step. The world's constant distancing from God scatters darkness around us. There are more and more questions and fewer and fewer answers.

And yet, in every situation, for the righteous man there is a light. A lighthouse that guides him. A star that leads him to Jesus. A candle that burns for the Bridegroom's arrival. A candlestick that still flickers...

Keep on being righteous.

God will take care of the light that shall rise in the darkness.

January 13

WHAT TO TEACH A CHILD ABOUT FINANCES?

"And not many days after, the younger son gathered all together, journeyed to a far country, and there wasted his possessions with prodigal living." – Luke 15:13

Most children learn the principles of financial education through their own experience, often late and with many pains and failures. It is much better if we, their parents, teach them from a young age some principles that will help them a lot in life.

1. Teach him how to save and spend wisely! Advise your child to save some of his money. He should not spend it all. He should be careful with money and have a budget for each thing so that, when he becomes a teenager or even a young adult, he will not spend all his money on clothes or as the result of being seduced by a tempting ad.

2. Teach him how to work hard to achieve something! When you make the mistake that many parents make and give your child money without them being a specific reward for the work he has done, you will raise him to take things for granted and think that he deserves it all. The easiest money to spend is the money you received without having worked for it.

3. Teach him how to avoid debts! The Bible has no positive verses about debts. On the contrary, it urges us to avoid them as much as possible or to resort to them only in cases of extreme emergency. Today's generation of teenagers borrows so easily only to buy things that impress others! In exchange for social media likes, teenagers from this generation are left with credit card debt, accumulating immense financial interest for the rest of their lives.

4. Teach him to give! The Bible teaches us that at least ten percent of what we earn should go to God. Teach your child from an early age to give from what he has saved, and when he grows up, he will never forget this principle.

Also, growing in this way will help him be altruistic, and when he matures, these principles planted in him will bear rich fruit in his family and community.

In conclusion, I end with the lesson of the prodigal son, from which, in addition to spiritual principles, we can also derive some financial lessons. The prodigal son is the symbol of the young man who does not know the value of work, nor of having savings. A young man who takes what the father offered him freely and spends it in debauchery. This lifestyle quickly ruins him, and he becomes bankrupt.

May God bless our children with healthy growth in this area as well!

January 14

WILLIAM BORDEN

"Yet indeed I also count all things loss for the excellence of the knowledge of Christ Jesus my Lord, for whom I have suffered the loss of all things, and count them as rubbish, that I may gain Christ." – Philippians 3:8

In 1904, William Borden graduated from high school in Chicago. Because his parents had built a profitable company, William received as a gift a trip around the world. Traveling through Europe, Asia, and the Middle East and observing people's needs, their illnesses, and their poverty, he wrote to his parents about his desire to become a missionary.

Freshly converted, William Borden wrote on his Bible two words of great value: *no reserves.*

He returned to the U.S. to continue his studies at Yale. His classmates testified that William's encounter with God was genuine, and his life showed continuous dedication to prayer and sanctification.

He established Yale Hope Mission, a mission that cared for widows, orphans, and homeless people, doing everything in his power to win them for Christ.

After graduating, William turned down several lucrative jobs and wrote two more words on the back of his Bible: *no retreats.*

He attended Princeton Theological Seminary in New Jersey and then set sail for China to dedicate his life entirely to missionary work. He stopped in Egypt to deepen his knowledge of the Arabic language, but while there, he contracted meningitis. In a month, the illness worsened, and at the age of 25, William Borden died.

The news travelled around the world, and many shook their heads, thinking, "What a wasted life!" However, to their surprise, two more words were found written in his Bible before his death: *no regrets.*

May God help us also to live a life with *no reserves, no retreats,* and *no regrets!*

January 15

THE JOY OF QUIET THINGS

"Then they are glad because they are quiet; so He guides them to their desired haven." – Psalm 107:30

Moments when the sea of life is calm are not very common. Amidst turmoil, scrutiny, questions, stress, and emotions, there are also a few moments of rest. Moments when the waves calm down. When leisure makes its way, and relaxation invites us to sit at its table.

The Bible encourages us to praise God for the moments when He intervenes! To rejoice in the calmed waves! Let's not count only the falls but also the rises!

"Oh, that men would give thanks to the Lord for His goodness, and for His wonderful works to the children of men!" – Psalm 107:31

Let us not focus only on our troubles even after they pass. There is this immense risk of being so focused on the past and so stressed about what will come that we cannot "catch our breath" in the pause between them, isn't it?

Take a break in the presence of God today and bring Him some words of gratitude. Let joy flood your heart and be thankful for the harbor you have reached after so many ups and downs. Lift your eyes to the heaven and, with tears of joy, say from the bottom of your heart, "Thank you, Lord!"

January 16

NO PAIN, NO GAIN!

"Yet it pleased the Lord to bruise Him; He has put Him to grief... But He shall see His seed, He shall prolong His days, and the pleasure of the Lord shall prosper in His hand." – Isaiah 53:10

No pain, no gain! This phrase, commonly used in English, means: *If there is no pain, there is no gain!*

When a grain of sand enters the inside of a shell, it causes a very deep wound. As a defense mechanism or as a consequence of pain, the shell secretes a liquid that isolates the grain of sand from the membrane. Pearls are the tears of shells.

Before conquering the top of a mountain, you must endure the pain of a difficult ascent.

Before being able to hold the baby in your arms, as a mother, you must endure the pain of giving birth to that baby.

Before winning a marathon, you must endure the pain of exhausted muscles and extremely stressful training.

Before reaching the shore, you must endure the pain of rowing.

That is how God planned everything. True pearls are born through pain. Through polishing, wood becomes smoother. Through striking, the piano produces beautiful sounds. Through rubbing, the violin plays delicately. Through tears, we become more sensitive. Through earth, we desire heaven more.

Jesus' crushing came before the joy of seeing a multitude of saved people. The cross was before the resurrection. The Garden of Gethsemane was before the ascension. The crown of thorns was before the crown of glory.

Obedience before reward. Running before eternal rest. Descent before ascent.

"And being found in appearance as a man, He humbled Himself and became obedient to the point of death, even the death of the cross. Therefore, God also has highly exalted Him and given Him the name which is above every name." – Philippians 2:8-9

If we follow in His footsteps, let`s also be prepared to travel the same path as His...

JANUARY 17

SPIRITUAL MALPRACTICE

"Faithful are the wounds of a friend, but the kisses of an enemy are deceitful." – Proverbs 27:6

Have you heard of malpractice?

Malpractice is nothing else but "incorrect or negligent treatment applied by a doctor to a patient, causing any kind of harm to him, in relation to the degree of impairment of physical and mental capacity."

Most of the time, malpractice meant the misdiagnosis of a serious condition. A superficial check for an acute illness that, not infrequently, ultimately led to the patient's death.

Do you know that malpractice also exists in our relationships?

If you notice that a friend of yours does the wrong thing and yet you avoid correcting him with love, this will ultimately lead to the temporary or eternal failure of that friend.

Do we want around us people who flatter us or people who tell us the truth?

Solomon reminds us that truth hurts, but later, it heals. The lie is pleasant, but later, it brings death.

It's painful to hear from a doctor about your illness, in real terms and with detailed consequences. But in order for you to follow the correct treatment, it is beneficial to hear these details.

It's the same in the spiritual realm. A person who truly cares about you will show you the areas where you need to improve, while a flatterer will tell you lies. He will tell you that you are fine, although your distance from God becomes more visible every day.

Tell your real friends the following words:

If you truly care about me, correct me! Tell me where I'm wrong! How can I improve if you don't show me the areas where I constantly fail?

Their advice will hurt you momentarily, but in the end, it will open your eyes and bring prosperity to the areas where you need to improve.

We do not like friends who hurt us by pointing out our flaws. But they are much more precious than the kisses of those who flatter us and who will later betray us...

January 18

GOD DOES NOT CALL THE LAZY!

"I went by the field of the lazy man, and by the vineyard of the man devoid of understanding; and there it was, all overgrown with thorns; its surface was covered with nettles, and its stone wall was broken down." – Proverbs 24:30-31

When God called Moses, he was tending the flock of his father-in-law.

When God called Elisha through Elijah, he was plowing with oxen.

When God called Gideon, he was threshing wheat.

When God called Peter and Andrew, they were mending nets.

God looked for busy people to call them into ministry. Diligent people to work in His field.

Too many people spend hours on the phone, waiting for God to work miracles through them. Too many people want to be missionaries on a certain continent, but they haven't talked to their colleagues and neighbors about Jesus yet.

Too many people desire the anointing but sit around with a bag of popcorn in their hands, doing nothing.

God will not show you step number 10 until you do step number 1. You will not see the end of the field if you don't start with the first row. You cannot think about victory until you start training.

Do what you can with what you have. Then God will empower you for more!

Be faithful in small things. Then God will call you to great things!

Enlighten the person next to you before God enlightens the crowds through you!

Feed one orphan before you think about building an orphanage!

Be a comfort to one elderly person before thinking of founding a nursing home!

Bind one wound before desiring to lead a hospital!

Take the first step, and then God will guide you to the next...

January 19

FRIEND OF JESUS OR OF CAESAR?

"Therefore, Pilate sought to release Him; but the Jews cried out, saying, 'If you let this Man go, you are not Caesar's friend. Whoever makes himself a king speaks against Caesar.'" – John 19:12

Pilate had a tough choice to make that day. The shouts of the Jews drowned out the voice of his conscience. Thoughts overwhelmed him. The inner voice told him not to condemn an innocent man to death. However, the shouting of the crowd threatened his friendship with Caesar.

Eventually, the crowd won, just as it does today. The shouts of the majority influence most people in their decisions. The world's standards cause many young people to fall in line, without any remorse, and join the trends promoted by the world's leaders.

The friendship of the crowd, for most, is more desirable than the friendship with Jesus. A free Jesus is not very appreciated. He will advise you on what to do. How to speak. How to dress. How to live.

The crowd wants a bound Jesus. A condemned Jesus. A Jesus who will no longer walk from place to place, evangelizing and healing.

History confirms that after that day, Pilate governed for another three and a half years and was then called to Rome to be judged by Tiberius. He lost both the friendship with Jesus and the friendship with Caesar.

Whom do you choose today? Who guides your steps? Do you let yourself be influenced by the world's trends or by the principles of the Kingdom of God? What fills your heart – hatred or love? Revenge or forgiveness? Sin or holiness? Darkness or light?

Every day we make choices. We choose based on our principles but also on the voices we listen to.

We choose based on the values we have in our hearts and the goal we have in life. We choose based on the actors we worship or based on the love for simple people who walked with Jesus. We choose based on the celebrities we appreciate or based on the heroes we take as role models.

We choose based on fleeting things or based on eternal things. Based on earth or on heaven. Based on the awards we desire. Based on the stages we want to be on.

We choose based on the glory we love.

"Nevertheless even among the rulers many believed in Him, but because of the Pharisees they did not confess Him, lest they should be put out of the synagogue; for they loved the praise of men more than the praise of God." – John 12:42-43

We choose. But do we understand that the glory of the world is temporary? That Caesar is on the throne only for a few years, while Jesus is eternal?

Caesar is temporary. Jesus remains.

Choose Jesus!

January 20

WHY STRESS IF IT DOES NOT HURT?

"They have struck me, but I was not hurt; they have beaten me, but I did not feel it. When shall I awake, that I may seek another drink?" – Proverbs 23:35

I have noticed that from the point of view of health, most people do not address certain medical conditions because it doesn't hurt.

Did you know that some of the sources of Alzheimer's disease settle inside our bodies 20 years before the disease makes its presence known in our everyday life? Did you know that a fatty liver will endure years of unhealthy eating before producing pain in the body?

Did you know that most young people do not worry about sugary drinks and excessive sugar consumption because it does not hurt? Did you know that cardiovascular diseases appear after years of unhealthy eating, and people do not refrain from anything because it doesn't hurt?

But I do not want to focus on physical health today, though it is important. Even if it does not hurt, the disease may still be there.

Lies, pornography, and envy do not hurt immediately, but they cause disastrous effects over time. When caught, it may be too late to regain trust, and the pain could be immense.

Today, take every action seriously, even if it does not hurt. Be responsible for every thought, word, and deed, as repeated harmful actions can lead to severe and possibly irreversible spiritual diseases.

Do not wait for it to hurt before you make a decision. Do not wait for the disease to advance before you stop doing what you are doing wrong.

Start a healthy life today, both physically and, more importantly, spiritually.

"Do not be wise in your own eyes; fear the Lord and depart from evil. It will be health to your flesh, and strength to your bones." – Proverbs 3:7-8

May God help us!

JANUARY 21

THE BATTLE OF THE MIND

Our greatest battle is the battle of the mind. It is there that we make decisions regarding our words, intentions, plans, and actions.

I have identified four sources of thoughts, and these are the following:

1. Thoughts that come from God

"My God put it into my heart to gather the nobles, the rulers, and the people, that they might be registered by genealogy. And I found a register of the genealogy of those who had come up in the first return, and found written in it." – Nehemiah 7:5

A person with a deep relationship with God will receive thoughts and plans inspired by Him, which will be reflected in that person's mind and soul. Thus, through the guidance of the Holy Spirit and through that person's spirituality, God will provide beneficial solutions in all areas of life.

2. Thoughts that come from our own minds

"David said to Abiathar, 'I knew that day, when Doeg the Edomite was there, that he would surely tell Saul. I have caused the death of all the persons of your father's house.'" – 1 Samuel 22:22

These thoughts come from our experiences, feelings, and character.

3. Thoughts that come from other people

Based on conversations with those around us, we share ideas, plans, and all sorts of thoughts. Joseph asks the cupbearer to remember him when he gets out of prison and to put in a good word for him, but when things went well, the cupbearer forgot.

4. Thoughts that come from the Devil

"During supper, the devil having already put it into the heart of Judas Iscariot, Simon's son, to betray Him." – John 13:2

If we open the door in our thoughts, the Devil finds a place to come in with his vile plans, with hatred, with thoughts of discontent or revenge. He will take every opportunity to stain our inner life and use it for his diabolical purposes.

I conclude with the advice of Frank Outlaw, and I pray that God helps us to implement it:

> "Watch your thoughts, they become words; watch your words, they become actions; watch your actions, they become habits; watch your habits, they become character; watch your character, for it becomes your destiny."

JANUARY 22

BETHEL

The fugitive Jacob had stopped for a night. Exhaustion took its toll. The fear that Esau would pursue him had not left his heart yet. He had no pillow, but a stone was good enough, if needed.

He fell asleep with difficulty, not knowing what the future would hold for him... His parents could no longer help him. And his relatives... who knows how they would receive him?

He dreamed something strange. A ladder to heaven. Standing at the top of the ladder, God made a series of promises to him that Jacob, after maturing, kept close to his heart in the years that followed.

Then he woke up with fear and said,

"Surely the Lord is in this place, and I did not know it." – Genesis 28:16

Before leaving, Jacob anointed the stone with oil and changed the name of the city from Luz to Bethel. The incident in that place was going to stay with him his entire life, and the experience he had there was the one that would give him the strength to stay close to God.

Sometimes, in life, you do not need spectacular things. In fear, in loneliness, with an unclear future in sight, it's enough to have what Jacob had: a stone, symbolizing human helplessness; a ladder, symbolizing God`s interest for mankind; and a drop of oil placed on the stone of remembrance, which is nothing else but the sign of a decision according to God`s will.

There is no elevator to heaven, only stairs. Life is a step-by-step ascent towards perfection. But the consolation that God is waiting for us at the top of the stairs gives us the strength to climb one more step.

January 23

THE CHILDREN WHO CAN END UP IN SLAVERY

Today, I read to my children the passage from 2 Kings 4:1-7. A widowed mother was on the verge of losing her children due to some debts. In a desperate attempt, she runs to Elisha for a lifesaving solution.

Elisha asks her, "What do you have at home?" When God performs miracles, He uses whatever little you have, whatever you already possess, whatever you have gathered so far.

She replied, "I have nothing in the house but a jar of oil!" She was unaware that her little was sufficient for God.

At the prophet's prompting, she brings pots from her neighbors. Empty vessels. She closes the door behind her children, then pours from the oil she had at home, and the miracle happens: all the empty vessels are now filled.

In total obedience to the man of God, Elisha, she goes and sells all the oil, saving her children from slavery.

I told my children that the Devil wants to make them slaves. To cigarettes. To alcohol. To disobedience. To rebellion. Slaves to gambling. To sports betting. To phones and computer games. To the many other bondages out there.

What can save us from slavery? The oil – a symbol of God's presence in our homes. If the vessels are filled with obedience, with fear of the Lord, with the Word, and with prayer, the Devil has no access in there. If the vessels are filled with the Holy Spirit, there are no vices.

> *"Do not be drunk with wine, in which is dissipation; but be filled with the Spirit." – Ephesians 5:18*

We have gathered many things in this life, but have we gathered what is most important, namely, oil?

We have been busy with many things, but have we done everything in our power, spiritually speaking, to save our children from the Devil's slavery?

January 24

WHAT DOES IT MEAN TO BE A TRUE MOTHER?

"He grants the barren woman a home, like a joyful mother of children. Praise the Lord!" – Psalm 113:9

To truly be a mother in the home, every woman should possess certain qualities.

Being a wife cannot fully cover the requirements for raising children; thus, in the following lines, I want to list the five most important qualities, and I pray that every mother reading these lines will desire to fully embrace them:

1. Love

A true mother unconditionally loves her children and is available for them anytime, regardless of circumstances.

2. Patience

Caring for children involves overcoming numerous challenges and requires much patience throughout their entire period of development. The ability to remain calm when the children are full of energy is a desirable quality that every mother should develop over time.

3. Altruism

A mother in the truest sense of the word will put her own needs secondary to the needs of her children. Often, she eats last and rests last, and these sacrifices should be appreciated and noticed by both her husband and her children and be rewarded with grateful words and mutual assistance.

4. Strength

Both physically and mentally, a mother puts in immense effort and needs much strength. Despair often knocks at her door, and the fact that results are not immediately visible often raises questions that may weaken her desire to continue the fight.

5. Empathy

Parenting also requires emotional connection with the child. They need understanding and compassion, and a true mother is there when her child needs her presence the most.

In conclusion, I want to motivate you, beloved mothers, with the story of the Chinese bamboo.

A Chinese farmer plants a bamboo seed. For about 5 years, only a tiny bud is visible. He diligently waters it daily. Perhaps it doesn't seem like a big deal to water a plant, but it becomes frustrating if there are no visible results for so long. During this entire period, the Chinese bamboo gives only small signs of existence above the surface.

However, its growth is happening underground. Its roots have a complex structure, spreading vertically and horizontally, taking shape. At the end of the fifth year, the Chinese bamboo suddenly grows to a height of about 80 feet in just 5 weeks.

The education and growth of your children are similar to this story. When you think that you can't take it anymore, that there is too much laundry and too much ironing, that it's too exhausting to cook every day, that the house needs cleaning again, remember that perseverance and patience, together with continuous involvement, bring amazing results.

The development of your children will not happen overnight but rather step by step. Sowing divine principles together with proper education will not yield immediate fruit, but over time, you will be able to enjoy the results of all the effort you made.

Be blessed, esteemed mother!

January 25

WHAT DOES IT MEAN TO BE A TRUE FATHER?

When you get married, you become a husband. When you have children, you become a father. The challenge of transitioning from a husband to a father is great and requires a Scriptural approach if you want to lead your family to God.

What should you, as a father who loves God, do in your family?

1. Love your family!

"Husbands, love your wives, just as Christ also loved the church and gave Himself for her." – Ephesians 5:25

Loving your wife and, of course, the children God has entrusted to you through her provides a perfect framework for exceptional development in all aspects of your family. Loving your family means putting your job, your car, your phone, and any other material thing in second place. Loving your wife and children means being kind, selfless, patient, and making the necessary time to interact with them as often as possible.

2. Lead your family!

"And you, fathers, do not provoke your children to wrath, but bring them up in the training and admonition of the Lord." – Ephesians 6:4

As a father, it is important to provide guidance and direction for your family. Teach your children to understand the concept of good behavior and to choose it! Discipline them when necessary and set clear boundaries in every area! Leaving all these things only on your wife's shoulders will exhaust her, and sooner or later, she will give up fighting. At the helm of the family is the man, and the direction must be towards heaven.

3. Be a good role model!

"Let no one despise your youth, but be an example to the believers in word, in conduct, in love, in spirit, in faith, in purity." – 1 Timothy 4:12

Most of the time, the children will do what the father does, not what the father says. Therefore, it is essential for the father to set a good example and to show through his actions what he is trying to convey in words. The lack of role models in our world is becoming more acute, and it would be ideal for our children to see us as role models, so that our personal example leaves a mark in their heart for a lifetime.

4. Pray for your family!

"Therefore we also, since the day we heard it, do not cease to pray for you, and to ask that you may be filled with the knowledge of His will in all wisdom and spiritual understanding." – Colossians 1:9

Despite all our efforts, we must admit that there are certain aspects that can only be accomplished by God. Therefore, every day, through prayer, we will entrust the present and the future of our children into His hands. We want our children's lives and growth to be blessed by the One who created the Universe and has a special plan for each one of them.

In conclusion, being a true father is about embodying love, leadership, and faithfulness every day. It is a commitment to not only guide and protect but to also nurture and inspire your family through Christ's teachings. By striving to fulfill these responsibilities, you create a legacy of faith and love that will resonate through generations.

JANUARY 26

HOW DO WE HANDLE CONFLICT?

"There was strife between the herdsmen of Abram's livestock and the herdsmen of Lot's livestock. The Canaanites and the Perizzites then dwelt in the land." – Genesis 13:7

Conflicts can arise unexpectedly, and for each of us, they are a real challenge. These situations reveal the character of both parties involved because, in such circumstances, the qualities of each of the two disagreeing parties can truly be observed.

In the following lines, I will present some methods to successfully handle a conflict:

1. Speak with respect!

"Abram said to Lot: 'Please, let there be no strife between you and me, and between my herdsmen and your herdsmen; for we are brethren.'" – Genesis 13:8

Please, thank you, I'm sorry, forgive me – these words always pour water instead of gasoline over the fire of conflict. They should not be absent from the vocabulary of anyone who truly desires a peaceful resolution of conflicts.

2. Speak on equal terms!

Although Abram was Lot's uncle, he says to Lot: we are brothers. Before God, people are equal. Humility, unity, and modesty will always lead to the elimination of conflict.

3. Do not let the conflict escalate!

The Bible says that the quarrel was between their servants, not between the two of them. However, Abraham knew that if he didn't take the initiative to solve it today, there was a good chance that tomorrow the quarrel would reach the masters, not just the servants. When the fire is small, it is easier to extinguish it...

4. Be ready to pay the price of peace!

"Is not the whole land before you? Please separate from me. If you take the left, then I will go to the right; or, if you go to the right, then I will go to the left." – Genesis 13:9

Abraham offers precedence to Lot. He is ready to lose the lush fields on the horizon in favor of the much drier and arid mountain, just for the sake of peace. This method was not entirely fair, but it was peaceful. Similarly, in our relationships, it is good to seek peace before justice...

5. Speak gently!

I notice kindness and gentleness in Abraham's speech. No shouts, no screams, and no unfounded accusations. He could have "rubbed it in" to Lot that he, Abraham, had made him rich; that he, Abraham, took Lot out of his country and brought him here.

The Bible says so beautifully:

"A soft answer turns away wrath, but a harsh word stirs up anger." – Proverbs 15:1

When you have conflicts, it is good to raise the value of your arguments, not the tone of your voice.

In conclusion, I would like to offer you a meditation worth considering:

One day, a wise man asked his disciples: "Why do people shout when they are angry?"

One of them replied, "We shout because we lose our temper."

"But why shout when the other person is right next to you?" asked the wise man again.

"Well, we shout to make sure the other person hears us," said another disciple.

The master asked again, "Still, couldn't we speak more softly, with a low voice?"

Nothing that was said was a satisfying answer for the wise man.

Then he spoke, "When two people quarrel, their hearts move away from each other. So in order for them to hear each other, they must shout louder, in proportion to the degree of anger. The more anger, the more shouts are needed to cover the distance between them. But when two lovers meet, their hearts come closer, so they speak slowly, gently. Sometimes, they are so close that they do not even need words, only whispers and murmurs. And when two human beings feel intense love, communication between them happens without words, through a simple look. Their hearts understand each other, showing that they are closely connected."

Then the wise man concluded, "Pay attention to the words you use when you have a conversation, and do not let your hearts be separated from each other, for a day will come when the distance will be so great that your hearts will no longer find the way back."

JANUARY 27

"JUST AS I AM, I COME TO YOU!"

"All that the Father gives Me will come to Me, and the one who comes to Me I will by no means cast out." – John 6:37

Charlotte Elliott was born on March 18, 1789. Charlotte received a Christian education and heard the Gospel and its principles numerous times. From a young age, her inclination towards poetry and music was evident.

Her passion for humorous poems and painting gradually distanced her from sacred values. Her appreciation for the world made her trust in her own abilities. However, at the age of 30, her life took an unexpected turn.

Due to a relentless illness, she became bedridden, and depression and disappointment began to take hold of her life. Her dreams shattered, and a bleak future cast its strong imprint on her being.

At the age of thirty-two, Charlotte was visited by a renowned Swiss evangelist named César Malan. He finally managed to make her understand the purpose of pain and Charlotte's need for salvation. The central truth that Dr. Malan impressed upon her was this: "You must come as you are, a sinner, to the Lamb of God who takes away the sin of the world. It does not matter that you are incapacitated – come as you are! What matters is that you are a sinner who needs salvation and must come to the Lamb of God who will take away your sin!"

On May 9, 1822, Charlotte came to saving faith. For the next 50 years, pain did not leave her, and the illness kept her disabled with pain that was sometimes hard to imagine. However, with the help of her faith, she managed to find a noble purpose in life and composed over 150 hymns.

In 1836, on a day when her entire family had gone for a fundraising project to support a school that her brother, Henry (a clergyman), wanted to start for the children of poor ministers, Charlotte was left alone at home, sick and a little sad. For her own encouragement, she began to dwell on the great certainties of her salvation – her Lord, His power, His promises.

Then, recalling Dr. Malan's words, Charlotte was suddenly overwhelmed with a sense of peace and thanksgiving. Taking her pen, she wrote the following lines:

Just as I am, without one plea,
But that Thy blood was shed for me,
And that Thou bidst me come to Thee,
O Lamb of God, I come, I come.

Just as I am, and waiting not
To rid my soul of one dark blot,
To Thee whose blood can cleanse each spot,
O Lamb of God, I come, I come.

Just as I am, though tossed about
With many a conflict, many a doubt,
Fightings and fears within, without,
O Lamb of God, I come, I come.

Just as I am, poor, wretched, blind;
Sight, riches, healing of the mind,
Yea, all I need in Thee to find,
O Lamb of God, I come, I come.

Just as I am, Thou wilt receive,
Wilt welcome, pardon, cleanse, relieve;
Because Thy promise I believe,
O Lamb of God, I come, I come.

Just as I am, Thy love unknow
Hath broken every barrier down;
Now, to be Thine, yea, Thine alone,
O Lamb of God, I come, I come.

This hymn was translated into dozens of languages, and hundreds of thousands of people have come to Christ through this song with a strong Scriptural foundation.

Billy Graham himself often used it in many of his evangelistic crusades.

After Charlotte's death, in one of her memory boxes, over 1,000 thank-you and encouragement letters were found from people touched by this song.

Isn't it wonderful to see how God uses people with physical problems to comfort other people who have spiritual problems? Isn't it moving that God provides grace in weakness? If a person dedicates himself to God, He will make that person a powerful candlelight for the salvation of others.

January 28

WHAT CAN WE LEARN FROM LIGHT?

"But the path of the just is like the shining sun, that shines ever brighter unto the perfect day." – Proverbs 4:18

The example of light speaks powerfully in our lives. Its properties can inspire us to live a life with purpose and a positive impact on those around us.

1. Light illuminates

Just as a candle helps us see the path, we must be a guide for those around us to help them carefully see the path on which they walk.

2. Light dispels darkness

Your presence as the light of Christ will dispel negativity from the hearts of those around you and, instead, bring hope and joy.

3. Light reflects

It is a particularly pleasant sensation for the eyes to observe how light creates special effects when reflected from certain surfaces. Similarly, we are called to reflect God's love to humanity wherever we are.

4. Light gives warmth

Light has the power to bring a sense of well-being by warming those around it. We are also called to bring, through our actions and words, a bit of warmth to frozen and despairing hearts.

May God help us truly be a light in a world full of darkness!

January 29

LESSONS FROM THE EXPERIENCES OF RICHARD WURMBRAND

"Remember those who rule over you, who have spoken the word of God to you, whose faith follow, considering the outcome of their conduct." – Hebrews 13:7

I had the privilege, from a young age, to read all the books of brother Richard Wurmbrand. They are a treasure of knowledge and evidence that persecution cannot defeat a Christian person who is completely dedicated to God.

In the following lines, I want to present to you 5 lessons I learned from his books and life, challenging you not to be satisfied with this summary but to read for yourself, if possible, all his masterpieces.

1. The importance of standing firm in the faith

Wurmbrand's experiences as a prisoner in the communist prisons demonstrate the importance of remaining faithful to the biblical doctrine and remain deeply rooted in the faith given once and for all to the saints. Such a faith can never be defeated.

2. The power of love

Wurmbrand's love for God and for his fellow men, even for his enemies, was a powerful force that sustained him during his time in prison and inspired others to follow Jesus. If he had replaced this love with thoughts of hatred or revenge, he would not have lasted through the 14 years of mental and physical torture. Love will always prevail.

3. The power of forgiveness

Wurmbrand's willingness to forgive those who wronged him was evidence of the transformative power of forgiveness. He saw a demonic struggle in the tormentors who made his life miserable every day and understood that behind that struggle was the Devil himself. Therefore, he forgave the people and fought, by faith, against the spirits behind them.

4. The importance of prayer

Wurmbrand's trust in prayer and his faith in the power of prayer were significant in his life and sustained him throughout his hardships. In times of trial, communication with God is essential because it is the only way we can access divine resources.

5. The need for unity

Richard's books always urge believers not to focus on differences but on similarities. Be ready to fight for unity because a united army cannot be defeated. Also, the unity of the church in difficult times is a force that the Devil cannot overcome. False rumors, communist lies, and the destruction of Christian literature did not succeed in destroying the church because it was united.

January 30

HOW TO BEHAVE WHEN FIGHTING THE DEVIL?

"Be sober, be vigilant; because your adversary the devil walks about like a roaring lion, seeking whom he may devour." – 1 Peter 5:8

The Bible teaches us that the Devil is a real being, the enemy of God and all Christians. However, believers should not fear him because they have been given authority over him through Jesus Christ. Here is some biblical advice on how to fight Satan:

1. Resist the Devil!

"Submit to God. Resist the devil, and he will flee from you." – James 4:7

There are circumstances when we must resist. I will not resist if I am in a nightclub or a dancing bar. I have no business being there. I must resist the Devil when he prowls around my home, in the church, on the street. I must look the other way. I must dismiss the incoming thought. I must refuse the tempting offer that violates Scriptural principles.

However, be careful! Resistance must be preceded by obedience to Jesus!

2. Put on the armor of God!

"Put on the whole armor of God, that you may be able to stand against the wiles of the devil." – Ephesians 6:11

A soldier cannot go to war without weapons. After putting on the uniform, the fighter must equip himself properly with the entire armor needed for the battle. An unequipped soldier will be easy prey, and any blow against him could be lethal.

3. Be watchful!

Peter urges us to always be on guard. Let us not forget that at every step, we have an adversary who wants to destroy us. If you think the Devil wishes you well, it is like believing that a snake wants to caress you when it coils around your neck.

4. Pray and fast!

"But this kind does not go out except by prayer and fasting." – Matthew 17:21

Our battles exceed the human dimension. We are not fighting with tanks or machine guns. We are fighting against powers in the heavenly realms, powers that are not intimidated by your education or your money. Battles in the unseen world are fought with prayer and fasting (in addition to the armor mentioned earlier).

I wish you to be an overcomer! Do not let any evil thought into your heart! Do not let any compromise or hidden sin open the door of your heart!

Be an overcomer in the Name of Jesus!

January 31

THE 4 TYPES OF TEMPERAMENTS

There are many different theories of temperament out there, but one of the best known one is the theory of the four temperaments, which classifies people into four different categories based on their dominant personality traits: *sanguine, choleric, melancholic,* and *phlegmatic.*

It is particularly important to understand these temperaments and their characteristics so that we know how to relate to others and be able to accept the fact that people are different.

1. Sanguine individuals

Sanguine individuals are extroverted, optimistic, and sociable. They are often described as enthusiastic, talkative, and impulsive.

2. Choleric individuals

Choleric individuals are ambitious and determined. They are often described as assertive, leadership-oriented, and temperate.

3. Melancholic individuals

Melancholic individuals are introverted, analytical, and perfectionist. They are often described as thoughtful, sensitive, and prone to depression.

4. Phlegmatic individuals

Phlegmatic individuals are calm, easygoing, and trustworthy. They are often described as patient, quiet, and emotionally stable.

The Bible encourages us to use the fruit of the Holy Spirit to develop self-control, thereby cultivating a peaceful and gentle spirit in our relationships.

"The fruit of the Spirit, on the other hand, is love, joy, peace, longsuffering, kindness, goodness, faithfulness, gentleness, self-control. Against such there is no law." – Galatians 5:22-23

It also encourages us to be humble and to consider others more important than ourselves.

"Let nothing be done through selfish ambition or conceit, but in lowliness of mind let each esteem others better than himself. Let each of you look out not only for his own interests but also for the interests of others." – Philippians 2:3-4

It is important to remember that no one is entirely a single type of temperament; rather we all have aspects of each type of temperament. Also, it is important to remember that our temperament does not define us – we can always work on developing our character and spiritual growth.

February 1

DO NOT QUARREL ON THE WAY!

"So he sent his brothers away, and they departed; and he said to them, 'See that you do not become troubled along the way.'" – Genesis 45:24

Joseph's brothers were returning from Egypt to their father, loaded with various goods. They had beautiful carriages. Provisions for the journey. Spare clothes. And for their father, they had a special gift: ten male and ten female donkeys loaded with the best of Egypt. In the famine that was rampant everywhere, these gifts were of immense value.

And yet, Joseph knew that material blessings are not enough. He knew that what you carry in your heart is more important than what you carry in your pocket or wallet.

Therefore, at the moment of their departure, he gave them a command: do not quarrel on the way (or do not become troubled on the way)! Joseph knew what it meant not to have peace. He knew what he had gone through years ago when he was sold by his brothers. He had felt firsthand what evil, quarreling, envy, and hatred meant. Thus, he did everything in his power for his brothers to live in peace, so that they would not repeat the dark history ever again...

Do you know people who have a lot of material wealth but lack the greatest wealth of all, namely, peace?

Have you ever passed by families that could buy whatever they wanted and yet they cannot eat together at the same table?

Have you met couples who drive luxury cars and yet cannot speak to each other due to a smoldering conflict?

Do you know why this happens? Because the greatest wealth of all is peace! Even if the table is not overflowing... Even if there are empty shelves in the fridge... Even if the car breaks down because it has too many miles on it...

I pray today that God helps you enjoy the presence of children who live in peace. And, last but not least, I pray that God helps you be a peaceful person.

Regardless of the losses you may experience, always make sure that you do not lose... your peace.

February 2

THROUGH YOU OR FOR YOU?

"So Paul and Barnabas spent considerable time there, speaking boldly for the Lord, who confirmed the message of his grace by enabling them to perform signs and wonders." – Acts 14:3

For us, God does many beautiful things every day. The sunrise we were able to see this morning, the heart that still beats, the legs that can still keep us balanced, a healthy mind, and countless other blessings God prepares for us daily.

Do you know, however, that God wants to make us more sensitive at a deeper level? He wants us not to remain with what He does for us but to use us in such a way that He does something through us.

Through Moses' outstretched staff, God parted the waters of the Red Sea.

Through Gideon, God delivered Israel from the Midianites.

Through Elijah's arms raised towards Heaven, God brought fire on Mount Carmel.

Through Hannah, He raised up a great prophet named Samuel.

Through David, Goliath was defeated.

Through Mary, God sent Jesus into our world.

Through Tabitha's hands, God blessed the poor with clothes.

Through George Müller, God fed over 10,000 orphans.

Through Hudson Taylor, the Gospel reached tens of thousands of Chinese.

Through David Livingstone, Africa heard about salvation.

Wouldn't you like to be the next one on the list of people through whom God does something?

Many times, we say: *Lord, have mercy on those who are in trouble!* But do you know that God's mercy wants to flow through us over them?

The angels will not preach the Gospel in our place. The archangels will not adopt orphans. The seraphim will not give gifts to poor children.

God is looking for mothers through whom He can send more children to earth.

God is looking for fathers through whom He can guide families toward heaven.

God is looking for intercessors through whom He can glorify His Name, by listening to their prayers.

There is a need for prophets through whom God can send warning messages to the planet.

Think today about how much God has done for you and how much or how little He has done through you...

What God does through you is more important than what He does for you. Through what He does for you, only you are blessed. But through you, many others can also be blessed...

February 3

IN DANGER FROM FALSE BELIEVERS

"I have been constantly on the move. I have been in danger from rivers, in danger from bandits, in danger from my fellow Jews, in danger from Gentiles; in danger in the city, in danger in the country, in danger at sea; and in danger from false believers..." – 2 Corinthians 11:26

Tomás de Aquino, also known in the Western world as Thomas Aquinas, was one of the most important theologians in the Western world. He delved deeply into the arguments for the existence of God, with his most famous work being "Summa Theologica."

He was a quiet, gentle, wonder-filled man who, in his youth, was often teased because of his innocence.

One day, some of his fellow monks hurriedly came to him and said, "Thomas, come quickly to see some pigs flying!"

Thomas quickly ran to the window, where he was greeted with bursts of laughter. After a minute of silence, he said, "I prefer to believe that pigs can fly than to think that my brothers would lie to me."

What kind of friends do you have? Who are the colleagues or neighbors you spend time with? Who are the "brothers" surrounding you?

Paul reminds us that among the dangers of the wilderness, among the threats from robbers, or the waves of the seas, there are also dangers among deceitful "brothers." They are the ones who smile when they are in front of you but speak ill of you behind your back. They are the ones who say one thing but do another. They are the ones who lie without blushing. For them, lying is not a mistake but a lifestyle. If caught, they won't regret lying but regret getting caught. So, you will be the one to be blamed... for catching them.

Paul said he faced dangers and was among pagans, but by listing the danger of deceitful believers last, he wants to tell us that a person who lies with the Bible in his hand is more dangerous than one who lies and does not know God. The one who claims to love the Lord but lies to your face more than one time is thousands of times more dangerous than the one who lies and curses God.

FEBRUARY 4

HAVE YOU SHARPENED YOUR AX?

"If the ax is dull, and one does not sharpen the edge, then he must use more strength; but wisdom brings success." – Ecclesiastes 10:10

"If I had only six hours to chop down a tree, I would spend the first four hours sharpening my ax," said Abraham Lincoln.

The ax in your hand is more important than your muscles, your strength, and the wood that needs to be chopped. The tool with which you chop the wood can make your life either difficult or easy. Superficiality and the attitude of "good enough" will lead you to a delayed final result and to making much more effort than if you had a well-prepared tool.

It is very tempting to quickly get to work, to enter the battle, to attack the problem as fast as possible. But preparation is much more important than the battle itself. To be wise does not mean to hit hard with the ax but to carefully sharpen its blade.

How much time do you dedicate to preparing each aspect of your life? In a fast-paced world where everyone has an opinion while very few are actually masters in a specific field, how much effort do you put into improving your skills?

Each of us was endowed with certain abilities. However, it is up to us to prepare beforehand everything necessary for those abilities to be used successfully.

Reading books in the field that interests you and that you want to master means sharpening your ax. Delving into the Bible in areas where you have spiritual gaps means sharpening your ax. The desire for preparation and continuous growth in the field of family life means sharpening your ax.

Therefore, when the wagon full of firewood arrives at your doorstep, all you have to do is roll up your sleeves and get to work. The sharpened ax will make you attack the problem with confidence, and the outcome will be victorious. As Lincoln said, those two hours of work will be efficient and sufficient because you spent four hours quietly sharpening the ax...

FEBRUARY 5

DID YOU BRING YOUR THOUGHT INTO CAPTIVITY?

"...casting down arguments and every high thing that exalts itself against the knowledge of God, bringing every thought into captivity to the obedience of Christ." – 2 Corinthians 10:5

In his letter to the Corinthians, Paul exhorts us to do something particularly interesting, if we truly understand the meaning of this verse: "...bringing every thought into captivity..."

In Greek, the word "captive" mentioned above is *aichmalótizó*, which means: a prisoner of war taken with a spear.

This type of military behavior is what Christ's followers should exercise over every thought. Through their thoughts, people are either conformed to the world or transformed into the likeness of Christ.

The thought we do not take as a prisoner of war will make us its prisoners! The thought we do not bind in chains will bind us in vices from which we will not easily escape.

Our thoughts are the primary source of inspiration for every word we speak or action we take. The most crucial battle takes place in our minds. Once a thought is accepted and passes through the filters of our principles, it will only be a matter of time before it is put into practice.

Have you taken captive the thought of revenge? Have you imprisoned the thoughts of hatred or unforgiveness?

Someone told me yesterday in counseling: every time I see those who did evil and took advantage of my father, that`s how many times I feel hatred growing in me, and this hatred keeps me tied up, preventing me from progressing on the path of salvation.

I wish you complete victory in the spiritual warfare of your mind!

It is a war that is not easily won but, once you win it, it will positively influence your entire life. Victories at the mind level are victories that will be visible in our words and actions.

Take captive every thought that is not in line with God's will!

Only in this way can you truly be free...

FEBRUARY 6

WHAT YOU GAIN AND WHAT YOU LOSE?

When the Devil gave Eve the forbidden fruit, he took away Eden in return.

When Esau accepted the lentil stew, he lost the blessing in return.

When Samson loved the embrace of Delilah, he lost his eyes in return.

When Judas received the silver coins for betraying Jesus, he lost eternity in return.

Most often, people look at what the Devil offers them but do not consider what the devil asks for in return. Blinded by the momentary glitter of the offer, they fail to comprehend what they lose in exchange for the offer.

Remember this: God offers you many things daily for free because that's what LOVE does!

The devil, however, will never offer you something that does not cost you anything. He is the most dangerous "solicitor," and his target is the destruction of your life and soul in exchange for fleeting sinful pleasures.

I was recently telling someone: the regrets of sin will always be greater than the pleasures of sin! The devil will always offer you something cheap in exchange for something precious. He will offer you earthly paradise, if necessary, just to take your soul:

> *"For what will it profit a man if he gains the whole world, and loses his own soul? Or what will a man give in exchange for his soul?" – Matthew 16:26*

Before you click on that dirty image, think about the loss of purity...

Before you, a wife, smile at the work colleague who is trying to flirt with you, think about losing your family and breaking your marriage vows.

Before you lie, think about the good name you are losing. You've worked for it for years. Is it worth losing it in two minutes?

Before you say "YES" to any sin, think about what you are losing, not just what you think you can gain!

If the blessings you have (the white garment of salvation, your name written in the Book of Life, a beautiful family, an exceptional reputation) are so valuable, why trade them for the devil's "trinkets"?

February 7

ARE YOU ABOVE GOD?

"And the Lord said, 'Because the outcry against Sodom and Gomorrah is great, and because their sin is very grave, I will go down now and see whether they have done altogether according to the outcry against it that has come to Me; and if not, I will know.'" – Genesis 18:20-21

So often I hear certain people rushing to spread rumors they have not personally confirmed! They make judgments and slander about situations they heard... something about. They can't remember from whom, but they know for sure that the person in question knows what they are saying. If, by chance, you find the person who gave them the information, you'll find out that they also heard it from someone else, and, in fact, no one confirmed.

Rumors reached the throne of God that Sodom and Gomorrah were living in "very grave" sins. So God sent His messengers to confirm, by sight, what they heard.

Did you read carefully? God did not rely on rumors to make a decision! This is confirmed by Isaiah when he talks about Jesus:

"His delight is in the fear of the Lord, and He shall not judge by the sight of His eyes, nor decide by the hearing of His ears." – Isaiah 11:3

Doesn't God hear well? Or why does He need to check? Do you know why? Because He knows there is an accuser, namely the Devil (Revelation 12:10), who brings before Him all kinds of accusations about people. Today too the Devil has people who work full-time for him, and they do it with great joy and satisfaction.

When someone accuses someone else, you have to check: is it, maybe, out of envy? Is it, maybe, out of malice? Is his intention to destroy that person's reputation and denigrate them?

Perhaps today the gossipers, the slanderers, the accusers, the envious, and the frustrated people can learn something from God: not to rely on what they hear, and never to spread a word that they haven't personally confirmed – they should not rise above God!

February 8

WHAT IS THAT IN YOUR HAND?

"So the Lord said to him, 'What is that in your hand?' he said, 'A rod.'" – Exodus 4:2

A rod, Moses would have answered.

A needle with which I poke Hannah, Peninnah might have said.

A needle and thread with which I make clothes for the poor, Tabitha might have answered.

A tunic soaked in blood, the brothers of Joseph might have answered without blushing because of the lie about selling their brother.

Stones we cast at the people of God, those who killed Stephen might have answered.

30 pieces of silver, Judas might have answered right after betraying Jesus.

A harp with which I praise God, David might have responded.

Some clothes and talents taken secretly from Naaman, Gehazi might have replied.

A pair of scissors I will use to cut Samson's locks, Delilah might have answered.

Trumpets and pitchers with torches, the 300 brave soldiers who fought with Gideon against the Midianites might have replied.

A mantle from Shinar, 200 shekels of silver, and a wedge of gold taken in secret, Achan might have answered.

Balak`s money received for the bad advice I gave to him about destroying Israel, Balaam might say, with a gleam of greed on his face.

A towel, Jesus might have answered on the evening of the Last Supper.

Also a towel, the one who buried the talent in the ground might have answered.

What do you have in your hand?

Do you know that God is interested in the answer to this question?

We will always have in our hands that which defines our character and intentions, our principles, and the hidden desires of our heart.

FEBRUARY 9

ARE YOU GATHERING A LOT OF STRAW?

"You shall no longer give the people straw to make brick as before. Let them go and gather straw for themselves. And you shall lay on them the quota of bricks which they made before. You shall not reduce it. For they are idle; therefore, they cry out, saying, 'Let us go and sacrifice to our God!'" – Exodus 5:7-8

Moses and Aaron went to Pharaoh. They asked for permission for the people to go into the wilderness and worship God. How did Pharaoh respond to their request? Simple. He asked that, for the making of bricks, the Jews should gather their own straw and be given more work. His ultimate goal? So they do not think about worship anymore...

Doesn't it seem to you that we live in similar times today? Pharaoh represents the diabolical system. The straw represents the temporary things we gather. What does the devil want? For us to be so busy with straw that we no longer have time for holy things. To give up worship for straw.

To give up fellowship for bricks. To sleep in on Sunday because we worked hard all week, right?

We have 8 hours of sleep out of 24. 8 hours of work. Then 4-5 hours a day for eating, shopping, spending time with our family, using the phone, etc. We have 2-3 hours left for holy things. And the devil takes those away too. He finds us a little gig to keep us busy.

He finds us some bales of straw on Facebook to compare them with ours. And so, our life passes by... And we wake up at the end of it realizing that for worship and offerings to the Lord we only had 2-3 years out of 80. We wake up, at the end, with large piles of straw gathered next to us, straw that we will leave here, while for eternity, we have gathered almost nothing.

What good is it that, at the end of my life, my pile of straw is bigger than yours? Do you know that Peter tells us that everything will burn?

"The day of the Lord will come as a thief in the night, in which the heavens will pass away with a great noise, and the elements will melt with fervent heat; both the earth and the works that are in it will be burned up." – 2 Peter 3:10

The only “advantage” then will be that the fire of those with more straw will be bigger... Is it worth it?

Let's decide that, from today on, we will rearrange our priorities. Straw should not be more important than holy things. Garbage should not be more important than pollen. Bricks should not be more important than fasting days. Nor should work hours be more valuable than worship hours.

Those who are desperate to gather straw all day will be disappointed to find, on the day of departure into eternity, that no straw bale can be taken beyond the grave...

FEBRUARY 10

THE LEDGER OF FORGIVENESS

"Jesus said to him, 'I do not say to you, up to seven times, but up to seventy times seven.'" – Matthew 18:22

The people who experienced those times in Romania after the 1989 Revolution probably remember that village stores used to sell certain foods 'on credit,' by keeping a ledger. The buyer who ran out of money was recorded in a notebook when they wanted to buy something, and the following month, when they got the child allowance, the pension, or the salary, they had to come and pay the debts written in the ledger.

Peter wanted to do something similar with forgiveness. In fact, his question was something like this: Lord, may I record in my ledger the name of the one who wronged me? Jesus said to him: No!

Oh, how many people say they forgive you but write you in the ledger of their hearts! You may think they have forgotten how you wronged them, but they forgave you only with their lips and wrote your name down 'on the ledger.'

There they underlined in red every mistake you made, and after a while, they will remind you about it. They will humiliate you and make you not be able to raise your eyes from the ground, although they say... they forgave you.

True love does not take such notes and does not remind you later about such things.

Love that comes from God does not point fingers after 20 years with that common phrase: "How come you`re mentioning this? Have you forgotten how many things you have done?"

True love does not keep scores. It knows that judgment belongs to the Lord. Ours is forgiveness, peace, forgetting, and kindness.

Forgiveness without a ledger is forgiveness from the bottom of the heart:

"So My heavenly Father also will do to you if each of you, from his heart, does not forgive his brother his trespasses." – Matthew 18:35

Allow me to ask you: Do you have many names written in your ledger? Do you have many who have wronged you, and you still keep a record of them?

The thicker the ledger, the thinner the forgiveness. The more names you have underlined as owing you apologies and reconciliation, and who, according to you, do not deserve your forgiveness, the more stressed and sicker you become, thus harming yourself.

God forgave us without a ledger...

Let's do the same with those who have wronged us...

February 11

HOW CAN YOU HAVE PURE THOUGHTS?

This is a question for which you would like to get a scriptural answer. It is a question by which you would like to find out how to avoid negative thinking, how to circumvent thinking that leads to disappointment, remorse, sin, and any other action that distances you from God.

So, how can you have pure thoughts?

Fight for a pure heart!

"For out of the heart proceed evil thoughts, murders, adulteries, fornications, thefts, false witness, blasphemies." – Matthew 15:19

Jesus tells us clearly: a dirty heart will give birth to dirty thoughts. Crystal-clear water does not come from a swamp but from a pure spring. You cannot have a dirty heart and a clean mind!

It is necessary to keep your heart clean through the Word of God. A house that you clean daily will not accumulate moisture, mold, or cobwebs.

Maintaining your heart through the cleanliness produced by the water of the Word will result in clean thoughts!

Fight for a pure circle of friends!

The company of dirty people will soil you too. Conversations with people who love sin will bring sinful thoughts into your mind.

Do you remember Amnon's friend?

"Now Amnon had a friend, whose name was Jonadab the son of Shimeah, David's brother. Now Jonadab was a very crafty man." – 2 Samuel 13:3

You know the end of Amnon's story, right? A crafty friend gives him advice that initially leads Amnon to sin and, later, to death.

Fight for a pure life!

Your thoughts will influence your speech and your life (actions).

Words and actions first have a thought behind them. And if you are aware that every action will be judged, should you not treat the cause (the thought) with great care, not just the effect (the action)?

"For God will bring every work into judgment, including every secret thing, whether good or evil." – Ecclesiastes 12:14

In conclusion, remember the advice given by the Apostle Paul:

"Finally, brethren, whatever things are true, whatever things are noble, whatever things are just, whatever things are pure, whatever things are lovely, whatever things are of good report, if there is any virtue and if there is anything praiseworthy—meditate on these things." – Philippians 4:8

FEBRUARY 12

MOSES` EXCUSES

"The Lord spoke to Moses, saying, 'I am the Lord. Speak to Pharaoh king of Egypt all that I say to you.' But Moses said before the Lord, 'Behold, I am of uncircumcised lips, and how shall Pharaoh heed me?'" – Exodus 6:29-30

Moses was 80 years old when God appeared to him in a burning bush and sent him to Pharaoh. He excused himself, saying that he had a difficult speech, both then and later too, hoping that this would exempt him from the specific mission God had in mind for him. However, God was not swayed by Moses' excuses and told him:

"Then the anger of the Lord was aroused against Moses, and He said: 'Is not Aaron the Levite your brother? I know that he can speak well. And look, he is also coming out to meet you. When he sees you, he will be glad in his heart.'" – Exodus 4:14

Doesn't it seem interesting to you that God does not heal Moses but rather He places Aaron by his side, his brother who was 3 years older?

We can learn two remarkable things from this passage today:

1. Nobody is perfect

One person may speak with difficulty, another may read slowly; one has a hard time explaining, another has a slower thinking process, and another is more impulsive; yet all these people have their own good qualities! Despite struggling with his speech, Moses was a very good leader. Aaron, despite remarkable communication skills, was a weak and easily influenced leader.

2. In life, we complement each other

Aaron complemented Moses. He spoke before Pharaoh and even before the Israelites, even though the message was not composed by him but received by Moses from God. Aaron could not boast, despite speaking excellently, and Moses could not consider himself more useful either, due to his speech impediment.

Whether in our family, at work, or in church, we must admit that we need each other. We should work in cooperation, not in competition. Electricity does not work with two positives but with a positive and a negative. No car will start if the terminals of its battery are both connected to either just the positive or just the negative!

We must accept ourselves the way we were created. What a grace that we are different! What a miracle that we are not clones! It would be a tragedy if we all liked to do the same things! The way God designed humans is marvelous! He put creativity in one, the gift of singing in another, the talent for drawing in another. Some feel comfortable speaking in front of a large audience, while others feel more comfortable discussing within a small group. One can build a house from scratch, while another is strictly focused on interior design.

Do not laugh at others' flaws because you have your own. Instead of laughing, mocking, or making excuses, it is better if you learn to work as a team. Appreciate that your negative can work with someone else's positive, and your positive can work with someone else's negative.

Let's seek solutions instead of excuses! Let's do what God has called us to do.

God does not need perfect people; He needs obedient people...

FEBRUARY 13

WHAT DO YOU ATTRACT WITH?

"Charm is deceitful and beauty is passing, but a woman who fears the Lord, she shall be praised." – Proverbs 31:30

I have the habit of reminding young people that it is crucial to be mindful of what they use to attract their future partners.

As a girl, do you place a huge emphasis on your body, sensuality, and looks? Then you will attract boys who only focus on a girl's body. Do you know what is the enormous risk? Besides the fact that you have to maintain your body as best as you can, don't forget that there will always be a girl with a more attractive body than yours. And the boy who was attracted solely to your looks will sooner or later go to someone else with a more appealing exterior.

As a boy, do you attract a girl with your money or your cars? Remember that you will never know for sure if she loves you for who you are or for what you have. And when you can no longer keep up, she will go to someone else, since there is always someone else out there with a thicker wallet than yours.

These examples can go on endlessly, but in conclusion, I believe it would be beneficial to emphasize who we are, not what we have. It is not wrong to have things, but it is essential not to prioritize wealth but character. Because Paul said:

"Therefore we do not lose heart. Even though our outward man is perishing, yet the inward man is being renewed day by day." – 2 Corinthians 4:16

And brother Nicolae Ciuriuc[5] added the following: "When beauty fades, all that remains is character."

Solomon gave us wise advice and understood that in those times, just as today, there were many women who attracted only with their "packaging":

"Do not lust after her beauty in your heart, nor let her allure you with her eyelids." – Proverbs 6:25

---

5 Nicolae Ciuriuc was born on August 6, 1959, in Horodiștea, Rădăuți-Prut, Botoșani, Romania. He was a Romanian Christian pastor, writer, and hymn composer.

I am so disappointed to see social media filled with pictures of barely and indecently dressed girls (to attract the boys, right?). Social media is filled with boys showcasing their cars and the vacations they can afford. They are full of teenagers seeking to become rich overnight. All these are traps that bring nothing but disappointment, frustration, and later, marriage failures – all because the emphasis was misplaced.

Garbage attracts flies, while nectar attracts bees... If you attract a materialistic woman who dislikes work but likes to spend money, you do realize you will be miserable for life, don`t you? If you attract a man without fear of God and only with sinful desires, you do realize that you won't be able to keep up with the fantasies in his mind, don`t you?

How good it would be if we all attracted others with our kindness. Our gentleness. Our peace. Our integrity. With our beautiful character. With fear of God! Let's hide, as much as possible, what we have, and display only what we truly are. This way, we will filter out the flies from the bees. We will filter out exploiters from honest people.

What do you attract with?

February 14

THE MOST EXPENSIVE WEDDING

It was July 29, 1981. Prince Charles and Princess Diana were heading to the altar of St. Paul's Cathedral in London. 3,500 guests followed them, and another 750 million people were watching on television the wedding of the century.

There were 10,000 pearls on Princess Diana's dress. The veil was 139 meters long, and the dress train was 7.5 meters long. 542 sequins and 132 pearls were placed on the bride's shoes.

The total cost? 48 million dollars. $600,000 was spent just to ensure security...

It is declared the most expensive wedding in human history.

Could it really be so?

The Bible says a much more expensive wedding awaits us. The location will not be in the cathedral of any European capital but in God's New Jerusalem. The guests will be from all the nations of the earth. The bride will be the Church.

The gold will be on the ground. The Bridegroom will gird Himself and serve us.

We will not need security. There will be no reason to be guarded anymore.

The price for expenses? It has already been paid through the sacrifice at Calvary. And the preparations have been ongoing for over 2,000 years. But, in addition to the preparations made in heaven, our preparation is also needed, the preparation of those who will participate in the wedding that takes place on earth:

> *"Let us be glad and rejoice and give Him glory, for the marriage of the Lamb has come, and His wife has made herself ready." – Revelation 19:7*

Do you know what is the greatest happiness we can ever have? To respond to the invitation that we are receiving to this wedding:

> *"Then he said to me, 'Write: 'Blessed are those who are called to the marriage supper of the Lamb!" And he said to me, 'These are the true sayings of God.'" – Revelation 19:9*

FEBRUARY 15

WHERE DOES YOUR STRENGTH COME FROM?

"So Dalilah said to Samson, 'Please tell me where your great strength lies, and with what you may be bound to afflict you.'" – Judges 16:6

We are familiar with various forms of power. Physical strength. Social status power. Emotional strength. Material power. Military power.

It is crucial to be aware that there is also spiritual power. We need this power or strength every day. Consider how valuable your soul is if both God and the Devil are contending for it! Don't you need power to resist the Devil?

Below, I list some sources of spiritual power:

1. The Gospel

"For I am not ashamed of the gospel of Christ, for it is the power of God to salvation for everyone who believes, for the Jew first and also for the Greek." – Romans 1:16

When Jesus was tempted by the Devil, He used the Gospel to resist those temptations. The Gospel contains the power of God, and the Devil knows this. Do you also know this? Have you made time every day to read the Gospel and then to live it out?

2. The Holy Spirit

"But you shall receive power when the Holy Spirit has come upon you, and you shall be witnesses to Me in Jerusalem, and in all Judea and Samaria, and to the end of the earth." – Acts 1:8

The more filled we are with the Holy Spirit, the more filled we are with power. We have the power to endure. We have the power of self-control. We have the power to love even those who do us harm. In this way, the Devil cannot prevail.

3. Prayer

"Watch therefore, and pray always that you may be counted worthy to escape all these things that will come to pass, and to stand before the Son of Man." – Luke 21:36

On the front lines, any soldier who can no longer communicate with the base is in danger of death.

If he no longer receives instructions, he does not know the enemy's location anymore, so he cannot prepare for the next attacks.

Our connection with heaven is established through prayer. The base is the place from where we receive the necessary instructions for the next steps. The more we pray, the more power we will receive.

4. Wisdom

"A wise man is strong, yes, a man of knowledge increases strength." – Proverbs 24:5

A wise person is powerful because he knows what decisions to make. The wise man knows that peace is often more important than justice; patience is more valuable than anger; it is often wiser to be silent than to speak casually.

Use these sources of power to be an overcomer!

February 16

LATE, LATER, AND TOO LATE

"Therefore, since a promise remains of entering His rest, let us fear lest any of you seem to have come short of it." – Hebrews 4:1

The Bible speaks about three kinds of comparative adverbs: late, later, and too late.

You might work until late at night to earn bread for your family, but do not forget that your effort needs the blessing of God in whatever you do:

"In vain you rise early and stay up late, toiling for bread to eat — for he grants sleep to those he loves." – Psalm 127:2

Jesus tells Peter that he will not leave this earth now but later:

"Simon Peter said to Him, 'Lord, where are You going?' Jesus answered him, 'Where I am going you cannot follow Me now, but you shall follow Me afterward.'" – John 13:36

In the book of Hebrews, the apostle warns us to be very careful not to come to Jesus too late!

"Let us therefore be diligent to enter that rest, lest anyone fall according to the same example of disobedience." – Hebrews 4:11

There are people who come to Jesus late. Bartimaeus cried out to Jesus as He was leaving Jericho. It was late, but not too late. Paul converted on the road to Damascus. It was late, but not too late. The thief cried out from the cross. He was later than anyone else, but not too late.

There are people who hear a sermon and are moved by it but repent later – after a few more years of evangelization. After a few more years of wandering in the world. They take the risk of coming later, and for some, it is good that it was not too late. But this enormous risk has led to a "too late" for the other category of people who procrastinate.

For those who watched Noah build the ark for decades but did not enter it, it was too late.

For Lot's sons-in-law it was too late. Although they were warned of the imminent punishment, they thought it was a joke.

It was too late for Samson not to lose his eyes after finding comfort in Delilah's arms and revealing the secret of his strength. It was too late for Dinah to regain her virginity after meeting Shechem.

It was too late was for the rich man in Luke 16 to ask for mercy.

It was too late for the five foolish virgins. They knocked on a closed door that never opened again

If you are reading these words, you should know that it is late.

Do not postpone your return to God – it may soon be too late.

February 17

SHORTCUTS WE MUST AVOID

"Then it came to pass, when Pharaoh had let the people go, that God did not lead them by way of the land of the Philistines, although that was near; for God said, 'Lest perhaps the people change their minds when they see war, and return to Egypt.'" – Exodus 13:17

Passing through the land of the Philistines was a shorter route to Canaan, but the Jews, recently freed from bricks and straw, were not physically and mentally prepared for war. Disappointment and frustration would have prevailed, and the regret of leaving Egypt would have set in as soon as they saw their brothers fall on the battlefield.

We also like shortcuts. To work a little and earn a lot. To go to church for an hour and receive spiritual power for a year. To read the Bible once a month and know the Word inside out. To offer a sandwich once a year to a poor person and reap the rewards of martyrs. However, most of the time, shortcuts defeat us. They take us into the middle of battles we will lose. They make us forget where we came from...

How wise it would be for us to understand that God has His plan of growth for each of us! How good it would be for us to understand that there are paths we must avoid! That there are wars we must not wage. That there are fires we must not ignite. That there are disputes we must not engage in. That there are questions we must not answer.

Am I ready to ask God for wisdom once again and accept His will in all the ways of my life? How many times did it seem to me that it would be better in one way, while God was trying to make me understand that my way would not bring me victory in the long run?

Is it not better to take the longer road with peace rather than the shorter one quarrelling?

Is it not better on a longer road with a clear conscience than on a shorter one with a stained conscience?

Is it not better on a more difficult road, but with your head held high than on a shorter one bowing down in shame?

Lord, guard us from the paths that seem best to us and help us accept the paths You have laid out for us!

FEBRUARY 18

MOSES, JOSHUA, AARON AND HUR

"So Joshua did as Moses said to him, and fought with Amalek. And Moses, Aaron, and Hur went up to the top of the hill." – Exodus 17:10

Joshua was in the valley fighting the Amalekites. On the hilltop, Moses held his hands raised to heaven for victory, and Aaron and Hur supported his hands when they grew tired.

At sunset, the fate of the battle was decided: the Amalekites were defeated, and the Jews turned to Joshua to congratulate him. He turned with tears in his eyes and pointed to the hilltop, to Aaron and Hur. But Aaron and Hur pointed to Moses. And Moses pointed to the heavens...

"Moses built an altar and called its name, The-Lord-Is-My-Banner." – Exodus 17:15

There are difficult, fierce battles today as well. The Devil wants to destroy families. He wants to stain the hearts and bodies of the youth. He wants to divide churches. He wants to kill souls. And when these wars are waged, we do not need tanks, machine guns, or ballistic missiles.

In spiritual battles, we need people to understand the place where God has placed them and to do their part there.

Joshua carries the sword – direct strikes on the front line. He is exposed to daily attacks; he will not succeed alone. He needs someone to watch his back, and that someone is Moses. With white hair, at the age of over 80, he could no longer wield the sword. He could no longer fight side by side with the youth. But he could hold his hands raised to heaven. He had a direct connection with God through intercession. It was not the first time God listened to him.

Next to Moses, there is still a need for Aaron and Hur. People who support God's work. People who support tired hands. People who bring a stone as support for the weary Moses. People who encourage. People who have uplifting words.

Do you understand why many spiritual battles today bring defeats? We have a better understanding as to why *Joshua* is sometimes defeated! Do you know that it is not always his fault? Can we take responsibility, and can we ask ourselves if we have done our duty in the place where God placed us?

If Moses were on the front line, and Joshua with his hands up, the battle would have been lost. If he had sent Aaron and Hur to wield the sword, while Moses and Joshua stayed in the tent for theological debates, the Jews would have been killed. When we do not understand our place and calling, the Devil gains ground...

Today, God calls us not to seek the culprits of past defeats but to personally check our place and the calling God has made to us, and thus prepare for future victories.

If you are called to Joshua's place, do what Joshua did: inflict considerable damage on the Amalekites.

If you are called to Moses' place, keep your hands lifted up. Victory on the frontline depends on intercession from behind the line.

If you are called to Aaron and Hur's place, support the work. Spiritually and materially. Through words and actions.

Do not pick up the sword if God told you to bring stones for Moses! Do not get involved in supporting the hands of intercessors if God told you that you should be in the valley on the frontline!

What are you doing at the pulpit when God told you that you must intercede in your room at home? What are you doing in the worship team when God called you to manage the financial expenses? Haven't you understood that God will not ask you about the place in which you liked to serve, but about the place where He put you?

Let us prepare and go be where our places are! No soldier will win the battle without discipline. No intercessor will be able to hold his hands up if they are not clean! No supporter will help Moses if he is 1,000 miles away, busy with something else.

I have seen so many people dissatisfied because they are not doing what they would like to do! So many frustrated commentators because Joshua is on the frontline, while they have to hold Moses's hands up. I have seen so many who do not know their place after years since meeting God... People who keep the score of the battle instead of raising Moses' hands.

The best soldier in this world is useless if he is not in the place the general sent him! The best intercessor is useless if, instead of holding his hands raised, he keeps them on the phone. Not even the best supporter has any impact if he sits sulking and dissatisfied because he does not like his work...

On your marks, get ready, go! Another battle awaits us on the horizon... And only then can we talk about building altars!

FEBRUARY 19

FIRST MY REPENTANCE OR OTHER PEOPLE`S REPENTANCE?

The most dangerous type of hypocrisy is that of a person who has a good reputation but a problematic character. To maintain his image, he always deals with other people`s problem, instead of addressing the issue of his character first.

When Judas saw Mary using expensive perfume to anoint Jesus' feet, he said:

> *"Why was this fragrant oil not sold for three hundred denarii and given to the poor?" – John 12:5*

When the prodigal son`s brother saw that his brother was coming home, he said:

> *"So he answered and said to his father, 'Lo, these many years I have been serving you; I never transgressed your commandment at any time; and yet you never gave me a young goat, that I might make merry with my friends. But as soon as this son of yours came, who has devoured your livelihood with harlots, you killed the fatted calf for him.'" – Luke 15:29-30*

When the Pharisee in the temple saw the tax collector daring to come for worship, he prayed like this:

> *"The Pharisee stood and prayed thus with himself, 'God, I thank You that I am not like other men—extortioners, unjust, adulterers, or even as this tax collector.'" – Luke 18:11*

Judas sold Jesus for thirty pieces of silver. The Pharisee continued on his way to hell, believing he was heading to heaven and that he was far better than the tax collector. The prodigal son's brother also had his friends, who were more valuable to him than the returning brother.

Before pointing fingers at others, let us not forget that there are three fingers pointing back at us. Before jumping to condemn others, it is better to focus on our own repentance. Before removing the speck from our neighbor's eye, let us deal with the log in our own eye, since we probably do not even see our neighbor clearly due to the log. Also, when attempting to remove his speck, we might end up pulling out his eye.

A doctor cannot heal others if he himself is bedridden. A judge cannot send anyone to prison if he himself is convicted of disgraceful acts.

Who will believe a shoemaker can repair shoes if he walks barefoot? Who will trust a car salesman if he himself walks on foot, without a car? Who will call a contractor to build him a house if that builder lives in a shack?

No one will believe my words if my actions are not right. People might be deceived by my image, but God sees my character, and sooner or later, it will be revealed.

A truly repentant person, no matter how low they are, will not hit others. The tax collector did not attack the Pharisee. Mary did not criticize Judas, and the prodigal son did not belittle his older brother nor ask him if he had more money to spend.

True repentance begins with me.

Only then can I lovingly and compassionately care for the one next to me...

February 20

HOW DO YOU MEASURE YOUR SUCCESS?

It is said that one day, Thomas Aquinas visited the Pope and found him in the Vatican treasury, surrounded by immense wealth.

The Pope looked at Thomas and exclaimed, "Look, Father Thomas, we can no longer say, 'Silver and gold have I none!'"

Without hesitation, Thomas replied, "Nor can we say what Peter said next, 'In the name of Jesus Christ of Nazareth, rise up and walk!'"

Thomas understood a truth that many do not grasp today: the success of a mission or a church is not measured by the money in the treasury, nor by the extravagant building, or the crowds attending the service. True success is measured by the work of the Holy Spirit and obedience to the Word of God.

The world we live in has its own operating standards, which differ from God's standards. The world values pride, while God values humility. The world appreciates greatness, while God appreciates meekness. The world values what is visible, while God values what is hidden. The world appreciates entertainment, while God values tears. The world values extravagance, while God values simplicity.

How do you measure your success?

By what you have in your wallet or by what you have in your heart?

By what people say or by what God says?

By temporal things or by eternal riches?

By quantity or by quality?

By words or by deeds?

February 21

THE CONDITIONS TO BECOME FUTURE LEADERS

"Moreover you shall select from all the people able men, such as fear God, men of truth, hating covetousness; and place such over them to be rulers of thousands, rulers of hundreds, rulers of fifties, and rulers of tens." – Exodus 18:21

When Jethro visited his son-in-law, Moses, he found him exhausted and overly involved. Not only was Moses tired, but the people who came for counseling, with every problem, big or small, were also weary.

Noticing this situation, Jethro gave Moses advice that is still valid today — work as a team and share the tasks. This team should consist of:

1. Competent people

A capable person is competent, skilled, clever, and talented in a specific field. He is a person who has earned a good reputation for being proficient in what he does.

You cannot ask someone skilled in laying tiles to do carpentry if he is not called to it. You cannot ask someone who skipped Romanian language classes to write books. You cannot ask someone who lacks musical knowledge to conduct an orchestra. Each of us has at least one area where we must excel and be competent.

2. Trustworthy people

Everyone, especially leaders, must be trustworthy. They must be people you can rely on, people you can count on. People who, if they say they finish a job in two weeks, will not take three months to do it. People who know how to keep the confidentiality of a confession. People who avoid gossip, lies, and hypocrisy. Only trustworthy people can be credible.

3. Enemies of greed

Leaders must be immune to bribery. They should not be for sale. Their eyes should not shine when they see gold. They should not show favoritism when they see the guilty person's thick wallet. Wise Solomon left us a warning worth considering:

"He who is greedy for gain troubles his own house, but he who hates bribes will live." – Proverbs 15:27

May God raise up leaders like these! Leaders who are promoted based on competence, not connections. People who have earned a good name, not people who have lost it. People with a "backbone," who fear God, and who cannot be corrupted.

FEBRUARY 22

THE 7 FACES OF THE HYPOCRITE

It is said that some people have only one cheek but multiple faces – this is the definition of a hypocrite. A double-faced person. The dictionary describes such a person as having insincere, feigned, and fake behavior.

You will not be able to avoid hypocrisy if you do not know its "qualities." You will not be able to avoid a hypocritical person if you don't understand their behavior.

Let's allow the Bible to describe the hypocrite:

1. He does what he does only so that others see him

"Woe to you, scribes and Pharisees, hypocrites! For you devour widows' houses, and for a pretense make long prayers. Therefore you will receive greater condemnation." – Matthew 23:14

Have you ever behaved nicely just because someone was watching?

Have you ever appeared more spiritual than you are just because another spiritual person was watching you?

Have you ever been very attentive to someone just because you knew you were being watched and wanted to make a good impression?

We live in a time when many things are done just for personal image! "Let it be said about me, let it be heard about me, let me be seen in a better light!"

2. He tells others to do but he does not do it

"Therefore whatever they tell you to observe, that observe and do, but do not do according to their works; for they say, and do not do." – Matthew 23:3

What we say has value if, first of all, we live what we say. People will be impressed not by our words but by our actions. The hypocrite will never motivate anyone because he says one thing and does another.

3. He seems good on the outside but is dirty on the inside

"So you also outwardly appear righteous to men, but inside you are full of hypocrisy and lawlessness." – Matthew 23:28

In the year 290 BC, Ptolemy I Soter, the king of Egypt, hired the architect Sostratus to build the Lighthouse of Alexandria so that ships could safely navigate into the harbor, avoiding the dangers posed by the rugged coastline.

In the end, Sostratus inscribed his name on a stone, covered it with clay and paint, and over the paint, with golden letters, wrote the king's name! He knew that, over time, the waves would hit the rock, causing the clay to come off, and thus eventually revealing his name!

4. He is preoccupied with trivial matters while ignoring the important ones

"Woe to you, scribes and Pharisees, hypocrites! For you pay tithe of mint and anise and cummin and have neglected the weightier matters of the law: justice and mercy and faith. These you ought to have done, without leaving the others undone." – Matthew 23:23

For a tree, the roots, trunk, crown, leaves, and its location in the garden are important, but the most remarkable of all is the FRUIT.

If I did not love the man who fell among thieves, what good was it that I dressed modestly? If I did not stop to help someone on my way to church, what good was it that I arrived there on time? If the Levite sang a solo that morning but did not stop to help like the Samaritan, what good was it?

The Devil wants us to argue over trivial matters and lose sight of the important ones!

5. He advises others but does not know the way himself

"Let them alone. They are blind leaders of the blind. And if the blind leads the blind, both will fall into a ditch." – Matthew 15:14

It's not wrong not to know, but it's wrong to pretend you do know. That is why a wise person admits it when he does not know and is willing to learn more. To avoid ruining his image, the hypocrite avoids learning.

The best map in the world is of no use if you do not know where you are! And if you do not know where you are, how can you guide others?

6. He clings to the trivial matters in the lives of others while he has serious sins in his own life

"Hypocrite! First, remove the plank from your own eye, and then you will see clearly to remove the speck from your brother's eye." – Matthew 7:5

The Pharisee prayed at the Temple and thanked God that he was not like the tax collector.

There is a terrible attitude among Christians: to hide sin in my life, I try to appear very holy by pointing out the sins of others. However, Jesus clearly says: you do not see well because you have a log in your eye! Would you trust a doctor who cannot see well to perform surgery on you?

Why must you pass an eye test before you get a driver's license? Because having a new car is useless if you cannot see six feet in front of you! If your car's headlights are dirty in winter, does it matter that your fuel tank is full?

Take care of your own problems before worrying about other people`s problems. Can a person with a broken arm extend a helping hand to someone who fell in a pit?

7. He applies mercy for himself, and justice for others

"But the ruler of the synagogue, indignant because Jesus had healed on the Sabbath, said to the crowd, 'There are six days on which work ought to be done. Come on those days and be healed, and not on the Sabbath day.' The Lord answered him, 'You hypocrites! Does not each of you on the Sabbath untie his ox or his donkey from the manger and lead it away to water it? And ought not this woman, a daughter of Abraham whom Satan bound for eighteen years, be loosed from this bond on the Sabbath day?" – Luke 13:14–16

The synagogue ruler considered it more urgent to observe the Sabbath than to heal a woman who had been sick for 18 years. He loved justice more than mercy. Had she been his daughter, he would surely have loved mercy more than strict law.

"François Fénelon was the preacher at the court of King Louis XIV of France. Every Sunday, the king and many people from the city attended the service. However, one Sunday, the king found the preacher alone in the entire church. 'What happened?' asked the king. 'Last week, I announced that it was possible for the king not to attend the service this Sunday because I wanted to show you how many people come to church for God and how many come for the eyes of the King of France!' replied François."[6]

Lord, help us stay away from any form of hypocrisy!

[6] https://barefootpreachr.wordpress.com/2011/06/06/empty-churches/

FEBRUARY 23

THE SENDER, THE MESSAGE, THE MAILMAN, AND THE RECIPIENT

"Write the things which you have seen, and the things which are, and the things which will take place after this." – Revelation 1:19

The one who writes a letter for someone is called the sender. The one who delivers the message is the mailman. And the one who receives the letter is the recipient.

There would be no message without a sender. It would not reach its destination without a serious mailman. And the message is useless if the recipient does not open and pay attention to it.

God is the sender of many messages to different people. He uses evangelists, writers, prophets, and other categories of people so that His messages reach their destination. But let's not forget that the focus should be on the sender and the message, not on the mailman.

God's message will address your character, not your comfort!

God's message will deal more with illnesses that are spiritual rather than physical!

God's message will have your eternal life in view more than your ephemeral life here!

God's message will focus on your family more than your workplace.

Are we paying attention to God's messages, or do we blame the mailman? Some people, to avoid accepting God's message, have tried to find faults in those delivering it. Perhaps the mailman is late with a delivery, perhaps his vehicle is older than you imagined, or perhaps his family has problems. But these do not give you the right to trample on the letters he brings.

I pray that we take God's messages seriously. Let`s appreciate those who make efforts to bring us this message, but above all, let`s be glad that God still speaks to us and let`s have the attitude He wants us to have!

February 24

SANCTIFIED PHONES?

"So rend your heart, and not your garments; Return to the Lord your God, For He is gracious and merciful, Slow to anger, and of great kindness; And He relents from doing harm." – Joel 2:13

Here is a headline from the internet: "An Italian priest sanctifies his parishioners' phones to protect them from fake news and shield them from hate on social media."

Father Don Giorgio Mariotti from Perugia believes that by doing this, the believers` devices "will be shielded from fake news published online and protected from the hatred that prevails on social media."

Hmm, seriously? So, if the phone is sanctified and I want to visit a website where people curse each other, the phone will not access that website?

I was shocked. I was amazed at the limited way of thinking of people who still believe that the phone is to blame when accessing fake news or inappropriate content.

As if the phone accesses a website on its own... I was amazed that there are still people who think gadgets need to be sanctified, but not our hearts.

Dear ones, haven't you asked yourselves: why does any country in the world, when judging a murder, send the murderer to prison, not the knife he used?

Why is the thief the one to be judged and not the weapons used in robbing a supermarket?

Is it so hard to understand that everything in this world is neutral, and the way in which we use it depends on our character?

Look at the prodigal son: money, while in the father's hand, was blessed. The same money, the same wealth, in the son's hand brought failure and bankruptcy. Was the money to blame? Certainly not; it was the character of the one using the money! Notice the tremendous difference Solomon makes when speaking of the righteous and the wicked in relation to their income:

"The earnings of the godly enhance their lives, but evil people squander their money on sin." – Proverbs 10:16

Is income to blame? The salary that goes into your account? Or do you think that some people receive blessed money, while others receive cursed money? No!

All money is the same. Plastic or paper cannot be holy or sinful. However, the way in which we earn and use money depends on our character.

Lord, wake us up! Let us not blame other things; let us understand that we need to change ourselves first and then begin to use the things around us beneficially for ourselves and for those around us.

February 25

THE SKY OF YOUR LIFE

The journey through life involves several stages, and the "sky" of our lives can take different forms, like the real sky:

1. Clear sky

Job. 11.500 cattle. 10 children. Everything was going well. It can be similar for us. Our children listen to us. Our salary is deposited on time. The doctor informs us, smiling, that the labs are perfect.

What does the righteous person do when he is going through good days? He prepares for bad days. Job built altars. Daniel prayed three times a day. It seems they both foresaw that the sky of life would not always be clear.

What does the sinful person do when everything goes well? He prepares only for continuous good times. He thinks that life is rosy forever. That is what the rich man in Luke 12 did. Except that the following night, his life was interrupted.

2. Partially cloudy sky

Isaiah tells Hezekiah to put his house in order because he will die. What does the righteous man do when the sky is partially cloudy? He turns to the One he served when the sky was clear:

"'Remember now, O Lord, I pray, how I have walked before You in truth and with a loyal heart, and have done what was good in Your sight.' And Hezekiah wept bitterly." – 2 Kings 20:3

What does the sinner do when the sky gets cloudy? Most of the people do not take God`s warnings seriously. That`s what Lot`s sons-in-law did:

"So Lot went out and spoke to his sons-in-law, who had married his daughters, and said, 'Get up, get out of this place; for the Lord will destroy this city!' But to his sons-in-law he seemed to be joking." – Genesis 19:14

When the Ninevites saw that the sky was getting dark, they repented. And God gave them another 180 years of clear sky, as confirmed by history.

3. Stormy sky

Both the house built on rock and the one built on sand go through the storm. However, the foundation makes the difference.

Daniel in the lions` den: his prayer in good times made the difference.

Job, on a heap of ashes, with a shard in his hand – unwavering in his faithfulness to God. Do you remember the altars from Job's sunny days? And his extraordinary testimony?

> *"For I delivered the poor who cried out, the fatherless and the one who had no helper. The blessing of a perishing man came upon me, and I caused the widow's heart to sing for joy." – Job 29:12*

The storm will cause losses. You might lose your health, your money, your material possessions, or your car. However, what is important is not to lose your faith.

In conclusion, the skies of our lives will always shift and change, bringing periods of clarity, clouds, and storms. The key to navigating these changes lies in our spiritual preparedness and steadfast faith. By building a strong foundation in God, we can face any weather with resilience and grace, knowing that our trust in Him will carry us through. As we embrace each phase of life's sky, let us remain anchored in our faith, preparing for the storms while cherishing the clear days, ever ready to turn to God in all circumstances.

February 26

HOW CAN I WIN OVER A PERSON WHO DOES NOT LIKE ME?

Benjamin Franklin had a political rival who made his life difficult. Instead of trying to gain his approval, Franklin took a different approach. Knowing his rival had a rare book, Franklin asked to borrow it. After returning the book with a note of gratitude, his adversary surprisingly became his friend.

This illustrates a psychological principle known as cognitive dissonance, where the tension from holding two opposing beliefs leads us to change one belief to resolve the conflict.

In Franklin's case, his rival had an unpleasant belief about him. However, after doing a favor to Benjamin, the rival was forced to accept another belief: "It is difficult to do favors to others, so I reserve this only for those I appreciate."

The secret of the principle used by Benjamin Franklin is as follows: if you want people to appreciate you, ask them to do you favors.

In other words, ask for their help. Make them feel happy when they know they can be of assistance. It is extremely difficult to help someone and continue to hate them. However, to ask for help, you must be humble.

How can you not love Job when he himself said,

"I go about mourning, but not in the sun. I stand up in the assembly and cry out for help." – Job 30:28

The help you seek from your adversary now will make him reflect more deeply on the relationship he has with you, and ultimately, you have a chance to win his friendship.

Ask for help! Ask for a favor!

In the end, you will gain a friend!

God can make friends even out of our enemies. But we must also desire this. The most beautiful life is one in which even if not everyone loves you, you do everything in your power to love and win them all. May God help us do that.

FEBRUARY 27

HOW MANY SECONDS CAN YOU LIVE WITHOUT GOD?

"For in Him we live and move and have our being, as also some of your own poets have said, 'For we are also His offspring...'" – *Acts 17:28*

It is said that a person can survive 40 days without food, 3 days without water, 8 minutes without air, but he could not live a single second without God!

I am amazed many times when I see the pride of some people who are overly confident in themselves, in their wealth, in their connections, and who do not want to hear about God. In their foolishness, they believe they can solve everything with money, or that they can have anything they want with a phone call to the right place, taking everything for granted. However, it is enough for God to withdraw His hand from their health for a few days, and then they become desperate, astonished by their human limitations and the constraints of their existence.

Could you have gotten out of bed this morning without His help? Could you have eaten today without Him giving you the appetite for food? Could you add at least two more days to the beats of your heart when its Creator says it is time to stop? If we cannot do the smallest things without God, shouldn't we walk humbly, as Micah says?

"He has shown you, O man, what is good; and what does the Lord require of you but to do justly, to love mercy, and to walk humbly with your God?" – *Micah 6:8*

Humility means acknowledging that in all things, we depend on Him; that every second you live is a blessing from Him; that every piece of clothing you wear is His mercy; that every glass of water is a grace from heaven; that everything you have is, in fact, from above:

"Every good gift and every perfect gift is from above and comes down from the Father of lights, with whom there is no variation or shadow of turning." – *James 1:17*

What should we offer in exchange for His blessings?

"Or do you despise the riches of His goodness, forbearance, and longsuffering, not knowing that the goodness of God leads you to repentance?" – Romans 2:4

Instead of contempt, let us have gratitude. Instead of looking down, let us look up. Instead of hardening our heart, let us turn in repentance toward Him.

On the day of judgment, no one will have any excuse. During his lifetime, every human being has felt in their heart the blessings that the Savior has offered them.

Be among those who have said "thank you" not just with their lips but through a life filled with humility, gratitude, and a lifestyle according to His will.

FEBRUARY 28

KEEP AWAY FROM ADULTERY!

"But whoever commits adultery with a woman lacks understanding; he who does so destroys his own soul." – Proverbs 6:32

The Barna Group statistics say that over one in three (35%) married men have extramarital sexual relationships, and one in six (17%) married women cheat on their husbands. Infidelity infects Christian marriages at the same rate in which it paralyzes marriages at a national level. Moreover, if a married man has one affair, it is likely that he will repeat it. Three-quarters of men who admit to having an affair also admit to having more than one affair, and 3 out of 10 (31%) admit to having had more than 5 different affairs.

Infidelity in marriage remains the primary cause of marital breakdowns worldwide. Why do people cheat on each other? The reasons are many, but I believe the most well-known reasons are: lack of fear of God, lack of respect, and lack of love that comes from a divine model.

I have repeated many times in sermons: the fundamental aspect to consider when getting married is to choose a partner who fears God – someone who has integrity, who keeps his word, who has an honorable character, and who listens to God. You cannot monitor your spouse 24 hours a day, and even if you could, you would live with continuous stress. However, if both spouses fear God, the relationship is not based on spying, interrogations *(Where were you yesterday? It seemed to me that you looked at someone else! You said you would be home by 5:00; why were you late?)*, but on trust.

When the fear of God departs, the agape love departs as well. Therefore, the Devil insists through sin to destroy your character. If a vessel is cracked in one spot, does it matter in how many other spots it is broken?

Adultery leaves behind a shattered family. It leaves behind tears and wounds that do not heal easily. Before adultery happens physically, it takes place in the mind of the person involved. A person does not cheat at work before he first cheats virtually through immorality. A partner does not make double meaning jokes until, before using such words, he has accepted immoral compromise in his mind.

God desires very much for us to keep our promise of a pure marriage, and this is called faithfulness to our spouse:

"And if you ask, 'Why?' Because the Lord has been witness between you and the wife of your youth, with whom you have dealt treacherously; yet she is your companion and your wife by covenant!" – Malachi 2:14

This Witness is always watching us. He made a record of the covenant we made. We chose our spouse and pledged our life-long fidelity. This fidelity is achieved every day through communication, transparency, sincerity, sacrifice, and anything else that is beneficial in a marriage.

Run away from adultery! Run away from any thought of infidelity! This sin is so vile and serious that it resembles a rope that, once cut, cannot be easily tied back together. This sin makes you lose your marital purity and brings with it regrets that you drag with you until the day you die! This despicable sin will shatter the trust your spouse has in you, and you will need years to restore it...

If you have fallen into this trap, make clear decisions for a complete change. Draw closer to God with many tears and much humility so that He may grant you forgiveness and help you never fall again.

March 1

SPRING OF THE SOUL

"The light of the king's face is life, and his favor is like a cloud of the latter rain." – *Proverbs 16:15*

The temperature rises. A snowdrop joyfully emerges through the melting snow. Brown and gray colors are replaced by bright ones, and the cold winds are slowly leaving.

The sun seems braver today. The trees will announce, through their flowers, that frost does not have the final word. Migratory birds, through their chirping, will offer us free access to reverie concerts.

It is the first day of spring.

The soul needs it too.

A smiling face and a heart full of kindness are signs that coldness and distance have melted away.

The fields near the village need the spring rains – but so does the field of your heart.

For a bountiful harvest, it is essential that God, through His attention, provides the care you need.

Spring brings growth to the soul. Time spent with God each day will bring you close to the source of water, and the fruit will not delay appearing.

Spring brings a new beginning to the soul. Forgiveness and healing of the wounds from the winter of your life can begin today if you turn your face towards Him.

Spring brings more light to the soul. The weeping of the night will be shorter, and joyful mornings will become more frequent. The light of God's presence will give you the victory you need.

I wish you a beautiful spring!

With parents who smile and are full of warmth! With children who melt the ice in your heart! With grandparents who welcome you with open arms!

March 2

ON THE EDGE OF THE GRAVE

When was the last time you meditated on your life in a house of mourning? When did you last think about the purpose for which you live, about the frailty of life, and about the importance of eternity while standing on the edge of a cemetery grave?

There, on the edge of the grave, you realize how fleeting human life is.

"Yet you do not know what tomorrow will bring. What is your life? For you are a mist that appears for a little time and then vanishes." – James 4:14

The dreams, plans, words, and deeds of the person who goes into the grave, they all come to an end. In the grave, there is no more childhood, marriage, jobs, credit cards, tiles, no more discontent to express to a colleague and nor more compliments to address to the spouse. That is the place where the dust covers the picture-perfect smile of the one who used to be alive, the place where the opinions of those around are not important anymore, nor are the *likes* of friends received for the vacation photos.

We all know how much time we have lived so far. On each anniversary, we do not actually celebrate the fact that we start a new year, rather, without realizing it, we smile on a day that should remind us that we have less and less to live. You must understand that all you really have is just TODAY! The moments from your past life no longer matter because you cannot change anything there!

What does ultimately really matter?

To live in the fear of God, in obedience to His will, and as a blessing to our fellow human beings.

"Let us hear the conclusion of the whole matter: Fear God and keep His commandments, for this is man's all." – Ecclesiastes 12:13

Meditation on the edge of the cemetery grave is very beneficial. It is like medicine: it does not taste like strawberries, but it heals through the bitterness it brings to the body. The more you realize how transient you are, the more this will make you humble and dependent on God, but also more active in what really matters.

Death makes everyone equal.

The first resurrection, however, will select those who have lived a truly useful life.

Life is the most beautiful gift. It is a unique event. It is a chance that we can only benefit from by being obedient to God, so that we may spend eternity with Him. Repeatable events can be corrected along the way. Unique events do not offer you a second chance.

March 3

IS BEING ALONE ON THE MOUNTAIN ENOUGH?

"Lord, by Your favor, You have made my mountain stand strong; You hid Your face, and I was troubled." – Psalm 30:7

The time when David slept among sheep was gone. So was the time when he fought with the lion or bear to protect the flock or when his clothes smelled like sheep and curd.

God had carried him with a mighty arm for years through the wilderness, while he was fleeing from Saul. The victory over Goliath had created immense envy in the heart of Israel's former king, and fleeing was the best solution.

The day of coronation had come. The day when God was fulfilling what He had promised. The palace servants were bringing him everything his heart desired. The granite he was stepping on was very different from the trodden ground of the fields. Comfort had replaced dirt. From the valley of the shadow of death, David had climbed to the highest peaks a man could reach.

When he wrote Psalm 30, full of joy and gratitude, David remembered all the deliverances of the Lord. At one point, he clearly expresses that he does not want to reach the top of the mountain if God is not present there. Success without the blessing of the Great Master would be a failure. In moments of glory, David feels a thought creeping in, reminding him of his achievements, and he fears that God will hide His face if he welcomes such feelings. The cutting of the palace's ribbon follows, and he would not want to claim the merits of the Lord as his own, since this would only cause trouble and discomfort.

I do not know how many valleys you have had in your life, but if you are on the mountain today, do you have the same mindset as David?

I have met people who were humble in the valley, but full of pride when things got better. While in the midst of failure, they had tears in their eyes but when they gained power, they became full of abuse. God distanced Himself from them when, instead of attributing their success to Him, they attributed it to themselves.

The mountain without God is just a high place from which you can fall. Large bank accounts without Him mean only more opportunities to sin. High positions without Him mean only places from which you can show off your power.

You should say what David said: ‘Lord, I do not want victory without You! I do not want peaks without Your presence! I do not want success without You impressing the value of humility on my heart.’

Only with God, the mountain is no longer about you but about what God can do from the top for the people in the valley. Or do you think you reached the summit just for your own sake?

March 4

DESPAIR AND BONDAGE

"So Moses spoke thus to the children of Israel; but they did not heed Moses, because of anguish of spirit and cruel bondage." – Exodus 6:9

The Egyptians` oppression over the Israelites was increasing at a fast pace. The slavery was becoming more and more severe, and the Israelites could no longer see any glimmer of hope on the horizon of their lives. Moses had told them extraordinary words from God, but they could not accept them:

> *"Therefore, say to the children of Israel: 'I am the LORD; I will bring you out from under the burdens of the Egyptians, I will rescue you from their bondage, and I will redeem you with an outstretched arm and with great judgments. I will take you as My people, and I will be your God. Then you shall know that I am the LORD your God who brings you out from under the burdens of the Egyptians. I will bring you into the land which I swore to give to Abraham, Isaac, and Jacob; and I will give it to you as a heritage: I am the LORD.'" – Exodus 6:6-8*

Something similar is happening nowadays too. The more someone is enslaved by vices such as sports betting, alcohol, cigarettes, pornography, debauchery, and many others, the more these vices will hinder him from hearing the voice of God.

Sin, at first, appears as a mistake. A small slip. Then it becomes a pleasure.

"I will just be betting $10 at the slot machines. Did you see that I won? Did you see the ecstasy that these drugs give me? Did you see how sweet immorality is?" This is how man thinks, and he is not aware that this pleasure comes at a high cost.

Sin becomes bondage. That is where the Devil wants to bring a person. And then, the person caught in sin hears a colossal lie: "Do you see that it is not worth living anymore? You have ruined your life, and God will never forgive you!"

If you are reading these lines, know that you are not reading them by chance. God is ready to offer you forgiveness and, in place of sin, to bring holiness in your life. In place of despair, to bring hope. But you must decide with all your heart to leave all the sinful places and abandon the wrong crowd.

To be ready to listen not only to the words of Moses but to the words of the entire Scriptures.

God's message is one of forgiveness, of hope, of cleansing. He has made extraordinary promises not only to the Israelites but also to us today. But this requires faith.

And faith is born only in a mind that has been washed from the filth of the past and is clean today!

Rise up!

The heaven that God has prepared for you is incomparable to the vices and bondage in which the Devil keeps you!

Canaan means freedom! Egypt means slavery!

Come with us to Canaan!

March 5

DO YOU LIKE TOYS?

This was the question one of the rescuers asked the little girl who had been buried for more than 17 hours under the rubble left in Turkey by the devastating earthquake on January 6, 2023.

What do you think her answer was?

"Mister, if you get me out of here, I will be your slave for life!" cried the desperate girl, directly avoiding the rescuer's question.

This scene made me think a lot. In critical moments, under the collapsed walls, the girl no longer thought about toys. Her savior asked her a question suitable for her age just to make her think of something beautiful, but the little girl understood that in such desperate life circumstances, toys are useless...

I thought about us. About our temporary "toys." About the food we like, the car we regularly polish, the house for which we worked for years. We hold on tightly to these things, like children holding on to the toys they do not want to share with anyone. And suddenly, life offers us an earthquake: bad lab results, unpleasant news, personal failures, and so on.

We desperately realize that toys no longer have any value, but life is the most important aspect, and we would give anything to get it back to normal...

I do not know what kind of "rubble" you are under right now but what I can tell you is that there is a Savior next to you who wants to help you.

You should say just like that little girl, "Mister, if you get me out of here, I will be your slave for life!"

And then you will see that the most beautiful freedom is found in serving Christ.

March 6

DON'T LOOK AT THE WALLS!

Brother Traian Dorz was summoned to the Securitate headquarters in Beiuș and interrogated more than once. During one of these visits, looking at the iron gates and at the intimidating walls, he was inspired with the song that says:

Don't look at the walls, at the iron gates,
At the grinding hatred, but look towards heaven!

Later, brother Nicolae Moldoveanu added music to these lyrics, also through divine inspiration. And for decades, this song has refreshed, encouraged, and comforted those with broken hearts.

We all have our own walls at which we look and wonder how we will ever get beyond them. The labs that are not within normal parameters. An insecure job. One of our children`s marriage on the verge of falling apart. An untrue rumor spread about us. And how many other walls are there?

My encouragement for you today is to look towards the heavens, not to the walls. To Jesus, not to people. To eternity, not to this temporary life.

Facing Jericho, the Israelites had no way to bring down those walls. All that was asked of them was... obedience. And God took care of the walls.

Facing the wall called famine, the widow of Zarephath gathered sticks for her last meal. All she had to do was obey. And God took care of multiplying the food.

Facing debt and the threat of losing her children, the widow in 2 Kings 4 had no solution. All that Elisha asked of her was... obedience. And oil flowed into the empty vessels, and the wall of debts collapsed.

Obedience seems strange. Marching around the walls of Jericho for 7 days? Making the last meal for Elijah while a widow and a child look at it as they starve? Asking for empty vessels from neighbors and pouring oil into all of them from a single jar that had only a little oil?

Do you know that God is not looking for people to operate bulldozers and bring down the walls themselves but for people who are ready to obey? Do not start demolishing; let God do it! You just obey!

Even if it seems strange. Even if the people on the walls laugh and mock you as you march around them. Even if neighbors ridicule you when you ask for empty vessels. Even if you give the last meal to the man of God...

The walls in front of us remind us of our human limitations. Of our need for something higher. Of having to look up. Of obeying God, no matter how much it might cost us.

Obedience seems strange.

But the falling of the walls will shatter the strangeness into pieces.

MARCH 7

THE DANGERS OF COMPLAINING

"All the congregation lifted up their voices and cried, and the people wept that night. All the children of Israel complained against Moses and Aaron, and the whole congregation said to them, 'If only we had died in the land of Egypt! Or if only we had died in this wilderness!'" – Numbers 14:1-2

The people of Israel had become extremely ungrateful. Frightened by the words of the spies sent to Canaan, they no longer had their eyes set on the fruits of the land that awaited them nor on God's promises but only on the negative news:

"But the people who dwell in the land are strong; the cities are fortified and very large. Moreover, we saw the descendants of Anak there." – Numbers 13:28

Their expectations had been high, but the reality on the ground looked entirely different.

They failed to understand that the chasm between expectations and reality could only be bridged by faith in God.

They began to complain. To turn to their leaders and rebuke them. Suddenly, they forgot all of God's miracles, and fear and panic caused mass complaining.

This deeply angered God, who pronounced a terrible verdict:

"In this wilderness your bodies will fall—every one of you twenty years old or more who was counted in the census and who has grumbled against me. Not one of you will enter the land I swore with uplifted hand to make your home, except Caleb son of Jephunneh and Joshua son of Nun." – Numbers 14:29-30

I want you to understand today that, just like the story of the Israelites, complaining will extend your wilderness experience. A journey that should have taken only 11 days ended up lasting 40 years due to lack of faith and its replacement with discontent and complaining.

A person who complains, who is always dissatisfied with his situation, who always grumbles about certain things, will remain in the wilderness of those states for many years to come. Complaining always makes you blame others instead of rising up and moving forward, understanding that there is a part you play, and another part that God will play.

Complaining prolongs the wilderness.

Faith diminishes it.

Look for reasons to be thankful today. Reasons for gratitude regardless of how vast your current wilderness is. The road to Canaan is not easy, but God has promised to be with us. Is it worth complaining? Is it worth grumbling? Is it worth staying in that state of dissatisfaction?

Research at Stanford University has shown that continuous complaining and dissatisfaction shrink the hippocampus, which is the control center of memory. Hippocampal damage is frightening, especially considering that it is one of the first brain areas destroyed by Alzheimer's.

Replace dissatisfaction, negative criticism, and complaining with gratitude! Do not look at what others have and you do not, but at what you have and others do not. Focus on solutions! If you see something negative, do not blame others; come up with helpful solutions!

The dissatisfied people, the complainers, and those who have thrown the responsibility onto others will never climb on the podiums of the world!

Rewards will go to the victorious people, to those who fought, who had faith, who said, "I can do all things through Christ who strengthens me!"

In Canaan will enter only those who encouraged the people, who spoke positively, who boosted morale, and who asked people not to look at the weapons of the Canaanites but at the power of God!

Be among the few!

Be among those who are grateful, thankful, and full of faith...

March 8

THE WOMEN'S POWER OF INFLUENCE

"Charm is deceitful and beauty is passing, but a woman who fears the Lord, she shall be praised." – Proverbs 31:30

God has endowed men with the power to lead and women with the power to influence. When a man and a woman understand their roles, they become exceptional tools in the hands of God, and the impact they have on others will be remarkable.

I invite you to explore together a few areas where a woman can exert her influence positively or negatively.

1. Influence in the life of the nation

In the book of Esther, we notice Esther's significant influence in saving the Jewish people. Putting her own life at risk, she saved a nation. By having the courage to approach the king and speak for her people, Esther proved that when you understand your place and calling, the results of your influence will make history.

2. Influence within the family, in the husband's life

In 2 Kings 4:8-11, a wealthy and faithful woman asks her husband to prepare a room in their house for Elisha. The husband agrees, and the upper room becomes a pleasant and useful surprise for the man of God.

In 1 Kings 21:5-7, we find another wealthy but unfaithful woman, namely Jezebel, the wife of Ahab. Finding out that Naboth refuses to sell his vineyard to her husband, Ahab, she brings false witnesses, and Naboth is killed. However, the joy of acquiring the vineyard did not last long because God's judgment for her negative influence was severe.

3. Influence within the family, in the children's life

The mother of the girl in Naaman's house remains anonymous in history, in terms of her name, but she instilled a remarkable character in her little girl through which God brought the solution to Naaman's leprosy.

Athaliah influenced her child negatively, and the Bible confirms that her advice was ungodly:

> *"Ahaziah was forty-two years old when he became king, and he reigned one year in Jerusalem. His mother's name was Athaliah the granddaughter of Omri. He also walked in the ways of the house of Ahab, for his mother advised him to do wickedly." – 2 Chronicles 22:2-3*

4. Influence in the life of servants

Hannah, Samuel's mother, had a decisive influence on the calling God made to Samuel. We can learn from her that mothers who talk to God will have children to whom God will talk!

Paul Black stated a great truth: "Apart from the power of the Holy Spirit, there is no greater power on earth than a praying mother. Mothers who have prayed have moved more mountains than bulldozers."

5. Influence in the lives of other women

Naomi had a profound influence on Ruth. At a decisive moment, Ruth would say these remarkable words to her mother-in-law:

> *"...wherever you go, I will go; and wherever you lodge, I will lodge." – Ruth 1:16*

Paul reminds Titus that older women can have a good influence on younger ones:

> *"The older women, likewise, that they be reverent in behavior, not slanderers, not given to much wine, teachers of good things—that they admonish the young women to love their husbands, to love their children..." – Titus 2:3-4*

Unfortunately, the example of Herodias shows us that there are women who decide to have a negative influence on the lives of other women. To ask for the murder of John the Baptist – isn't this a diabolical influence?

> *"The daughter of Herodias herself came in and danced, and pleased Herod and those who sat with him. The king said to the girl, 'Ask me whatever you want, and I will give it to you.' She went out and said to her mother, 'What shall I ask?' And she said, 'The head of John the Baptist!'" – Mark 6:22, 24*

6. Influence in the children's marriages

Lemuel's mother decided to influence her son toward a blessed marriage, through some wise advice (Proverbs 31). She paints a portrait of a prudent, wise, diligent, and honorable woman for Lemuel. The experience of life teaches a serious mother what advice to give her children in respect to choosing a spouse who will be a blessing!

Today, I pray that God will bless all women! Your influence, esteemed sisters, is undeniable.

Strong people have strong mothers behind them. Devoted ministers have been shaped by God through women like you.

Never underestimate your power of influence! Stay close to God and to the principles of Scripture so that the influence you spread around will be a true fragrance from God and a real blessing for those over whom it will overflow!

MARCH 9

I DO NOT BELIEVE IN IT, BUT I LIKE IT!

At funerals, in most parts of Romania, services include various elements: almsgiving, boiled wheat dish, memorial services, etc.

The memorial service is a prayer in which we come to the aid of the deceased, praying for the forgiveness of their sins. The underlying idea is that the dead cannot pray for themselves anymore, so they need our help and prayers. According to folk beliefs, if you do not perform the memorial service, the deceased cannot rest in the grave, and the sins that prevent them from reaching Heaven cannot be forgiven.

Giving alms means helping with the forgiveness of the deceased's sins and the salvation of his soul. Those who have departed from this world can no longer do anything to cleanse their souls of sins, so the living relatives act as mediators, as intermediaries.

The boiled wheat dish symbolizes the very body of the deceased, as wheat is the main food of the human body.

At the wake and funeral, all the people who are present gather around the deceased, hold onto the boiled wheat dish, join hands as a sign of love connection with the departed, and shake the dish while saying, "eternal remembrance." This shaking symbolizes the shaking of the earth at the resurrection of the Savior. In this way, the souls of the living enter into communion with the deceased, just as wheat grains come together in the dish.

At such an event, someone asked his colleague, "Do you believe in what's happening here?"

"I don't believe in it, but I like it," was the colleague's reply.

I thought deeply about this answer. If we look in the Scripture, none of the three customs described above has a scriptural basis. The Bible clearly states that after death, there is nothing but judgment:

"And as it is appointed for men to die once, but after this the judgment." – Hebrews 9:27

"For we must all appear before the judgment seat of Christ, that each one may receive the things done in the body, according to what he has done, whether good or bad." – 2 Corinthians 5:10

"For the Son of Man will come in the glory of His Father with His angels, and then He will reward each according to his works." – Matthew 16:27

The Bible clearly states that the deeds of the deceased accompany him, and after death, no modification can be made to those deeds:

"Then I heard a voice from heaven saying to me, 'Write: Blessed are the dead who die in the Lord from now on.' 'Yes,' says the Spirit, 'that they may rest from their labors, and their works follow them.'" – Revelation 14:13

Those who have lived in obedience to God rest because they lived a faith accompanied by deeds worthy of their faith. Others, like the rich man in Luke 16, have remorse and eternal torment because their deeds were in obedience to the Devil.

You see, deep down, people understand that after death, forgiveness is no longer possible. You cannot do good deeds on behalf of the deceased, just as you cannot collect his pension after he died. The "file" of that person's life has been forever closed. And yet, even though people understand that nothing can be done, they find pleasure in these customs.

Do you know why? Because these things tell you that you can live however you wish, do whatever you want, and that, at the end, at the funeral, everything will be fixed through a proper funeral service. But if you have not asked for forgiveness of sins on your own, why do you think that others can ask on your behalf? If you have not prayed to God personally, why do you think others can pray in your place after you die? The Bible tells us of only one Mediator:

"For there is one God and one Mediator between God and men, the Man Christ Jesus." – 1 Timothy 2:5

The surviving relatives cannot act as mediators because this would mean that the Bible is lying and that certain things can be corrected after death. Today, I encourage you not to do whatever you like, but whatever is true. Do not rely on what others do for you after you die; instead, repent now and live every day with God until the end of your life.

March 10

SEVEN DAYS

"After seven days, the waters of the flood came upon the earth." – Genesis 7:10

Noah worked for decades to build the ark. Then the animals entered, and Noah with his family went inside the ark. But the rain did not start immediately. The door of the ark remained open for another 7 days.

Have you thought about the mockery Noah faced from people during those 7 days? Can you imagine the sarcastic looks from neighbors towards the family staying inside the ark and waiting for rain that did not come? Why were they not moved by the fact that the animals entered the ark by themselves?

Before punishing a nation, God will always send it a warning. Before the rain began, Noah's hammer had banged for decades as a sign of mercy from heaven. The open door during the last 7 days was the last chance for the people of that time.

The Ninevites received 40 more days and took full advantage of them.

Nebuchadnezzar had 12 months for repentance, and yet he ignored them. Belshazzar had only a few hours.

Judas had 3 and a half years but did not repent.

God does the same today. No mortal person will leave this life before having the opportunity to hear God's warning. Though nature, through history, through the Bible, and through many other forms, God speaks. He knocks on the door of our hearts, hoping we will open our eyes, see His mercy and grace, and repent:

"Or do you despise the riches of His goodness, forbearance, and longsuffering, not knowing that the goodness of God leads you to repentance?" – Romans 2:4

Every passing second is another grain of sand slipping from the hourglass of God's mercy and patience for you. And with each passing second, life goes by, and the time of mercy becomes shorter.

Do not keep God outside!

Do not wait for the door of the ark of salvation to close.

When the rain starts, it is too late... Can you imagine how those people shouted when the first drops of water began to drip?

Can you imagine how they pleaded for their children in front of the ark? How they apologized to Noah for all the decade-long mockery?

Decades.

7 days.

A few hours.

The closed door.

Are you inside or outside?

MARCH 11

THE NON-PRODIGAL SON

"But he was angry and would not go in. Therefore, his father came out and pleaded with him." – Luke 15:28

He is the son who stays at home. The one who does not cause big problems. The one who does not squander his inheritance in wild living. The one who does not want to go inside the house because, well, why share the father's joy for a brother returning from the pigs?

He had his own friends. But he had not dared to leave like his brother did. He had plenty of scenarios in his mind. But for him, the taste of the party is enjoyed in secret. What was important was his reputation. 'I would like to have fun too, but what will the brethren say? I would leave too, but I would not want anyone to know… What should I do?'

The non-prodigal son is the devout person in the church, the one who cannot rejoice in the forgiveness God grants to the one returning from a life of sin. Someone once said: 'If God forgives even a man like this, I do not need such a God…'

The non-prodigal son was in the house but not at home.

He was near his father physically, but his mind was with his friends. The fattened calf was not meant to be shared with the brother who wasted the wealth but with his "respectable" friends.

The non-prodigal son is the one who serves and then he rubs it in. He serves like a slave, not like a son…

"But he answered and said to his father, 'Lo, these many years I have been serving you; I never transgressed your commandment at any time, and yet you never gave me a young goat, that I might make merry with my friends.'" – Luke 15:29

He is always looking over the church fence. 'What a good time are those guys having and how miserable am I, stuck with these parents who keep me indoors all the time. Prayer again. Fasting again. Going to church again. I'm so fed up…'

The non-prodigal son cannot rejoice in someone else's salvation. He wants heaven without forgiven sinners. He wants eternity without his neighbors who, in his opinion, are irredeemable.

The Bible says he was angry. He has the appearance of righteousness, is an excellent conservative, but when it comes to a quarrel or scandal, just watch and see this righteous man get all red in anger. Watch him throw words at others. He does not drink, does not go clubbing, does not beat his wife. But gossip is his specialty. Anger takes over when something does not please him. He makes everyone else's problems his business but fails to deal with his own.

There is no deeper spiritual death than that of someone who judges others, who has a forked tongue and who cannot rejoice in the salvation of others. The sickest person is the one who claims not to need a doctor, who says he is healthy even though he is full of gangrene. The person who talks back to his parents and then goes to relax playing the guitar. The person who has a password on his phone so that no one knows what he watches is more dangerous than the one who rolls in the mud, then hears a sermon, and truly repents. The non-prodigal son shakes hands with everyone, hugs them, and then throws mud at them behind their backs. The non-prodigal son is part of the Pharisees who say, 'Are you saying we are blind too?'

For the prodigal son, returning home means a new life. Immense joy. Tears in his eyes, new decisions, and then... back into the house.

For the non-prodigal son, repentance is an unwanted chore. The father is a tyrant. His brothers are the ones about whom he says, 'Who does he think he is to teach me?' His brother's T-shirt bothers him. His hairstyle is too outlandish. His shirt is not tucked in. 'What is he doing at church looking like this?'

Joy in the church. A day of celebration. Candidates in white outfits. The non-prodigal son is still sulking. No one paid attention to him. No one noticed the Bible under his arm. No one asked him to give an exhortation from the pulpit. 'That guy preaching again? Hmm... Are they really baptizing this one too?

Heaven forbid, only 5 candidates to the baptism in water? Oh, who am I sitting next to? Look at what this guy is praying about... he wants to show off again. What about that singer? I think she got up there only to show off what she knows.'

In the hallway are the joyful pastors and parents bringing flowers. The non-prodigal son is still angry. He found something else in the service that he does not like. Everyone is excited, yet he remains grumbling. 'When I was baptized, brother, it wasn't like this... it was not just anyone who could enter the baptism water, brother... Oh, those days, those prayers we had in the past... Ever since this pastor came, nothing works well anymore...'

He who squanders at home is more guilty than the one who squanders outside... The one pretending in front of the father is more dangerous than the one pretending away from the father. The one who hits you and smells of brand perfume is more dangerous than the one who hits you and smells like pigs.

The prodigal son, even while far from the father, has a great chance of returning home someday. The non-prodigal son, while at home with the father, is unrepentant and has every chance of remaining... unrepentant.

The non-prodigal son did not understand that everything the father forgave him for is infinitely greater than what he needs to forgive his brother for.

The prodigal son was dead and is now alive.

The non-prodigal son was dead, and now... he is still dead.

March 12

BITTER HERBS

"They shall eat the flesh on that night; roasted in fire, with unleavened bread and with bitter herbs they shall eat it." – Exodus 12:8

We like strawberries. Oranges. Clementines. Cream puffs. Savarins. What about grapefruit? What about horseradish or lettuce stems? What about dandelion and arugula?

Most of the time, sweetness makes us sick, while bitterness heals us. Bitter foods are rich in polyphenols, flavonoids, isoflavones, and glucosinolates that have chemo-preventive effects. They can block the metabolic activation of carcinogens and can stop the development and multiplication of cancer cells, promoting the destruction of cancer cells. They can also protect the body from harmful free radicals.

Christian life with too much sweetness harms spiritual health. It is sweet to be praised, to be glorified, to be popular and always appreciated.

But in this sweetness, the cancer of pride can easily sprout, and then bitter herbs are needed.

Mockery. Suffering. Unjust slander. Avoidance. Marginalization. Betrayal. Hatred. And many other bitter herbs.

Thank God not only for meat, fruits, and pastries but also for bitter herbs.

Without them, the soul becomes sick and then dies...

Just as physical health relies on a balance of tastes, spiritual health thrives on a balance of experiences. The bitterness we endure refines our character and draws us closer to God.

MARCH 13

75 SECONDS

"Therefore, thus will I do to you, O Israel; because I will do this to you, prepare to meet your God, O Israel!" – Amos 4:12

The devastating earthquake that struck Turkey and Syria on February 6, 2023 lasted for only 75 seconds but left behind over 50,000 dead, hundreds of thousands injured, and millions of homeless.

In 75 seconds, a person's life can change.

75 seconds turn a homeowner into a homeless.

75 seconds turn children with parents into orphans.

75 seconds turn men and women into widowers and widows.

75 seconds turn businesspeople into unemployed individuals.

75 seconds leave grandparents without grandchildren or grandchildren without grandparents.

75 seconds. That's all it takes to lose everything you have gathered in a lifetime. All dreams collapse, and all plans are canceled. The diplomas you have earned no longer matter, and the money in your accounts cannot help you.

The boss can continue at work without you. The world moves on without you. The insurances you have been paying for do not go with you into eternity...

Isn't it true that life comes to its sunset so fast?

Do not let the matters related to your soul and the place where you will spend eternity be dealt with in the last 75 seconds of your life! You cannot make up in 75 seconds for what you have not solved in decades.

Prepare now for the moment of your departure.

Everything can change in 75 seconds.

March 14

THE EARTHQUAKES OF THE BIBLE

There have been earthquakes not only in recent history, but also in biblical history. The tectonic movements of the Earth's plates are not sporadic events; they have occurred throughout history, on special occasions.

The Bible tells us that the earth quaked when the Creator of the Universe died on the cross:

"Then, behold, the veil of the temple was torn in two from top to bottom; and the earth quaked, and the rocks were split." – Matthew 27:51

There was also an earthquake on the day of the resurrection:

"And behold, there was a great earthquake; for an angel of the Lord descended from heaven, and came and rolled back the stone from the door, and sat on it." – Matthew 28:2

Another noteworthy earthquake happened on the day of the release of Peter and John from prison:

"When they had prayed, the place where they were assembled together was shaken; and they were all filled with the Holy Spirit, and they spoke the word of God with boldness." – Acts 4:31

In the Philippian jail, while Paul and Silas were praising the Lord, and the prisoners were listening, another earthquake occurred:

"Suddenly there was a great earthquake, so that the foundations of the prison were shaken; and immediately all the doors were opened, and everyone's chains were loosed." – Acts 16:26

Interestingly, no one left the prison even though they were free. The presence of God was so powerful that people preferred to stay in the cold cell with God rather than outside without Him!

Is the earth the only one that should quake? Shouldn't our hearts be more moved than the tectonic plates when hearing the Gospel? Shouldn't our hearts be stirred at the remembrance of the events at Calvary or the joy of the resurrection? The earth did not remain indifferent when it witnessed the events involving its Creator. Can we remain indifferent?

March 15

FROM BELOVED SON TO DESPISED SERVANT

The parable of the prodigal son is unique in the Bible. It is preceded by two other parables: the one about the lost sheep, where the loss is 1%, and the one about the lost coin, where the loss is 10%. However, when the son leaves his father, the loss is 50%.

The prodigal son did not want to wait until his father passed away. The calls of friends from afar, the clinking of glasses, and the temptation of revelry were calling him eagerly. Therefore, he asked for his share of the inheritance much sooner. Then, he gathered everything and probably left without even hugging his father.

He went far away. He could not have a good time close to his father. How can you gamble, surrounded by cigarette smoke and immoral magazines, with a father who prays near you? A father who reads Scripture, who lives a righteous life. It would be disturbing. Sinful entertaining is incomplete when you are near righteous people.

There, far away, flattering words from friends came one after another. The one who pays the bill, in this case the prodigal son, had to be praised, to make sure that he would pay the bill for the next feast as well. However, one thing is certain: if you keep taking money out of a bag without putting anything back, it will surely empty quickly. Eventually, when he had nothing left to offer, his friends left him and moved on.

From a beloved son, he became a servant tending to pigs. The husks used as pig food had become the food he longed for. There, in filth and solitude, he understood that the blessings of the father, used without the father's blessing, become a curse.

Health, life, time, and everything God offers will become a curse when you use them without Him. The devil takes everything, and then he laughs at you. What is the solution then?

To return.

The image of fresh bread eaten at home, near the father, would not leave his mind. But, before that bread, he kept repeating a prayer in his mind:

"I will arise and go to my father, and will say to him, 'Father, I have sinned against heaven and before you, and I am no longer worthy to be called your son. Make me like one of your hired servants.'" – Luke 15:18

He left the pigs. In rags and with the stench of the pigsty, shame overwhelmed him.

What will my father say? Will he blame me for squandering his wealth? Will he accept me? Will he...?

Looking in the distance, through the back of the garden, his eyes lit up. There, under the blooming trees, smelling like spring, with open arms, full of mercy and tears in his eyes, his father was waiting for him.

What a precious embrace! But why does he not say anything about the wasted silver coins? Why does he not blame me for my pig stench?

A new robe for me? A ring? But... dad, can I ever become your son again?

Come, his father said. *Come in the house! Let us rejoice!*

He has the same words for you today.

Do not focus on the years you have spent without Him. On the health He gave you and for which you never said *thank you.* On the time spent with friends who took advantage of you...

He tells you just this... *Come back!*

Do not wait until you lose everything! Do not wait until it is too late. The world's pleasures, its debauchery, the illusion of fulfilled dreams are just chains keeping you away from the Father...

Come back!

The desolation in your soul, the smell of sin, and the rags of an unclean heart will never give you joy.

True fulfillment is the white robe, communion with the Father, and... being home!

Come back!

Any despised servant can become a beloved son again!

MARCH 16

THE CHARACTERISTICS OF THE PEOPLE WHO LIVE ON THE STRAIGHT STREET

"And the Lord said to him, 'Arise and go to the street called Straight, and inquire at the house of Judas for one called Saul of Tarsus, for behold, he is praying.'" – Acts 9:11

Ananias was sent by God to the street called Straight, where Paul was. The main clue God gave him was that Ananias was praying.

First, the people who are on the straight path pray. Not just in the hospital, not only during exams, not only when they have problems. They always pray. Prayer is a complete dependence on God and His will.

Prayer shows our human limitations and acknowledges our dependence on the One who created the Universe. When we kneel down, we recognize that above us there is Someone who has solutions to every problem we face.

Secondly, people on the straight path are healed of blindness.

"Immediately there fell from his eyes something like scales, and he received his sight at once, and he arose and was baptized." – Acts 9:18

Just as there is physical blindness, there is also spiritual blindness. There are people who cannot see that it was God who has taken care of them until now:

"And yet I taught Ephraim to walk, taking them by their arms; but they did not know that I healed them." – Hosea 11:3

Spiritually blind people only see this life. Oh, how they need God to open their eyes to realize that they need forgiveness, repentance, and salvation!

Thirdly, people on the straight path get baptized: "then he arose and was baptized." Baptism is the public testimony of a change that occurred in private. First comes prayer, then an openness to repentance, and only then baptism.

"Repent, and let every one of you be baptized in the name of Jesus Christ for the remission of sins, and you shall receive the gift of the Holy Spirit." – Acts 2:38

At the same time, people on the straight path receive power.

"So when he had received food, he was strengthened. Then Saul spent some days with the disciples at Damascus." – Acts 9:19

In our world there is military power, physical power, social power, and material power. The battles fought in these areas, between people, are fought with the specific "weapons" of each field. But in the battles we fight against the unseen demons, we cannot overcome with tanks or physical strength. We need spiritual power, power received through the filling of the Holy Spirit:

"But you shall receive power when the Holy Spirit has come upon you, and you shall be witnesses to Me in Jerusalem, and in all Judea and Samaria, and to the end of the earth." – Acts 1:8

But also power received through the Gospel:

"For I am not ashamed of the gospel of Christ, for it is the power of God to salvation for everyone who believes, for the Jew first and also for the Greek." – Romans 1:16

Additionally, those who live on the straight path understand their calling from God and get involved in ministry:

"Immediately he preached the Christ in the synagogues, that He is the Son of God." – Acts 9:20

In the Church, there is no unemployment from a spiritual point of view. Neither are any pensions to be given here – only in heaven. Therefore, we are called to contribute to the advancement of the Gospel. Some are called to preach. Others are called to make packages for the poor. Others to visit those in the hospitals. Yet others to evangelize in prisons.

Jesus told us that the harvest is great, but the laborers are few! Wouldn't you want to be one of the few who contribute to the work of God and who will be rewarded eternally by the One who called them to serve?

Are you on the straight path today? I did not ask if you are Pentecostal, Orthodox, Baptist, or Catholic. The name of the denomination you belong to is not important; what matters are the characteristics listed above.

The path we choose is not easy, but it is straight. It is not comfortable, but it leads to heaven. It is not popular, but it is the only one that guarantees eternal life in the end. I invite you to come on the straight path as well!

March 17

CORRECT ATTITUDES TOWARD THE BIBLE

"For I am not ashamed of the gospel of Christ, for it is the power of God to salvation for everyone who believes, for the Jew first and also for the Greek." – Romans 1:16

The Word of God is not just another book on our shelf. It is not just another collection of meditations or life advice. The Bible is the inspired Word of God, written by 40 writers over a period of 1,500 years, and it has the power to change a person's life.

What are the four steps that everyone should take when it comes to the Bible?

1. Reading the Bible

Do not complain that God does not speak to you as long as you keep your Bible closed. Reading the Bible daily does nothing else but bring God's message into your heart.

Unfortunately, over 82% of Christians only read the Bible on Sundays during congregational services.

Make time to read the Bible! Change your priority list so that what God wants to tell you every day comes first in your life!

2. Learning the Bible

"This Book of the Law shall not depart from your mouth, but you shall meditate in it day and night, that you may observe to do according to all that is written in it. For then you will make your way prosperous, and then you will have good success." – Joshua 1:8

The second step is memorizing and studying the Holy Scripture. When you reach this step, you become interested in the basic themes of the Scripture.

You meditate on its principles and want to see where else in the Scripture it talks about a particular subject.

You are ready to memorize important verses and often meditate on those words.

Instead of filling your mind with news, politics, sports, and other transient and useless things, you decide to take a few verses and meditate on them during the day.

3. Applying the Bible

"Whoever comes to Me, and hears My sayings and does them, I will show you whom he is like." – Luke 6:47

At this step, the Scripture has already passed beyond just the eyes and is no longer just information in your mind. You have decided to let the Word change your thinking and your speech, and your actions will be in line with God's will.

You have decided to listen, not just hear. To fulfill, not just talk. To live in accordance not with your own will but with the will of the Author. Only at this step will those around you notice a change in you and be amazed. Only now you can start to preach both with words and actions the timeless truths of Scripture and have every chance of being believed because the change is already visible in your personal life.

4. Defending the Bible

"And in the days of these kings the God of heaven will set up a kingdom which shall never be destroyed, and the kingdom shall not be left to other people; it shall break in pieces and consume all these kingdoms, and it shall stand forever." – Daniel 2:44

This is the step that the fewest people reach. This is the step that hurts the most and for which the Christian is most deeply mocked. It is a step avoided by most.

Imagine how few people reach this step if only 18% of Christians read the Bible! How many are the ones who study the Bible? How many are the ones who apply it? Is there anyone left to defend it?

May God help us to be Christians not only at the census but every-day-Christians. Christians not just recorded in a church registry, but Christians whose names are recorded in the Book of Life. Let us read the Word of God, learn it, apply it, and be ready at any cost to defend it.

Let us not forget what Howard G. Hendricks said: "Dusty Bibles always lead to dirty lives."

March 18

IF GOD EXISTS, WHY IS THERE INJUSTICE?

Sometimes we are confronted with pertinent questions regarding God and His existence. Atheists and others use such questions to challenge us, and most of the times we cannot just throw Bible verses at them because they do not believe in the Bible.

The most common questions people ask sound like this: *If God exists, why did He allow that woman to be killed by her husband? Why is there so much suffering? Why do innocent children die? Why are there orphans?*

We should always start with the aspect of love and free will. Love can only exist if the person who loves has free will. Would you like your partner to be a robot? To love you because it has been programmed to? Certainly not.

From here, we can go one step further: since man has the freedom to decide, he can choose between good and evil. If someone chooses to waste their money on drinking and gambling, it will implicitly bring the misfortune of poverty and bankruptcy upon their children, right?

If you ask God to stop someone from entering a bar and waste his money on bad things instead of buying shoes for his children, then there's no more free choice! Why don't you ask God to pull your leg back when you're crossing the street and a car is coming? And if you do ask such a thing, how far can God go to cancel your freedom of conscience and action?

Even the fact that you ask such questions is part of your free will. If God had made us robots, we would not ask whatever questions we want but only what He would dictate. God does not want robots with Him in heaven, but people who love Him willingly.

God is love, and in order to nullify your free will, He would have to nullify, in fact, His love because His love makes Him give you the freedom to choose. And God cannot nullify Himself!

Then we must emphasize that we live in a fallen and sinful world:

"For all have sinned and fall short of the glory of God." – Romans 3:23

And the ruler of this world is the Devil:

"I will no longer talk much with you, for the ruler of this world is coming. He has nothing in Me." – John 14:30

Sin is precisely man's desire not to listen to the will of God but to the will of the evil one. And sin brings suffering! Abortion, murder, lying, robbery, theft – they all bring suffering! Don`t you think that the poverty of some parts of the world is a result of the greed of other countries? Aren`t wars the result of the sinful desire of some nations to conquer more? Do you know that many who end up in prisons have been abused when they were young, in one form or another, and these traumas have haunted them all their lives? God is love, but He is also justice. Man can choose good or evil, but in the end, he will have to give account for what he chose:

"For we must all appear before the judgment seat of Christ, that each one may receive the things done in the body, according to what he has done, whether good or bad." – 2 Corinthians 5:10

The fact that the atheist (or the non-practicing Christian) refuses to believe in God and finds all sorts of questions or reasons to nullify His existence in his conscience is nothing more than a childish way of saying: *I do whatever I want, and I don't want to be held accountable by anyone for what I do...*

Do not forget, however, that a blind man can say that the sun does not exist, but he cannot cancel the warmth he feels on his skin.

On the day of judgment, no one will have any excuse. The God they mocked, refused, cursed, or did not want to believe in, is, in fact, the God who offered them health, time, life, strength to work, and other necessary resources through which He knocked on the door of their hearts. Decades of patience and forbearance intertwined with blessings from God had only one purpose: repentance!

"Or do you despise the riches of His goodness, forbearance, and longsuffering, not knowing that the goodness of God leads you to repentance?" – Romans 2:4

March 19

AFTER 53 YEARS

The year is 1968. A platoon of Americans, who did not know each other very well yet, was fighting on the front lines in Vietnam. Suddenly, a shell hit a tree, and from there some shards rebounded into Fred's leg. Dale was nearby. With cool-headedness and great courage, he ran to Fred. Blood was flowing continually. The leg had been torn apart. With exceptional skill, Dale applied a tourniquet and dragged Fred off the battlefield.

"See you back home, Fred," Dale shouted before returning to battle.

Ashland, Illinois. 2021. A car stops in the front yard of a farm after having driven for 579 miles. Fred comes out of it. First, he puts down his healthy leg, then the one with the prosthesis. With a smile on his face and tears in his eyes, he heads towards Dale. A melancholic and grateful meeting was about to take place after 53 years.

They knew nothing about each other during all this time. Fred wondered if his savior had managed to escape the front, and Dale wondered if Fred was still alive.

They reminisced about the war, telling each other about those painful and challenging years on the front lines... Only those who have been through war know how to appreciate the years of peace...

Have you ever thought about how the meeting in heaven will be? The people you fed, helped, or talked to about Jesus will come to you and hug you. What unique moments we will experience! We will remember planet Earth as a distant dream. No more tourniquets. No more bandages. No more shivering from the cold. No more cancer. No more medication. No more pain.

Maybe today you did a good deed and are not sure if it was worth it. Maybe you go back to the frontline, like Dale, and continue the fight, while the one you helped has not even managed to say thank you...

Keep going!

Someone is alive because you did the right thing at the right time. Someone enjoys his life because you reached out when he was on the edge. Someone praises God because your money helped him and was used for a bottle of medicine.

Keep going!

There are still tourniquets to apply. Trenches to dig. Wounds to dress. Houses to build. Clothes to warm those who shiver... When the war is over, we will look each other in the eye and say this: *It was worth it!*

It's worth making every effort today for a joyous meeting beyond the clouds...

Heroes are not those who come out of the war unharmed, but those who have helped wounded people get home...

March 20

WHAT IS DEATH?

"Abraham breathed his last and died in a good old age, an old man and full of years, and was gathered to his people." – Genesis 25:8

Have you ever wondered what happens when someone dies? Beyond the biological or physical aspect. Beyond the ceremony, the preachers, the wreaths, the coffin, or the burial.

First of all, death is an **addition**. By no means an end. Not a finality. But an incorporation into your people. Into the people who have already departed. Into the midst of those who await on the other side.

Secondly, death is a **relocation**.

"His winnowing fan is in His hand, and He will thoroughly clean out His threshing floor, and gather the wheat into His barn, but the chaff He will burn with unquenchable fire." – Luke 3:17

The chaff is moved into the fire, and the wheat is moved into the barn.

Each one is moved to the place they have prepared for themselves during their lifetime. The chaff is the leftover husks of grains. It is a worthless person, in the figurative sense from the dictionary. People who lived only for themselves, disobeying God. Wheat means something valuable. A rich harvest. The good part of the threshing.

What else is death? A **reward**.

"For we must all appear before the judgment seat of Christ, that each one may receive the things done in the body, according to what he has done, whether good or bad." – 2 Corinthians 5:10

There will be a reward for the evil done (meaning eternal condemnation) or a reward for the good done (eternal reward). Nothing hidden will remain hidden, and everything will be rewarded:

"For God will bring every work into judgment, including every secret thing, whether good or evil." – Ecclesiastes 12:14

Does the thought of death scare you? Do you become terrified when you hear this word? That means you do not have hope. You do not have assurance. You do not have a biblical perspective on it.

It means you need to look at it with different eyes and prepare for it. As Isaac the Syrian said: "Prepare your heart for your departure... If you are wise, you will expect it every hour... And when the time of departure comes, go joyfully and say: 'Come in peace, I knew you would come, and I have not neglected anything that could help me on the journey.'"

March 21

CIA INTERROGATION TECHNIQUES

Among the interrogation techniques of the United States Central Intelligence Agency (CIA) are the following: isolating, creating addiction and fear, depriving of sleep and natural light, stripping of self-respect.

Why does the CIA use such techniques? Because they yield results. Because the prisoner can be controlled in this way, and any information can thus be obtained from him.

Does it not seem to you that the technology we use today employs the same techniques as the CIA?

More and more teenagers and young people are isolating themselves. They have an increasingly chaotic sleep schedule. They have come to depend at every step on their mobile phones. They get easily irritated. They are increasingly gripped by anxiety and depression.

Someone said a very profound truth: "When phones were tied with a wire, humans were free. Now phones are wireless, and we are bound."

Paul reminds us of a very important aspect that can be applied in the field of technology:

> *"All things are lawful for me, but not all things are helpful; all things are lawful for me, but I will not be brought under the power of any." – 1 Corinthians 6:12*

Do you use technology to change the world around you, or does technology change you? Do you use the phone to solve your problems or to have more problems? Do you use social media to select valuable things (sermons, songs, testimonies, Christian quotes) or to rummage through the world's garbage?

I conclude with Peter's warning:

> *"While they promise them liberty, they themselves are slaves of corruption; for by whom a person is overcome, by him also he is brought into bondage." – 2 Peter 2:19*

Modern slavery does not happen to people from Africa. *Uncle Tom's Cabin* was a great truth, but that story has reached its sunset. Slaves are no longer on plantations, but in their beds with phones in their hands.

The past focused on photography; the present focuses on video content. And through this content, if we are not extremely vigilant, the Devil takes us as slaves. And he makes the slaves do whatever he wants...

Be a slave of Christ, not of the phone! Be the master of technology, not its slave!

Beware of the CIA's interrogation methods.

Today they are used more than ever in history...

MARCH 22

VALUES AND DECISIONS

"Finally, brethren, whatever things are true, whatever things are noble, whatever things are just, whatever things are pure, whatever things are lovely, whatever things are of good report, if there is any virtue and if there is anything praiseworthy—meditate on these things." – Philippians 4:8

Our life is filled with decisions. We decide which school to attend, what career to have, what kind of car to buy, or what type of house to build. But there are decisions that involve a commitment, such as the decision of marriage or the decision of baptism.

Our values determine the decisions we make.

If you are a girl who loves purity, morality, honor, and who wants to offer these values to your future husband, will you decide to go out on a date with just anybody, at any time? Absolutely not. But why make such a decision? Because of your values.

Judas sold Jesus for money. The decision to betray Him was made because of the non-value called greed.

The prodigal son loved his father's wealth more than he loved his father. The decision to use the blessings received from his father without accepting his presence or advice turned out to be disastrous and led him to failure.

At the same time, he loved his friends more than his family. Surrounded by loads of money, he thought that his friends respected him, but later, he painfully realized that he was loved because of what he had, not because of who he was. When he ended up feeding a cruel master's pigs, he realized that you have friends only when you are on top, and they leave when you go bankrupt...

Moreover, his value was entertainment. Sin. Revelry and banquets. That is why he decided to leave as far as possible from home. He could not enjoy all these things if he stayed close to a godly father. Debauchery took control, and the son's clothes were soon exchanged for a servant's clothes.

The true values of life are not those presented by Hollywood. Narcissism, hypocrisy, obscenities, abortion, adultery, Marxism, and many others only push those who have such non-values into ruin on all levels.

True values are repentance, integrity, faithfulness to your spouse, altruism. Heaven. The white robe. Salvation. Humility and obedience. Purity and faithfulness. And those who have these values will make decisions that reflect them...

Look today at the decisions you have made in recent years. What do they say about your values?

I'm not asking you to change your decisions.

I'm asking you to change your values.

Then the decisions will change on their own...

March 23

THE SPIDER'S WEB

It is said that in the third century, when Saint Felix of Nola was persecuted and was fleeing his enemies, he hid in a cave.

A spider wove a web at the entrance, sealing it and making it appear as if no one had entered inside for months. As a result, the pursuers passed by without finding him.

Coming out into the daylight, Felix stated, "When God helps us, a spider's web becomes a protecting wall; and without His help, a wall is no more protection than a spider's web."

Many times, we believe that if we stand in the shadow of a strong wall, we will be well protected. The wall of money, the wall of our comfort, the wall of high-profile friendships, the wall of a secure job, the wall of our health. However, more than once, God has shown us that if He is not first in our life, that wall is like a spider's web.

On the other hand, in small and mundane things that we did not think could help us in any way, we saw God`s hand. That insignificant person who put in a good word for you. That moment when His hand protected you when you crossed the street. That colleague who defended you in front of the boss. And how many other moments, which you thought were of little importance, ultimately worked for your good?

Small things for some, but still significant for people who walk with God...

A stone in David's sling and yet, a dead Goliath...

A den of lions and yet, a saint who comes out in the morning unharmed...

A fiery furnace and yet, a God who makes a wall between the fire and the three young men...

A board nailed next to other boards for many years in a row... and a flood that cannot sink an ark...

A Joseph sold by brothers as a slave and yet... a future prime minister.

A mother with 12 children. Yet, not a day without food provided...

Believers who start building a church and do not even have the money for the foundation. Yet, the inauguration took place the same year.

A pregnancy about which the doctor says that the baby will have deformities. Yet, a healthy child...

How many other victories have we not seen? Spider webs for some, but for us, they have been walls on which we climbed and shouted for joy because God gave us extraordinary victories.

Do not laugh at the spider web behind you...

It might be the wall allowed by God for your salvation.

March 24

WHERE IS IT BETTER?

"To everything, there is a season, a time for every purpose under heaven." – Ecclesiastes 3:11

Young children want to become students. Students want to become employees. Employees want to be children again.

The teenager playing in the yard looks at the plane flying in the sky and says, "How nice it would be to be up there!" The pilot from the plane says, "How nice it would be to get home as soon as possible and be with my family!"

Single people want to have a happy family. Did you know that there are married people who unfortunately would like to be single again?

There are employees who would like to be employers while many employers would like not to have the headache they have and be employees instead.

There are people in the church who wish they could lead the church while some of those who lead it wish they could sit once again somewhere in the back, on a bench, without this great responsibility weighing on their shoulders.

These examples can go on endlessly, and the question is: where is it better?

I believe the correct answer is to live each day where we are and with the status we have. It does not help us at all to carry along, every day, regrets or dreams, unfulfilled desires, or unsatisfied wishes.

Beautiful things are done at the right time. Under God's guidance, in accordance with the principles of Scripture, with passion and quality. This way, we will not have regrets or frustrations but daily joys and fulfillments.

Enjoy the day of today!

Do what you need to do wherever you are.

And tomorrow, you will be happy with what you did today.

March 25

THE NEED FOR BALANCE

"For what profit is it to a man if he gains the whole world, and loses his own soul? Or what will a man give in exchange for his soul?" – Matthew 16:26

Have you ever seen people who have gained a lot of money, but the depravities of life have destroyed them by consuming all their wealth?

Have you ever seen people who have become extraordinarily successful in their careers but lost their families?

Have you heard of people who have won valuable medals but have not accomplished anything in the spiritual realm?

If you have destroyed your health through various sinful addictions and thus become a burden to your family, what have you achieved?

Also, if you have destroyed your health and have millions of dollars in your accounts, what have you gained?

We see people who are financially accomplished on all business magazine covers, but are they fulfilled in their families? Do those in high social positions also have access to heaven guaranteed?

Do you notice how much need we have for balance in all areas of life?

We must be careful about what we eat. We must be mindful of how much we work. We must be cautious about how much we spend. We must develop a character that is the master, not the slave of the things around us.

Having a balanced life is not easy. We see examples of failures at every step of the way. Maintaining self-control while walking on the thin wire called life is a continuous challenge. Packing only what is valuable in the luggage of eternity requires extraordinary wisdom.

I believe the correct order matters enormously. First, God. Then family. Then material things.

On the death bed, no one will regret not having $10,000 more in their pocket. Nor will they lament driving a cheap car instead of an expensive one. Nor will they say, "What a pity I didn't work overtime hours at my job..."

The bond that binds our life is love. The essence of living is hidden in its fulfillments. The spiritual life and the family life should be our priorities, while the educational, material, and social aspects should be only temporary things we use.

When we mistake the temporary for the eternal, we end up with regrets. When we confuse values with non-values, we end up in failure.

I pray today for you, dear reader, to understand the need for balance and priorities.

Living a balanced life requires intentionality and discernment. We must actively choose to invest our time and energy in what truly matters, ensuring that our actions align with our values. This often means saying no to distractions and superficial pursuits that promise immediate gratification but leave us spiritually and emotionally empty.

In this fast-paced world, it is easy to lose sight of what is truly important. We must remind ourselves that the pursuit of wealth, status, and material possessions is fleeting. Instead, we should seek to build meaningful relationships, cultivate our faith, and contribute positively to our communities. Only in the correct order does life make sense.

MARCH 26

WHAT DOES ACCEPTED SACRIFICE LOOK LIKE?

"When you offer a sacrifice of thanksgiving to the Lord, offer it of your own free will." – Leviticus 19:5

When we serve, we do it with the belief that God will accept our sacrifice. Who would want to reach eternity and find out that a large part of the sacrifices he made out of love for God were not actually taken into consideration? When is our sacrifice accepted? What does the Bible say about this?

The sacrifice is accepted when our relationships with others are correct.

"Therefore, if you bring your gift to the altar, and there remember that your brother has something against you, leave your gift there before the altar, and go your way. First, be reconciled to your brother, and then come and offer your gift." – Matthew 5:23-24

God does not want me to sing while someone cries at home because of me. The joy from heaven should not be overshadowed by the pain I caused to my neighbor's heart. Our sacrifice is accepted when we make every effort to have relationships of peace, forgiveness, and tolerance with those around us.

The sacrifice is accepted when it is done without personal interest.

"But all their works they do to be seen by men." – Matthew 23:5

People's *likes* are fleeting. God's appreciation is eternal. Which is the glory you long for?

"For they loved the praise of men more than the praise of God." – John 12:43

The interest behind our sacrifice must be to glorify God. When the craftsman uses the hammer in a beneficial way, it is not the hammer that is praised but the craftsman. If God has prepared the good deed in which you should walk, do not forget that all the glory must be His, and yours should be humility and gratitude that He used you.

The sacrifice is accepted when it is without blemish.

"Your lamb shall be without blemish, a male of the first year. You may take it from the sheep or from the goats." – Exodus 12:5

God does not want you to give the poor the ripped pants nor the shirt you have worn for two years.

Quality is absolutely necessary. Because when we give something to someone, we are actually giving it to God. Do you want to give worn-out, ripped, patched, and useless things to the One who holds the Universe in His hands?

The sacrifice is accepted when it is done with joy.

"So let each one give as he purposes in his heart, not grudgingly or of necessity; for God loves a cheerful giver." – 2 Corinthians 9:7

Would you like someone to give you a gift and, while preparing it, to see the regret on their face? Or would you like them to always bring it up many days after giving it to you?

Our joy must be complete when we can be of service to God's ministry. One of the greatest joys in the church should be the voluntary money offering. Giving from the heart, not with regret. Offering with satisfaction, not grumbling.

May God help us bring offerings that are accepted!

They are becoming rarer and rarer...

March 27

FOREIGNERS, GUESTS, OR CITIZENS?

"So then you are no longer strangers and foreigners, but fellow citizens with the saints and members of the household of God." – Ephesians 2:19

A **foreigner** is a person from outside a country. A **guest** is someone who visits you from time to time. But an heir, after your death, is neither a foreigner nor a guest but a **son**.

Paul beautifully describes this process. A foreigner can become a guest if he desires to come closer to the House of God. Then, from a guest, he can become a son through faith in Jesus Christ:

"But as many as received Him, to them He gave the right to become children of God, to those who believe in His name." – John 1:12

It is self-evident that a foreigner or a guest will behave however he wishes, speak however he has been taught, and do whatever he wants. I cannot tell my guest how to dress, what to talk about, or how to behave when he visits me. But an orphan who has been adopted and who becomes part of the family will have to obey the new principles in that household. My child is not a guest but a son.

Now do you understand why so few people want to become sons of God, and most of them want to remain foreigners or guests? They want that because, in this way, they can live however they wish and, from time to time, visit a place of worship as a guest.

Do you truly want to be a son? Let the words of the Father shape your life. Let the principles of Scripture mold your character.

Paul also uses the comparison of citizenship in this whole process of explaining our status. A foreigner comes to a country and then leaves, but only a citizen enjoys the full rights of that country.

Moreover, just like in the case of a son, a citizen has not only rights but also obligations. He enjoys freedom in that country, certain privileges, but must also conform to the laws of that country.

When we become citizens of Heaven, we live according to the laws of Heaven. I call you today not to be a foreigner. Nor a guest. But to be a son of heaven. Only the sons of God will enjoy the eternal inheritance of paradise...

MARCH 28

COMFORTING METHODS

"And our hope for you is steadfast because we know that as you are partakers of the sufferings, so also you will partake of the consolation." – 2 Corinthians 1:7

Often in our lives, we go through certain problems and troubles, and in those moments, a comforting hand matters enormously.

The storms of life will filter your friends, and you will easily notice who among them are people who stand with you and who are those who leave you when things get hard. You will be able to recognize the comforters and the judges.

When God tests someone through suffering, He also tests our attitude toward that person. Will you mock him, or will you encourage him? Will you point fingers, or will you comfort him? Will you be there for him, or will you pass by with indifference?

I will list below several biblical methods by which a person can be comforted:

1. Through Family

When Noah was born, he was seen as a comfort to his parents:

"He called his name Noah, saying, 'This one will comfort us concerning our work and the toil of our hands, because of the ground which the Lord has cursed.'" – Genesis 5:29

Joseph was a comfort to his brothers:

"'But now, do not therefore be grieved or angry with yourselves because you sold me here; for God sent me before you to preserve life.' So he comforted them and spoke kindly to them." – Genesis 50:21

Rebekah was a comfort to Isaac:

"Then Isaac brought her into his mother Sarah's tent; and he took Rebekah, and she became his wife, and he loved her. So Isaac was comforted after his mother's death." – Genesis 24:67

So, through a life partner, through children or through siblings, comfort should not come as a surprise to us but should be something normal. After all, biologically, the family is the closest to us.

2. Through those close to us (neighbors, relatives)

When Lazarus died, Mary and Martha were comforted by the Jews who knew them:

"Then many of the Jews who had come to Mary, and had seen the things Jesus did, believed in Him." – John 11:19

There are times when we need to be near those who are close to us. We need to weep together with them so that the burden of pain is carried on more shoulders, making it easier to bear.

3. Through servants

Paul sends Tychicus to comfort the Colossians:

"All my state shall Tychicus declare to you, who is a beloved brother, a faithful minister, and a fellow servant in the Lord. I am sending him to you for this very purpose, that he may know your circumstances and comfort your hearts." – Colossians 4:7-8

A word of edification, encouragement, or comfort from those who watch over the flock of Christ should not be a rare thing.

4. Through the Word of God

"For whatever things were written before were written for our learning, that we through the patience and comfort of the Scriptures might have hope." – Romans 15:4

The Word of God gives us the hope we need in trials. It gives us hope when everything seems to have collapsed. It provides guidance when we are at the major crossroads of life.

5. Through the Holy Spirit

"Nevertheless, I tell you the truth. It is to your advantage that I go away; for if I do not go away, the Helper will not come to you; but if I depart, I will send Him to you." – John 16:7

The fullness of the Holy Spirit will bring you comfort in the difficult days of life. The Holy Spirit can comfort a person's heart through a song, a poem, a message, and many other means.

6. Through personal testimony

"But it is still my consolation, and I rejoice in unsparing pain, that I have not denied the words of the Holy One." – Job 6:10

The person who lives beautifully has the inner comfort that, when going through troubles, he is not, in fact, punished by God but tested. A student who prepares for the exam will not be stressed out during the examination but happy to expect a good grade. The tests of life do not come in order to defeat us; rather, they have a much more precious goal:

> *"That the genuineness of your faith, being much more precious than gold that perishes, though it is tested by fire, may be found to praise, honor, and glory at the revelation of Jesus Christ." – 1 Peter 1:7*

If things are going well for you today, look for someone near you for whom you can be comforting. But if you are going through trouble, I pray that, through the means listed above, you may be encouraged, edified, and filled with the hope that the One who directs the whole Universe has not abandoned you!

March 29

THE STEPS TAKEN BY THE GOOD SAMARITAN

One of the most wonderful parables told by the Savior Jesus Christ is the *Parable of the Good Samaritan.* It is the parable of a man who, though on a journey, chooses to interrupt his plans in order to take a man wounded by thieves to an inn.

What Jesus emphasizes from the beginning is that the religious individuals passed by and avoided the place where the man struggled between life and death. Religion does not save, only mercy does. Many are religious, but few are merciful...

The first step the Samaritan took was that he "came to the place" where the wounded man was. He went to the scene of the incident. He went there up close. Not to take pictures, not to judge, nor to give his opinion. He went to help. He went to see the wound as closely as possible, to see the needs of the one wounded by thieves, and when he saw him, he felt compassion for him...

Today, dear reader, I would like to ask you something important: do not judge anyone until you have been at the scene. Do not judge, do not give your opinion, and do not spread useless rumors until you have been there – to see the pain, to see the injury, to see the deep wounds. And when you arrive there, get some mercy. Only mercy overcomes judgment! Only mercy takes the next steps!

What are these next steps?

Binding the wounds. We are not called to make the wound bigger, but to close it. To bandage it gently, to place the tourniquet where the bleeding is heavy, and to stop the flow of death.

Then we should use oil and wine. They were used in the Middle East to soothe the pain of the wounded. The wine disinfected and the oil alleviated the pain.

Do we have this blessed emergency kit? Both materially and spiritually speaking? Words of encouragement, but also material solutions? How do the wounded people we meet on the short path of life feel – healed by us or left lying there? Changed and touched by the resources with which God has blessed us, or left on the roads where the thieves lurk?

"Go and do likewise," Jesus told the teacher of the law. "Go and put it into practice," He tells us today.

In a world full of thieves who want to kill the soul and the body, Jesus is still looking for Samaritans who have the necessary remedies and who are willing to change their plans to make room for the plans of others. We have so many poor, orphans, widows, and lonely elderly people whom the "thieves" of poverty, illness, vices, or deep disappointments of life have left lying in pain. Surrounded by gloomy judgments, they long for relief. An encouraging conversation. A kind word. A sandwich or a pair of sneakers.

Be a Samaritan!

There are so many priests, Levites, curious people, people who give their opinion without having been at the scene, gossipers, slanderers...

Be a Samaritan!

MARCH 30

THE PRINTED BIBLE

"Sanctify them by Your truth. Your word is truth." – John 17:17

In the early 1400s, duplicating the knowledge found in books was a task that took months or even years. As a result, owning a book was extremely expensive, a luxury that only the wealthiest people could afford.

Historians tell us that a hand-copied book in the 14th century could cost as much as a large house. Of course, manuscript writers were few, and the profession was very well paid.

While many people sought these well-paid jobs, a German named Johannes Gutenberg had a similar goal. He wanted to write many books, but he wanted to do it differently. Gutenberg began experimenting with his idea around the year 1440. About a decade later, he succeeded in creating the first printing press: the Gutenberg Press.

Although it took Johannes Gutenberg almost a decade to build this machine, when he finished, he managed to reproduce 200 copies of the Bible in three years, which was considered a miraculous achievement at the time. Only 46 of these printed Bibles have survived to this day.

In 1468, on February 3rd, nearly 13 years after his exceptional invention to which we owe much of the progress, education, and development of our culture and civilization, Gutenberg died in utter poverty. The place where his lifeless body was buried remains unknown to this day... This is the paradox and destiny of someone considered by many historians and specialists to be the most important inventor in history.

The first complete translation into Romanian of the Bible was finished in 1688 (known as the Bucharest Bible) by Radu Greceanu[7] and Șerban Greceanu[8] with the help of Șerban Cantacuzino[9] and Constantin Brâncoveanu[10].

Two main Romanian translations are used today. The Romanian Orthodox Church uses the Synodal Bible, the standard translation of the Romanian

[7] Romanian translator and collaborator on the first complete translation of the Bible into Romanian in 1688.

[8] Collaborated with Radu Greceanu on the first complete translation of the Bible into Romanian in 1688.

[9] Assisted in the translation of the first complete Bible into Romanian in 1688.

[10] Contributed to the completion of the first complete translation of the Bible into Romanian in 1688.

Orthodox Bible, published with the blessing of Patriarch Teoctist[11]. Protestant denominations mainly use the Dumitru Cornilescu[12] translation, first published in 1921, although the use of older translations is not to be neglected.

In 1989, the Revised Cornilescu Bible was published, and this edition attempted to be as close as possible to the original manuscripts, with grammatical forms being corrected and adapted based on the evolution of the modern Romanian language.

Will we ever understand the enormous efforts made by our ancestors so that we can enjoy a printed Bible? Doesn't it seem to you that, most of the time, we take everything for granted, being so ignorant of the price others have paid for us to enjoy many things we possess today?

Do not let all these efforts be in vain! Get yourself a Bible and read it! Let its profound message transform your life, and you will find the Truth.

Because only when you are conquered by the Truth will you find true freedom...

---

[11] Leader of the Romanian Orthodox Church who endorsed the Synodal Bible, the standard translation used by the Romanian Orthodox Church today.

[12] Translator of the Bible into Romanian, known for the 1921 edition that has become widely used among Protestant denominations in Romania.

March 31

SEVEN QUALITIES OF AN EXCEPTIONAL LEADER

"Let no one despise your youth, but be an example to the believers in word, in conduct, in love, in spirit, in faith, in purity." – 1 Timothy 4:12

There are many bosses, but few leaders. Why? Because being a boss does not require great effort, while being a true leader requires exceptional qualities. What are these qualities?

1. Respect

Leaders respect the people they are responsible for. They do not treat them with superiority, do not talk down to them, and do not try to impose respect but to earn it.

2. Authenticity

Leaders are authentic. They will display their real personality and avoid being hypocritical or pretending to be different from what they are. Although the pressure to act in an unauthentic way is great on their shoulders, they will stick to their values and will not be ashamed of them.

3. Communication

You cannot be a leader without being a good communicator. We cannot guess the thoughts of those around us, but through communication, we can identify their needs and come to their aid.

4. Modesty

The boss is full of pride and uses those under him to improve his own image. The leader, however, is modest and uses this quality to remain connected to the team he coordinates.

5. Responsibility

A true leader takes responsibility for his actions and, at the same time, expects those around him to do the same.

6. Vision

A true leader does not have only short-term goals. He has a clear, long-term vision for the team he coordinates. Without a clear target, no one knows the steps to follow.

7. Empathy

A true leader will always be a warm person. He will understand that his team is made up of people who also have their own worries and troubles. When he asks them, "How are you?" he will be truly interested in the answer.

Be a leader, not a boss! Be a role model, not a tyrant!

These qualities are necessary both in the family and at work. In church, but also in the community.

There are plenty of bosses.

You should be a true leader!

April 1

HOLINESS, FRUITFULNESS AND THEN MINISTRY

"I beseech you therefore, brethren, by the mercies of God, that you present your bodies a living sacrifice, holy, acceptable to God, which is your reasonable service." – Romans 12:1

People are impressed by the gifts, but God seeks the fruits first and foremost. Before we go to the end of the earth, God first wants us to go into the upper room. A life filled with deeds – and only afterwards our words will be believed by people.

Love must come before prophecy. Self-control before singing on a stage. Holiness before performing miracles. Otherwise, you will be put to shame. Renounce your flesh before being filled with the Spirit. Be on your knees before you can stand up. Dig deeper into the Word and live it before you preach it. Have personal experiences and only then you can talk about the experiences of other people.

If you keep this order, then church programs will be transformed into divine services. Pentecost will no longer be just a memory, but a reality. The House of the Lord will truly become a house of prayer.

Ministry without a foundation of holiness is like a tree without roots. It may appear strong and vibrant on the outside, but the first storm will reveal its weakness. Our character is the soil in which our ministry grows. If that soil is rich in the nutrients of God's Word, prayer, and obedience, the fruits of our labor will be abundant and lasting.

Moreover, the authenticity of our ministry is tested not in the spotlight, but in the quiet moments of our daily walk. It's in the secret place of prayer and the unnoticed acts of kindness that our true character is formed. When we prioritize our private devotion over public display, we align ourselves with God's heart, making our service more powerful and genuine.

Holiness and character, therefore, are not just personal pursuits but communal blessings that pave the way for true revival.

April 2

THE CONTEST WITH FEW CONTESTANTS

"And let our people also learn to maintain good works, to meet urgent needs, that they may not be unfruitful." – Titus 3:14

God never called us to compete in receiving and collecting.

He never called us to compete by comparing our cars with the cars of our neighbors, nor the height of our house with that of our relatives.

God called us to compete in a competition of good deeds, altruism, and sacrifice.

"The earth receives everyone, but heaven chooses," said Grigore Vieru[13].

If you want to be part of the world's history, you must accumulate as much as you can. But all that we accumulate for ourselves will become straw, hay and reeds.

On the other hand, if you want to be part of God's history, seek to be the first in the contest called "good deeds." That is where the straws become gold, the sandwiches offered to orphans become precious stones and sweating for God becomes diamonds for the crown of glory.

True fulfillment in life comes not from the abundance of our possessions, but from the richness of our hearts. When we share what we have with those in need, we mirror the compassion of Christ. This selflessness transforms our temporary belongings into eternal treasures.

Consider the parable of the Good Samaritan. He did not pass by the suffering man but stopped, tended to his wounds, and provided for his care. His actions were not driven by the hope of reward, but by genuine love and mercy. This is the kind of competition God calls us to—one of empathy and action.

Ultimately, the legacy we leave behind is not measured by our wealth but by our willingness to serve. In God's eyes, our success is defined by our dedication to uplifting others. Let us strive to be remembered not for what we owned, but for how we loved and served those around us.

---

13 Renowned Moldovan poet and writer, known for his significant contributions to Moldovan and Romanian literature, including works that reflect themes of love, patriotism, and social justice.

April 3

WISE OR FOOLISH?

"A fool has no delight in understanding, but in expressing his own heart." – Proverbs 18:2

For a wise man it is not so hard to admit that he does not know everything and that he still has a lot to learn. It`s not hard for him to admit that only through a humble character and through a thirst for knowledge he can acquire even more wisdom.

One the other hand, the fool has an answer for each question. He thinks he knows everything and is eager to demonstrate it. He's characterized by pride and when pride and foolishness meet you are shocked by the diversity of foolish ideas that emerge from such an encounter.

Be a wise man! Ask questions even if others may laugh at you at school. Try to learn more and more at your workplace, even if your colleagues mock you. Most of the time it is the fools who laugh at others, not the wise men. So be wise enough to keep on going, regardless of other people's attitude.

The wise man asks questions. He is humble enough to ask questions. The fool cannot humble himself to do this because he fears he would damage his false image which he built with so much effort.

Be a wise man! Surround yourself with wise people, with good books and with God's Word, the supreme source of wisdom. Seek to know the truth as much as you can. As much as possible, be busy doing what is good. The fools will surely be busy doing evil...

The path of wisdom is paved with humility and a desire to grow. A wise man never ceases to seek, to ask, and to learn, understanding that wisdom is a lifelong journey. In contrast, the fool's path is marked by arrogance and stagnation, leading to a dead end.

True wisdom comes from recognizing our limitations and striving to overcome them through continuous learning. It involves listening more than speaking, observing more than showing off, and seeking to understand more than to be understood. This approach not only enriches our own lives but also positively impacts those around us.

April 4

THE PEOPLE WE MOURN

"He was thirty-two years old when he became king. He reigned in Jerusalem eight years and, to no one's sorrow, departed. However, they buried him in the City of David, but not in the tombs of the kings." – 2 Chronicles 21:20

Live your life in such a beautiful way that when you leave this world the people around you will mourn, and heaven will rejoice.

There have been kings throughout history whom nobody mourned and there have also been ordinary people like Tabitha whom everyone wept for.

When the wicked leave this earth the corner shop sells no tissues.

"When it goes well with the righteous, the city rejoices; and when the wicked perish, there is jubilation." – Proverbs 11:10

Would you like to be mourned when you leave this earth? Then start sharing your kindness, mercy, and love. Choose words that edify, not discourage your neighbor.

We mourn people who, although may have been far physically from us, were always close to us in spirit.

These are the kind of people who don't wait for a tragedy to happen before they help someone; they help someone each day.

We mourn people who give us a call even when they do not need anything from us, except to see if we are doing well.

We mourn people who do not wait for Christmas to give an orange to somebody. They give themselves every single day.

We mourn people who weep, not people who complain. These are the kind of people who fast and pray for the nation, for their neighbors and their brethren.

We mourn people whose car is always dirty – dirty from carrying clothes for the poor and packages for the needy and from taking brothers and sisters to and from the church or the hospital. I know several such ministers who work this way around the country; these are people who do not show up on YouTube, but who will show up on the big screens of heaven on the day of rewarding judgement.

We mourn people who do not look at their watches when they talk to us. These are the kind of people for whom the most precious time is invested in their neighbor.

The people we mourn are those who lived in fear of the Lord. They are the kind of people whose heart would have beaten faster if they had cut off the edge of Saul's robe. Some people lie and steal without shame. No one will mourn such people. The people we mourn are those who come to church regardless of the weather outside.

The people we mourn are those who give us calls, not *likes.* These kinds of people were concerned with their neighbors` pain, even if their own pain was probably greater.

Wouldn't you like to be such a person?

You can start today!

APRIL 5

SAND OR ROCK?

"Therefore, whoever hears these sayings of Mine, and does them, I will liken him to a wise man who built his house on the rock... Therefore, whoever hears these sayings of Mine, and does them, I will liken him to a wise man who built his house on the rock." – Matthew 7:24,26

Ruins or solid walls? Shaky ground or stability?

The storm will test the foundation of your house, not the flooring of your house. It tests your personal relationship with God, not what you show on the outside; your character, not your reputation; the holiness of your life, not the beauty of your words; your integrity, not just your ministry.

In vain we waste money to buy new curtains for our house, if its foundation is cracked. What is the use of expensive windows if the foundation does not have reinforced concrete? What use can you have for a 10-story house if its foundation is only 5 inches deep?

Let us read the Word of God. Let us hear the Word of God. Let us fulfill the Word of God. This way we won't be scared by weather reports. We will go victoriously through our daily difficulties, adversities, and trials, because God always helps the man who not only hears but also obeys His voice.

Building our lives on the solid rock of God's Word ensures that we are prepared for any storm that comes our way. It is not enough to merely listen to sermons or read the Bible; we must integrate its truths into our daily lives. This means living out our faith in every decision we make, every interaction we have, and every challenge we face.

When we prioritize our relationship with God, we fortify our foundation. This spiritual discipline involves regular prayer, sincere worship, and a deep commitment to live according to God's commandments. By doing so, we cultivate a resilience that withstands the fiercest storms, because our strength is rooted in something unshakeable.

Contrast this with those who build on sand – fleeting pleasures, societal approval, material wealth. These are temporary and unstable. When life's inevitable trials strike, their foundations crumble. But those who build on the rock of Christ will stand firm, their faith and integrity unscathed, shining as a testament to God's enduring power and love.

April 6

LOTS OF TROUBLES, FEW FRIENDS

"A friend loves at all times, and a brother is born in adversity." – Proverbs 17:17

When the prodigal son left his home taking half of his father's wealth he was quickly surrounded by friends. When you pay the restaurant bill, when everything goes your way, when you are on the mountain and have lots of things to share with others, then you will also have lots of friends.

Life, however, does not lack valleys. When you find yourself at the ICU, in personal failures, disappointments or in all sorts of financial holes, there are not too many people willing to stand by your side.

When Job ended up financially bankrupt even his servants stopped answering him. The few friends still by his side started to judge him unfairly.

There are not too many friends who give you a call when you are sick, who stay close to you when you fail an exam or when you go through foggy times. The sieve of troubles shows us that many are willing to share a meal with us, but few are willing to pull at the same yoke.

When the fuel price went up, I saw lots of people in line at the gas station waiting to fill up their tanks. I don't think there was even one of them waiting to fill up somebody else's tank. Why not? Because most people are only interested in obtaining personal gain out of a friendship, not the gain of the other.

If the fingers at one of your hands are enough to count the friends you have when you go through troubles, don't be upset. Rather, value them and make sure you too are such a friend for others.

If you find yourself alone, don't give up the race to Heaven! When nobody else comes along, God will!

April 7

BEING AVAILABLE IS MORE IMPORTANT THAN BEING ABLE

"Thus Noah did; according to all that God commanded him, so he did." – Genesis 6:22

God didn't choose to save Noah because he was an expert in building arks, but He gave Noah the ability to build the ark because he was available to obey.

God doesn't choose people for their gifts and abilities; there are lots of gifted people who work according to their own mind. Rather, God looks for people who are ready to fall on their knees before Him and say, "I want to do Your will, not mine!" The people who are willing to obey will be taken by God from their lowly states and equipped for great works.

Stop complaining about your lack of gifts. Be ready to give up your will, your time, and your expectations and then give yourself to Him entirely.

Over the years you will be astonished when, looking back, you will see how God equipped you because of your obedience.

Then, when you finish building the ask of your ministry, according to His plan, He will come to close the door.

"...the Lord shut him in." – Genesis 7:16

When He closes the door, only those who obeyed Him completely will remain inside.

By the way, the Titanic sank.

Noah's ark did not.

April 8

BE CAREFUL IN THE PLAIN OF ONO!

"Now it happened when Sanballat, Tobiah, Geshem the Arab, and the rest of our enemies heard that I had rebuilt the wall, and that there were no breaks left in it(...), that Sanballat and Geshem sent to me, saying, 'Come, let us meet together among the villages in the plain of Ono.' But they thought to do me harm." – Nehemiah 6:1-2

Nehemiah was done building the wall. He was done with the dust and the trowel. They only had to put up the gate doors, some finishing touches here and there, and do some cleaning. Nehemiah and his people were working with the trowel while Sanballat and Tobiah were giving their opinions. Those who are a stumbling block for the ministry cannot be happy for the accomplishments of others. Envy does not leave them alone. If that was not their idea, if they weren't the center of attention, they could not enjoy the other people's wall.

Four times they called Nehemiah to meet them, to let others put up the doors, to let others finish up the work. That's all the Devil wants: things that are half done. Meetings with the people who discourage, with those who kill dreams.

I like Nehemiah's answer:

"So I sent messengers to them, saying, 'I am doing a great work, so that I cannot come down. Why should the work cease while I leave it and go down to you?'"– Nehemiah 6:3

He understood his work. He understood his call. He knew that at the inauguration he couldn't say, "Remember me, Lord!" if he met with the people from the Ono plain: with the blamers, with the score keepers, and with the ones who set up roadblocks. No! He had to be next to those who were involved and be a role model!

I don't know in what ministry you are involved. I don't know if you have identified your calling. What I can tell you is that Sanballat and Tobiah still live today. They are not just certain individuals, but they can be anything that stops you from continuing the work God gave you!

Their call sounds very nice. They don't have a problem with you, but with the ministry that God gave you to do.

They want to convince you to come down in the valley, while God wants to bring you up on the mountain.

They want to make you give up. To leave the field and go back to the bleachers and be on their side. Be careful because they are not sent by God!

"Then I perceived that God had not sent him at all..." – Nehemiah 6:12

I have seen the spiritual setback of many who mocked those who were involved. They would laugh at them all day long and call them names. They would always blame others. They would build their mansions in the plain of Ono but not secure a place in Heaven.

Ignore them! Focus on the work that God entrusted you with. With humility, courage, and obedience to the leaders of the Lord, continue to work with your trowel, with your cement mixer, pouring water on the hands of Elijah or doing whatever else is necessary.

Be careful about the plain of Ono! There is no magnificent landscape over there – there is only the waiting room of hell. And when God shuts the door, only the ones who listened to Him completely will remain inside.

April 9

PESSIMIST, OPTIMIST OR NEUTRAL?

"Then Caleb quieted the people before Moses, and said, 'Let us go up at once and take possession, for we are well able to overcome it.'" – Numbers 13:30

Winston Churchill said that our attitude is a small thing that makes a huge difference. It defines our personality and represents what people see about our thinking and our vision.

When the 12 spies sent by Moses to spy in Canaan came back into the camp, they were divided into two categories: 10 of them had a negative attitude and 2 of them, Joshua, and Caleb, had a positive attitude.

People with a **negative attitude** ignore the beautiful things of life and always see the bad ones. They always compare themselves with the ones who are better than them and complain about how bad their own life is. Instead of seeing every opportunity as a chance, all they see is a problem.

They are characterized by anger, distrust, and frustration. This is why they rarely make any progress in any area of life. They always blame others for their own failures, and they never want to change or get out of the pit in which they are.

People with a **positive attitude** always try to see the good things in life. While the pessimist considers the problem bigger than God, the optimist considers God bigger than the problem itself. Joshua and Caleb did not look at how big the giants of Canaan were; rather, they looked at how big their God was.

The person with a positive attitude is always joyful and influences those around him with this special character trait. He is a sincere and courageous person. He works hard wherever his involvement is needed and always has the same vision as Joshua and Caleb:

"We are well able to overcome it." – Numbers 13:30

A third attitude that a person can display in many situations is **neutrality.** In this category belong the people who are neither doubtful, nor hopeful. These people live their life ignoring both its joys, and its troubles.

They do not belong to either side. They are not emotional, and they do not get involved; although they are present, they have no comment. They are content with their lifestyle, even if this lifestyle is often a mediocre one. They are neither the last nor the first in their class. The house they build does not fall apart, but it is not ready for move-in either. Their usually comment is, "It works this way too...".

Your attitude will define you or it will destroy you, and then it will influence those around you... Most of the time, people are drawn to those with a positive attitude, to those who inspire trust, who are motivated to fight for what they want until they get it. Be a person with a positive attitude! Attitude makes the difference both when you are in the wilderness and when you are entering Canaan!

We need orange juice. There are already too many grapefruits and lemons.

April 10

HOW CAN I UNDERSTAND GOD'S CALL FOR ME?

"But you are a chosen generation, a royal priesthood, a holy nation, His own special people, that you may proclaim the praises of Him who called you out of darkness into His marvelous light." – 1 Peter 2:9

For each one of us God has several calls. The first 3 that we will mention are general calls (they are for everybody), and the last one is specific for each individual.

The first call that God has for each one of us is **the call to REPENTANCE.**

It is absolutely necessary to have a moment in our life when we become aware of the fact that we have upset God by living a sinful life and that we must ask for forgiveness of our past. Then, believing in the sacrifice at Calvary, we will receive the forgiveness of sin and the promise of salvation. This event is called regeneration - the conversion of the sinful man and the renewing of his mind. This is how he passes from the Devil's kingdom into God's kingdom.

Before asking ourselves, "What is God`s plan for me?" it's very important to put ourselves into the hand of God. I cannot use a tool that is not in my hand or in my workshop.

The second call that God has for us, after the call to repentance, is **the call to HOLINESS.**

"For God did not call us to uncleanness, but in holiness." – 1 Thessalonians 4:7

Being born again is an event (it happens just one, like the birth of a child), while holiness is a process (like the growth of the child).

Again, I want to point out that holiness comes before serving.

"Therefore, if anyone cleanses himself from the latter, he will be a vessel for honor, sanctified and useful for the Master, prepared for every good work." – 2 Timothy 2:21

Before a woman can use a vessel for cooking, she must make sure that the vessel is clean. If you put even the best food in the world into a dirty vessel, it compromises the food and, under no circumstance, it does NOT cleanse the vessel. The cleansing of the vessel is done with water, not with food. The Word, which is the water of life, will keep your life clean:

"Your word I have hidden in my heart, that I might not sin against You." – Psalm 119:11

Every day, the man of God needs to stay away from sin and live a holy life. If he happens to make a mistake, this is merely an accident, not a lifestyle. It is one thing to walk through the ditch and another to just accidentally slip into it, then get up from it and be more careful in the future.

The third call that God makes to every one of us is **the call to OBEDIENCE.** No owner can use his animal to carry burden if it doesn't obey. No cook can use a vessel, no matter how clean it is, if it doesn't stay where it is supposed to stay (personifying this example).

It's not enough to know that my child does not do anything foolish, if he doesn't listen to me when I send him to do a good thing.

The Bible teaches us that **"TO BE"** is more important than **"TO DO."**

"Having confidence in your obedience, I write to you, knowing that you will do even more than I say." – Philemon 1:21

The fourth call that God makes to every one of us is **the call to MINISTRY.**

"...ministry, let us use it in our ministering; he who teaches, in teaching; he who exhorts, in exhortation; he who gives, with liberality; he who leads, with diligence; he who shows mercy, with cheerfulness." – Romans 12:7-8

Let me repeat this: this is the fourth call, not the first one! The order matters a lot! It's not enough to serve! My child may know how to dig the whole yard; if he doesn't listen to me WHEN and WHERE he should dig, he might ruin all the tomatoes I planted in the greenhouse!

On judgment day a lot of people will have a huge surprise because they served, but they did not respect the order of the four calls! There will be people who have served but did not live a holy and fully obedient life!

"But He will say, 'I tell you I do not know you, where you are from. Depart from Me, all you workers of iniquity!'" – Luke 13:27

How can you understand your ministry? Start by looking at what you CAN do. I cannot tell whether I can cook or not if I don't try it a few times. I cannot tell if my gift is sewing clothes, like Tabitha, unless I try to do it.

When God gives you a gift and you discover it, you realize that you love to do that thing, and it gives you a huge satisfaction. Be careful! Do not make the following confusion: if I like to preach, everyone will surely applaud me for what I do. Do not mistake the challenge of ministry (which we will discuss later) with the satisfaction and the joy of ministry!

Furthermore, when God gives you a gift and you start using it, you will notice that people are encouraged or edified by that gift. The women who surrounded Tabitha on the day of her death had been touched and affected by her service. If I have a gift from God and am called to use it, the people will not get bored or fall asleep while I'm using my gift. By observing the impact, you can check your gift!

Last, but not least, serving is a blazing fire inside you. If you have the gift of singing and one day you don't sing, you feel that something is not all right. If you have the gift of interceding in prayer and one day you do not do it, you feel that something is missing.

I wish, from the bottom of my heart, that you discover your calling! There is nothing more important than to reach the end of your life and be able to gladly look back and know that you said "YES" to all of the four calls: repentance, holiness, obedience, and ministry.

April 11

HONORED BY PEOPLE OR BY GOD?

"Then Balak said to Balaam, 'Did I not earnestly send to you, calling for you? Why did you not come to me? Am I not able to honor you?'" – Numbers 22:37

In my lifetime I have met quite a few people who believed that they were the center of the universe. They believed that their money, their connections, and their own person were the key factors for receiving honor. These people have a very good opinion about themselves and a very bad one about everyone around them.

Be careful with such people! The honor they give to you does not come for free. They will forever call in a favor because of something they did for you or because they lent you a helping hand.

The honor that God gives is of a whole different nature. It comes as a reward for your humbleness, for your fear of God and for your beautiful testimony. When Mordecai refused to bow down before Haman and did not choose to flatter the enemy of Jewish people, we notice that the man in charge with many of the Kingdom's matters was very disturbed by this. However, did you notice how nicely comes God and gives honor to Mordecai through a set of circumstances synchronized by none other than the Hand of the Almighty?

Let's desire God's appreciation. The appreciation of people is short-lived and most of the time it is a trap.

It is true that we should appreciate and honor one another. But we should do this freely, without any hidden interest. Only appreciation that comes from a pure heart has value. But such kind of appreciation is rarer than 24-karat gold...

One day, God will honor the man who was humble, honest, and who feared the Lord by giving him heaven. He will raise him up to the highest level, after having allowed him to walk his whole life through deep valleys in order to shape his character.

What greater honor can a man have than receiving God's honor as a gift, and the grace of living an eternity with Him?

Seek the honor of God! Make this endeavor the goal of your life! At the end, you will see that it was totally worth it!

April 12

66 CHANNELS

I asked a widow if she ever gets bored during the day, having been alone for more than 15 years since she lost her husband...

"Not at all!" she answered me. "I have in my room a TV with 66 wonderful channels! This year I watched all of them, and now I'm watching them a second time. I'm watching the 'Ezekiel' channel now..."

As a minister, I have noticed that each family that valued and honored the Bible remained standing by God even though they went through problems and trials. I have also noticed that if they neglected the reading of the Bible, they also neglected living it and, sooner or later, that family drifted away from God.

"The Bible should be the daily bread, not the cake on a special occasion," said Victor Hugo.

You can't love God if you don't respect His Word.

"If you love Me, keep My commandments." – John 14:15

In order to respect His commandments, we must know these commandments.

Do not postpone the reading of the Bible until you are on a hospital bed, nor until you take your college exam or until you need help. When you do this, you try to bring God closer by catching up in a few days with what you did not do for years. The Bible is not the spare tire of the believer, but the steering wheel of his life.

Our decisions, our victories or failures, our ideals and our plans must be closely linked to the Bible. You cannot ignore the Bible and have a life of victory. You cannot disregard the Word of the Lord and reach the finish line victoriously, the place where all the prizes are given to those who lived a holy life.

Sir Walter Scott, the famous English novelist, on his deathbed asked his son-in-law Lockhart to read something from the book.

"From which book?" Lockhard asked, looking at the 20,000 volumes covering the walls.

"There is just one book: the Bible!" answered Scott.

Edmond Barke, the great English statesman and matchless speaker, states, "All my life I read the Bible, in the morning, at lunch and in the evening. This habit was very useful to me."

William Gladstone, an English statesman, four times prime minister, wrote in the foreword of a popular edition of the Bible, "In the solitude of the room, in the silence of the night, on the bed of suffering, facing death, everywhere the Holy Bible is by our side; its words heal and comfort, lead and guide, strengthen and guide to all that is good."

Today is a new opportunity to open the Book. Open it gladly!

April 13

CHOOSE THE POSITIVE EXAMPLE!

"Nevertheless, the children of Korah did not die." – Numbers 26:11

Korah, Dathan, and Abiram were the heads of the rebellion against Moses. God punished them harshly, opening up the ground to swallow them.

The Bible emphasizes something very important, namely that Korah's sons chose NOT to follow in their father's footsteps in his reckless behavior. We also noticed that Dathan and Abiram had a brother, Nemuel. He also refused to join his brothers' folly.

I have noticed that most people choose negative role models very easily, even if they have some good examples in their family or among their friends. Later, when they are asked how they ended up like this, they immediately point fingers at their drunkard father, at their classmate who smoked in the school's bathroom or at their teacher who fell in love with a minor. This is how they try to explain their own fall but omit to say that they also had some positive examples whom they ignored.

Our life is full of choices. The role models that we have in our hearts will guide our steps to Heaven or to hell.

It is more tempting to choose evil. It`s more tempting to give the blessing of eternity for a life full of sinful pleasures. It is more tempting, but not more beneficial.

Look for a positive example around you, wherever you are! It's impossible not to find one. Look at the steps that person took to become a role model for others.

What we admire will influence us. If I see a person ruining his life with alcohol, adultery, immorality or lies, it is clear that if I follow his footsteps, I will have both a destroyed family and an eternity without God. Why should I choose the negative?

Of all the examples around you, choose to follow the footsteps of the person who loves God and sacrifices for Him.

When the negative role models will have to stand before God and give account for the life they lived, the words you will hear are these: eternal life...

APRIL 14

APPEARANCE OR CHARACTER?

They say every person has a beautiful smile in front of a camera.

There is a unique desire inside us to behave in front of others differently than when we are alone. What people see is our appearance, but what we are when nobody sees us shows our true character.

One of the faces of hypocrisy is reflected when there are notable differences between our appearance and our character.

The value of a person is not given by his appearance, but by his character. A person should be the same both in the church and in society, both in the family and at work, both on social media and in private.

Be a man of character, so that when people find out how you are in private, they will not be surprised, but rather discover that you are the same person both in private and in public.

God knows each one of us and He sees beyond our appearance. Eliab had a gorgeous image in the eyes of the people, but God considered him a rejected man.

David, on the other hand, did not turn heads; he was an insignificant child, a shepherd, a young boy without many *likes,* but a boy whom God appreciated and whom God made king because of his distinguished character.

Eliab never asked God to look into his heart, because people who are concerned with their own appearance are not at all interested in God's opinion about them – they care only about other people's opinion.

David knew that God looks beyond our clothes, beyond what is visible and, thus he was able to say something only men of character can state:

> *"Search me, O God, and know my heart; try me, and know my anxieties..." – Psalm 139:23*

Celebrities are built on appearance. Heroes are built on character.
Fame comes and goes! Virtues stay!

April 15

PRAYER IS NOT AN OPTION, IT IS A NECESSITY!

"Pray without ceasing." – 1 Thessalonians 5:17

The most important aspect in a relationship is communication. In a marriage, the car can be replaced by walking, the house can be replaced by a condo, the microwave by a stove, etc. But communication cannot be replaced by anything. Without it, the partners are slowly growing apart from each other, just like a fire that has no more fuel.

It is exactly the same in our relationship with God. Prayer cannot be replaced by anything else. It is not optional, it is necessary. Fire, light, and water are not optional things! When you transform a necessity into an optional thing, you are definitely headed for failure.

Prayer does not depend on a specific place, nor a specific state of the soul, but it is a communication channel that must be kept open in any moment of the day: when I wake up, when I'm about to eat, when I put on my seatbelt, when I park, when I sit down at my desk, etc. A few words of thankfulness and a few requests to God in moments like these matter a lot!

Not the length, the grammar, or the shouting of the prayer matters, but the heart of the man that utters it. My wife is not impressed by my speech, but more than that, she wants to see honesty and commitment in what I tell her.

Continuous prayer is nothing but a continuous state of dependency on God. How long could I breathe without His air? How many steps could I take without His continuous protection? How many days could I work without strength in my hands?

Oh, how much we need to pray for guidance at the roundabouts of life, for protection in the lions' den, for appetite in the green pastures, and for company in the valley of death!

A special quote of Ravenhill says, "We must pray in order to live a holy life! We must live a holy life so that we can pray!"

Let's pray!

April 16

THE PASTURE BEFORE THE JORDAN OR THE ONE IN CANAAN?

"Now the children of Reuben and the children of Gad had a very great multitude of livestock; and when they saw the land of Jazer and the land of Gilead, that indeed the region was a place for livestock... Therefore, they said, 'If we have found favor in your sight, let this land be given to your servants as a possession. Do not take us over the Jordan.'" – Numbers 32:1,5

God took the Jews out of Egypt in order to lead them to Canaan. They were almost at the border when the children of Reuben and the children of Gad came with an odd request: they asked to remain outside of the Land and the main reason was that there were good pastures for the livestock. They did not wait to cross the Jordan to see how the pastures of Canaan were, to see God's promises in the Land.

Our life is full of choices. What is the main factor to consider when making a decision? The livestock? The car? The house? The pasture? The material?

Oh, I saw so many marriages in which what mattered was the visible: the color of the car, the color of the eyes, the value of the mansion. For many people, the inner values are not so important: kindness, fear of the Lord, Agape love, a beautiful character...

Naomi went to Moab because there was a huge financial crisis in Israel at that time. Do you know what she said when she returned?

"I went out full..." – Ruth 1:21

So I wonder: why did she leave in the first place? That means that the abundance to which she refers here is not material. She had a different kind of abundance: the family that she lost in Moab in the meantime. Why? Because spiritually speaking, Moab has a price tag.

My dear, let's ask for more guidance from God so that the main factor in our choices in life is not the material. Let us not miss the crossing of the Jordan to the heavenly Canaan because of fleeting pastures.

It is not a sin to have abundance; we use material things all the time, but we must be careful not to tie our hearts to them.

If the pasture of this world is more important than the pasture in Psalm 23, it is possible that, materially speaking, you are wealthy, but spiritually speaking, you are surely bankrupt...

When Lot had to choose, he looked to Sodom and Gomorrah:

"And Lot lifted his eyes and saw all the plain of Jordan, that it was well watered everywhere." – Genesis 13:10a

He initially pitched his tents *as far as* Sodom. It doesn't say: *in* Sodom. This means that he probably said, "I will stay apart. I will stay close, but I will not go inside." But one day he did go inside and then all his life was tormented. (2 Peter 2:8)

If my barn is full of "livestock" but my children fall in love with Sodom and Gomorrah, what have I gained? If my accounts are full and my prayers are tearless, am I still burning for God? Sodom and Gomorrah do not offer anything to us for free. If I do not have 30 minutes a day to read the Bible because the "livestock" and the "pastures" take up the most of my time, then what have I achieved?

Abraham chose the mountain, not the clover nor the lucerne. He chose with his heart connected to God and with his eyes looking towards Heaven. On the mountain there is not so much grass for the livestock, but the air is cleaner. The prayers are more sincere, and the presence of God is much closer.

We must work. It is absolutely necessary to be diligent and care for our families, to work honestly in order to help others who desperately need our help. But let us not forget: if we do not cross the Jordan because our heart is too connected to the livestock and the pastures, we lose everything.

Our Canaan is the Heaven of God. Our values are eternal. I do not want to let my work make me lose my prayer time. I do not want to let money take the place of the joy of salvation. I do not want the temporary to swallow up the eternal.

It's not such a big deal to leave Egypt behind and the truly important thing is to reach Canaan.

Let's get ready!

We can see Canaan right in front of us!

APRIL 17

THE SACRIFICE THAT PRECEDES THE JOY

We look at the great men of the Bible and we wish to get where they got, but we cannot do that without making the sacrifices they made.

Every joy hides a matching sacrifice.

If you want to enjoy the fragrance of a rose, you must feel the pain of the thorns.

If you want to enjoy the view from the mountain top, you must deal with the weariness of climbing some dangerous paths.

If you want to enjoy the sunrise, you must wake up earlier than others.

Consider Abraham, who became the father of many nations. His journey to joy involved the heart-wrenching willingness to sacrifice his own son, Isaac. This act of faith and obedience brought him to a place of immense blessing and fulfillment, demonstrating that the pathway to divine joy often runs through the valley of personal sacrifice.

Reflect on Moses, who led the Israelites to freedom. Before he could experience the joy of the Promised Land, he endured the sacrifice of leaving the comforts of Pharaoh's palace, facing the hardships of the wilderness, and bearing the weight of leading a rebellious people. His perseverance through these sacrifices ultimately led to the fulfillment of God's promise and the joy of deliverance.

Finally, Jesus Christ Himself exemplified the ultimate sacrifice that precedes the ultimate joy. He endured the agony of the cross, despising its shame, for the joy set before Him – the redemption of mankind. His resurrection brought immeasurable joy to the world, a testament that the greatest joys come through the greatest sacrifices. Let us follow His example, embracing our sacrifices with the hope of the joy to come.

Don't be afraid of today's sacrifices.

They are just the preceding steps of tomorrow's joy.

April 18

JESUS VS. HISTORY

"...that at the name of Jesus every knee should bow, of those in heaven, and of those on earth, and of those under the earth..." – Philippians 2:10

History does not record any king who was born in a manger, except King Jesus.

History does not record any king who wore on his head a crown of thorns, except King Jesus.

History does not record any condemned man who asked for the forgiveness of those crucifying him, except the "Condemned" Jesus.

History does not record any human being who conquered death, except for the One who is alive forever and ever.

History does not record any groom who came down from His glory in order to invite His bride to a wedding that will not take place on Earth, except for our Groom, Jesus.

History does not record any shepherd who became the sacrificial lamb for his flock, except for the Good Shepherd, Jesus. He laid down His life for His sheep, enduring the ultimate sacrifice to bring us the ultimate joy of eternal life with Him.

History does not record any light that shone in the darkness and was not overcome, except for the Light of the World, Jesus. His life and teachings continue to illuminate the path to salvation, dispelling the darkness of sin and despair.

History does not record any healer who took upon Himself the wounds of humanity to provide healing for all, except for the Great Physician, Jesus. By His stripes, we are healed, and through His suffering, we find restoration and peace.

History does not record any servant who washed the feet of his followers to set an example of true leadership, except for the Servant King, Jesus. His humble service teaches us the profound joy found in serving others and putting their needs above our own.

Some people have a past, others have a present, but only the ones who live in obedience to Jesus have a future.

I wish you a bright future.

April 19

THE SHOUTS OF THE KING: "FATHER, FORGIVE THEM!"

"Then Jesus said, 'Father, forgive them, for they do not know what they do.'" – Luke 23:34a

The most negative "achievement" that man had throughout history was to crucify his Creator. To put on the cross the One who came to offer him eternal Salvation.

There, in front of the cross, the crowd was impatiently waiting for His first word. Often times, the tongue of those being crucified was cut off due to much cursing and bad words against their executioners.

Jesus preached gentleness in the Sermon on the Mount. The people were curious to see if that sermon could now be fulfilled. What would the One who said, *"I am gentle and lowly in heart"* do?

He asked for forgiveness for the ones that had no clue about what they were about to do. They were condemning Life to death. They were nailing the hands that fed the crowds. They were putting on the cross the feet that walked all His life for the benefit of others.

He could have answered the mockery, and yet Peter tells us that He did not. He could have said to them, "I will show you on Judgement Day what you did! You will pay for this! We will see in 3 days who was right!"

He chose not only not to threaten or get revenge, but rather to defend the guilty; to pray for them!

Instead of using His last moments to prove His innocence and instead of complaining about His pain, He chose to pray. He shouted with all of His strength for us. Doesn't this shout pierce you? Don`t your eyes shed tears when you see His perfect love?

There, among all those who spat on Him and hit Him, I see you and I see myself. I see me, the one who wrote these lines, and I see you, the one who reads them.

The King's shout for forgiveness moved me so much that I decided to change my life! I was pierced by His prayer, and I finally understood that at the cross justice was taken over by mercy. Mercy for us, justice for Jesus. A transfer willingly made by the one who was guilty – me, to the One who was not guilty – King Jesus.

Jesus knew that the circle of hatred can break only if you turn the other cheek. The King stood between Heaven and Earth and, instead of returning the blow, He asked for forgiveness for His executioners.

For me and for you.

But this forgiveness takes effect only in the life of the person who admits his guilt.

Like Ioanid said,

And now Jesus, the condemned
He's asking you: 'Yes or no?
Are you guilty or not?'
I answered, 'Yes!' and I was forgiven.
I answered, 'Yes!'
What about you? What about you?

April 20

THE SHOUTS OF THE KING: "TODAY YOU WILL BE WITH ME IN PARADISE!"

"And Jesus said to him, 'Asssuredly, I say to you, today you will be with Me in Paradise.'" – Luke 23:43

Jesus already shouted, minutes before, "Father, forgive them!" But nobody answered, "I admit, I am guilty, I am the one who needs forgiveness!" Only the thief…

"And we indeed justly, for we receive the due reward of our deeds." – Luke 23:41a

A stained criminal record. A life of shame about which he did not want to talk to anyone. Most likely, he never witnessed any miracle of Jesus, he never heard any sermon of Jesus, and yet something moved him. A grain of faith sneaked into this sinner's heart, and that faith made him admit his sin and admit the holiness of the King.

Jesus did not look at how many sins the thief had, but at the depth of his repentance. What a paradox: the Priests, with the Law in their hands, were standing by the cross to make sure that the King is dead, while the criminal, the thief, the robber looks at Jesus and tells Him,

"Lord, remember me when You come into Your kingdom." – Luke 23:42b

Grace had just bypassed those who bragged about being sons of Abraham. Grace jumped over to a man who said, *"Lord, remember me! I am guilty but remember me when You come into Your kingdom!"*

There are people who have only one chance in life, and they take full advantage of it. There are other people who have countless chances, but they waste all of them… Why? Because they always say they are good people, they never hurt anyone, they never break into anyone`s homes; they think that others need salvation, not them.

While dying, the King found the type of man for whom He had come. With His hands nailed on the cross, the King opened the gates of Heaven for a poor thief.

Why?

Because the Son of Man came to save the lost: the people who, instead of pointing fingers to others, point their fingers towards themselves.

The doctor can only heal the patient who admits he is ill.

The King can only offer Paradise to those who see their sin and realize that, without Jesus, the eternity will be a disaster.

Where there's humility, there's grace.

Where there's regret, there's hope.

In a life in which Jesus is called King and Lord, the paradise starts today...

April 21

THE SHOUTS OF THE KING: "WOMAN, BEHOLD YOUR SON!"

"When Jesus therefore saw His mother, and the disciple whom He loved standing by, He said to His mother, 'Woman, behold your son!'" – John 19:26

With a broken heart, Mary was looking at the cross on which her Son was hanging between Heaven and Earth. The words of Simeon were coming true,

"Yes, a sword will pierce through your own soul also, that the thoughts of many hearts may be revealed." – Luke 2:35

Separation hurts. Its depth can be understood only by those who have been there. At bus stops, airports, or train stations, for a day or for many years, separations in your soul leave a scar that cannot be easily healed.

Love is not about bypassing suffering at all costs but about passing through suffering by paying a price. Jesus preached,

"And everyone who has left houses or brothers or sisters or father or mother or wife or children or lands, for My name's sake, shall receive a hundredfold, and inherit eternal life." – Matthew 19:29

And now the time had come for these words to be fulfilled for Himself.

The King did not leave until He left His mother in the care of the one who loves in any circumstance. John was by Jesus` side not only at the multiplication of the bread, but at the cross too. Not only when He entered Jerusalem, when people acclaimed Him as King, but also when they mocked Him and spat on Him.

John was a man of few words but much action. That's what love does: "noise" with its actions, not with its words. The interest of others, not my own. Resting his head on Jesus' chest, John learned to synchronize his life by the heartbeats of the One who was the perfect embodiment of the Agape love.

John receives what love receives: more responsibility, more care, more reasons to sacrifice. And, in the end, in eternity, a bigger reward.

In our lifetime, we will surely come across separations too. Walking with Jesus will cost you a lot. Are you ready, in your pain, to comfort those who are also in pain, like Jesus did?

Jesus thought about others when almost nobody was thinking about Him anymore.

"Father, forgive them!", He shouted for his killers. *"Today you will be with Me in Paradise!"*, He shouted for the thief. *"Woman, behold your son!"*, He shouted for the closest person on Earth...

This is how Agape love sacrifices: by filling the holes in the souls of those who are left behind.

However, separation is short-term. The thief met with Jesus again on the same day. Mary, a couple of years later. John, some decades later.

We, the followers of the King, will be separated from Him for just a few moments.

And when we meet again in His presence, we will never separate again.

See you soon!

April 22

THE SHOUTS OF THE KING: "MY GOD, WHY HAVE YOU FORSAKEN ME?"

"And about the ninth hour Jesus cried out with a loud voice, saying, 'Eli, Eli, lama sabachthani?' that is, 'My God, My God, why have You forsaken Me?'" – Matthew 27:46

Beating humiliates the body of a convicted man and spitting humiliates his soul. Jesus did not answer anything to the mocking, the beating, or the spitting. Without saying a word, He watched how the soldiers "cast lots" for His shirt; He was silent when He was unjustly condemned to a cruel death, but something made Him shout loudly, *"Father, why have You forsaken Me?"*

More profound than any pain caused by people was the pain caused by being separated from the Father. God turned His head away from His Son who was carrying our sins; He looked at us. In all eternity, this was the only moment when the Son was separated from the Father, and this separation could only be described by a desperate shout...

There, on the cross, the Son of God showed to the world the feelings of the One who carries all the sins and who has to die for them. He showed everyone what an awful solitude and what a separation from God can the burden of sin bring.

People who play with sin should be terrified. Their separation will be eternal, not just temporary, like the one Jesus had. He was a holy Person who died instead of us. If you don't accept His sacrifice and you don't change your life, you will have to die for your own sins, but that death will be eternal...

This is why, on judgment day, no one will find any excuses. If God turned His face from His Son because He was carrying our sins, do you think He won't turn His face from the man who all his life denied the existence of God and, despite the divine goodness, he lived a life full of sins?

If, for just a few hours of carrying the sins, Jesus shouted with all His might for the presence of the Father, can you imagine the shouts of those who will suffer in hell for millions of years?

Jesus, as divinity, could not have been left by God because God cannot leave God. But Jesus the man, in those moments, truly felt the pain of separation and the broken connection between man and God, because of our guilt...

If we look deeper, we realize that God does not leave anyone, but it is the man who leaves Him. It was not God who hid from Adam, but Adam who hid from God...

It would be so good to understand that it is not the spring that leaves the thirsty hiker! The water spring remains there. The hiker, however, can choose not to drink and, with parched lips, illogically blame the water for many years.

We refuse to drink and then wonder why we are thirsty. We refuse to listen and then we are surprised by failure. If we refuse to choose Love, why are we shocked by the consequences of hatred?

Christ shouted with all His might so that you should no longer have to shout. Christ bore your sin so that you could bear His righteousness.

Every year, the Romans crucified more than 30,000 convicts. The only Convict crucified for the sins of others was our King. Because God left Him, we were able to get close to Him and in His wounds, we found healing.

I want to be with God always... Don`t you want it too?

April 23

THE SHOUTS OF THE KING: "I THIRST!"

"After this, Jesus, knowing that all things were now accomplished, that the Scripture might be fulfilled, said, 'I thirst!'" – John 19:28

Parched lips. Dry mouth. Exhausted body. The heat of the day. Six hours on the cross. History confirms that the greatest torment a crucified person could endure is thirst.

Jesus was human like us. He endured hunger (Matthew 4:2), He went through periods of thirstiness (John 4:7), He felt fatigue (John 4:6), He needed sleep (Mark 4:38). He wept at the tomb of Lazarus and was angry with the money changers in the Temple. The human emotions did not bypass Him, and among the divine shouts on the cross is also the human shout of a thirsty man.

When you go through illness, trouble, rejection, physical needs or material needs do not forget that He also felt them. He can fully understand you and He can come to your help.

On the other hand, the King's shout on the cross also referred to the thirst of a man who was oppressed by the guilt of sin and who longed for complete deliverance. Sin desolates and dries up the human soul, and Jesus, who was carrying the burden of our sins, showed us how deeply should shout the person who is burdened by guilt when he wants to be freed in the way in which only the Water of Life can free.

He said in the Sermon on the Mount: *"Blessed are those who hunger and thirst for righteousness, for they shall be filled!"* (Matthew 5:6)

Sin does not satisfy. Sin always asks for more until it ends up taking your soul. Only walking with Jesus in holiness can quench the thirst inside of us. There, on the cross, Jesus reminded us about what He had preached. The thirst for righteousness is not an option, but a necessity.

Thirsty, on the cross, He gave us all the Water of Life. Stripped of his clothes by the soldiers who cast lots for His shirt, He clothed each of us with the robe of righteousness. Carrying a crown of thorns on His head, the King was preparing crowns that will be given to us at the end of the marathon of life – to all those who lived a renewed life.

Sometimes, without realizing what you say, you too probably shout, "I'm thirsty!" Although you are surrounded by many friends, your spiritual hunger is often not satisfied. We have hundreds of kinds of water and juices and yet, our soul stays thirsty...

Don't smother this shout! Tell Jesus, "Lord, I am thirsty for the Water of Life! I'm thirsty for an awakening in my life and the life of my family! I am thirsty for a holy life, free from sin!"

And He who understands your thirst will answer. He will not give you vinegar and gall, but the fulfillment you long for.

APRIL 24

THE SHOUTS OF THE KING: "IT IS FINISHED!"

"So when Jesus had received the sour wine, He said, 'It is finished!' And bowing His head, He gave up His spirit." – John 19:30

Someone said, "I didn't stop because I was done, I stopped only to get some rest."

Jesus stopped. But He had also finished. The plan to save man had been completed. There was nothing else to add. Jesus fulfilled, through His life, over 300 Old Testament prophecies.

The masterpiece of human salvation was completed! God's love was crying out forgiveness for us, but His justice was asking man to pay for his sins. In His absolute wisdom He had an extraordinary way of reconciling justice with mercy: His Son. Love for us, justice for His Son.

Jesus never did things half-way. He did not feed 2,000 out of the 5,000. He didn't just heal one of Bartimeus's eyes. He did not calm a quarter of the storm. He never promised something and did not fulfill it!

The King taught us how to finish what we started. Not without obstacles, not without temptations. Should you continue to preach the Gospel when 70 disciples abandon you? Should you continue to pray in Gethsemane when those in whom you invested the most sleep nearby? Should you endure all the mockery of the man you created, dying for him?

Yes. All the way to the end!

"Now before the Feast of the Passover, when Jesus knew that His hour had come that He should depart from this world to the Father, having loved His own who were in the world, He loved them to the end." – John 13:1

The love that goes all the way to the end is the love that looks beyond the nails. Beyond the opposition. Beyond the offence. It overcomes any obstacle in order to finish the race in a remarkable way. If Jesus had given up, our whole eternity would have been compromised today...

We should get rid of this illness once and for all – the bad habit of starting and never finishing what we started; of promising and then lying, *"I don't remember, brother!"* I met many people who wanted to rest before they even started to work... Such people would say, *"I'm just the person with the idea! You must take care of work and the costs!"*

Oh, how easily we give up! How many jobs we quit from! How many friendships we start and then end them too early! How many children are abandoned by irresponsible parents! How many families destroyed because partners did not keep their covenant to the end...

God will not judge us by our success, but by our faithfulness. He will not judge us by our intentions, but by our deeds. He will not reward our promises, but their fulfillment. Staying in the fight until the end is the biggest challenge.

"To him who will overcome..." says Revelation. Not to him who starts the race. Not to him who has great momentum in the beginning but gives up after a few days. Overcomers. Those who go to the end. Despite the thorns, despite the gossip, despite the opposition.

We do not quote what Paul said when he began the race. But we are extremely happy to be able to say his final words: *"I have fought, I have kept, I have run."* It is an amazing grace to be able to speak about the past with joy, after having reached the finish line with a lot of enthusiasm.

To look back and be able to say, "It is finished! I did the work that God entrusted me to do!"

When you reach the finish line with flying colors, that finish line will be only the beginning of eternal joys.

Here, it ended, but there, it merely begins: an eternity with the One I served.

And in eternity we will never have to say: "it is finished...".

April 25

THE SHOUTS OF THE KING: "FATHER, INTO YOUR HANDS I COMMIT MY SPIRIT!"

"And when Jesus had cried out with a loud voice, He said, 'Father, into Your hands I commit My spirit.' Having said this, He breathed His last." – Luke 23:46

When you have a goal in life it is very important not to change it every day. A steady goal means years of struggle to achieve it. If you change it every day, you may just run around in a circle.

Jesus' lifetime goal was to do the will of the Father who sent Him (John 5:30). He always "synchronized" His watch with the Father's watch and His words, with the Father's words.

At the end, when He accomplished everything, the certainty that He obeyed God in everything made Him know where He was going. Looking back, He was able to also look ahead.

This shout tells us that Jesus never lost sight of His purpose and did absolutely everything He could do to achieve it. He removed any obstacle from His enemies, family, disciples, and even from the thief who asked Him to get down from the cross. Being freed, He headed to the Father. Like a bird you release from her cage, so Jesus knew that in a few minutes the cage of His body would open, and the Father would receive Him in glory...

At the end of our lives, not many of the things we struggle with now will matter anymore. Death will not ask us what kind of car or house we had, nor how much we had in our bank account, nor if our phone was expensive or cheap. At the end, when we cross the finish line, all that shall matter is if we lived in God's will. We find the Father's will for our life in the entire life of the Son, as Paul says:

"...that I may know Him and the power of His resurrection, and the fellowship of His sufferings, being conformed to His death, if, by any means, I may attain to the resurrection from the dead." – Philippians 3:10-11

Today I pray that you set this goal above everything else. May you desire to know the Son as much as possible because whoever knows the Son knows the Father. May you understand the call to salvation, to obedience, to sanctification, and to ministry. NEVER let anything remove this goal from your mind: the resurrection from the dead. Only those who entrust their spirit into the hand of the Father will be part of the first resurrection.

When you make a payment, you receive a receipt. This is how that company proves that your money was deposited into its accounts.

Do you know what is the proof that the payment of our sins has been deposited into God's account?

The resurrection of Jesus.

Pilate does not have the last word. Nor do those who spat and mocked Jesus. Nor does the nail-banging hammer. Nor bankruptcy. Not even cancer. Not even the accident. The last word belongs to the Father. And the Father received the spirit of the Son. Those received by the Father will live forever. Therefore, if He raised, He will also raise us from the dead:

> *"Blessed and holy is he who has part in the first resurrection. Over such the second death has no power, but they shall be priests of God and of Christ, and shall reign with Him a thousand years." – Revelation 20:6*

True happiness is not found in devices. It's not found in alcohol. It's not found in immorality. Happiness belongs only to those who have cleansed their past through the sacrifice of Christ and then live a holy life.

Entrust your life into the Father`s hand, and at the end it will be easy for you to also entrust your spirit...

April 26

THE IMPORTANCE OF CHARACTER IN MANAGING YOUR FINANCES

Money is neutral. Just like a knife. If you are an angry person, the knife can make you a murderer. But if you like cooking, the knife is essential and will help you on the way to becoming a master chef.

Money is not inherently evil, but the love of money is bad. Money is not bad or good. It becomes evil or good depending on our character. If you are a selfish person, money will make you even more selfish. If you are a compassionate person, money will help you be even more generous.

I met people for whom poverty was a blessing, and others for whom it was a reason for rebellion. I met people for whom money was a blessing, and people for whom it was a curse.

Few are those who can say, like Paul, "I know how to live humbly, and I know how to live in abundance". Knowledge and character are more important than money. "To be" is more important than "to have."

Abraham was rich, but he followed God everywhere. The rich young man could not do this. Job, whether rich or bankrupt, remained close to God. The right relationship with God implies a correct relationship with the material things.

Before you think about money, think about your character. Spend daily time with God, be full of the Holy Spirit, read the Bible to learn from the experiences of others, and then the Lord will bless you with as many blessings as you can handle.

First take care of your income and then think about spending. Financial education according to the biblical model spares the Christian family from many problems.

A person's habits, character traits and abilities to work hard and gain certain financial blessings will then help him manage them correctly as well.

A pious man, a humble man, regardless of the wealth he has or the monthly salary that goes into his account will remain the same due to his character and due to his relationship with God. He acknowledges that everything he has is the blessing of the Lord and the result of his diligence and seriousness.

On the other hand, a man who does not acknowledge God's involvement in his life will become arrogant, proud, and selfish because he takes all the credit for what he accumulated.

Be grateful. Be modest. Be a hardworking and upright man. In this manner, the blessings will not cease to follow. And when they do show up, they will make you more grateful and more responsible because of your character.

April 27

THE VALUE OF SILENCE

"Jesus kept silent and answered nothing." – Mark 14:61a

There are times in life when we must talk. But there are also moments in life when silence is of great use.

The man who speaks little and only when he has to is, most of the time, one who thinks before he speaks. He thinks about what he has to say, how to say it, and when to say it.

The wise man knows when to be silent. He does not answer evil with evil, nor to mockers with mockery.

Don't answer back! You will not change the gossiper and the mocker by having tense debates. Life is too short to waste it in verbal conflicts.

We have enough people who like to talk more than to act. We have enough people who think they know everything, and you cannot teach them anything.

Be a man of value. In time, you will see that you never learn anything new unless you are silent.

Someone said, "We are the masters of the unsaid words, but slaves of those we let slip out." Silence will keep you away from many troubles:

"Whoever guards his mouth and tongue keeps his soul from troubles." – Proverbs 21:23

The greatest people spoke little and worked hard. Non-constructive criticism did not stop them from working, nor did those who gave their opinion without even being asked. So what if they say untrue words about you? Prove to them by your actions that they are not right.

"The silence of an intelligent man is worth more than a thousand words of a fool," said Cato the Elder.

Why do good people keep silent when they are provoked? Because, in addition to their silence, they also have some other values, such as common sense, respect, and harmony.

The fish is caught when it opens its mouth.

Watch out for the bait around you. They are full of hooks inside.

April 28

THE VALUE OF TRUSTING GOD

"But as for you, you meant evil against me; but God meant it for good, in order to bring it about as it is this day, to save many people alive." – Genesis 50:20

The years in prison taught Joseph at least two lessons of immense importance: that you cannot control everything in life and that the end of the life of a person who trusts in God is not the dungeon, but the Kingdom.

There are things in this life that we can control, but there are other things that strictly pertain to the One who rules the Universe. When circumstances that we cannot control come our way, only faith can help us keep our calm, peace, and hope.

I cannot control the rain, but I can buy an umbrella. It is not the storm itself that should worry me, but my reaction to the storm.

The special beauty in the believer's life is that absolutely everything works for his own good. This truth, however, can only be accepted through faith and through a daily walk with God.

I cannot change the curse into a blessing. But God can! I cannot change evil for good. But God can!

Only the man of faith can live with hope and peace no matter the circumstances he goes through.

Only such a man can rely on God even when he does not understand why his labs are off, why he gets stones from his friends instead of bread, or why he was abandoned by those who told him they would be close.

The man of faith knows that easy roads lead nowhere, while the difficult ones have, at the end, a unique view: Heaven.

April 29

CHANGE BEGINS WHEN YOU ADMIT YOUR WEAKNESSES

"Two men went up to the temple to pray, one a Pharisee and the other a tax collector. The Pharisee stood and prayed thus with himself, 'God, I thank You that I am not like other men—extortioners, unjust, adulterers, or even as this tax collector. I fast twice a week; I give tithes of all that I possess.' And the tax collector, standing afar off, would not so much as raise his eyes to heaven, but beat his breast, saying, 'God, be merciful to me a sinner!'" – Luke 18:10-13

When you meet God, you have only two options: with great satisfaction and pride you tell Him your good points or with great humility and repentance you tell Him your sinful state.

When I go to the doctor because your head hurts, you don't say, "Doctor, I have a great heart, a liver that works well, and sprinting legs." You cannot get a treatment for your headache as long as you keep talking about your healthy organs.

The closer you get to God, the more you notice the need for change. Your sinful state and His holiness will create inside of you, if you come with humility and sincerity, a real repentance and a deep desire for change.

When there is humility and repentance, there is also the grace of forgiveness.

"I tell you, this man went down to his house justified rather than the other; for everyone who exalts himself will be humbled, and he who humbles himself will be exalted." – Luke 18:14

Change begins when you recognize your weaknesses. Change begins when you come into the presence of God with the mirror, not with the binoculars. When you look through binoculars you always see "enlarged" everything that others do. When you look in the mirror you see yourself and you see your sins.

Do not make the following mistake: if we see in the mirror that our shirt is dirty, we will change the mirror… The solution is to change the shirt, not the mirror.

Humility accepts change. The humble person admits the state in which he is, points the finger at himself, like the thief on the cross, and says:

"Depart from me, for I am a sinful man, O Lord!" – Luke 5:8b

When you see yourself so sinful and unworthy that you ask God to depart from you, a miracle happens: He comes closer, and when He comes closer, He comes with forgiveness, grace, and salvation.

Change begins when you recognize your weaknesses. Change begins when you come into the presence of God with the mirror, not with the binoculars. When you look through binoculars you always see "enlarged" everything that others do. When you look in the mirror you see yourself and you see your sins.

April 30

10 DIFFERENCES BETWEEN A BOY AND A MAN

"Brethren, do not be children in understanding; however, in malice be babes, but in understanding be mature." – 1 Corinthians 14:20

Each man`s road to maturity passes through a period of childhood, one of adolescence, and one of youth. The problem is that age does not always bring the necessary maturity.

Maturity depends very much on the relationship with God and on how each person relates to life and the purpose for which he lives.

I will list several differences between a boy and a man, not to denigrate boys, but to challenge them to an acute desire to become mature.

These differences are extremely important in our relationships, but especially in the steps towards marriage.

1. Boys promise, while men act. A real man will be ashamed if he did not fulfill what he promised, while a boy will have no problem with it. The boy promises a lot and accomplishes little, while the man promises a little and accomplishes a lot. Boys impress with promises, men with action.

2. Boys are selfish, while men are altruistic. Boys are like children. Everything is only for themselves. They always ask, "What do I get out of this?" They want to be pampered and to receive all the attention. Boys want adventures, while real men want to start families and be responsible for them. Boys choose by looks, while men choose by character. Boys flirt, while men really love. This is why so many families fall apart. Because if you marry a boy, he will always find a better woman to fulfill his selfishness. A man, on the other hand, will value the covenant he made and will act with selflessness for an entire lifetime.

3. Boys act out of duty, while men act with responsibility. The boy takes the garbage bag to the dumpster because his wife or his mother told him to do so. The man will identify the need before anyone tells him and will act because he is responsible. Boys feel frustrated when they need to act. They do not want to be bothered. Real men are not waiting to be told. They notice when they need to intervene, and they do it joyfully.

4. Boys have excuses, while men have plans. Boys point fingers at others and always find excuses. They always find excuses for not having a chance in life like others who have succeeded. They always complain and do not want to do anything to get out of their failure (spiritual, material, family, social). Real men point fingers at themselves. They know that the solution in life is to have a purpose that, through discipline and continuous sacrifice, you can achieve. This is valid on all levels.

5. Boys seek to impose their respect, while men seek to earn their respect. Boys raise their voices in a discussion. Men raise the value of the arguments. Boys slam the table, put on their sunglasses even when it rains outside, and have a lot of guts and arrogance, thinking that in this way they will impose their respect. Real men, however, seek to gain their respect through deeds worthy of a special character. The role models of real men are heroes, not celebrities.

6. Boys need someone to take care of them, while men look for someone to take care of. Not few women told me that they ruined their marriage lives. How? Believing that they were marrying a man, and after the wedding they realized that he was, in fact, a boy who needed a lot of attention, who expected his food to be brought in bed and his clothes to be picked up from the floor after him. Boys feel as if they live in a hotel all their lives. Boys are immature, just like young children – except they don't throw tantrums with their feet but with their mouths. Real men are attentive, well-mannered, respectful, and when they enter a relationship of friendship and marriage, they see the needs of their wife and offer the necessary care.

7. Boys do whatever they want, while men do the right thing. The minds of the boys who have not yet matured remain at the same stage as when they were children. They do whatever they like, whatever brings them personal satisfaction. It does not matter that others suffer because of their irresponsibility. For them, all that matters is to feel good. Men, however, do the right thing. They do what is moral, what leads to the consolidation of the relationship in which they are involved.

8. Boys waste time, while men value their time. Boys did not understand the value of time. For them, the priority is to play (yes, I know a father with children who plays for many hours a day on his phone), socializing endlessly, sleeping in, and going to bed late. A club life, or life at the mall every day, to watch the escalators rolling. These boys one day turn 40 years old and, when they look back, they realize that they have accomplished nothing. And, believing that someone else is to blame, most of them continue to waste their time, forgetting that, in fact, that time is their own life. At the end of their life, on the hospital bed, they yell at the doctors to do something. They would like to extend their lives because they have no hope of getting to Heaven. Wasting your life leads to losing your eternity.

Men value time. They know that they have only one life (not like in the video games where you have more lives). For this reason, they live it responsibly and want to leave a good name behind them. They are always watching the hourglass of time and seek to live a life worthy of being given as an example to others.

9. Boys go to the gym, while men go to work. Boys value their looks enormously. They value their shape-revealing T-shirt, their tight pants, their sneakers that draw the people`s attention. They value muscles and dumbbells. For them, it doesn't matter that they are still renting at the age of 40; for them it is important that they just got new clothes from Zara. For them it doesn't matter that they don't have any money set aside for hard times. The important thing for them is to have all the perfume brands and also, when looked at from behind, to show a V muscle shape.

Real men are more preoccupied with the interior than with the exterior. More with the mind than with the muscle. More with the knowledge than with showing off. They know that a family requires responsibility, involvement, and diligence. They have conquered their wife with these qualities and have understood that the woman next to them is not impressed by dumbbells, but rather by a husband who works hard at his job and at his house as well.

I did not say we shouldn`t eat healthily. I did not say there was no need for physical activity. I did, however, want to make it clear that the beautiful exterior with an unmatured interior will ruin your life. I know too many people who go to the gym every day, but who cannot pick up the mop in the house, because it is too hard for them. I also know others who buy size S clothes (although they have a size L body), believing that a shape-revealing garment makes them more attractive and can make up for the lack of education. There are too many young people who spend hundreds of dollars a month for muscle building and no dollar for a book in a whole year...

10. Boys are born, while men are formed. Yes. All males are boys by birth. They all went through most of these steps. There was an age when each one of us thought that being "cool" is nicer than being honest. We thought that a shape-revealing T-shirt and showing your abs is more important than a good resume. Yes, we were all boys on some of the points above. It's understandable...

However, there comes a time when you must realize that you have to become a man. You must want to grow, to mature. Life has too little to offer to boys and a lot of precious things to give to men. It is the same way with eternity.

It's okay to admit you are still a boy and to want to become a man. Any map in the world helps you if you know where you are and you know the destination to which you are heading. It is tragic, however, to believe that you are a man while still being a boy.

I hope that the female gender hears me as well: it is extremely difficult to marry a boy and raise boys who want to later become men. I wonder if you understand me. Are you sure you do? Then read these pages carefully before turning your head to look at the boys you mistake for men... Remember that it is extremely easy for you to impress a boy, but very hard to impress a man. Boys seek passionate love, while men seek sacrificial love. Boys tell you what you want to hear (so that they win you over), while men tell you what you need to hear.

MAY 1

YOUR FACE

Your face is unique among billions of faces on the planet. It is something you always carry with you and cannot get rid of.

Your face says a lot about your character. Its expressions are nothing but a reflection of your feelings. Looking at your face, people can see your heart...

When Laban noticed that Jacob had been blessed by God, his countenance, that is, his face changed.

> *"And Jacob saw the countenance of Laban, and indeed it was not favorable toward him as before." – Genesis 31:2*

After 20 years of work, Laban could not believe that Jacob had surpassed him through seriousness and diligence. Envy immediately seized him, and his face betrayed him. Jacob had no other alternative but to leave. It is dangerous to stay close to envious people...

When Hannah went to the temple, the wrinkles on her face clearly showed Peninnah's stings.

She could not hide the tears she had been shedding for years. She went before God, prayed with whispers, and afterward, she left. And the Bible says that her face was no longer the same.

When you unload your burdens in front of people, your face might remain unchanged. When you unload your burdens before God, your face will surely change...

Moses went up the mountain where he spent 40 days in fellowship with God.

> *"So it was, when Moses came down from Mount Sinai (and the two tablets of the Testimony were in Moses' hand when he came down from the mountain), that Moses did not know that the skin of his face shone while he talked with Him." – Exodus 34:29*

While on the mountain, Moses used the most powerful face concealer: the glory of God. He did not know that his face was glowing, but everyone who saw him knew... This is the beauty we lack: we should not be aware of how holy we are – instead, those around us should be the ones who notice it. It is a great blessing when God is reflected in us...

Stephen, the first martyr, on the day of his execution had the face of an angel:

"And all who sat in the council, looking steadfastly at him, saw his face as the face of an angel." – Acts 6:15

You cannot have the life of a demon and the face of an angel. Stephen was full of power and grace. He lived serving God with total and unconditional dedication. The people who live such a life have faces of angels...

Do you want to have a special face? A pleasant sight for those around you? Then you should value the shaping of your character. You should value a life fully dedicated to God, both in private and in public.

What is inside is visible on the outside.

MAY 2

YOUR TIME AND GOD`S TIME

"All things have their time, and every work under the heavens has its appointed hour." – Ecclesiastes 3:1

On October 13, 1884, delegates from 25 countries gathered in Washington to agree on a universally recognized standard for measuring time, possibly with local adjustments based on time zones.

They decided that the reference time would be established based on the Prime Meridian that passes through the Greenwich district in London, south of the River Thames.

Since 1884, Greenwich Mean Time (GMT) served as the unique reference for time for many years. In 1972 it was replaced by the Coordinated Universal Time (UTC), a highly precise standard, very close to the first but with a slight difference in the measurement base.

While GMT is based on the Earth's rotation, which has certain variations, the UTC system is based on atomic time which is much more precise and capable of eliminating the influence of variations caused by the Earth's rotation.

However, most often the public does not know the details regarding the atomic time, and thus still uses the term Greenwich today. This is not entirely wrong, since the differences are very small – in seconds or fractions of a second.

What do we learn from this? We learn that, in order to relate well to ourselves and to each other, we must first relate to a standard.

God's time is our spiritual standard. By this, we understand that we should not ask God to change His schedule according to ours, but we should strive to adjust our schedule according to His.

Some people struggle all their lives to set God's clock forward or backward, instead of adjusting their own clock to God's.

Perhaps it is the time of salvation for you today! Perhaps it is the time for self-examination! Perhaps it is the time for awakening. The time to reconcile with the person next to you because you do not know when there are only 15 minutes left until the midnight of your life. Synchronize with God's clock! It never runs behind!

May 3

ALONE WITH GOD

"But Jacob was left alone..." – Genesis 32:24

There was a time in Jacob's life when he was near his mother at home. Then near his father, dressed in his brother's clothes. Later, he was near Laban, because in life, there is a time for marriage as well.

However, the most significant event in his life was when he was left ALONE.

Do not forget: there is a time in life when, if you want a real encounter with God, you must remain alone. Not with colleagues, not with neighbors, not with your mother, not with friends, but ALONE.

The trials of this year have no other purpose for you but to make you remain alone with God. When you are alone, you no longer rely on those close to you, nor on gifts or phones, but only on God.

And after you have remained alone with God, there will be a sign, a change!

"The sun rose on him as he passed Penuel, and he limped on his hip." – Genesis 32:31

In fact, this limping is nothing but a sign that only from that day on, Jacob started to walk upright...

The beauty of this is that after you meet God, you will desire a change for those around you as well:

"Jacob said to his household and to all who were with him, 'Put away the foreign gods that are among you, purify yourselves, and change your garments.'" – Genesis 35:2

I wish you the most beautiful solitude: the one spent with God. There, you are never alone...

May 4

SHOW ME YOUR TONGUE!

"Death and life are in the power of the tongue, and those who love it will eat its fruit." – Proverbs 18:21

Derek Prince tells a story from World War II taking place in an English hospital in North Africa. A doctor was attending to his patients who were sick with dysentery. Every morning, he greeted each patient with the same two sentences: "Good morning, how are you feeling?" and "Show me your tongue!"

The doctor was less concerned with the answer to the question and always looked very carefully at the patient's tongue. Based on his observation, he made a diagnosis...

Even if the patient said that he was feeling well, his true physical health could only be evaluated by the appearance of his tongue.

We can apply this situation in the life of faith in a very clear manner.

God is not impressed by what we say about our own condition... He knows that our spiritual health is truly reflected in the way we speak.

The Bible uses some highly relevant comparisons to show us how important the tongue is.

1. The Bridle

"For we put bits in horses' mouths that they may obey us, and we turn their whole body." – James 3:3

A horse can be controlled by a bridle`s bit. Its physical strength can be coordinated by its master so easily through the bridle in its mouth. Similarly, in life, you will notice that a person who controls his tongue and mouth can also control his body. Whoever is master over his words is also master over his body. The opposite is also true...

2. The Rudder

"Look also at ships: although they are so large and are driven by fierce winds, they are turned by a very small rudder wherever the pilot desires." – James 3:4

A ship needs wind and masts to be propelled, but only the rudder can decide the destination of that ship.

A ship with a favorable wind but a broken rudder can hit rocks. On the other hand, a ship with a not very fast wind but a rudder well-managed by the helmsman will reach its destination.

Your tongue determines the destination towards which you are heading.

3. The Fire

"Even so the tongue is a little member and boasts great things. See how great a forest a little fire kindles!" – James 3:5

Forest fires wreak havoc every year worldwide. Many acres of dry vegetation burn up without anyone being able to stop them – often due to a tiny match thrown out by accident.

On the website of the Emergency Inspectorate, in a fire prevention document, I noticed the following sentence: "WARNING, with just one match, you can set a whole forest on fire! Periods of drought and strong winds favor the outbreak of fires of dry vegetation and woodlands. The wind accelerates the drying of the soil and the vegetation, increasing the risks of fire propagation over long distances."

In the same way, fires can break out in our lives as well. Families and even communities can be set on fire from a word spoken by someone carelessly. We must tread carefully through wind and drought, and not play with fire.

In conclusion, let us not forget that God checks our spiritual condition when we least expect it, and the statement to which He seeks an answer is, "Show me your tongue!"

I have seen people who thought they were very strong in their relationship with God but failed miserably when it came to having a conversation without getting all fired up and saying words that hurt and put others down.

David's prayer should be ours as well:

"I said, 'I will guard my ways, lest I sin with my tongue; I will restrain my mouth with a muzzle, while the wicked are before me.'" – Psalm 39:1

In this way, the helm of our ship will indicate the direction to the heavenly port, and we will avoid the fire with all our might.

And what if someone else ignites it, what should we do?

We should pour water on it, not gasoline.

May 5

MOMENTS OF RELIEF

"Pharaoh, seeing that there was relief, hardened his heart and did not heed Moses and Aaron, as the Lord had said." – Exodus 8:15

If God does not punish the person who lies, it is because He gives him a moment of relief...

If God still sends rain over the crops of the person who curses Him "to His face," it is because He gives him a moment of relief...

If God still grants physical health to the person who steams with hatred and envy, it is because He gives him a moment of relief...

If God still grants life to the person who makes the days of his neighbor bitter, it is because He gives him a moment of relief...

If God still gives an appetite for food to the person who ruins the appetite of everyone around him with his sourness, it is because He gives him a moment of relief...

If God still provides warmth to the person who freezes many hearts with his presence, it is because He gives him a moment of relief...

When God gives you a moment of relief and does not punish you according to the merit of your deeds, He does it for you to repent, not for you to harden your heart...

Value the respite of His patience! Do not sigh in relief, thinking that He does not see you and does not know you! Come with tears of repentance, and the respite He gives you after the blessed forgiveness will have eternal proportions...

May 6

A GOOD NAME

"A good name is better than precious ointment, and the day of death than the day of one's birth." – Ecclesiastes 7:1

A good name means a good reputation. It means being trustworthy, keeping your word, and being a man of good character.

A person with a good name leaves only quality things behind. You want to be around such a person because he is someone you can learn from.

A good name is earned over many years but can be lost in just a few minutes.

The most expensive perfume ever made, Shumukh, was launched in Dubai and cost $1.29 million. Currently, there is only one bottle of this limited edition available, and its value will continue to increase over time.

The Bible says that a good name is even more valuable than Shumukh because what cannot be bought with money, one`s character, is worth more than all the money in the world. A good name spreads a more beautiful and powerful fragrance than any perfume.

Only for a person with a good name, the end is worth more than the beginning.

You cherish and appreciate someone with a good name. When they finish their work, when you see what they have accomplished, you realize that the promises from the beginning have been fulfilled.

Today, you have a new opportunity to add value to your good name.

You have the opportunity to leave behind a fragrance stronger than Shumukh.

May 7

A BROKEN HEART

"The Lord is near to those who have a broken heart and saves such as have a contrite spirit." – Psalm 34:18

We have all experienced sad and unpleasant days in life. Hearts that weep, lament, and hide from the curious eyes of people.

Interestingly, most of the time, people want to know about your trouble only so they can tell others about it, not to lend you a helping hand.

Most people do not get involved when they see someone nearby with a broken heart.

Those who are defeated are set aside, placed on the stretcher of indifference, and admitted to the hospitals of futile promises.

How good it is that God does not act like men! For God, a broken heart means a distress call asking for closeness. An opportunity for lifting up, encouragement, and restoration.

Stop being sad! His love is not indifferent to the cry of a broken heart.

When our hearts are shattered, God sees each fragment and tenderly gathers them. He doesn't ignore our pain or dismiss our sorrow. Instead, He meets us in our brokenness, ready to mend with His healing grace what is torn apart.

In times of despair, we might feel abandoned by everyone around us, but God's presence remains constant. He whispers comfort into our anguish, reminding us that we are not alone. His promises are steadfast, providing a refuge in the storms of life.

God specializes in turning our mourning into joy. He can transform our deepest wounds into testimonies of His faithfulness. Our broken hearts become testimonies of His power to restore, heal, and bring new hope to our lives. Trust in His unfailing love, for He is close to the brokenhearted and saves those who are crushed in spirit.

May 8

A MAN OF HIS WORD

"...undiscerning, untrustworthy, unloving, unforgiving, unmerciful." – *Romans 1:31*

One of the great traits of a person with an exemplary character is that he keeps his word. He fulfills his promise. And if he cannot do that, he does not let you wait in wander; instead, he calls you in advance and humbly apologizes for being late or unable to attend the meeting.

The Bible warns us that breaking your word is a sin that reveals unseriousness and indifference towards the one to whom you promised something. A weak person promises and does not follow through. A person with significant flaws in the foundation of his character is ready to say grand words and not fulfill them.

What you *possess* is reflected in your reputation and image. What you *are* is reflected in your character. You can have any position in church, hold important roles in society, or have outstanding degrees; if you are not a person of your word, it all amounts to nothing!

Be a man of your word! Keeping your promise is becoming increasingly rare. And what is rare is valuable!

A friendship with a man of his word endures. A partnership with a man of his word lasts. A family with a spouse of his word lasts a lifetime.

Whoever does not keep their word surely has other enormous flaws in their character.

And if the vessel is broken in one place, does it matter in how many other places it is broken?

May 9

PRAYERS IN WAITING...

"My voice You shall hear in the morning, O Lord; in the morning I will direct it to You, and I will look up." – Psalm 5:3

The main purpose of prayer is not to change God but to change ourselves.

Prayer makes you dependent on God! Not on your salary, not on your knowledge, not your friends, but on God!

In some prayers, God is silent because if He were to speak, we would not understand His answer. He will answer later when we are prepared and ready to accept His response.

It is not the waiting that is the secret but waiting in secret. Waiting after you have shared your secret with God.

He will answer at the right time. All I should be concerned about is prayer, and while I wait, He will be concerned with preparing the answers to my prayers.

In the quiet moments of waiting, our faith is refined. Like gold tested by fire, our trust in God's timing strengthens as we lean into His promises. It's during this period that our character is molded, teaching us patience, humility, and unwavering faith.

We often desire immediate answers, but God's timing is perfect, aligned with His greater plan for our lives. While we wait, He works behind the scenes, orchestrating events and preparing our hearts for the blessings to come. His answers, though delayed, are always on time and exactly what we need.

In the process of waiting, we grow closer to God, learning to rely on Him more deeply. Our relationship with Him deepens as we experience His faithfulness time and time again. Remember, the wait is not wasted; it is a vital part of our spiritual journey, transforming us into the image of Christ.

Many people have expectations, but few are those who wait after they have prayed.

Be among the few.

May 10

HITLER VS. ISUS

The principle of Hitler: “You must die so that I can win!”

The principle of Jesus: “I had to die so that you could win...”

Anything that is conquered by force will eventually fall apart. Anything that is conquered by love will forever endure.

Terror demands the sacrifice of others, while love demands your own sacrifice.

Pride fuels selfishness, while humility fuels altruism.

Do you want something temporary? Do you want a destroyed family? Do you want friendships that are doomed to fail? Then you should mix pride with selfishness and dictatorship.

Do you want something that will last? Then you should mix humility with unconditional love and daily sacrifice; you will be amazed by exceptional results.

The world’s ideology says your rise depends on the crushing of others. Christianity says your crushing is actually the uplifting of others.

A candle does not burn for itself but for those around it.

“You are the light of the world...” – Matthew 5:14

Love without sacrifice is a lie. The lie says: you must burn so that I can be well. The truth says: I will burn so that you can be well.

The surest thing in this world is death. We will all die one day, but only those who have burned for a good cause will experience the first resurrection.

Those who have died here, illuminating the path for others, shall live beyond. Those who have lived here, lighting their own path, shall die on the other side.

May 11

I AM NOT AFRAID...

"He said to them, 'Why are you fearful, O you of little faith?' Then He arose and rebuked the winds and the sea, and there was a great calm." – Matthew 8:26

I am not afraid of storms in life. I am afraid of drifting away from Jesus in good times...

I am not afraid of hospitals in life. I am afraid of the days when I am healthy...

I am not afraid of poverty. I am afraid of the moments when I have money in my wallet and put only a coin in the offering plate...

I am not afraid of exams. I am afraid of missing classes...

I am not afraid when the car breaks down, and I cannot drive it anymore. I am afraid of the moments when it does work, but I'm headed in the wrong direction...

I am not afraid on a plane when most people say their prayers during takeoff and landing. I am afraid that I will end up praying only at such times...

I am not afraid of the day when I will close my eyes for good. I am afraid that today, while my eyes are still open, they might look where they should not...

I am not afraid of wolves. I am afraid of straying from the Good Shepherd.

It is not the dirt on the carpet that I fear the most. I am afraid of the filth in the heart that can be easily hidden under the rug of hypocrisy.

I am not afraid to lose something material. I am afraid of losing tearful prayers.

I am not afraid that I am not known by important people. I am afraid that He might say on Judgment Day that He does not know me.

I am not afraid that friends do not visit me. I am afraid that Jesus might pass by my house... Seek Jesus when the weather is good, so He can be with you in the boat. And then, when the weather changes, there will be Someone to stand beside you and guard you.

And when He is in your boat, He knows which harbor to anchor in. Let Him take the helm.

MAY 12

TODAY`S CHRISTIANITY

The paradox of today's Christianity is that it desires great victories with minimal investment.

We want to see miracles with five minutes of prayer. By reading one chapter from the Bible each week, we hope to have the strength to resist the temptations that come our way each day.

With one weekly church service, we deceive ourselves that Heaven is waiting for us.

The paradox of today`s Christianity is that it invests heavily in worldly matters and yet it believes that great treasures are waiting for us in the afterlife. We want comfort here and joy beyond. We would like as few people as possible to know that we are believers, and yet we want God to know us. We wish for the coin placed on the offering plate to bear more fruit than those dollars deposited in the bank account.

The paradox of today's Christianity is its constant struggle to reconcile the flesh with the Spirit. "How are you, brother?" "Praise the Lord, it is good to be with Him." This is the answer of today's Christians when they meet before a church service.

But when they say their goodbyes after the service, they greet each other with a casual "bye" or "see you," being in a hurry to leave.

We brag to one another about clothing, houses, and cars but do not ask each other about the fellowship with God that we had this week.

On Sunday morning, five minutes before 9, we are not worried that we might be late, and yet, when the clock shows five minutes before noon, we are impatient and stare at it if the preacher shows no signs of reaching his conclusion.

The paradox of today's Christianity is that it promises much and costs very little. We preach about the Lord's grace and love, and very rarely about "...take up your cross daily and follow Me." We talk often about a salvation being already guaranteed to us and very seldom about "...work out your salvation with fear and trembling."

The youth group sings about "my eyes weep without stopping," but the tears are absent. You cannot cry on Sunday during worship time if you have not lived with God from Monday to Saturday.

Dear ones, it`s time to live a reality, not a paradox. A real walk with God, not just a church service experience. A life of kneeling every day so that we can stand in the face of trial. A song from a pure heart, not just from the lips.

Would you like to reap a bountiful harvest? Then you must start investing: tears, sacrifice, intercession, fasting, vigil – then you will end with songs of joy. (Psalm 126)

Oh, Lord, we really want great victories. But help us to invest accordingly!

May 13

QUALITY VS. QUANTITY

One of the greatest mistakes Christians make today is to label success by quantity. How wrong this is! Nowhere in the Bible was God interested in QUANTITY first, but in QUALITY.

Sensing that in the last years of history there will be an increase in quantity, Jesus asked so suggestively regarding quality:

> *"I tell you that He will avenge them speedily. Nevertheless, when the Son of Man comes, will He really find faith on the earth?" – Luke 18:8*

When Jesus provided free bread, thousands were present, but at the cross, you could count them on your fingers.

The true quality of those who follow Jesus is seen not in freedom but in persecution. Not at the same table with Jesus but at the cross with Him. Not on Sundays in church but during the week in hospitals and nursing homes.

"For many sat with Him at the same table, but too few pulled at the same yoke with Him," said Traian Dorz.

Do not be drawn to crowds, to popularity, to sensationalism.

Be drawn to quality, to faithfulness.

Crowds come and go.

The faithful person remains...

May 14

INCOME AND EXPENSES

Alexandre Dumas once said, "Money is a good servant but a bad master." It is either we that use the money, or the money that uses us.

The Bible provides valuable advice not only about family, spiritual and social aspects, but also about finances.

The wise advice of Solomon is to think about how to earn money before thinking about how to spend it. Having a steady income before making a specific expense is a sign of wisdom.

Take care of your income first, and only then think about making expenses. Being financially educated according to the biblical model will spare the Christian family from many problems.

Jesus said,

"For which of you, intending to build a tower, does not sit down first and count the cost, whether he has enough to finish it?" – Luke 14:28

If you spend more than you earn, you will never progress, and you will never get out of trouble.

Before buying something, ask yourself, "Do I really need this? Am I buying it because it is useful, or am I just buying it to impress others? Am I buying it just to use it once a year, or is it something that helps me in my daily life?"

Be careful about personal or family expenses. Keep a daily record of both your income and your expenditure. The cause of break up for 22% of the families has to do with money problems. Unjustified expenses coupled with insufficient or inconsistent income lead to marital problems that sometimes become irreversible.

Our children will learn how to handle money by watching us, their parents. 86% of those who save money acknowledge that they learned it from their parents. So, if I am a balanced and efficient parent, there is a good chance that my children will be the same. Children do what parents do, not what parents say...

Place great value on living a balanced life, even in the financial area! This way, you will be spared of many problems that can arise from its absence!

MAY 15

THOUGHTS

"Let this mind be in you which was also in Christ Jesus..." – Philippians 2:5

Our mind is like a mill. If you feed straw into it, it grinds and produces fine straw. If you feed stones, it produces sand. If you feed wheat, it yields flour. It is never empty.

It constantly grinds and yields whatever you have put in it.

You are what you think. You talk about what you think. Your actions are the product of your thoughts.

Do you let your mind grind the actions of others who have upset you?

The words they said that humiliated you? Then it will grind hatred, resentment, and revenge.

Do you constantly compare yourself with others in your mind, being dissatisfied with what they have and you do not? Then the chaff of envy will quickly flow into the sack of your life.

Do you think about appearing important? About making it clear that things cannot happen without you?

Then the sand of pride will flow into your speech and your behavior, quickly reaching the eyes of those around you, carried by the deceptive wind of pride.

Wouldn't you rather fill your mind with good thoughts instead? To think like Jesus? Reflect on how you can strip off the "self" and clothe yourself with modesty. Accept that the greatest value is obedience to the will of God, and be concerned with understanding and applying it...

If you think like Jesus, you will speak and live like Jesus. And then you will reach the divine place where Jesus is.

Nourish your mind with positive thoughts. With reasons for gratitude. With divine ideals and holy goals. With questions about how to become holier, more respectful, and more compassionate. Thoughts about how to love more. About sacrifice and giving. Thoughts that God will approve of and open the door of fulfillment for them.

Count your blessings in your mind, and then you will see how your heart will be filled with joy, and tears of gratitude will appear in your eyes.

Think more about eternity. About the millions of years you are preparing for.

"Set your mind on things above, not on things on the earth." – Colossians 3:2

And then act accordingly. Train your mind. Make it a library of values. Organize each drawer and put the jewels of love in them.

Be careful when you start to "ponder" deeply. Make sure you lie down in an armchair, not in a place with thorns and thistles. Make sure you stop to rest, when you are weary, at an oasis with palm trees, not near a deep chasm. You decide what you bring into the house of your mind. The carpet should not be placed over filth but over a clean floor. A sofa does not belong in a stable, but in a living room.

You are the interior designer of your mind. You can turn your mind into a bat cave or a picture-perfect living room.

"The mouth speaks out of the abundance of the heart," said the Savior...

The words we speak are the windows of our minds through which those who hear us can tell what is inside. A clean mind only utters clean words.

Our deeds come out through the door of our minds. If a group of spiders, accompanied by bugs and mice, has come out of the house of a mind, that means that there no one is living in that house... it is an abandoned building.

It is a place that has not been cleaned up for years, and the dust is thicker than the shoe sole...

"You cannot keep birds from flying over your head, but you can keep them from building a nest in your hair," someone said.

Perhaps you need to clean up your mind. The water of the divine Word can cleanse everything.

And when you are done cleaning, put the shoe-cleaning mat in front of the door.

"Shoes off, please!" should be written on it.

"Why?" asks a muddy thought with an insolent tone. "Why can't I enter like this?"

You should answer without hesitation: "Because here, every morning, the fragrance of heaven is sprayed, and cleanliness is maintained on a daily basis."

May 16

WITH GOD IN DROUGHT

"He went and did according to the word of the Lord..." – 1 Kings 17:5

Sometimes, we think that if we serve God, we will have available for us, throughout our entire lives, a Swedish buffet, high-quality filtered water, and exceptional comfort. We think that the world will carry us in its arms, and everyone will appreciate us... But this is far from reality.

Our life is often like that of Elijah. With dangers, limited resources, and Ahab chasing us. With obedience that requires sacrifice. Elijah did not complain that the water from the brook was not drinkable. That its pH was too low. That the food brought by ravens was close to the expiration date.

Elijah understood that if God wants to send you somewhere, He will take care of you.

Whether He does it through a full fridge or through a slice of bread and butter, that is up to Him. What is up to me is my obedience.

In times of drought, God took care of Elijah through an insignificant brook, through some ravens, and through a penniless widow. Never doubt God's resources!

In difficult times, if you stay close to Him, you will understand that, according to His Word, ravens can give up their piece of meat for your sake, the water from the brook can quench the greatest thirst, and the last meal of a widow can satisfy better than the luxurious meals of kings (1 Kings 17).

The secret is to act according to the Word of the Lord. In a time when most people follow the advice of their friends or their own ideas and other material advantages (ignoring the spiritual ones), you must be the person who loves the Word and fulfills it.

Despite the wilderness, despite a dried-up brook, and ravens that might not come on time, I must continue to act according to His Word.

You should do the same.

May 17

WHAT DOES YOUR HEART TELL YOU TO SEEK?

"My heart says to You, 'Your face, Lord, I will seek.'" – *Psalm 27:8*

In our world, full of materialism, many hearts may say: look at the store offers, look for a car with more horsepower, search for a better condo, find a cheaper rent.

A pure heart, however, speaks with tenderness and encourages you to seek, above all else, spiritual values.

Those who seek the face of God will turn their backs on sin.

Those who seek the face of God will see more often the face of the orphan, the widow, and the pauper who longs for a piece of bread.

Those who seek the face of God will look into the mirror of the Word more often, so their face can reflect the features of the most beautiful Face in the Universe.

To seek the face of God is to pursue the highest purpose of our existence, to commune with the Creator in intimate fellowship. It is to prioritize spiritual enrichment over fleeting earthly treasures, knowing that true fulfillment is found in His presence alone.

When we seek God's face, we align our hearts with His will and experience the transformative power of His love. Our perspective shifts, and we gain clarity in discerning His voice amidst the noise of the world. Each moment spent in His presence brings us closer to Him, deepening our faith and strengthening our resolve to walk in His ways.

In seeking God's face, we discover our true identity as His beloved children, chosen and cherished beyond measure. His face becomes our refuge in times of trouble, our guiding light in the darkness, and our source of unwavering hope. As we fix our gaze upon Him, His glory illuminates our path, leading us ever closer to the abundant life He has promised.

Those who seek the face of God on this earth will never grow tired of looking at it with joy in Heaven.

May 18

BEARS AND MOCKERS

"So he went up from there to Bethel; and as he was going up the road, some youths came out of the city and mocked him, and said to him, 'Go up, you baldhead! Go up, you baldhead!' So he turned around and looked at them, and pronounced a curse on them in the name of the Lord. And two female bears came out of the woods and mauled forty-two of the youths." – 2 Kings 2:23-24

Bethel, meaning "House of God," a place where God was supposed to be *well-known* and *welcomed*, a place where He was supposed to *feel at home*, had become an idolatrous place (1 Kings 12:29).

God had sent multiple times prophets with special messages to awaken Bethel and all of Israel (1 Kings 13:4, etc.). There was also a school for prophets there.

Elijah had passed through there, so the people of that place were not strangers to the law of God, nor to the warning messages of the prophets.

Elisha was passing through Bethel. He was well-known there. People were talking everywhere about Elijah's ascent to heaven and Elisha's mission to continue Elijah's work. Therefore, this incident of mockery was not at all directed at an unknown person; it was not the mistake or the rushed judgement of some kids who wanted to laugh at a person without hair.

The Hebrew word used for "youths" is "na'ar," the same word used for Joseph at the age of 17 (Genesis 37:2).

Ishmael was described as "na'ar" when he was over 13. Shechem, who abused Dinah, is described as "na'ar." David is described as "na'ar" when Saul says,

"You are not able to go against this Philistine to fight with him; for you are a youth." – 1 Samuel 17:33

So, these were not 5-year-old kids teasing an old man but teenagers who knew exactly at whom they were yelling, who knew Elisha`s mission and yet, who chose to directly and deliberately mock him!

When they told him, "Go up, you baldhead!" they were essentially saying, "If you claim to be Elijah's successor, go up to heaven, baldy, just like your teacher did."

Baldness was considered somewhat shameful. It was one of the consequences of leprosy, but here it was also considered a sign of the man's physical and mental deterioration.

Consequently, these young men did not only laugh at an old man, but they simply acted with a devilish intention of mocking the man of God and the work of the Holy Spirit within him. **When you mock the vessel, you automatically mock its contents.** In other words, they were saying, "Leper! You and your prophecy! We are not afraid of you! Go up! Go up!"

This is the Devil`s method to oppose God`s work by mocking the messenger and mocking the Word of God! He points his finger at small things in a person`s life (in this case, lack of hair) in order to denigrate his entire call and work.

Elisha cursed them. What does this mean? That he cursed them with vulgar language or answered back in the same way, mocking them? No! It means that he pronounced a judgment upon them! He presented their condemnation, just as God did in Deuteronomy 11:26.

We have the freedom to choose. We have the freedom to ignore the blessing and thus automatically choose the curse. I repeat, what Elisha did was just show them that, through their deliberate and intentional attitude, they chose curse.

When we do not choose the good, the obedience to God and holiness, all that remains for us is ignorance, death for sin, and curse. Without God and without obedience to Him, there is no protection and no happiness.

What was the punishment of the Law for disobedience? Most often, the shortening of life. Elisha did not call the bears from the woods. The bears were just God's way of punishing those young men immediately.

Oh, is God harsh to punish them instantly? Like Ananias and Sapphira?

His justice can do that. He is God and can do whatever He wants. (Psalm 115:3)

What do I have to learn from here? The fact that God has given us the freedom to choose. But what does man do? He continues to sin because God does not always punish immediately.

> *"Because the sentence against an evil work is not executed speedily, therefore the heart of the sons of men is fully set in them to do evil." – Ecclesiastes 8:11*

"See?" someone said not long ago. "I have cursed, and lightning has not struck me!" And what else? "I have committed adultery, I have lied, stolen, deceived; do you see that nothing has happened to me?" So what? This should humble you and make you come with many tears before God.

If you have not been punished, it is because of His great mercy and patience with us. But beware! God is patient, but not endlessly patient!

Let's pay attention to the words we speak. We boast with 2,000 years of Christianity, but we swear like sailors. We mock Saint Peter with jokes, and we also mock the priests and pastors, the church and holiness. We joke about the Holy Spirit and make fun of those who live according to the Word of God written in the Holy Scriptures.

An entire Romania mocks the young people who go to church and applauds those who come from the nightclub at 5 a.m., praising them for doing well. **Mothers who have children are humiliated with harsh words, while women having affairs are applauded... Those who seek education are ridiculed, while those who prefer entertainment are appreciated.** We do what the children of Bethel did, but on a much larger scale...

Be careful with your words!

> *"For by your words you will be justified, and by your words, you will be condemned." – Matthew 12:37*

God does not take lightly our attitude towards the messages He sends us! By the way, did you know that blasphemy against the Holy Spirit is never forgiven (Matthew 12:31)? This blasphemy is nothing but unbelief. And if you do not believe that God is speaking to you, you can never be forgiven for your sins... If you oppose His message, you cannot receive His blessing.

Let us repent, dear ones! Let us "repent of the sins committed," as the Romanian language dictionary (DEX) says. Repentance is not a suggestion but a command.

> *"Truly, these times of ignorance God overlooked, but now commands all men everywhere to repent..." – Acts 17:30*

Let's not forget that mockery, arrogance, and ridicule are also sins. Let's stop laughing at people who call us closer to God...

And then, instead of punishment, God will give us forgiveness. Instead of a curse, we will receive His blessing, and instead of hell, we will receive Heaven...

May 19

YOU REAP WHAT YOU SOW!

"Sow for yourselves righteousness; reap in mercy; break up your fallow ground, for it is time to seek the Lord, till He comes and rains righteousness on you." – *Hosea 10:12*

To harvest weeds, you do not need to sow anything. They grow on their own.

A soul untouched by the plow of the Gospel and the rain of salvation to prepare the soil of the heart will yield a crop of thorns: the weeds of envy, hatred, and lies.

Thorns flourish where the master allows laziness. Where the Bible is closed, and prayer is absent.

However, those who sow righteousness in the spring of life will rejoice in a great harvest in the eternal autumn. Those who sow with tears, love, and good deeds will have an amazing harvest.

Just as a farmer diligently tends to his fields, we too must diligently tend to the garden of our hearts. We must cultivate a heart that is receptive to the seeds of God's Word and the showers of His grace. Through prayer, meditation, and obedience, we can ensure that the soil of our hearts remains fertile and free from the thorns of sin.

As we sow seeds of righteousness and faithfulness, we can trust in God to bring about a bountiful harvest in due time. Though the process may require patience and perseverance, we can rest assured that God is faithful to His promises. In the end, the harvest of righteousness will far outweigh any temporary trials or struggles we may face along the way.

What will you sow today?

MAY 20

WHOSE VOICE DO YOU LISTEN TO?

"My sheep hear My voice, and I know them, and they follow Me." – John 10:27

The voice you listen to determines the destination you are heading towards.

The voice of the Lord Jesus is unique. The devil has many voices. What do you listen to every day? Which voices are calling you?

You cannot change the path you are on until you change the words that reach your ears and then your heart.

"My sheep do not listen to a stranger's voice; I know them, and they follow Me." – John 10:5

Do not let strangers steal your eternity. Run away from sin. Sin tastes like an orange for a moment and then like grapefruit for a lifetime.

You take the first step; the rest of the steps are prepared by the "stranger."

From dawn, you will start receiving multiple invitations from various voices. Choose the voice of the One who died for you! Put the rest on silent!

In a world filled with noise and distraction, it can be difficult to discern the voice of the Good Shepherd amidst the clamor. Yet, His voice is the only one that leads to true life and freedom. As His sheep, we must train our ears to recognize His voice above all others, for it is the voice of love, truth, and salvation.

When we heed the voice of the Good Shepherd, we find ourselves on the path of righteousness and peace. His voice guides us through the trials and temptations of life, leading us safely to green pastures and still waters. Let us tune our hearts to His voice each day, knowing that He alone holds the keys to abundant life and eternal joy.

MAY 21

FOCUS ON THE TARGET!

"I press toward the goal for the prize of the upward call of God in Christ Jesus." – Philippians 3:14

On April 13, 1970, 56 hours had passed since the launch of the Apollo 13 mission. The three astronauts were about 200,000 miles from Earth. Suddenly, a malfunction in the electrical system caused an explosion that jeopardized both the mission and the lives of the astronauts. After repairs that lasted 36 hours, with all kinds of makeshifts (towels, duct tape, small plastic tubes), the three crew members managed, after another 45 hours, to move from the lunar module "Aquarius" back to the command module "Odyssey" to re-enter Earth's atmosphere.

Do you know what was one of the main reasons the astronauts eventually landed in the Pacific Ocean safely?

Despite limited electricity, an almost frozen cabin, and too much carbon dioxide present, they successfully overcame all obstacles due to a small secret: there was a very small window in the lunar module, and to re-enter the atmosphere safely, without navigation equipment, they kept the Earth in their sight at all times.

Our life is a journey with many challenges. Like the astronauts of the Apollo 13 mission, we encounter things we did not know beforehand and for which we have not prepared enough. Just as the crew members desperately wanted life on Earth, we desperately desire eternal life.

The problems that arise, the exams we go through, the pains, shortages, and troubles can be overcome if we always keep Heaven in our sight.

With our eyes fixed on Heaven and our hands on the plow. With our eyes fixed on Heaven and the power of the Holy Spirit in our hearts. With our eyes fixed on Heaven and our feet running for what truly matters.

Failures. Cancer. Disappointments. Friends who turned their backs on you. Sweet words that turned bitter. Loneliness or depression. All these and many more show you that Earth is becoming more and more insecure. Our earthly tent module has more and more deficiencies, and its only salvation is the transformation into a glorious body.

When? How? In what way? Why? Why me? Why now? Another one? Isn't it over already?

I do not know how to answer all these questions. However, God has answers to all of them. Some answers we receive in class, others in verifying the assignments, and yet others only on the heavenly podium.

I, however, have a single goal: to challenge you not to lose sight of the Target, looking through the window of your heart. In times of crisis, in chaotic and hopeless moments, that one point you fix your eyes upon can restore your strength and clarity to survive.

And this point is Heaven. In Philippians, Paul tells us what he looked at during the race. And in Timothy, when he was at the end of the race, he tells us what the target looks like up close:

> *"Henceforth, there is laid up for me the crown of righteousness, which the Lord, the righteous judge, will award to me on that day, and not only to me but also to all who have loved his appearing." – 2 Timothy 4:8*

Lunar landing is the term used for the moment a spacecraft reaches the moon. Splashdown is the term used for the moment an object descends from flight and skims on the sea until it stops. Landing is the word used for the moment an aircraft returns to the Earth's surface.

Do you know what is missing from the dictionary of every language on Earth? The term used for the moment we "reach" Heaven.

We will discover it there... if we do not lose sight of the Target.

See you at the Heavenly Awards Ceremony.

May 22

COLD OR BOILING?

On Pentecost, above each disciple a tongue like fire rested, not an icicle. The Holy Spirit ignited a fervent passion within them, empowering them to spread the Gospel with boldness and conviction. This divine flame symbolizes the transformative power of God's presence, turning timid hearts into courageous witnesses. Just as fire brings light and warmth, the Spirit's fire in us brings enlightenment and fervor, melting away indifference and igniting a zeal for God's kingdom.

Cold or boiling? Active or passive? Is it possible that the things for which we should be cold are exactly the ones for which we burn, and vice versa? The world often entices us to be passionate about fleeting pleasures and indifferent to eternal truths. Yet, Scripture calls us to burn with a holy passion for righteousness and to be cold towards sin and worldliness. It is a daily choice to align our desires with God's will, allowing His Spirit to kindle our hearts with the right kind of fire.

The flame burning in your heart for Heaven will melt the ice in your neighbor's heart. Be concerned about your flame, not about someone else's ice. Our lives are testimonies of God's love, and our fervent devotion can inspire and transform those around us. When we live ablaze with the love of Christ, others will be drawn to the warmth and light emanating from us. This divine warmth has the power to soften the hardest hearts and draw them into the embrace of God's grace.

Burning consumes you, but it is better to become wax, illuminating others, than an iceberg, sinking ships. Our willingness to be consumed for the sake of Christ reflects our commitment to His mission. Like a candle that melts to provide light, our sacrifices and acts of love illuminate the path for others, guiding them towards the Savior. In contrast, a cold, unyielding heart can cause harm and lead others astray. Therefore, let us choose to burn brightly, even if it costs us, for the glory of God and the salvation of souls.

Have you found the cause for which the Master has asked you to burn? It's getting colder outside; ignite, oh Lord, the fire within our hearts!

MAY 23

FAN OR PLAYER?

Jesus did not call us to click "likes" for the pictures of orphans but to make sandwiches for them. The cheapest form of friendship is the "like" button, and the most expensive one is sacrifice.

You will learn in life that the world has too many bystanders and too few who truly care.

A candle that does not burn is like a lamp used only for decor.

It is not the shelf with candles that makes a difference, but the flame.

You boast about what others have done for the Lord. But how many can testify about what you have done for Him?

Fans keep the score, but players sweat. At the end, it is not the pile of popcorn crumbs in the stands that matters but the score on the field. It is not the fans that have the final say but the coach. No true player stops running because of the supporter who is eating popcorn while booing.

The sweat of the player is more valuable than the brand perfume of the fans in the stands.

Be a player! Get down from the stands! Come to practice, not just to holidays!

The score of the game of your life will determine your eternity.

Stop seeking the fans` applause; make the Coach happy.

He has the final word: "Come!" or "Go!"

May 24

MARIO FROM NISTRIA

Nothing seemed to disturb the peace of the village on the morning of November 9, 2013. A warm sunrise heralded a beautiful day for those in Nistria.

From the horizon, on a country road, a bus with young people from Deva, Hațeg, and Hunedoara[14] slowly approached this forgotten village, bringing a ray of hope.

Soon, the bus was surrounded by about 40 children with sparkling eyes, delicate hands, and rosy faces. Some, barefoot in November, looked with curiosity at something new, something changing for their undisturbed countryside.

The young people started singing, the villagers gathered one by one, and in the yard of an unbeliever, we were allowed to proclaim the Gospel.

We told them that it was sad to be poor for a lifetime, but it was tragic to be poor for eternity. That receiving oil and sugar today is in vain if, on Judgment Day, you receive hell because you lived without God. People wiped away tears from their wrinkled and troubled faces that were now beginning to gain a glimmer of hope.

At the end, the parents went to receive food packages, while the children remained in that yard, wanting to sing more about the One who can transform a melancholic childhood into one full of grace. "This little light of mine..." reverberated powerfully in an area full of darkness and sin.

Two families promised us that from now on, every Saturday afternoon, they would gather to learn more about the One who has mercy on the poor and sees the tears of those in need. A father with seven children told us that he lives with 130 lei a month but that from now on, he will read the Word of God so that he could have a future and a hope. His mother, the children's grandmother, told us that she entrusts them all into the hands of the Creator. A girl asked the young people for a Bible, and one of the sisters gave her Bible forever.

I met Mario at the gate. At two years of age, he showed me his dirty little hand and told me about "mom" and "dad." I pulled him towards me, thinking

[14] Deva, Hațeg, and Hunedoara: Cities in Transylvania, Romania.

that my daughters had never gone to bed hungry, while he, on the contrary, rarely fell asleep with a full stomach. But I saw in the eyes of this child that he glimpsed the hope of another world: a village where the center tavern would go out of business, where dad would no longer argue with mom, and where children, at 10 PM, would be praying at home instead of wandering the streets.

When the bus turned around, I leaned between the seats and wept. We were leaving, but Mario and the others from Nistria remained with hands raised and eyes glimpsing a brighter future.

If I wish for anything, it is to see Mario grow up and, in a few years, serve along with other children in a church planted today.

And we hope it will last until the day of the rapture when we will be taken to a place where children will not shiver on the street in November, nor jump for joy for having received 8 lbs. of flour and a bottle of oil.

They will live eternally with the One they heard about for the first time nine years ago, today, and from now on.

Pray for all the children from Romania. Let us weep with those who weep. And one day, we will recognize them in Heaven when they come to embrace us.

See you soon, Mario... Here, on earth, or beyond. Above.

May 25

FORGETFULNESS & LOVE

"When Joseph's brothers saw that their father was dead, they said, 'Perhaps Joseph will hate us, and may actually repay us for all the evil which we did to him?'" – Genesis 50:15

Joseph's brothers believed that his forgiveness would last only as long as their father was alive, but Joseph had been trained for forgiveness not for a few years but for a lifetime. He named one of his children "Forgetfulness" and the other "Fruitfulness" because love will never bear fruit in you if you cannot forget what the one beside you has done to you.

In a world that forgives only until it has the chance to remind you about what you have done, I wish you forgiveness intertwined with forgetfulness. Not just an apparent forgiveness, for the eyes of the family or the pastor, but a lifelong forgiveness so that we can pray without being ashamed: "...and forgive us our debts, as we forgive our debtors"!

Years later, when a "goodhearted" person who wants to stir up the past will remind you of what your brother did to you, your only answer will be some tears in your eyes and a stretched out helping hand:

"So they spoke to Joseph, saying, 'Oh, we beg you, please forgive the trespass of the servants of the God of your father.' And Joseph wept when they spoke to him. 'Now therefore, do not be afraid; I will provide for you and your little ones.' And he comforted them and spoke kindly to them." – Genesis 50:17, 21

If you give out roses, you will have their fragrance on your hands...

May 26

THE TEXAS KILLER

Salvador Ramos. A young man who, on May 25, 2022, immediately after turning 18, became the focus of national and international news. Not for a good deed, but because, after seriously injuring his grandmother, he stole a car and went to an elementary school in Uvalde, Texas, where he fatally shot 19 children and 2 teachers.

Every effect has a cause. Every abnormal behavior has a combination of abnormal factors behind it. What are these factors in the case of Salvador Ramos and many other children?

Firstly, the boy had been the target of mockery since childhood because he stuttered. He experienced what is called "*bullying*": an act of physical, verbal, or psychological violence. In school, many students target weaker children and try to dominate them through verbal or physical aggression (hitting them, pointing out their physical flaws, insulting them, or nicknaming them).

Secondly, Ramos had *issues with his parents*. Swearing and verbal violence were not absent from their home. Neighbors testified to frequently hearing fights between the boy and his mother. Eventually, she kicked him out of the house.

Moreover, Ramos had *problems with loneliness*. He isolated himself from others, feeling rejected. From this isolation to depression, there was only one step. Violent computer games were part of the environment in which he believed he found himself, but these games turned him even more into a wild beast.

What do I learn from this, as a parent?

I learn that I must be careful with my child's education. God has entrusted us with His inheritance, and without the involvement of His Word in raising the child, sooner or later, that child will end up destroying his life. The wise Solomon warned us long ago:

"A child left to himself brings shame to his mother." – Proverbs 29:15

Some destroy their lives by seeking revenge on others, as in Ramos's case. Others ruin their lives seeking escape in vices. Some end up in depression and then suicide.

No one, however, ends up there all of a sudden. Family problems are an inheritance that the child carries with him everywhere! Educational deficiencies are gaps that cannot be covered for the rest of his life. *The lack of the first formative seven years at home cannot be replaced by anything!*

Good education cannot exist without parents whose main goal is to obey God. Parental authority is guaranteed by remaining under the authority of God's Word. The family where God is present enjoys harmony, peace, and unity. And these values are transmitted to the child's character.

I also learn, as a parent, that I need to pay attention to my child's friends. Through communication with him, I need to find out about his behavior and the behavior of his peers when they are not in my presence. If my child has a speech defect, a health issue, or anything else, I will not humiliate him further; instead, I will talk to him about the other values he has, trying to balance out the faulty behavior of his peers.

At the same time, it is necessary, as a parent, to pay attention to *how my child spends his free time*. Daily playtime is necessary, but the priority is learning, involvement in household chores (age appropriate), and involvement in serving God (learning to play a musical instrument will take up much of his time and keep him busy with an important activity through which he will develop).

Ramos's combination of factors was lethal: *academic failure, social failure, family failure, and fascination with games promoting violence*. If these factors had been positive, the lives of 21 people would have been saved.

Ramos would have had a bright future and might have influenced others positively...

Perhaps America will wake up. Perhaps Romania will wake up. Perhaps families will wake up. **To understand that when you remove the Bible from schools, only weapons remain.** When God is not involved in a child's education, the Devil automatically gets involved. When parents are more concerned about money than about their children, they will weep for the rest of their lives.

Let's keep our children close. Let's tell them about Esther and Moses. About Ruth and Daniel. Let us, as parents, be role models for them. Let us guide them towards God. Let's put the Bible, not the phone, in their hands when they learn to read.

Let us, as parents, go to Church and take them with us. Let's involve them in good deeds. Let's spend time with them.

Children are the only inheritance we take with us for eternity...

It is worth investing in them because this investment lasts forever.

May 27

"I AM..."

God said to Moses, "I AM WHO I AM." And He added, "Thus you shall say to the children of Israel, 'I AM has sent me to you.'" – Exodus 3:14

Every Israelite had his own burden, his own problem, his own loneliness and turmoil. In their suffering, they cried out for relief, for someone who could understand their pain. God's declaration of *"I AM"* echoed with profound hope and assurance.

When God said, *"I AM,"* they could fill in what they needed: *"I AM your Savior," "I AM your Deliverer," "I AM your Protector."* Each person could hear in those words the promise of God's intimate and personal involvement in their lives. He was a present help in times of trouble, ready to meet their deepest needs.

God does not have a fixed name because any name you choose would diminish His attributes! His infinite nature and boundless power cannot be contained within human language. This invites us to seek Him in new and deeper ways, knowing He is always more than we can comprehend.

If you understand this principle, your relationship with God will undergo radical changes! You will see Him as a constant, dynamic presence in your life. Your prayers will transform into heartfelt conversations, filled with the expectation that God is actively listening and responding. The realization that "I AM" is with you in every circumstance can bring unparalleled peace and confidence.

The next time you are in distress or facing problems, and you do not know who could help you, remember that Someone is waiting for you and saying, *"Come to Me, I AM...!"* This invitation reminds you that you are never alone. In your moments of greatest need, the Almighty God stands ready to be whatever you require – your comfort, your strength, your guide.

Don't forget: no one in the Universe can speak in the present about themselves for an entire eternity, except the One who says, "I AM..." Praised be His Name forever and ever! While everything else changes and fades, He remains constant and eternal. Our worship and adoration flow from this truth, as we honor the everlasting, unchanging nature of our God.

May 28

THE SALT & THE CHRISTIAN

"You are the salt of the earth. But if the salt loses its flavor, how shall it be seasoned? It is then good for nothing but to be thrown out and trampled underfoot by men." – Matthew 5:13

Any ingredient in a meal can be substituted. Salt cannot. Any person in this world can be replaced. But a true Christian cannot.

Salt leaves behind a good taste. So does a true Christian. You desire to have them around, to be influenced by the joy of salvation and the peace in their hearts.

I have not seen any ads for salt. Because something you cannot live without doesn't need advertising. A Christian who needs advertising might not be wanted by anyone...

Salt has no value if it stays in the saltshaker – only in the food. It is easy to be a believer at church. True repentance, however, is seen outside the saltshaker.

Salt preserves:

"Then He went down with them and came to Nazareth and was subject to them, but His mother kept all these things in her heart." – Luke 2:51

A Christian living with God holds His Word in high regard in their heart.

Let us be salt! There is enough pepper.

May 29

THE PATH OF LIFE

"The Lord went before them by day in a pillar of cloud to lead the way, and by night in a pillar of fire to give them light, so as to go by day and night." – Exodus 13:21

The path you walk on indicates the destination you are heading towards.

Life is a one-way street. You can turn back the clock but not the time.

Therefore, it is vital to have full assurance that the path you are on has the correct destination.

Pay attention! I did not say it is important for the road you are on to be paved or asphalted, to be a national road or a highway. The direction is more important than the speed.

The only path with the right destination is the one where God goes before you. It is the path where you can see His footprints. The path where you can say like Paul when nearing the end:

"Be imitators of me, as I am of Christ." – 1 Corinthians 11:1

Be careful on the road of life. There are many intersections, and the signs pointing to exits to other roads are brightly colored and attractive. They sparkle like falling stars, but, in the end, they lead to death...

The sign "Ahead only" is valid only if you are on a road where God goes before you.

Only His Son was able to say: "I am the WAY, the truth, and the life."

May 30

PAY ATTENTION TO CLOTHING!

"And there a woman met him, with the attire of a harlot, and a crafty heart." – Proverbs 7:10

The way a person dresses says a lot about their character. A wise and principled person will invest more in what is not visible (character, knowledge, and principles) than in what is seen. However, an "easy" person will seek to draw attention to their body. Lack of wisdom and scriptural values will be evident when that person is more naked than dressed...

Clothes should not put on display our financial potential. Wanting to show off how much money you have through expensive clothes means nothing but a confusion of values. A person's worth is not determined by what they wear or have but by who they are.

Moreover, clothes should not advertise your body. Tight clothes and skimpy attire are characteristic of people who, through their bodies, manipulate and destroy families, thereby preparing others for a fall into immorality...

Be a person with values! Show through modesty that you are not "for sale." Let common sense be evident in this area. Dress in such a way that the gentleness and modesty of your character are not contradicted by the clothes you wear.

Whoever values the inside will express it through the outside!

Dress in such a way that people will desire your company for your character, not just for your appearance...

Value what is promoted by the Bible, not by Hollywood.

"Do not love the world or the things in the world. If anyone loves the world, the love of the Father is not in him. For all that is in the world—the lust of the flesh, the lust of the eyes, and the pride of life—is not of the Father but is of the world. And the world is passing away, and the lust of it; but he who does the will of God abides forever." – 1 John 2:15-17

Dress in such a way that your maturity, personality, and prestige are well represented.

A city with values does not have walls and gates made of foam. Inner values are kept hidden, and the gates to them must be securely closed...

A crafty heart has its specific clothing. Infidelity, eroticism, and a self-centered personality are visible in the way most people dress.

Be different! A godly heart only goes hand in hand with modest clothing.

Beauty attracts the eye... Character attracts the heart.

The exterior passes. The interior remains...

May 31

LEARN TO APPRECIATE!

"Many daughters have done well, but you excel them all." – Proverbs 31:29

We are so rich in words when we have the chance to correct someone and so poor when it comes to saying a few words of appreciation.

Appreciation is for the soul like salt for the food. It adds that taste of a small verbal reward to a loved one who has made an effort to accomplish something.

Appreciation is the verbal gratitude of a thankful heart. It is the medal you offer to the person beside you after their daily run. It is the dose of motivation your neighbor needs to continue their sacrifices.

Learn to appreciate! To bring a word of thanks! To take the time to say a word of praise when most people get up from the table and leave in a hurry.

If you are an employer, appreciate your employees! They will feel valued, and the quality of their work will increase.

If you are an employee, appreciate your employer! The effort to run a company is immense, and sometimes a simple word of thanks along with your quality work will make your boss's day easier.

Appreciate your mother! Her sacrificial love needs a look in the eyes and a word of gratitude for all the years of work when she asked for nothing in return except... obedience and respect.

Appreciate your father! Take his calloused hands in yours from time to time and say a heartfelt "thank you."

Appreciate your wife! Flowers that do not receive daily light, warmth, and moisture will wither.

Appreciate your husband! Turn your home into a haven with a few words sweeter than honey.

Appreciate... Look around at the people who have done you even the smallest good and tell them a word of appreciation.

Be water for the dry soil of the heart beside you. Be a cool breeze for a heart that has withered under the scorching heat of sacrifices that so many do not notice...

Appreciate...

And you will be appreciated in turn.

June 1

HABITS

"Not forsaking the assembling of ourselves together, as is the manner of some, but exhorting one another, and so much the more as you see the Day approaching." – Hebrews 10:25

The actions we repeatedly and automatically perform are called habits. Those that yield positive results are called *good habits,* while those leading to negative outcomes are *bad habits.*

Another classification of habits is based on their nature. Motor habits are related to our physical activities: running, standing, sitting, etc. Others are intellectual habits: observing, thinking, etc. However, the most significant habits are those tied to expressing our character: always speaking the truth, being respectful, working diligently, maintaining cleanliness, etc.

Habits impact every area of our lives: health, relationships, finances, career, and spiritual life.

The habit of constantly relying on loans and spending recklessly will ruin your life. The habit of recording every expense and evaluating where you can save will greatly help you over time.

The habit of desiring to learn more and, with a humble attitude, asking questions when you don't know, will help you progress at work. The habit of being closed off and unable to set aside your ego to seek help will keep you stagnant for a long time.

Daniel had the habit of praying three times a day because he had started practicing this regularly in the past. Our present is actually the result of decisions made in the past. Our future will depend on the habits we have in the present.

When Jethro came to Moses, he found him exhausted from working too much. Following the advice he received from his father-in-law, Moses changed the habit of working alone instead of working as a team.

The habit of reading Scripture every day will gradually build the spiritual maturity you need to overcome the daily challenges of the world we live in. The habit of attending church for fellowship services was beneficial for Paul (Acts 17:2) and certainly is beneficial for us. Job had the habit of interceding for his household, and it would be good for us to have the same habit (Job 1:5).

Let us be careful about the kind of people that we allow around us! The habits of our friends will influence us for better or for worse:

„Do not be deceived: 'Evil company corrupts good habits.'" – 1 Corinthians 15:33

The challenge for today is to think about a bad habit in your life that you should eliminate and, at the same time, to think about a good habit in someone else`s life that you could adopt. Looking at a good role model and wanting to be like them is not enough. To get where that person is, you need to do what that person did!

Do you understand now why most people, when they see someone who has succeeded in a certain area, speak ill of them, unfairly judge them, and envy them? It is easier to have these negative attitudes (which, for many, are already habits) than to make a habit of the sacrifices that such people have made. Therefore, most people keep staying in the ditch and in their bad habits. Hippocrates said: „Before you heal someone, ask him if he is willing to give up the things that make him sick!"

They say that it takes 21 days of repeated action for it to become a habit.

Shall we start forming a good habit today?

JUNE 2

THE ALTRUISTIC BELIEVER

"A friend loves at all times, and a brother is born for adversity." – Proverbs 17:17

In his everyday service, the selfish believer asks himself, whenever he does something, "What's in it for me?" On the other hand, the altruistic believer asks himself, "What's in it for my neighbor?"

Today, I experienced the grace of an altruistic believer who "wasted" his time with me, investing it in eternity. His selfless act reminded me of the true essence of Christian love, which seeks not personal gain but the well-being of others.

There are many believers who put some money in the Sunday offering plate just because they do not want their neighbor to see them putting nothing. However, what we truly need are people who give of their time during the week when only God sees them! These quiet acts of service are the true measure of a heart dedicated to God and neighbor.

Lord, let there be more of such individuals! Inspire us to be generous with our time and resources, not for recognition, but for the sake of love and kindness.

Be an altruistic person every day for someone who needs your friendship! In a world that often focuses on self-interest, your small acts of selflessness can make a profound difference. Embrace the call to serve others with a joyful heart, reflecting the love of Christ in all you do.

JUNE 3

TODAY`S SACRIFICE

"Therefore I run thus: not with uncertainty. Thus I fight: not as one who beats the air. But I discipline my body and bring it into subjection, lest, when I have preached to others, I myself should become disqualified." – 1 Corinthians 9:26-27

Both in the Bible and in everyday life, we encounter two main ways of sacrifice: one for this life and one for the life to come. Both are based on the following principle: sacrifice something valuable today for a better tomorrow.

Moreover, the purpose of today's sacrifice can be either your own well-being or the well-being of others.

A life without sacrifice breeds mediocrity. That is, routine, rust, and eventually ruin.

If you want to become the village drunkard, you do not need to make any sacrifices. However, if you want to become a successful doctor, you will have to sacrifice outings with friends and evenings spent at the movies.

The challenge of our generation is not to go with the flow. Not to be among those who make no effort but settle for failure, for wasted youth, and for broken families.

We must learn that only what is born out of pain, out of effort, out of continuous struggle and diligent work can later on claim the crown.

Be a fighter! Sacrifice today what you like for a better future you will have later.

This applies both in material and spiritual aspects.

.

June 4

THE TEMPTATION OF COMPARISON

"Now godliness with contentment is great gain." – *1 Timothy 6:6*

You scroll through social media. You notice the vacation they took that you could not afford. The car they bought last week, while you still drive your ten-year-old vehicle. You notice their clothes, their careers... their smart children who already know English at the age of 7. "Oh, what a romantic evening they have! What a restaurant they can afford! How much they love each other..."

Questions flood your mind. "Look at them, with their brand-new kitchen! Wow, who knows how much money they are making..." You scroll further down. "Oh, but didn't they use to rent? What?! A new house??? Hmm..."

Frustration starts to creep into the corner of your heart.

You begin to have regrets and look for someone to blame. Why them and not me? Why their children and not mine? Why is her husband capable of that, while mine "is good for nothing"?

When we long for something that others have and we lack, we become envious and unhappy because that thing is missing in our lives.

The comparison game is a game you play endlessly without ever winning. You will always find someone who has more than you. Someone with children who seem better than yours. Someone with a more understanding wife than yours.

Most of the time, however, social media pictures do not show the whole reality. They do not tell you that maybe the vacation is funded with a credit card; that the car is on lease; that the picture of the smiling children took ten failed attempts; that the *perfect* face came after dozens of filters and retouches; that the fantastic career was achieved at the expense of sending the children to daycare...

Have you ever seen Jesus, during His *time* on earth, being impressed by someone's house? By someone's designer clothes? By outward appearances? Was He frustrated that Caesar had dozens of rooms in the palace, while He had nowhere to lay His head? Absolutely never did Jesus praise someone for external *values* but only for inner ones.

He was amazed at the faith of the centurion but never impressed by the gold in the Temple. He publicly praised the faith of the Canaanite woman but was never impressed by someone's fishing boat...

Have you considered that the family you envy might have significant marital problems? That the cool boy with 3,000 *likes* from friends might be contemplating suicide? That the *gorgeous* girl who displayed her newly bought dress yesterday recently had an intense argument with her parents?

We do not know what is behind each picture. And we should not care. *Life is too short to waste time comparing ourselves to others.*

You are unique! Your life experience is unique! To be truly happy, your youth does not need the approval of others but the blessing of God. And happiness is not even the goal of our life here – holiness is. And holiness does not pair up well with envy. Gratitude does not go well with judging other people`s lives. Comparison will never be a sister to joy...

Let your values be inner values. Gentleness, gratitude, and faith in God may not receive praise from people, but I assure you, you will be appreciated by God.

Stop the sin of comparing yourself to others! Stop wasting your money, time, and energy trying to reach the level of others. Use what you already have and invest significantly in personal development!

What we have is a blessing only if we know how to use it wisely. That is why "TO BE" is more important than "TO HAVE."

When we depart for eternity, we will leave everything behind.

The house. The vacation. The tiles. The phone.

Only our deeds will follow us.

I have decided that the act of comparing myself with others shall not be among those deeds.

You should do the same...

June 5

THE SCHOOL OF LIFE

"For I consider that the sufferings of this present time are not worthy to be compared with the glory which shall be revealed in us." – Romans 8:18

The troubles you go through before knowing God reveal that evil has a demonic influence on your being, and the only salvation is Jesus.

After knowing Him, the troubles you face become a school where the Savior tests you. As a reward for going through them without complaining, you receive great rewards in heaven.

"For our light affliction, which is but for a moment, is working for us a far more exceeding and eternal weight of glory." – 2 Corinthians 4:17

This is the significant difference between a non-believer who despairs when faced with trouble and a believer who, in the same situation, holds onto the hand of Jesus more tightly!

In the suffering you go through, I pray that these words motivate you:

"I hold on tight. Not to a rope, as it may break. Not to a person, as he may leave. Not to a dream, as it may shatter. Not to a plan, as it may be canceled. I hold on to God tightly. When the devil seeks to bring me down at any cost, God lifts me up without any cost. Because He loves me. Therefore, know that I hold on tightly. I haven't let go. Take away anything you want from me but let me have God!" (Alina Ilioi-Mureșan)

June 6

TRUE SERVICE

"Serve the Lord with fear, and rejoice with trembling." – *Psalm 2:11*

If we place ourselves in the foreground while serving, God becomes less visible. True service, however, is one in which God is clearly visible, while man, being just an instrument, takes a secondary place.

Unfortunately, we live in a time when man is exalted and applauded, while God is often eclipsed by the glory we receive.

True service does not impress but searches the heart.

True service does not value the voice, the oratorical skill, the style, but a life of holiness. The gift offered on the altar has no value if the life of the giver is not in harmony with the Father and with his fellow humans.

Today, we have instruments, concerts, programs, sermons, but one thing is increasingly lacking: the fear of the Lord. Without it, all is useless.

With it, even if the elements mentioned above are missing, the sacrifice is accepted.

I am afraid of serving without tears and of joy that does not make you tremble with amazement and gratitude before your Creator.

"Praise Him" through your life, through your voice, through your existence. You have been given the grace to worship Him. But do not forget to do it with the respect He deserves and the humility He desires.

Only then your service will be accepted. The fragrance of your sacrifice will be pleasing to God, and the joy of entering His presence will overwhelm you.

June 7

PRICE VS. VALUE

"The Lord is not slack concerning His promise, as some count slackness, but is longsuffering toward us, not willing that any should perish but that all should come to repentance." – 2 Peter 3:9

The price is what we pay for something. The value is what we receive in exchange for that price. Often, however, we are deceived because those who sell us certain things at a low price make us believe that only the price has decreased, not the value. We often time realize that along with the decrease in price, some of the quality of that product has also been lost.

T. Mann, looking from a different perspective, said something exceptionally true: "For us humans, the value of a thing increases in direct proportion to the difficulty of acquiring it." And sometimes, this difficulty is not measured only by the price but also by the time we spend waiting for that thing.

I do not know what are the things that you have been asking from God. What I can tell you is that God's answers are always valuable. He does not lower the quality to offer that answer at a discounted price. But are we ready to pay the price?

In many situations, the price means prayer, intercession, days of fasting, worries cast upon Him, loneliness, unanswered questions, and turmoil. And all these have no other purpose than to make you depend more on Him...

Should I still hope? Faith seems to have diminished. The fog is too dense. When, I wonder?

While asking these questions, do not forget that the value of the answer increases.

Instant gratification is the term used today for what we receive immediately. Young people click and get the internet page in 2 seconds. Everything is at the push of a button. Turnkey. The faster the answer, the less we value what we receive. The child who receives the LEGO after the first tantrum gets tired of it after 2 hours. We want everything to be instant.

In such times, God says, "Wait! Pay the price! All in their time! Pray more! Hope more! Believe more!" Persistent prayers do not change God but prepare us for His answer!

I baptized a mother for whom her son prayed for 14 years. On the same day, I baptized a man for whom his mother prayed for 22 years.

Two weeks later, I met someone in Spain who told me, “My mother prayed for me for 25 years!”

When God delays, He does it so that we value more the day of the answer. If He fulfilled every desire instantly, we would treat Him differently.

He is God. And even if it seems late to us, He comes at the right time.

Continue to pay the price! You will be amazed at the value of the answer received from God!

JUNE 8

IN THE VALLEY BEFORE THE MOUNTAIN

Each of our lives goes through both problems and victories. Through both hardships and joys. Most of the time, victories are visible, but the preparation for them takes place in secret.

Many saw Elijah on the mountain when fire came down from heaven. However, no one saw him at the Brook Cherith, eating the pieces of food that the ravens brought him.

People see when you are on the mountain, but only you and God know how many valleys full of tears you have passed through.

Do not be discouraged! The valley prepares you for the victory on the mountain.

Athletes train privately, unseen by anyone, during the weekly workouts.

People only see them during the game, but athletes know that the full stadium is not the secret; the secret is the sweat from the times when the stadium was empty.

Weightlifters who reach the world's major competitions have at least 10 years of training behind them. Without noise, without applause, unseen by anyone.

The examples can go on indefinitely, but the lesson is the same.

If today you are in the valley, do not despair! The valley shapes you to remain humble on the day of victory on the mountain.

People who do not have valleys in life will not withstand the thin air of the mountain. A building without a foundation will not withstand an earthquake, and a tree without roots will not withstand the storm.

June 9

DEEDS, NOT JUST WORDS!

"Little children, let us not love in word or in tongue, but in deed and in truth." – 1 John 3:18

Promises cost nothing when spoken. But they cost you if you want to actually fulfill them.

People fall into two categories: those who promise much and do little, and those who promise little and do much.

I do not know what kind of promises you made in the past. But what I do know is that true value is not in words but in deeds.

Sweetness that relies only on promises becomes bitter later if there are no deeds to back it up.

The marriage covenant made with promises accompanied by stomach butterflies will soon break if the deeds are absent.

The covenant with God on the day of baptism will soon erode if the deeds of faith are not present.

Love is measured by the quality of the deeds, not the quantity of the words.

Paul told the Galatians to clothe themselves with the garment of love.

"But above all these things, put on love, which is the bond of perfection." – Colossians 3:14

When the garment of love is on the hanger, the only thing you hear are sweet words and promises.

When the garment of love is truly worn, deeds come naturally.

Deeds, not just words!

June 10

LIFT UP, DO NOT BRING DOWN!

The way we treat those around us reflects our character.

When an accident happens, you can be just a *curious* onlooker. You can just give your opinion about the fact that the person in the accident was not wearing a seatbelt or was driving too fast.

Or you can be a *reporter,* an exaggerating reporter. One who will say you are in a coma, even if you just broke your arm. Why? Because flashy headlines attract clicks. Exaggerations sell well on the market of curiosity.

You can also be a *police officer*. You will hand out fines or check for skid marks.

But it is most desirable to be a *doctor*. Have you ever seen a doctor chatting on the phone while the injured person was dying in front of him? Or giving his opinion about whether or not the injured person was wearing a seatbelt?

Oh, what a great need we have for *spiritual doctors*!

For people who know how to perform spiritual resuscitation, who know how to lift up the fallen, as Paul did with Eutychus.

We have enough curious onlookers and reporters. Police officers? Everywhere you turn. God forbid you fall into their hands on a difficult day...

The worldly Christian crushes the fallen person. The spiritual Christian lifts him up.

Be a person who lifts up! A person who bends down! Be like the Samaritan to the man fallen among thieves.

The one who bends down will be rewarded one day. By whom?

By God, who keeps track of all the efforts of the spiritual doctors.

JUNE 11

THE WINDOW DURING THE STORM

"You shall make a window for the ark, and you shall finish it to a cubit from above; and set the door of the ark in its side. You shall make it with lower, second, and third decks." – Genesis 6:16

The greatest hurricane that came upon mankind was the flood in Noah's time. The Bible says it rained so much that no patch of land was visible.

In those stormy days, Noah could still look at the sky. Even if it was cloudy, a glimpse of the sky is more valuable than any patch of land.

God told Noah to make a window in the ark, above, because it is crucial that during the storm, you look only towards Heaven.

No matter what trouble you go through, no matter the illness or problem you have, do not forget that there is a window through which you can look towards Heaven, and that is the Bible.

When the words of people no longer help us, the Word of God remains.

When the earth no longer has even one "patch" of safety to offer, the Bible remains as the only window that provides security.

When things are in constant change, do not look down, but look to the Heavens.

On our knees, through the window of God's Word, we receive the peace and tranquility our hearts so desperately need.

The earth may be flooded. Heaven will never be...

JUNE 12

YOU ARE NOT ALONE IN THE DEN!

"The angel of the Lord encamps all around those who fear Him and delivers them." – *Psalm 34:7*

We were not promised to be saved *from* danger but *in* danger. We cannot avoid the valley of the shadow of death, but we are promised that there, in the valley, the Lord will be with us.

Old Daniel, with white hair, being over 80 years old, descended into the lions' den. The condemnation said nothing more than that he bowed down to the King of kings and the Lord of lords.

He did not panic in front of the den. He did not take antidepressants. He did not despair. He knew that those who have God on their side when things go well will also have Him close when things go wrong.

The angel sent by God worked the "third shift" that night so that the lions could not get near Daniel. The lions thought they would have a tasty meal, but they realized that saints are not to be eaten.

I kept wondering: why was the Angel in a hurry to leave, after Daniel was taken out of the den? After a night of watching over him, couldn't he stay a few more minutes to also protect Daniel's adversaries?

I understood, then, that when the Angel of God comes, he does not look at our education, nor at what kind of cars we own, or what kind of connections we have. He has a clear mission: to protect those who have something more precious than anything material: the fear of the Lord.

Daniel had prayed even before the den. His adversaries probably prayed with loud cries only in front of the den, but their prayers came too late, because they were made only in times of trouble.

I also understood that those who fight against the saints, instead of becoming saints themselves, will face the judgment of God. The greatest punishment is not a night with the lions, but eternal hell, a horrifying place for those who have no fear of God.

I do not know how you woke up this morning. But do not forget to kneel down and call on God like Daniel. Do not wait until you get close to the den to pray. Do not wait until you end up in intensive care to make a change.

Start a life with God today when the sky is clear, and everything is going well.

And when you find yourself in the lions' den, God will not forget about you.

Do not worry about the depth of the den, the roar of the lions, or those lying in wait. Be concerned not to lose the fear of the Lord!

JUNE 13

QUALITIES NEEDED IN A MARRIAGE: LOVE OF GOD

"You shall love the Lord your God with all your heart, with all your soul, and with all your strength." – Deuteronomy 6:5

Those who have a correct relationship with God also have a correct relationship with their spouse. Whoever loves God also loves their spouse. Putting God first in one's life will always lead to making family decisions based on this extraordinary value.

God is perfect love. A person who loves God will receive that love from Him and will extend it to his spouse. A wife who listens to God will appreciate her husband.

The love of God will keep your spouse away from sin. The love of God will lead your spouse to make obedience to God the primary purpose of your home.

Do not risk the next decades of your life (and maybe even eternity) by choosing a spouse who does not have an authentic relationship with God. If he does not love the Bible, he does not love God! If he is not involved in ministry, he does not love God! If he does not have friends with spiritual values, he does not love God! If he only goes to church on Easter and Christmas, do not be deceived: he does not love God!

If your future spouse loves sin, he does not love God! If he enjoys sinful entertainment, parties, lies, gossip, he does not love God! If he values the body more than the character, he does not love God! If he slams the door in front of his parents, he does not love God! If he is jealous and constantly judges others, he does not love God! A person who has a negative opinion about everyone else usually has too high an opinion of himself... And someone who has a high opinion of himself, and a negative opinion of others will seek change from others, not from himself. He will always blame you for everything that is wrong in your family...

The person who loves God can pin-point a moment in his life when he has met Him. He loves his fellow human beings, his eyes are directed towards Heaven, and his hands are on the plow of the sacrifices needed in life. Modesty is a quality he possesses, and the desire to mature and draw closer to God is evident in his words and actions.

He will not take dating and marriage lightly but be very responsible about it. He understands that it is not eros love that sustains a marriage but AGAPE love.

God is the one who established the family. Let Him be the architect of your family. Look for a spouse who is ready to build according to His plans, but do not forget: only if you love God first will you be able to find such a spouse...

June 14

QUALITIES NEEDED IN A MARRIAGE: RESPECT

"Honor all people. Love the brotherhood. Fear God. Honor the king!" – 1 Peter 2:17

Respect in a relationship is one of the most crucial factors contributing to the health and harmony of a marriage. Every person is born with the desire to be loved, appreciated, and respected. The marital nest is the setting where each person contributes to the happiness of the other. The two spouses are not perfect, but they are willing to communicate with each other. The way they communicate is one of the methods in which they show respect daily. Listening to each other, encouraging each other, and saying small daily appreciative words are gestures that demonstrate mutual respect.

Communication consists of the words we say (7%), the tone in which we say those words (38%), and the gestures we make while speaking (55%).

Respect must be present in all three components of communication. Beautiful words, a calm and gentle tone, and our gestures should prove that we value the other person's opinion and are willing to consider their ideas or views.

A respectful partner will not humiliate you with derogatory words, will not make you feel like a "pawn," will not verbally or emotionally abuse you, will not coerce you through threats, and so on. Respect simply allows the person beside us to think freely, unobstructed by any outburst of our own and entirely open to express the thoughts that trouble them.

Be very careful when choosing your future spouse! If the girl you are dating does not respect her father, she will not respect you either. If the boy with whom you have started talking about marriage does not respect his mother, he will not respect you either.

A disrespectful person cannot hide for long. Their attitude, words, and gestures will eventually reveal their true character.

As a girl, do not just look at how the boy behaves with you! He may respect you because of the image he wants to project to you... Pay close attention to how he behaves with those around him, with whom he is not involved in an emotional relationship like he is with you. Whoever respects their family, friends, colleagues, and boss will surely respect their spouse too...

Too many girls overlook the disrespectful tone of a boy just because he drives an expensive car. Too many boys overlook a rude and arrogant girl just because she has a beautiful body. Do you think material *values* can compensate for the lack of good manners? Do you think that someone who does not know how to say *please* when asking for something deserves to be given decades of your life just because they have a thick wallet? The verb *'to have'* will never compensate for the lack of the verb *'to be'*...

If you want a spouse who respects you, try to have this value yourself first.

Whoever values others will be valued himself.

Whoever waters others will be watered himself as well.

Whoever truly respects will choose only someone respectful...

June 15

QUALITIES NEEDED IN A MARRIAGE: DILIGENCE

"For even when we were with you, we commanded you this: If anyone will not work, neither shall he eat." – 2 Thessalonians 3:10

I was seven years old when I learned to milk a cow. Around nine, I mowed alfalfa with the scythe for the first time, and by the age of twelve, my brother and I were taking turns in the kitchen, washing dishes. I used to wonder, upset: "Why? Why don't our parents let us play all day? Why are waking up early for school and then daily chores necessary?"

Today, I understand. Recently, I got back home at 5 a.m. from a church service. After a few hours of rest, together with my wife and our first four children, I went to work in the backyard greenhouse. Not because we cannot afford to buy a pound of tomatoes from the market, but because we understood that if it is hard when you are young, it will be easy when you are older.

Preparing for marriage should not happen at the altar, 10 minutes before the wedding blessing... Diligence is not strengthened with the phone in your hand all day. This quality, which is becoming rarer with each passing day, is formed when the child is young, if he has responsible parents. It is good for the child to know how to use a hoe but also how to carry a suitcase. It is good for him to be familiar with both the dishwashing sponge and the studies for a school degree. With using a mop for cleaning the floor and with typing on a computer.

I thank God every day for blessing me with a diligent wife. Raised in a family with 12 children, she learned the meaning of industriousness. She learned to tie tomato vines but also to study for five years in college. To take the cow to pasture and, at the same time, to keep up with interior design.

In the Bible, we do not find anything positive about LAZINESS. On the contrary! Scripture warns us that laziness is like a bulldozer that destroys the house:

"When the hands are lazy, the rafters sag; when the hands are idle, the house leaks." – Ecclesiastes 10:18

Diligence, however, is a treasure:

"The lazy man does not roast what he took in hunting, but diligence is man's precious possession." – Proverbs 12:27

The woman who can be praised at the city gates for her deeds is the diligent woman:

"She seeks wool and flax, and willingly works with her hands." – Proverbs 31:13

Oh, I have met so many families in which an industrious woman married a lazy man! Or vice versa...

In which children are disoriented. In which the diligent one must do the work of the "lazy" one as well... Oh, how hard it is in those families! Oh, how many sighs are there where only one of the spouses pulls at the family "yoke"... It is not enough to be diligent. We must also do quality work. I have seen many diligent people who have made a mess of their own work. They finished quickly but worked poorly. They forgot what the apostle Paul says:

"Whatever you do, do it heartily, as to the Lord and not to men..." – Colossians 3:23

Diligence goes hand in hand with QUALITY and INTEGRITY. A person who works hard produces quality, and what they promise and complete is of immense value. Oh, what a blessed home such a person has! What exceptional children can be raised by parents like these, who pass on these values without which no family can last...

It is of immense value to have a spouse who knows what work means. Such a person will be careful with spending money because they know how hard they are earned. Those who work hard spend reluctantly. Those who earn money easily will spend it quickly. Rebecca drew up dozens of buckets of water for Eleazar's camels. She did not get muscle soreness, and she did not have to lie in bed for two weeks to recover because she was used to hard work. If Isaac had not chosen such a girl, everything he gathered with Abraham would have gone "down the drain"...

Pay attention, dear ones! Open your eyes widely! Ask your future spouse what they know to do... If he is still in school, ask him what he worked on during summer breaks. If he has finished school a few years before, ask him where he has worked so far and what he did with the money he earned. If an employer asks you for a resume and is not willing to hire you if you are a slacker, even more so for a marriage relationship, you should be interested in what your future spouse knows to do.

If he only works his "mom and dad's pocket," as a boy wrote on Facebook in his profile "job" rubric, then run away from him quickly! If she was raised in luxury, spending the day in tanning salons, pampered by a mother who did everything in the house so that the young "miss" had time for manicures, pedicures and outings every day with friends, then run away from such a person! You will not be able to change her!

"What is crooked cannot be made straight, and what is lacking cannot be numbered." – Ecclesiastes 1:15

I know MANY cases where the young "miss" had a very messy room, but when she went out, she was covered in fake eyelashes and brand perfumes! The boys who were attracted by the false image created by these lazy girls had no idea what a mess was behind them! I have talked more than once with girls who worked abroad, cleaning the houses of many such "ladies" and were horrified by the fact that the public image of those women was not at all representative of what was going on in their home!

Our elders used to say that in the past, when you went to ask for someone's hand in marriage, in some areas of the country, you would ask for a glass of water in order to check how clean that glass was. Often, they would open the wardrobe by surprise to see if the character matched the image. Is it surprising then that those families stayed together for a lifetime, while many families today do not even last through the honeymoon?

I was horrified to meet families in which the husband, a diligent man, earned thousands of dollars a month, while the wife was spending the whole day shopping in the city. Women whose sweet voices you constantly hear saying, "Sweetheart, sweetheart," but who, in 3 days of "shopping," empty the wallet of their husband.

If you have come across such a "diva," then you have had the chance to see how "sweet" the journey of life is. A grapefruit squeezed to the last drop.

Did you know that there are people who feel good after 10 hours of work? And, at the same time, there are people who get a headache at the mere thought that they must go to work? They get "seasick," even though they live on dry land all day...

Receiving children from God is a great blessing. But receiving them and raising them requires diligence.

Waking up earlier than the children is a sacrifice made for decades during your marriage. Cleaning, ironing, homework, and other activities in which the two spouses help each other will bear fruit only if there is diligence. Whether you are a girl or a boy, do not forget that changing diapers is closely related to "I love you."

I conclude by saying that if you are a "nobody" before marriage, you will surely become "somebody" after marriage. "Somebody" to take out the trash. "Somebody" to vacuum. "Somebody" to...

Try to be a "somebody" even before the wedding day. "Somebody" who helps with household chores. "Somebody" who cooks... "Somebody" who fixes the door latch. "Somebody" who...

How many people wish to be such a "somebody"? Open your eyes widely, dear young people who want to get married! Study Proverbs 31 carefully! The happy home of love has this priceless diamond called: diligence.

June 16

QUALITIES NEEDED IN A MARRIAGE: VISION

"She considers a field and buys it; from her profits, she plants a vineyard." – Proverbs 31:16

It seems that the inventor of GPS said that the most important thing about this device is to know where you start and where you are heading. Without a starting point and without a destination, the GPS is of no help.

This is true on every level of life: spiritual, material, familial, social, etc. Without a specific target, the most imposing ship on the ocean will navigate in circles. Without a specific purpose, the best marathon runner will run in vain. Without a clear vision, two young people getting married will be disappointed that their family is going nowhere...

The woman in Proverbs thought hard. Considered. She made up a plan in her mind. She had a purpose for waking up in the morning. She knew why she had to save money.

She understood that vigilance in all matters is necessary for the blessed future of her family. Do you have a vision? It means you guard over your things of value...

"She watches over the ways of her household..." – Proverbs 31:27

If you do not see your marriage as a future home where you can raise children for Heaven, how will you be able to go on every day? If you do not have a spouse with a holy goal, what will you work for your whole life? What good is it to be the richest person in the cemetery if you have not achieved anything spiritually?

The strongest missionaries in Christian history began thinking about serving God from the moment they encountered Him. Therefore, they chose a spouse accordingly. If you want to serve, but she wants to go to the movies, your shared vision will soon break apart. If having children is a blessing for you, but she wants to maintain her perfect body until the age of eighty, then you will have conflicts about the transient things at the expense of the eternal investments.

Ask your spouse about his vision. What does he want from life? What does he work for every day? How many books (besides the Bible) has he read to grow spiritually? How interested is he in God's work? What does he desire from you as his spouse? What brings him satisfaction in life? Is he a supporter or a player? Is he preoccupied with thoughts like, "One more day is passing, I am closer to the pay day"? Where does he see himself in 5 years?

What did he do with the money he earned so far? What did he spend it on? Is he content to live on rent for the rest of his life? Does he often say, "The Lord will take care of it," while casually eating popcorn and throwing a stone at someone who has accomplished something in this life? Does he always have endless excuses instead of taking action?

Do you know that there are young people who have two weeks left until graduation and still do not know if they want to go to college or do something else? Do you know that there are young people who have heard that in a particular field you can earn a lot of money, and yet they make no effort towards it?

We all know about Jim Elliot, the missionary killed by the Auca tribe when he went to proclaim the Gospel to them. But what kind of training do you think this martyr had to be ready for God's work?

Philip James Elliot was born on October 8, 1927, into a Christian family from Portland, Oregon. His father was a preacher, dedicated to ministry. He read from the Scripture to his four children daily, praying with and for them. His mother, after studying medicine, opened a medical practice near their home to be closer to her family. Their home was always open to guests and missionaries, teaching the children to be welcoming and open as well.

Faith and discipline were the foundation of their family. Each child had his own chores to do in the household. Fellowship in prayer and songs of praise were ever-present. Growing up this way, Jim, at just 6 years old, was already "preaching" to his little friends about salvation, while swinging at the playground, telling his mother, "The Lord Jesus can return anytime He wants. He can take our whole family with Him because now I am saved." The children heard the Lord's calling from an early age and were prepared to follow Him. From the age of fourteen, they became personally responsible before the Lord for their actions.

When parents know what they want in life, they will raise children who will be a blessing to society and to God's ministry. Such children will have a good name and will influence others. When your vision for marriage is that together with your spouse and children, you will reach Heaven, it means that every day you will do everything in your power to reach this goal.

Look for a visionary spouse! Be careful, I do not mean a dreamer! Not someone who dreams of palaces but changes his job every two weeks. A visionary who knows what he wants in this life and is willing to put in daily effort to get there...

We trust in God! We pray for the future! But this is not enough! We must ask for guidance from God and have a purpose to strive for. No one reaches Heaven "accidentally." No one will have children dedicated to God and Scriptural principles "accidentally."

Everything requires work and sacrifice. Self-denial and closeness to God. But at the core of these things, there must be long-term planning.

Everything we do here has an eternal counterpart. If you have Heaven in your sight, you will choose a spouse with the same vision. And one day, on the platform of eternity, at the last station, you will reach the destination together. With a fulfilled vision. With God's plan fully unfolded for your family life.

And with eternal rewards.

June 17

QUALITIES NEEDED IN A MARRIAGE: ALTRUISM

"...does not behave rudely, does not seek its own, is not provoked, thinks no evil ..." – 1 Corinthians 13:5

Tolstoy said: "If you feel pain, you are alive. If you feel other people`s pain, you are a human being." In daily life, but especially in marriage, it is not enough just to be alive. You need to be a human being. A person of agape love. A spouse who seeks the well-being of the other.

The question, "What's in it for me?" is asked only by selfish people, by people interested only in their own benefits. Marriage to a selfish person guarantees failure. A selfish person will always seek to be served, not to serve. To be waited upon, not to wait on others. To be loved, not to love. To fulfill themselves, not to meet the needs of his spouse.

The altruistic person will put their neighbor above themselves, as Paul advised the Philippians:

"Do nothing out of selfish ambition or vain conceit. Rather, in humility value others above yourselves." – Philippians 2:3

When you see the person next to you as more important than yourself, you will always behave proactively, not reactively. What does this mean? It means that you will notice the needs of others and intervene without waiting for them to beg for help. It means that you will come with a mindset of service, with the desire to get involved, with the motivation to contribute to the needs of the family. The reactive person waits for a good deed to be done to them, and only afterwards reacts to that kindness. The proactive person takes the initiative to get involved.

The husband needs altruism in his relationship with his wife. The wife needs altruism in her relationship with the children. Both of them need to help each other. Only in this way can a house become a home. Only in this way does verbal love become practical love.

True love forgets itself. True love is willing to face any danger just to help those in need. Altruistic love is the only love that does not calculate its own benefits but gets involved regardless of the cost.

The altruistic spouse sacrifices his time for the family's sake. Through daily work, he sacrifices his earnings for the benefits of his family members. He will never use the phrase "each one with his own piggy bank." He will not love conditionally. He will not do something only in exchange for rewards.

The heart of an unconverted person is not capable of true altruism because it is a sinful heart. Therefore, it is extremely important for your future spouse to have an authentic relationship with God. Through the Holy Spirit and the reading and fulfillment of His Word, divine altruistic love will descend into your spouse's heart, and your marriage will be a corner of heaven.

Do not put feelings before principles when talking to a person with the purpose of getting to know him better. Check if he or she has an authentic conversion and love for others. If they serve their community with altruism, there is a high chance they will do the same in the family. If they are compassionate with the poor, widows, or orphans, there is a high chance they will plant mercy in the home you dream of having. If they offer a specific part of their salary to God first, it means that deep in their heart, there are values like generosity and charity.

Avoid a selfish person! Keep your distance from someone who only knows how to assert their own rights! Do not get emotionally involved in any relationship where the partner primarily seeks personal gain. Small gestures will reveal their true intentions. Whoever waters others will also be watered. Whoever casts their bread upon the waters will joyfully gather it later.

The candle is like altruistic love. It burns for others, not for itself. It consumes itself endlessly to light the way for others.

And when only wax remains, it can be said of those who burned for God and family: "It was worth the burning!"

JUNE 18

QUALITIES NEEDED IN A MARRIAGE: FLEXIBILITY

"The wisdom that is from above is first pure, then peaceable, gentle, willing to yield, full of mercy and good fruits, without partiality and without hypocrisy." – James 3:17

When was the last time you met a stubborn person? Did you wish to spend more time with them? Can you say that it was an encounter worth repeating, and that the dialogue was memorable?

I doubt it.

Five minutes with a stubborn person can ruin your entire day. Meeting someone who sticks only to their own ideas, even when easily proven wrong, is not an event you want to frame on your wall.

If five minutes with a stubborn person are hard to bear, how about spending 50 years with that person? That is the question you should ask yourself before saying "YES" in marriage.

Did you know that even God does not desire the company of stubborn or stiff-necked people?

"Go up to a land flowing with milk and honey; but I will not go up among you, lest I consume you on the way, for you are a stiff-necked people." – Exodus 33:3

The term "stubborn" appears ten times in the Bible, and it is never associated with something positive. It denotes rebellion, disobedience, and inflexibility.

A spouse who truly seeks the well-being of his marital relationship will not behave like a child who grips tightly onto his toy, screaming and kicking. He is ready to let go and knows when to back down for the sake of harmony within his family.

Stubbornness is, in fact, a refusal to change. Marriage, on the other hand, changes us, matures us, and helps us grow! Through flexibility, harmony, and altruism, both spouses draw closer to each other and to God.

The stubborn person is very selfish and proud. The flexible person is altruistic and humble. The stubborn person seeks his own happiness. The flexible person seeks the happiness of his spouse! The stubborn person believes he is always right! The flexible person does not seek justice first, but harmony. Stubbornness destroys, flexibility unifies.

The stubborn person demands sacrifice from his spouse, while the flexible one sacrifices for his spouse!

Stubbornness may seem powerful, but, in reality, it is a significant weakness of character!

Wisdom from God possesses the crucial quality without which no marriage can endure: flexibility. Such people can easily adapt and allow themselves to be molded and swayed towards what is good.

Be an adaptable and flexible person. And then your company will be desired by another adaptable person for the next few decades of your lives...

June 19

QUALITIES NEEDED IN A MARRIAGE: HONESTY

"Who can find a virtuous [honest] wife? For her worth is far above rubies." – Proverbs 31:10

The most valuable thing you have is your character. The most precious quality of character is integrity. Being known as an honest, truthful person whom you can rely on is worth more than anything else.

In the covenant of marriage, you cannot enter without a trustworthy spouse. Marriage is more than a one-day stroll. It is more than a business partnership. It is more than a contract. It is a covenant! The next few decades will be mountains and valleys. Clouds and sunshine. Fields with flowers, but also deserts. You can navigate through all of this successfully only with a person who has a good name, who does more than he says, who gives more than he receives, who runs more than he stands...

Fidelity is another important aspect of honesty. It is closely linked to purity. To cleanliness. Clean food does not clean a dirty vessel; on the contrary, it gets spoiled by that dirty vessel. If you are a girl, do you dare enter into marriage with a boy who spent his adolescence in adulterous cohabitation? As a boy, do you dare enter into a relationship with a girl who has been in the arms of several other boys? What guarantees do you have that, after marriage, she will not do the same? Oh, yes, I know that through sincere repentance, the Lord can grant forgiveness. But have at least a few years passed since that person returned to the Lord and restored the good name they had tarnished?

"You can only lose somebody's trust once," said Nicolae Iorga[15].

Do you want a blessed marriage? Do you desire the Lord's blessing in the coming years? Then do not accept compromise! Do not joke around! Do not be a person who says one thing today and something entirely different tomorrow. If your spouse is capable of lying, remember that he is capable of doing anything else too! Do you want the Devil as your father-in-law? Then why continue dating a person without integrity?

---

[15] Nicolae Iorga (1871-1940) – Renowned Romanian historian, politician, and prolific writer known for his contributions to Romanian historiography, literature, and cultural advocacy.

Where light appears, darkness disappears. Where there is warmth, coldness does not penetrate. Where there is honesty, there is no room for anything else. Where there is fear of the Lord, there is no doubt.

Integrity is for marriage like cement is for a foundation: it holds both the iron and the sand together. Whether you rent or own a mansion, whether you walk or drive a beautiful car, it does not matter. With an honest spouse, the relationship endures. A virtuous woman is a crown to her husband:

> *"A virtuous woman is a crown to her husband, but she who causes shame is like rottenness in his bones." – Proverbs 12:4*

An honest man will be a blessing to the family and the community. Even in the financial realm, there will be security and trust. Did you know that in one Old Testament circumstance, the king said there was no need for a committee of auditors when he noticed how honest those working in the House of the Lord were?

> *"They did not require an account from the men into whose hand they delivered the money to be paid to workmen, for they dealt faithfully." – 2 Kings 12:15*

I pray that God raises more honest young people. Honest families. People of their word who raise children of their word!

Be a person of integrity!

And you will find an honest spouse!

JUNE 20

YOU CAN ONLY GIVE WHAT YOU HAVE...

"You prepare a table before me in the presence of my enemies; You anoint my head with oil; my cup runs over." – Psalm 23:5

The cup of my life is always filled with something specific. It can be filled with bitterness, turmoil, and anger, and then I will contaminate those around me with these negative feelings. Or it can be filled with joy, peace, and hope, and then I can offer plentifully to others from my own abundance.

How is the filling with these positive gifts achieved? Through fellowship with God, obeying His Word, and fellowship with wise people.

Jesus said, *"I am the light of the world."* – John 8:12. But in Matthew, we have a remarkable addition: *"You are the light of the world."* – Matthew 5:14. This truth speaks very clearly: if you are connected to light, you offer light. If you are connected to the Lord of Peace, you offer peace.

One day, when David woke up, he realized that the travertine and marble of the palace did not belong to him. He understood that the path from being a shepherd to becoming a king was opened by God, by the One who is the source of our goodness. He felt that his cup was full of gratitude and of the goodness of God, and he exclaimed:

"The king said, 'Is there still anyone of the house of Saul, to whom I may show the kindness of God?' And Ziba said to the king, 'There is still a son of Jonathan who is lame in his feet.'" – 2 Samuel 9:3

Do you notice the beauty of David's question? *"I want to offer kindness because I have kindness in my cup."* Yes, but this filling with kindness did not happen overnight but through years of shaping in the wilderness. First, David was kind to Saul; when he could have harmed him, he did not, and now David is exceptionally kind to Saul's grandson. The continuation of this remarkable story can be found in 2 Samuel 9, but one thing is very clear: you can only offer what you have accumulated. When the cup overflows, everyone will see what we have been gathering...

June 21

WORLDLY SUCCESS VS. GODLY SUCCESS

Everyone desires success, whether it be financial, familial, or spiritual. However, the problem lies in the fact that God sees success differently than how people perceive it...

People were looking at the wealthy individuals offering large sums of money at the Temple. Those who gave more received more recognition—from people. The widow offered a small amount but was appreciated by Jesus. Success in the Kingdom of God is not about how much you give but about what is left at home after you give. God also looks at the motivation behind your giving. Are you doing it to be appreciated by people? Then, your giving is in vain. Are you giving to be appreciated by Jesus? Then, your giving is meaningful.

The sons of Korah said:

> *"For a day in Your courts is better than a thousand..." – Psalms 84:10*

Going to church is viewed by godless people as a failure, as second rated. They would never exchange a day at the mall for a day at church.

Those who have a godly perspective realize that the most valuable moments are in the presence of God.

The world we live in finds pleasure in money, wealth, and connections. Paul, looking from God's perspective, said:

> *"Therefore I take pleasure in infirmities, in reproaches, in needs, in persecutions, in distresses, for Christ's sake. For when I am weak, then I am strong." – 2 Corinthians 12:10*

How do you see success? Through the eyes of the world or through the eyes of God?

On the evening of the Last Supper, Peter looked at the door to see if any servant would come in to take the towel. He was shocked when he saw that Jesus, the Greatest Theologian, the Mightiest Doctor, the Supreme Scientist, the Creator of the Universe, and the Incarnation of Divinity, bowed down to wash their feet. At that moment, he understood the practice of what Jesus had said shortly before:

"...and whoever desires to be first among you, let him be your slave." – Mark 10:44

I am very nervous and harbor hidden fears that I might be captivated by people's calculations and love their success formulas, only to find out in the end that, in fact, God's formulas are the only ones that matter. Don't you feel the same?

I wish you success, but not the success the world pursues.

Why not?

Because success without God is the greatest failure.

JUNE 22

THE DANGER OF WORRY

"...casting all your care upon Him, for He cares for you." – 1 Peter 5:7

One of the most common snares that the Devil uses to entangle people is worry—a sin that turns your eyes away from God to other things. From faith to unbelief. From trusting in His promises to uncertainty about tomorrow.

There is a difference between caring for something and worrying about it. I care for my children, for my family and I do my part to take care of them. But I do not need to take headache pills because of worrying about their future. What I do not know is already in the hands of the One who knows all things.

Peter doesn't say to give Jesus a portion of your worries. Peter says, "cast all of them." Why?

Because worry will block your spiritual progress. It will hold you back and keep you spinning in a whirlpool from which you cannot easily escape...

Nothing escapes the eye of God. He knows everything, He understands everything, and He has mapped out the entire course of world history. The Bible tells me:

> *"But the very hairs of your head are all numbered. Do not fear therefore; you are of more value than many sparrows." – Luke 12:7*

If He is in control of everything, why should I, a mere mortal, a handful of dust, live with the stress of daily worries?

Oh, how many times has worry succeeded in drowning out the Word of God's promises from your heart?

> *"The seed sown among thorns is he who hears the word, and the cares of this world and the deceitfulness of riches choke the word, and he becomes unfruitful." – Matthew 13:22*

I have seen so many people who cannot rejoice! People who lack peace, who lack patience! Why? Because of their worries...

Worry makes the heart heavy:

> *"But take heed to yourselves, lest your hearts be weighed down with carousing, drunkenness, and cares of this life, and that Day come on you unexpectedly." – Luke 21:34*

And a person with a heavy heart certainly does not walk confidently on the path that God has laid out for him... He sighs constantly, breathes heavily, and sees possible threats to his life in everything. He complains about everything, always has tissues ready, and medications close by.

Today, God wants to make an exchange with you: you give Him your worries, and He gives you His care...

What do you think? Is it worth it?

I said "YES."

And it was worth it.

June 23

WATCH YOUR SPEECH!

"The Angel of the Lord said to Balaam, 'Go with the men, but only the word that I speak to you, that you shall speak.'" – Numbers 22:35

One of the major differences between humans and animals is articulate language. Many animals have a tongue, but humans were endowed by God in such a way that they can arrange sound sequences to produce spoken words.

The Bible urges us to be particularly careful with our words. Our speech can be influenced by our thoughts, our desires (whether holy or sinful), our peers, and what is in our hearts, etc.

The way someone speaks says a lot about that person. Insults, verbal violence, obscene language, complaining, dissatisfaction, lying, and many other sins of the tongue are characteristic of proud individuals, people who strike, hurt, and trample over others in life in order to fulfill their cunning purposes. We must be very careful to avoid such forms of speech to the best of our ability:

"For 'He who would love life and see good days, let him refrain his tongue from evil, and his lips from speaking deceit.'" – 1 Peter 3:10

Watching your speech is necessary to avoid hurting those around us:

"There is one who speaks like the piercings of a sword, but the tongue of the wise promotes health." – Proverbs 12:18

We can be spared many troubles in life if we are wise in our speech:

"Whoever guards his mouth and tongue keeps his soul from troubles." – Proverbs 21:23

Balaam was warned to speak only words from God. These are the words that bring benefit to us (because we are in obedience), but also benefit to those around us.

However, Balaam did not listen. He had prophetic words, but he also gave advice that led to the spiritual downfall of many.

What words have you spoken today with your tongue?

"Pleasant words are like a honeycomb, sweetness to the soul and health to the bones." – Proverbs 16:24

June 24

BALANCE

"For God has not given us a spirit of fear, but of power and of love and of a sound mind." – 2 Timothy 1:7

In a heated parliamentary session, Nicolae Iorga, with a distinctly superior posture, asked I.C. Brătianu, who was the prime minister of Romania at the time:

"What can a historian learn from an engineer?" Brătianu responded sharply and emphatically, "Balance, Professor, balance!"

We need **balance in every area of life.** Its absence will lead to abuses that, later on, will lead to a collapse in that area. A person who does not have a well-established balance in everything he does will sooner or later destroy himself and negatively impact those around him.

We need **balance in our speech.** Too easily, we give our opinions about someone without even having shared a cup of tea with that person.

Too quickly, we show that we know everything, that we are masters of the image of any person, and later, with regret, we realize that we painted a distorted portrait. Balance in speech is characteristic of a self-disciplined person. Someone who can control themselves, who has a cool head, who cannot be easily provoked. Our words show the measure of our character. Only what is inside can come out...

"A fool vents all his feelings, but a wise man holds them back." – Proverbs 29:11

We need **balance in work** as well. The daycare will not compensate for your lack of involvement in your family. The Sunday school with a drawing of David and Goliath once a week will not solve your lack of involvement in your child's education—a non-involvement caused by too much involvement in material things. If we work 12-14 hours a day to make a lot of money and then spend that money on hospital treatments for illnesses caused by stress, what have we achieved? If our spouse suffers because of our greed, can we compensate with money for what has been destroyed by our lack of balance?

We need **balance in clothing.** A balanced person values modesty over sensuality, the interior over the exterior. The height of our values is seen in how we dress.

People who spend thousands of dollars on clothes and too little money on a useful book show no prudence and balance. Investing in appearance at the expense of character shows a significant lack of wisdom.

We need **balance in the way we nourish ourselves.** An unbalanced diet will produce diseases that you will later try desperately to get rid of, but the chances of success will be slim. Let the "knife of measure" never be missing:

> *"When you sit down to eat with a ruler, consider carefully what is before you; and put a knife to your throat if you are a man given to appetite. Do not desire his delicacies, for they are deceptive food!" – Proverbs 23:1-3*

If you always struggle to get up from the table, you will surely find yourself in the doctor's office soon enough. "We eat to live, not live to eat" are words that should remind us of... balance.

All things have their right time. There is a need for **balance on a daily basis.** Do not try to cram everything into a single moment. Do not struggle to have in one week what others have gained in 20 years! Beautiful things that are not done in their time become unpleasant. The lack of balance in our lives will make us disgraceful and worthy of being pointed at as negative examples.

Balance and self-control are exceptional values. Prudence is the characteristic of a wise person, while its absence is attached to fools:

> *"Every prudent man acts with knowledge, but a fool lays open his folly." – Proverbs 13:16*

On the list in Galatians 5, as the last value mentioned but not the least important fruit of the Holy Spirit, is self-control.

What can we practice more intensely in our daily lives starting today?

Balance, dear ones, balance!

June 25

A FIRE OF STRAW OR A FIRE OF WOOD?

"When there is no wood, the fire goes out ..." – Proverbs 26:20

Straw ignites the fire but cannot sustain it. Wood, however, can ensure a long-lasting flame. Straw promises much but burns out quickly. Wood, on the other hand, offers the necessary endurance.

In the spiritual realm, we can use this comparison to ask ourselves, "Is my fire for Jesus made of straw or of wood?"

Typically, individuals who live Christianity only through the physical senses rely heavily on straw fire. Do not get me wrong! Straw is good, but if you do not have wood afterward, everything goes out. The fire from singing, preaching, uplifting meditation, or a touching testimony is good. But you cannot live only with these! After hearing a moving sermon on Sunday, you need to continue putting wood on the fire to keep it burning all week: fasting, private prayer, daily Bible reading, walking by faith. What good is it to have a beautiful Sunday, if during the rest of the week I am not ready to put the wood of my personal time to keep the flame burning?

People who are on the verge of death are often brought back to life through resuscitations. However, this does not help if that person, after recovering, does not eat, does not drink water, does not move, etc., to sustain his life. If they rely only on the fact that another resuscitation is coming in a few days, can we say that they have "life abundantly" (John 10:10)?

Too many Christians today live only with fires of straw. Someone told me, "Brother Cristi, I have come forward at the altar call 15 times so far!"

Oh, how easy it is to ignite a fire! Oh, but how hard it is to maintain that fire – whether it's the family fire or the spiritual fire. So much enthusiasm on the wedding day. So many flowers and hearts. And afterward, who puts the wood in the fire? Who sacrifices himself? Who takes the time for communication, for mutual assistance, for involvement?

Love without sacrifice is just passion. Christianity without continuous burning is just a mere religion.

I am so glad to see people who are enthusiastic about Jesus not only on Sundays at church but also at work, on Wednesdays.

With tears in their eyes not only during the fervent preaching of a pastor once a month but with tears on their cheeks in the company of orphans and widows when needed. People who burn not only on the day of baptism but also in the years of service that follow.

Too often we come with the attitude that someone else should put their wood on our fire. His preaching. His ministry. His money. His time. But what about you?

What have you put on the fire today? How is your fire? Have you let it turn to ashes, or are you still doing everything possible to keep the flame burning?

I do not want mine to go out. I do not want to resort to straw again. I do not want to start over.

I am going to put a few more logs on it.

I will come back later...

June 26

WHOM DO YOU WALK WITH?

"And Jephthah fled from his brothers and dwelt in the land of Tob; and worthless men banded together with Jephthah and went out raiding with him." – Judges 11:3

Jephthah had a period in his life when he preferred people without values over people with values. He chose to band with people of no account rather than staying close to his brothers. Other translations describe these "worthless men" as unscrupulous people, capable of any evil, rebellious individuals.

Our circle of friends influences us. Our character values are the average of the values of the five closest people in our lives – of those with whom we spend the most time or admire privately or publicly.

There is a big difference between making friends and choosing friends. There is a big difference between meeting someone and spending time with that person.

We, humans, were created to socialize and feel good in the company of other people. But this socialization is not without effects. It influences our language and thinking, our actions, and our values.

The prodigal son left his family to spend time with friends. He preferred to lose the closeness of his father in favor of the profligate. He chose to detach himself from the one who loved him unconditionally and attach himself to those who loved him for their gain. After losing everything in the company of sinful buddies, he eventually understood that true friends are rare. He realized that many who give you 'likes' while you have something in your wallet will not even give you a call when you are alone and bankrupt. He experienced firsthand what the wise Solomon said:

"Wealth brings many friends, but the poor is separated from his friend." – Proverbs 19:4

Our friendships today will define our values tomorrow. If you are in the company of God-fearing people, you will be a God-fearing person and will say like the Psalmist:

"I am a companion of all who fear You, and of those who keep Your precepts." – Psalms 119:63

Euripides said, "When you are unhappy, do not count on friends." Why? Because everyone crowds around you only when you are happy. When you celebrate success. When the wallet is thick...

I was amazed to see how many politicians and reporters recently associated themselves with the success of David Popovici[16] after he won two swimming competitions at the world championships. I am absolutely disgusted to see how many people are now writing about him, wishing to "parade" with his name after he "took" the gold. Where were these people when David woke up at 5 in the morning for training? They were probably turning on the "other side" and continuing their sleep...

David knew that if you want to train, you have to say *no* to strolling with people. If you want success on any level, you have to stay away from those who waste time and practice the sport called "giving opinions." David knew that if you want to excel, you have to stay away from mediocre people, from those who say, "You will not succeed! Forget it, others have tried and failed!" For an earthly medal, David made incredible efforts, both in organizing his time well and in choosing his friends wisely. He confessed that he spent most of his time with his father and his coach. David knew that if you waste time with those who love to sit around and eat popcorn, you will never have the gold cup in your hand.

Do you want to be a person of value? To reach the heavenly reward? To make the Coach happy? The One who "enlisted you as a soldier"? Then be careful with your circle of friends! Stay close to people who are by your side in "training," just as they are on the "competition" day.

Life is short. Time is valuable. The sand in the hourglass of our lives is flowing down second after second. Therefore, I will pay attention to whom I talk on the phone. With whom I communicate on social media. I will choose carefully the people to whom I respond. I will not waste my time with mockers. Nor with proud people. I will be selective. I will stay around wise people. Around those in my family whom God has entrusted to me. I want to be of real help to those who are truly my friends. I want to learn from humble people and from those who spend more time with God. I will stand by honest brethren.

I will not walk around with just anybody... You should do the same.

[16] A prominent Romanian swimmer, known for his remarkable achievements in freestyle swimming.

June 27

HONEY FROM THE HOLY WORD

"How sweet are Your words to my taste, sweeter than honey to my mouth!" – Psalms 119:103

If David took a spoonful of honey in the morning and then a verse from the Law, the taste of honey paled when compared to the taste of God's Word.

For some people, the Word is no longer like honey but bitter like grapefruit, because they have distanced themselves from Him and have found another kind of honey, like Samson's, from a carcass, a pleasure found in dead things.

But I recommend honey from the comb, like Jonathan, because our lives are often bitter with trials, suffering, and ridicule. The best remedy is a spoonful of honey from the Holy Word, in the morning, on an empty stomach.

And then the face cheers up, and the heart gains strength to fight another day.

When we start our day with the sweetness of God's Word, it sets a positive tone for all that follows. Just as honey provides natural energy and nourishment, so does scripture invigorate our spirits and minds. The wisdom and comfort found within the Bible's pages can uplift our souls, offering us strength and guidance throughout our daily challenges.

Moreover, sharing the honey of the Holy Word with others can spread its sweetness far and wide. When we encourage family, friends, and even strangers with the verses that have inspired us, we participate in a divine cycle of nourishment and growth. This spiritual honey not only enriches our lives but also fosters a community grounded in faith and love, turning bitterness into blessings.

Have you taken your spoonful of honey from the Bible's honeycomb today?

JUNE 28

GOOD DEEDS ARE NOT FORGOTTEN

"Then Peter arose and went with them. When he had come, they brought him to the upper room. And all the widows stood by him weeping, showing the tunics and garments which Dorcas had made while she was with them." – Acts 9:39

Honest and faithful people will forget what you did for yourself, but they will not forget what you did for them, in the Name of the Lord, with a heart full of love.

People will forget that you had a nice suit, but they will not forget if you bought them a nice suit.

People will forget that you had plenty of food, but they will not forget if you fed them.

People will forget that you had a refrigerator, but they will not forget if you bought them a refrigerator.

People will forget the size of your house, but they will not forget if you provided them shelter when they had none.

People will forget the car you drove, but they will not forget if you gave them a ride when they were stranded.

People will forget the vacations you took, but they will not forget if you helped them when they were in need of a break.

The most wonderful thing is for the answer to the prayers of others to come through you.

On the day of the funeral, it would be good if people cried with sadness because you have departed, and not be joyful that you did...

June 29

FROM "KNOWING" TO "DOING"

"I will show you whom he is like who comes to Me, hears My words, and DOES them." – Luke 6:47

The flawless speech of the doctor about your illness, the prescribed medications, and the stamped prescription do not help you at all if you do not follow the treatment.

The approval of the first house loan by the most renowned bank in Romania, the eloquent explanations of the clerk, and the signed contract do not help you at all if you do not have the necessary resources.

The best refrigerator in the world cannot satisfy you if you do not open it and eat the food inside.

The most expensive wallet is worthless if it is empty.

The best clothes have no value for you if they hang on the rack in the store.

You can have the keys to the most reliable car in the world, but if they are only for a test-drive car, it is useless for you.

Going to church, listening to the best sermons and songs do not help you at all if you do not fulfill the will of God.

Knowing about God is one thing, and walking with God is something else entirely. Calling yourself a Christian because it looks good in the census is one thing, and having your name written in the Book of Life is something else entirely.

We will be judged not by success but by faithfulness. Not by sacrifice but by obedience!

June 30

HORIZONTAL OR VERTICAL RELATIONSHIPS?

"Behold, I stand at the door and knock. If anyone hears My voice and opens the door, I will come in to him and dine with him, and he with Me." – Revelation 3:20

It is not bad at all to know people with influence, people who can put it a good word for you in a critical moment. People who can lend you a helping hand at a crossroads in life where you cannot find the right way out.

What is painful, however, is that the world seeks friends and relationships horizontally but forgets that the most important relationship they can have is vertical.

It is pointless to have connections with important people horizontally if you do not have a personal relationship with Jesus vertically.

What good is it to sit at the table with the most influential people in the world if you are not sitting at the table with Jesus?

At the end of history, it will not matter how many people you have known, but only if you have known the One who became Man for us and died for our sins at Calvary.

For when the trials of life come, it is not the horizontal connections that will sustain you, but the strength of your vertical relationship with the Savior.

True peace and fulfillment do not come from the accolades and acknowledgments of people but from the assurance of God's love and grace.

In the grand scheme of eternity, the depth of your vertical relationship will far outweigh the breadth of your horizontal ones.

July 1

COME WITH US!

Moses said to Hobab the son of Reuel the Midianite, Moses' father-in-law, "We are setting out for the place of which the Lord said, 'I will give it to you.' Come with us, and we will treat you well; for the Lord has promised good things to Israel." And he said to him, "I will not go, but I will depart to my own land and to my relatives." – Numbers 10:29-30

Jethro (also known as Hobab or Reuel) was Moses' father-in-law. Moses had worked for him for forty years before God sent him to Egypt to deliver the Israelites from the Egyptian slavery. After the miraculous exodus from Egypt, Jethro hastens to meet his son-in-law and is amazed by what he hears from him. The miracles of God and His divine intervention on behalf of the Jewish people had become known among all the surrounding nations.

After a while, Jethro wants to return to Midian, but his son-in-law tells him, "Come with us!" A call of faith! A call for Jethro to leave Midian and journey towards Canaan!

A call to which Jethro answered by excusing himself and saying, "I cannot...". Still, Moses insists:

"And if you go with us, indeed it shall be that whatever good the Lord will do to us, the same we will do to you." – Numbers 10:32

We do not know for certain whether Jethro was persuaded or not. Sometimes it is easier to make excuses than to change... What I do know is that the call is the same for you: "Come with us!"

Under the inspiration of the Holy Spirit, composer and poet Simion Buzduga[17] wrote:

We are journeying to the Promised Land
On the holy path of victory!
Jesus lovingly guides us
Like an eagle guarding its young.

---

[17] Simion Buzduga was born on April 29, 1961, in the village of Vicovu de Sus, Suceava County, Romania. Over time, he has served God through the talents received from above, being a book author, poet, composer, and talented conductor who founded several choir groups. He has also served as an elder and pastor both in Suceava County and in America; currently, he is serving in Romania.

O Canaan! O Canaan!
You are closer every year...
O Paradise! O my Land,
Soon I will enter you...

We have come out of the *Egypt* of this world. Out from under the bondage of sin. Out from under the power of the devil who tormented us every day with the lusts and desires of the world, but who would have eventually given us hell...

We have departed from *Egypt,* forgiven through the sacrifice of Jesus on Calvary for all we did there, and now we are heading towards the heavenly Canaan. It is true that it is not easy in the wilderness of this world. Every day we depend on God's resources and His guidance. There are challenges everywhere, and the temptation to give up tries to sneak up in many people`s hearts. But we continue to move forward. Why? Because...

> *"...we do not look at the things which are seen, but at the things which are not seen. For the things which are seen are temporary, but the things which are not seen are eternal." – 2 Corinthians 4:18*

Don't you want to come with us? Sooner or later, the wilderness will end. The weariness, trials, and hardships of life will cease, and then, in eternity, we will enjoy the presence of God and eternal rewards...

Yes, it is not easy! Scorching sand. Thirst. Occasionally, an oasis that appears for your soul... Sickness. Accidents. Unanswered questions. People staring at you. This is what happens to you in the world if you want to serve Jesus... But the Lord warned us beforehand.

We press on! And we cry out at every step to all those around us: *Come along! Come out of the mad rush of the world. Egypt will fall sooner or later, but Canaan is eternal!*

Streets of gold. Jasper stones. The river of life clear as crystal. The tree of life bearing twelve kinds of fruit. Angels and saints together. Choirs singing flawlessly. Tears wiped away forever. These are just fragments of what Canaan offers eternally.

Are you still thinking about it?

I urge you once again: Come with us!

JULY 2

THE VALUE OF SPEAKING WELL OF OTHERS

"Jonathan spoke well of David to Saul his father..." – 1 Samuel 19:4

Jonathan, who had the throne assured in terms of succession, spoke well of David to Saul, even though he had every reason to find faults and give Saul additional reasons to continue fighting against David. He could have been envious of David because he clearly saw how God was preparing him to ascend the throne. Yet, he spoke well of him. What an amazing character! What a good name!

He also could have remained silent and said nothing, neither good nor bad. Like Absalom:

"But Absalom spoke to Amnon neither good nor bad. For Absalom hated Amnon..." – 2 Samuel 13:22

No human being is able to see what is inside our hearts, but through the words we speak, they can discern what is within us.

It is not enough simply to decide not to speak ill of someone. We must decide to speak well of them.

A good person speaks well of others.

A wicked person speaks evil. Frustration, envy, lust, and many other spiritual viruses cause the wicked person to speak evil of others. However, they forget that when they throw mud, their hands also get dirty.

Today, we have the opportunity to speak well of someone. Tomorrow, the same.

And one day, this will become a habit that will say more about you than all of your friends combined could ever say.

July 3

PAINFUL "ROMANIAN" STATISTICS

"But when the Son of Man comes, will He really find faith on the earth?" – Luke 18:8

Did you know that 29.5% of Romanians do not believe in Resurrection, and 35% do not believe in life after death? And if we add the 12% of undecided Romanians, we reach conclusions that deeply concern us. This means that almost half of the Romanians live only for this life. Their thoughts extend only to the grave. They have only the desire to live life to the fullest in the present moment because everything ends at the grave anyway. They have the false impression that you can do whatever you want, because everything will be erased at the end of life...

What is even stranger is that in Romania, 99% of the people state that they are Christians. But what kind of Christians? Because the half that is left are Christians without resurrection. Christians without faith.

Christians without the Bible. How can you call yourself a Christian if you do not believe what the Bible says?

> *"For the Lord Himself will descend from heaven with a shout, with the voice of an archangel, and with the trumpet of God. And the dead in Christ will rise first. Then we who are alive and remain shall be caught up together with them in the clouds to meet the Lord in the air. And thus we shall always be with the Lord." – 1 Thessalonians 4:16-17*

In the last 50 years, over 24 million children have been killed in Romania. Every 5 minutes, an abortion takes place in Romania. A murder. Committed by one of the 99% of the people who declare themselves Christians, right?

Prisons are full. Do you know why? Because the churches have emptied. If the churches were filled, we would see the opposite effect: the prisons would empty.

In 1990, one in six marriages ended in divorce. In 2020, one in three couples end up in court to divide their assets and children. The washing machine and refrigerator are easy to divide. But what about the children? How do you handle that? Who will ever be able to measure the traumas of those fragile beings in whom the shock of their parents' separation leaves deep marks for the rest of their life?

We have more comfort than the people before us. State-of-the-art technology. Everything "at the touch of a button" in our homes. Fast cars. Better conditions. And yet, we have lost something... We have lost what was most important...

We have lost the "Lord's Prayer" that used to be recited in schools. We have lost the greeting "God bless you!". We have replaced the city entrance signs that used to say, "God bless you!" with the EU emblem. We have lost common sense and respect that used to accompany the fear of God.

We have lost shame. We clearly see how much shame Romanians have from the way in which they dress. People have lost the shame of cohabitation with a partner, without making a marital covenant. The shame of talking back to your parents is also about to disappear. The shame of making promises by the thousands in electoral campaigns and then running the country without fulfilling any of them can surely be declared "null". The Romanian looks you in the eyes, while you see clearly that he is lying, and you wait for his cheeks to blush. But you wait in vain.

We have lost trust in each other. The Christian who is a Christian only on paper is no longer a man of his word. You lend them money and you never see it again. Hypocrisy is at home in Romania. A pound of tomatoes is worth more than the word of many Romanian people. The promise of most *Christians* today is not worth $.50.

We have lost courage – the courage we need to call sin by its name. The courage to live with dignity at school and at work. To speak about God and to live with God. To raise children with the Bible in hand. We have lost that courage not to lie, but to speak the truth regardless of the consequences. To "have a backbone" in every moment of our lives. We have always fooled ourselves with the phrase "a bowed head does not get chopped off by the sword" and thus we have become hunchbacked. We bow our heads before anyone. We accept any law. We accept any person. We have lost our head without even realizing it.

We have lost silence. We remained silent when we should have spoken, and we spoke when we should have remained silent. We talk incessantly. Unending conversations. We have started to idolize the phone and hate the book. Teenagers "talk" a lot, but through emojis and *likes.* Out of ten pages of conversations, I do not think there is one sentence from which you could learn something. We socialize a lot, but we are increasingly lonely.

The statistics worry us. What will tomorrow look like? How bleak will the future be if there are increasing differences between what we say and what we do?

When the light goes out, darkness comes in naturally. When practicing Christians fade away, the non-practicing ones flood the space. They just did not declare themselves atheists because it does not look good on the census.

But in their hearts, they are still without God. And the person who lives without God is capable of anything...

Jesus does not seek inflated statistics. Nor holy days on the calendar. Nor saints on the walls of churches. Jesus seeks true faith. And that faith dwells in people who are Christians every day. People who truly believe. Who not only talk the talk, but also walk the walk – the creed that for most Romanians ends like this: *"I look forward to the resurrection of the dead and the afterlife."*

JULY 4

THE LAW OF CAUSE AND EFFECT

"Do not be deceived, God is not mocked; for whatever a man sows, that he will also reap." – Galatians 6:7

At the moment of creation, God established a universal law, a simple yet extremely important law, namely: for every effect, there is a cause.

This law demonstrates that there is no such thing as luck in life. Victory and success are not accidents, but rather the results of steps (causes) that you have taken diligently in a previous period.

Nature is neutral. The earth is neutral. It does not look at you as a person, at how much money you have, what kind of connections you have, or what diplomas you have obtained. It does not look at whether you have blue or green eyes, blond or brunette hair. The ground, regardless of who you are, will yield what you have sown. Did you plant corn? You will reap corn. If you did not plant anything, you will have weeds and thistles.

Many people live in a world of excuses. They complain daily, are pessimistic, blame fate, and do nothing. That is why they encounter thorns that grow in the field of a lazy man.

We, humans, are all created equal. None of us was created with supernatural powers. None of us was created with the ability to plant tomatoes and harvest cucumbers. No one can have a rich harvest by being on the phone and staring at the unsown garden soil.

What sets us apart? Action. Sowing. Sweat. Effort. Goal. The purpose for which we live.

Today is a summer day. The sun does nothing but bring to ripeness what you planted a few months ago.

It is the same in life: whatever a man sows, that he will also reap...

Do you want a rich harvest? An outstanding effect? Work on the cause, on the sowing, and the fruit will be commensurate.

July 5

MUTUAL LOVE

In a marriage, it is not enough for just the husband to love his wife or just the wife to love her husband. Mutual love is essential, forming the foundation of a strong and lasting relationship, fostering trust and understanding.

We know that each of us is valuable to God. We are His creation, His offspring:

> *"Therefore, since we are the offspring of God, we ought not to think that the Divine Nature is like gold or silver or stone, something shaped by art and man's devising." – Acts 17:29*

This reminds us of our worth and the intimate relationship we share with our Creator. To reach Heaven, it is not enough for God alone to love us. This love must be mutual. Our faith journey is a partnership with the Divine, where we actively choose to love and follow Him.

Similarly, a thriving marriage requires both partners to actively love one another. It's a continuous exchange of affection, respect, and support, reflecting the mutual love God desires from us. Mutual love means sharing joys and sorrows, supporting each other's dreams, and growing together in faith.

Just as we respond to God's love by loving Him back, in marriage, both partners must continually nurture their love for one another. This mutual commitment strengthens the bond and creates a resilient union.

Let us strive for mutual love in our relationships and with God, fulfilling our purpose to love and be loved in return.

July 6

THE JOY OF SALVATION AND THE JOY OF SERVICE

"The seventy returned with joy, saying, 'Lord, even the demons are subject to us in Your name.' And He said to them, 'Nevertheless do not rejoice in this, that the spirits are subject to you, but rather rejoice because your names are written in heaven.'" – Luke 10:17,20

We feel a pleasant sensation when we do something for God, when we intercede for someone, when we visit a sick person, when we send some money to a family in need.

Let us not forget that what God has done for us, by sending His Son to die for our sins, will never be equaled by what we can do for Him.

Therefore, the joy of salvation is paramount. It must be accompanied by the joy of service, but it should never be inferior to it.

The joy of salvation should always be greater than the joy of service.

What God has done for you is greater than what you can do for Him.

The attitude of a true Christian does not involve boasting about what he does for the Lord, but rather constantly praising His name, as a sign of gratitude for the gifts received from Him.

I am glad that I serve, but I am even more glad that I am saved.

Do you have both these joys?

July 7

FAITHFUL

We would like God not to abandon us in the difficult moments of life, but are we ready not to abandon Him when we need to testify about Him?

The Plain of Dura is the place where you must stand up for God, while your colleagues kneel daily before their idols. It is a battleground of faith, where your commitment to God is put to the test amid the pressures to conform.

The Plain of Dura is the place where people question your faith, mock you for choosing God, and where you continue not to be ashamed of His name. Here, your unwavering loyalty to God is displayed for all to see, demonstrating the strength of your convictions.

In the Plain of Dura, your faithfulness to God becomes visible. In the fiery furnace, the faithfulness of God to you becomes evident. It is in these moments of trial and testing that God's presence and protection shine brightest, affirming His promises to those who stand firm.

The Bible speaks a great truth:

"Therefore whoever confesses Me before men, him I will also confess before My Father who is in heaven. But whoever denies Me before men, him I will also deny before My Father who is in heaven." – Matthew 10:32-33

When we remain faithful before men, Jesus promises to remain faithful to us before the Father. This mutual faithfulness is a testament to the strength of our relationship with God. Our public declaration of faith is not just a duty but a profound opportunity to align ourselves with God's unwavering love and commitment, knowing that He stands with us in every trial.

July 8

DO YOU HAVE NUMBER 1 IN FRONT?

"One of the servants answered and said, 'Look, I have seen a son of Jesse the Bethlehemite, who is skillful in playing, a mighty man of valor, a man of war, prudent in speech, and a handsome person; and the Lord is with him.'" – 1 Samuel 16:18

The story goes that a young girl came to her father and said, "Dad, I found an amazing guy!" The father took a sheet of paper and a pen and asked the girl to list the qualities of that young man. She began to say, "He is handsome." And the father wrote a zero on the paper. "He is respectful." And the father added another zero. "He is intelligent." And the father added yet another zero... Puzzled, the girl asked, "Dad, why are you putting all those zeros when I am listing such outstanding qualities?" The father asked, "Does he have God with him? Is he a believer, a young man who fears the Lord?" And the girl replied, "Oh, yes!" Then the father put the number 1 in front of those many zeros...

The father continued, "You see, every quality you mentioned is special.

But these qualities have no value unless God is first, in front of all of them. What gives value to a person is his relationship with God."

When the Spirit of God departed from Saul, another spirit came. Why? Because when the cup of life is empty of the presence of God, it will soon be filled with the presence of demons. Seeing the desperate situation, the servants all came up with a suggestion that seemed very good at first glance:

"Let our master now command your servants, who are before you, to seek out a man who is a skillful player on the harp. And it shall be that he will play it with his hand when the distressing spirit from God is upon you, and you shall be well." – 1 Samuel 16:16

The servants wanted to find a special young man. Talented. With a terrific voice. Skilled at playing the harp. And yet, it was not enough. A wise servant understood that the spirits do not get scared if someone can sing like a baritone. This servant understood that the Devil does not flee if someone can play any song on the piano flawlessly, with their eyes closed. That is why this servant listed David's "zeroes" (he can sing, he is also a mighty man of valor, a warrior, speaks well, he is handsome) which became values only after, at the end, he added that number 1 in front:

"And the Lord is with him." – 1 Samuel 16:18

Oh, how many beautiful young people we have! How many valiant people who speak well! Beautiful from head to toes. Swift as deer. Intelligent. They can vocalize for hours. They can list all the capitals of the world, that`s the kind of memory they have. They have been endowed with these gifts since birth. And yet, how many of them use the gift that God has given them, to His glory?

This is why talent is not enough. Nor is cleverness. Nor height. Nor beauty. All the gifts you have are special, but not sufficient. There are so many people singing in clubs... So many dedicating their lives to the Untold[18]... So many selling their bodies for a flattering "I love you"... So many talented young people in the arms of the Devil because they have not understood that it is not enough to be endowed with special gifts – you must have an authentic relationship with God and use those gifts for His glory.

When the prodigal son left his father with the inheritance in his pocket, everything he received became a curse for him. The same money that was a blessing for his father turned him into a prodigal, when he remained with zeros without the 1 in front.

Money, health, time, life, relationships are beautiful. But if you use them without God, they will destroy both your life and your eternity. However, if you acknowledge that God has given them to you and you listen to Him every step of the way, He will guide you so that these values are a blessing for you and for those around you.

Thank you, Lord, for all the gifts you have given us. For everything you have put in us... But help us not to forget the number 1 in front...

---

[18] Music festival that takes place annually in the city of Cluj-Napoca, Romania, having over 100.000 young people in attendance.

July 9

LISTEN FIRST, SPEAK LAST!

"You know this, my beloved brethren. But let every man be swift to hear, slow to speak, slow to wrath..." – James 1:19

Speaking in haste is a significant temptation for anyone.

However, it is wise to keep our ears open when we need to listen to what our neighbor is saying.

It might be that a person who seems insignificant in your eyes will give you meaningful advice.

You might hear the cry of an orphan, a widow, or the silent weeping of an elderly person.

It could be that, when you are truly ready to listen, God will speak to you through someone.

It might be that, when you are swift to *listen,* in a group of people, you will learn things you would not have heard from your peers if you had rushed to *speak.*

We often rush to speak and leave the listening for later. Then we realize that we have spoken what we should not have.

The Apostle James offers exceptionally wise advice: "*listen first, speak last.*"

When you speak last, you have the chance to quietly listen to everything everyone else has said, carefully consider it, and only then express your opinion or offer your advice.

July 10

SPIRITUAL SENSORS

"The Lord will guide you continually, and satisfy your soul in drought, and strengthen your bones; you shall be like a watered garden, and like a spring of water, whose waters do not fail." – Isaiah 58:11

When I was in kindergarten, we played an interesting game: one child was blindfolded, and another one hid a toy that had been shown to everyone before. After the whole group saw where the toy was hidden, the game began. The blindfolded child started searching for the toy. As the child approached the hiding spot, the others would shout, "fire, fire, fire." When the child moved away from the object, the children would shout, "water, water, water." The game continued until the toy was found, and then it restarted with another child.

This game was nothing more than a game based on sensors. However, these sensors were not technological but imaginary. Approaching or moving away from a particular place gave the blindfolded child a way to approximate the hiding place.

Our lives are filled with hiding places. In some, we find beautiful things. In others, venomous *snakes* are ready to bite us. In some places to which we are guided by our *sensors*, we find oases of water in the midst of the world's *desert*. In others, we find deserts like the Sahara, and we unknowingly move away from the *palm trees* where we would have found shade and the joy of a cool place for our souls.

Technology has invented motion sensors. Rain sensors. Distance sensors. Cars that can automatically brake when the sensor detects a nearby danger. Alarms that can be triggered when an intruder is detected in a specific place at a certain time. However, these sensors are useful only as long as they are clean. They may not be defective, but if, for example, mud has covered the car`s distance sensor, that sensor will no longer be able to detect anything else because it cannot pass through the obstacle that has covered it.

The sensor that God has placed in us since birth is our conscience. It serves as a guide during our lives. Over the years, everyone's conscience becomes tainted. If a person does not personally encounter Jesus Christ, his conscience will become increasingly "dulled." The sensor that once told them that stealing an eraser is not a good thing will no longer function, not even if he steals a truck. The sensor that was recently triggered by a lie, causing a blush in his cheeks, will malfunction to the point where the person will lie and smile while promising you the world.

Repentance and being born again act as a reset for the internal sensors. Everything that has malfunctioned over the years is renewed, as Paul says:

"That you put off, concerning your former conduct, the old man which grows corrupt according to the deceitful lusts, and be renewed in the spirit of your mind..." – Ephesians 4:22-23

Then, when you are filled of the Spirit of God, another sensor is added to these spiritual sensors: **guidance.**

"For as many as are led by the Spirit of God, these are sons of God." – Romans 8:14

Under the imprint of the Divine Word and under the guidance of the Spirit placed by God in us, this sensor will help us navigate slippery roads, hiding places with "snakes," pitfalls of compromise, and many other places where the Devil seeks to destroy us.

These renewed sensors must be kept clean every day. Through prayer, reading the Bible, fellowship with those who also take care of their sensors, the ability to detect intruders increases, and our proximity to Heaven becomes more evident. Inner alarms are triggered for an inappropriate word, a bad joke, or even a tiny bit of envy. These spiritual *sensors* transform our soul (mind, reason, and will) and give our personality a Christ-like character.

Samson had extraordinary promises regarding the journey ahead. However, because, step by step, he got closer to the Philistines and refused to listen to the sensors of the Holy Spirit, his conscience was "dulled". He reached a point where, when Delilah asked about being *tied* and *overcome,* nothing was activated in his conscience. He was on the edge of the abyss, and the sensors were not functioning at all! Eventually, he ended up bound and imprisoned to the enemies. Not only were his spiritual sensors killed by his negligence, but he also lost his eyes, the most powerful physical sensors he had.

"Delilah said to Samson, 'Please tell me where your great strength lies, and with what you may be bound to afflict you.'" – Judges 16:6

How about your own spiritual sensors? Does the Holy Spirit still convict you of the "little foxes that spoil the vines in bloom"? Do you still feel regret for speaking when you should have been silent? Does an alarm still go off when your eyes wander to a place where they should not look?

Take great care of your sensors! A beautiful car without brakes ends up over the cliff. An expensive house without an alarm becomes prey to robbers. And a person's soul without the guidance of the Holy Spirit ends up forever in the *lake of fire.*

Ask God today for a renewal of your mind, your thoughts, your speech. Drawing near to Him and His Divine intervention will reset the senses that God has placed in you. The water of the Word will remove the mud deposited on the sensors and make them functional again.

And when others choose evil, you will choose good. When others choose cursing, you will choose blessing. When others choose death, you will suddenly hear something you have not heard since childhood: "Fire, fire, fire!"

July 11

JESUS CHRIST IS THE LORD!

"And that every tongue should confess that Jesus Christ is Lord, to the glory of God the Father." – Philippians 2:11

A close-knit family recently went through a tough trial. As they were waiting for the birth of their fourth child, a baby girl (after having three boys), complications appeared during pregnancy. At the last checkup, a little time after the seventh month, the doctor mentioned it would be a premature birth but assured them that everything was going to be fine. However, the following Sunday, the mother, sensing that the baby had not moved for a while, went for another checkup with her husband. On the way, the husband tried to comfort his worried wife, saying, "The Lord is in control of this situation. Let us pray that we can accept His will. Jesus Christ is Lord."

The woman went inside the waiting room, while her husband returned to the car.

After a few hours, the doctor delivered the heartbreaking news to the mother: "The baby girl has died." After having three boys, the family was especially looking forward to having a baby girl. Her birth would have brought immense joy, but in His sovereignty, God chose to take her to Himself. Upon receiving the painful news, the mother sent this text message to her husband: "Our little girl has gone home. Jesus Christ is Lord."

I was deeply moved to tears when I heard this testimony. Do you know why? Because there still are people who acknowledge that the God who gives is also the God who has the right to take away. That the God who offers can also take back. That the God who takes you up the mountains may also lead you through deep valleys.

Later, the baby's mother wrote on the family chat group: "Our little girl was born, but she was born for eternity... Praise be to God for everything!"

I am moved when I encounter such extraordinary testimonies because I have met people who, for a toothache, cursed God. People who spit out curses because they lost a twenty dollar bill. Individuals whom God blessed with health and who never thanked Him for it yet became frustrated and angry with the Creator when their health was lost.

Are we aware that the God who gives can also take away? Cotton Mather, a 17th-century Puritan, lost 13 out of the 15 children that God gave him.

Additionally, he became a widower twice. Despite going through all these hardships, whenever he lost a loved one, he knelt down with tears in his eyes and accepted God's will.

Can you say, "Jesus Christ is Lord"? Can you say it like Job?

"The Lord gave, and the Lord has taken away; blessed be the name of the Lord." – Job 1:21

We have become accustomed to a God who fills our refrigerator. Can we accept a day when the pantry is empty and still praise Him?

We have grown accustomed to a well-paid job. Will we still praise Him when we end up on unemployment benefits?

We have become accustomed to having a healthy child. But if God gives you a sick one, how will you relate to Him?

Recently, I attended the funeral of the 36-year-old wife of one of my colleagues at the company where I work. Two daughters, aged 5 and 9, were left orphans. Camelia, with cancer throughout her body, served in Sunday School until a month before her death. She made sandwiches for homeless children until she fell ill and went to the hospital for her final treatment. She always had a smile on her face and never complained about her physical illness.

At the end of the funeral service, I sat on the curb of another grave, next to my colleague, Cosmin. We cried together, looking at the fresh flowers placed on his wife's grave.

There, in the cemetery, where every dream ends, where every plan comes to a close, both of us acknowledged, tissues in hand and teary-eyed, that the God who gives also has the right to take away.

Do you know where the secret lies?

If we do not thank Him for the good weather, we will not be able to thank Him for the storm. If we do not acknowledge Him when we are healthy, we will not be able to accept the moment when our health is taken away. If we do not walk with Him on the mountain, what will we do without His presence in the valley of the shadow of death?

Umbrellas are made on sunny days but are opened in the rain – if you have acquired one in time... If you have a strong and sovereign God when the sea is calm around your boat, He will still be there when the storm comes.

Jesus Christ is Lord...

July 12

DO YOU UNDERSTAND WHAT YOU ARE READING?

"So Philip ran to him, and heard him reading the prophet Isaiah, and said, 'Do you understand what you are reading?'" – Acts 8:30

There are over 130 million unique books worldwide. Considering the average lifespan of 79 years, for a person to read all the existing books, he would need to read 1.8 million books each year, a practically impossible feat.

Nevertheless, we read. More or less often, books come into our hands, and we either skim through them hastily or read them attentively. The information conveyed by these books enters our minds, influencing our imagination, our creativity, and even our day-to-day life decisions.

Is it necessary to be selective in this domain? Should we filter what we buy and what we do not? What we read on electronic devices or in printed books? Certainly!

Reading influences us. Our values can change due to reading, and our perspective on life can be profoundly affected by what we read.

The famous Ethiopian was reading from the book of the prophet Isaiah, one of the 66 books of the Bible. Even though he did not understand anything, he kept on reading. His soul longed for a fulfillment that his position, wealth, and possessions could not provide. The fact that he read the right thing changed his life.

The Bible is the book that, by the grace of God, we have in printed form. The first complete translation of the Bible into Romanian was made in 1688. For centuries, people could not read the Bible in their native language! They attended church and listened to its reading in Slavic and Latin, understanding very little.

How blessed we are to have the Bible on the internet, on our phones, and on our shelves. By reading it, we can also have it in our hearts.

In Hunedoara[19] County, in the year 2022, a brother passed away at the age of 72. Until the age of 45, he had only read the Bible twice. At 45, after passing through a serious illness, he made new decisions to draw closer to God, and from the age of 45 to 72, he read the Bible 157 times.

---

[19] A county in Romania, located in the Transylvania region.

In the USA, in California, the mother of a friend, a retired lady in her 70s, had read the Bible 137 times when I visited her son in 2021.

This is another remarkable proof that those who love God also love His Word. Through prayer, we speak to God, and through reading the Bible, He speaks to us.

Oh, how many alternatives the Devil has to draw us away from Scripture! I notice with pain so many people who read science fiction, romance novels, detective stories, etc., without knowing that these novels are written under the influence of demonic spirits that have negative effects on those who read them. If the information we allow into our minds is not pure and true, it will affect our thoughts and experiences, leading us out from under God's protection. I personally know young people who drifted away from God after reading philosophy and psychology.

It is essential to keep only the Word of the Scripture as the foundation of the literature we peruse. The Divine Word is the basis for all life choices. If you read the Bible, you will be blessed with spiritual discernment and heavenly wisdom at every step of life and you will be able to stay away from sin:

"I have hidden your word in my heart that I might not sin against you." – Psalm 119:11

First, read the Bible. Then study it. Meditate on it. Finally, it is desirable to memorize it. When our minds are filled with God's Word, the whispers of the Devil find no place to enter.

"All Scripture is given by inspiration of God, and is profitable for doctrine, for reproof, for correction, for instruction in righteousness." – 2 Timothy 3:16

By reading the Scriptures, we will be taught. We will be cautioned and corrected. We will become wiser and prepared for the works that God wants to do through us and with us:

"That the man of God may be complete, thoroughly equipped for every good work." – 2 Timothy 3:17

Certainly, you can comfortably explore other Christian books. But only after you have read the Bible at least once – so that you can select books written by people who walk with God every day. People who live what they write. Who have a relationship with God and write under the inspiration of the Holy Spirit.

Do you understand what you read? Are you selective about what you read?

Do you have access only to information or also to revelation?

Let us read! But let us read only what is valuable! Life is too short to engage with the rest...

JULY 13

THE MANDATORY SPORTS OF A CHRISTIAN: ROCK CLIMBING

"All who compete in the games go into strict training. They do it to get a crown that will not last, but we do it to get a crown that will last forever." – 1 Corinthians 9:25

Spiritual life resembles physical life in many ways. In the above verse, Paul showed us that athletes have certain rules to follow and endure certain disciplines to be accepted in the game. In the end, they receive a medal that gathers dust over the years. In heaven, however, we will receive medals for eternity if we play by the heavenly rules in spiritual sports.

One of the mandatory sports for every Christian is *spiritual rock climbing,* manifested through the desire to reach heights and overcome the obstacles of ascent to ultimately enjoy the magnificent view:

"From the end of the earth I will cry to You, when my heart is overwhelmed; lead me to the rock that is higher than I." – Psalm 61:2

When many settle for a one-minute prayer a day, you are called to be an intercessor! When most step back, you are called to stand in the gap. When most stay at the barbecue in the plains, you are called to mountain training...

Moses was a strong climber. He spent 40 years in Egypt, then 40 years in the school of the wilderness. In the last year of the wilderness, he said: *Let me try something more! Let me go beyond the comfort zone!*

"Moses was tending the flock of Jethro his father-in-law, the priest of Midian. And he led the flock to the back of the desert, and came to Horeb, the mountain of God." – Exodus 3:1

When you desire more from a spiritual point of view, you will encounter the burning bush of God! You will discover your calling. You will hear your name called, and you will understand that there is a higher purpose for which you live.

Not long after, Moses ascended **Mount Sinai**. There, he received from God the commandments. These are laws that are not pleasing to the world. However, we forget that without rules, chaos ensues. In the stands, supporters may choose to behave as they please, but on the field, the athletes follow clear rules.

Moses also climbed **Mount Nebo**. It was his final ascent. From there, God showed him the earthly Canaan into which he did not get to enter. Yet, we understand from the event of the transfiguration during the life of the Lord Jesus that Moses entered the heavenly Canaan.

I challenge you today to desire more from this life. We were not created just to build a house, plant tomatoes in a greenhouse, or lay tiles in the bathroom. We were created to serve as a praise of His glory and fulfill the plan He made for us.

I did not say that rock climbing is an easy sport. Not at all! It is risky. Climbers often need climbing ropes, sometimes jugs, slings and cords. Similarly, spiritual mountaineers need faith, consecration, fasting, and prayer to climb higher and aim for loftier goals. They need sweat, effort, self-control from worldly pleasures, and reliance solely on God.

I conclude with the words of Jim Elliot, spoken shortly before he went to the Auca tribe and died as a martyr: “Father, make of me a crisis man. Bring those I contact to decision. Let me not be a milepost on a single road; make me a fork, that men must turn one way or another on facing Christ in me.”

He desired spiritual heights, not just a warm seat in church, not just a name on a membership list. He wanted to be a mountaineer climbing towards new summits.

Prepare yourself for the next mountain to climb.

It is visible on the horizon.

July 14

THE MANDATORY SPORTS OF A CHRISTIAN: BOXING

"So I run, not with uncertainty. I box, not as one beating the air." – 1 Corinthians 9:26

Someone once said that the most harmful additives are not in processed meats but within us. I believe there is truth in that.

As long as we live in our human nature, we have to fight an ongoing battle. Not with neighbors, not with in-laws or parents. The greatest struggle is with ourselves. In order to overcome our old habits, we need continuous training in what I call: **boxing with the flesh.**

The fact that God has forgiven you of sins does not mean the fight is over. The new birth is an event, and then comes sanctification, an ongoing process.

The Holy Spirit, along with God's Word and our spirit (awakened and brought to life by the other two), engage in a continuous battle with our soul with the purpose of transforming it.

Before conversion, my will was following my own ideas and whatever seemed right to me. After conversion, my will must submit to God's will. This requires daily *boxing*.

My desires before conversion were sinful. I enjoyed what God disapproved of. I felt, loved, and followed instincts that tainted my life. Now, I must love what God loves. And God loves humility, modesty, piety, gratitude, and more.

My reasoning before conversion was a place where sinful thoughts gathered for counsel. Then, based on those thoughts, I was speaking and acting according to the world's sinful commands. Since conversion, Paul says:

> *"Now this I say and testify in the Lord, that you must no longer walk as the Gentiles do, in the futility of their minds. They are darkened in their understanding, alienated from the life of God because of the ignorance that is in them, due to their hardness of heart." – Ephesians 4:17-18*

Even if you have repented and started a new life, various thoughts will still come knocking at the door of your mind. Invitations to sin, desires for revenge against those who wronged you, replies with a tone as demanding as those who shout at you, and many more.

Do you desire victory? Do you seek more daily sanctification? Do you long for long-term victories? Do not forget about boxing. Punch! But not other people; punch yourself. Bite your tongue, if necessary, but endure! Always speak the truth, even if it causes you to suffer! Turn the other cheek, even if it hurts!

Pray for your enemies! Do good to those who dislike you! Bless those who prepare snares for you!

The person who fights with himself will never be defeated.

You cannot fight on two fronts: against yourself and against others. If you do, you will spare yourself and punch them. You will end up doing what mockers do: "personal attacks," words of insult, being merciful with yourself but *just* with others... You may win some battles, but what good is it if you ultimately lose the war?

> *"I discipline my body and bring it into subjection, lest, when I have preached to others, I myself should become disqualified." – 1 Corinthians 9:27*

When you feel that your human nature is asserting its rights, give it a day of fasting.

When you sense that pride is surfacing, impose silence on yourself as a punishment. When temptation seems too close, run away!

I read about kings who conquered empires but could not conquer themselves. Great men who won immense territories but lost their families due to sins of immorality. Renowned names that gained millions of 'likes' but could not control themselves when faced with the temptation of drugs.

Samson killed a lion weighing about 400 lbs., but he was defeated by a *lioness* named Delilah, probably not weighing more than 130 lbs. He carried gates weighing hundreds of pounds on his shoulders but could not hold a secret. He used a donkey jawbone to kill a thousand men, yet a hairdresser turned him from a king into a miller. From a free man into a prisoner. He used his fists always for others but never for himself.

Self-control comes after years of boxing with your own flesh.

You cannot acquire "cold blood" by standing next to an iceberg; it becomes that way after years of boxing with yourself.

Self-control can turn a slave into a king. Its absence will turn a king into a slave.

I stop here.

Today`s training starts in a few minutes...

JULY 15

THE MANDATORY SPORTS OF A CHRISTIAN: ATHLETICS

"I have fought the good fight, I have finished the race, I have kept the faith." – 2 Timothy 4:7

Our journey with God is a marathon that takes many years, not a 2-minute sprint. In a marathon, everyone starts with enthusiasm, but few finish with flair. Both the marathon's distance and its direction must be considered. It is pointless to have great speed if you are running in the wrong direction. In a marathon, the direction is more important than the speed...

In the end, everyone runs. But some, as the apostle stated, run towards debauchery, immorality, and sin. And while running in the wrong direction, they collide with those running correctly:

"They are surprised that you do not run with them in the same flood of dissipation, speaking evil of you." – 1 Peter 4:4

After leaving the marathon of sinful living and transferring to the marathon of faith, let's not forget that one of the most crucial qualities in an athlete's life is perseverance. It is that strong desire to win or at least to continue until the end:

"Therefore, my beloved, as you have always obeyed, not as in my presence only, but now much more in my absence, work out your own salvation with fear and trembling." – Philippians 2:12

Salvation is received as a gift but is maintained through the daily race with God.

Paul is aware that the prize is awarded at the end, not in the middle of the marathon.

"Not that I have already attained, or am already perfected; but I press on, that I may lay hold of that for which Christ Jesus has also laid hold of me. I press toward the goal for the prize of the upward call of God in Christ Jesus." – Philippians 3:12, 14

The length of the marathon varies for each individual. For some, it is 36 years; for others, it is 70. But neither the distance nor a good start is enough. The most important thing is to cross the finish line well.

After running to fellowship meetings, to church services, to widows and orphans, to rehearsals, to evangelism nights, to soup kitchens for children, and to wherever God sends you, you will have eternal joy, and you will feel that the race was worth it.

Do not stop! Do not say, 'I give up!' Do not let any sin stop you! The devil is furious with you because you switched teams! He will try to put many obstacles in your way, but you keep going! He will continue with various gossips and insults, trying to make you stop. He knows that the years you lose fighting with mockers will drain your strength, and it will be so hard to return to the race.

Instead of running shoes, I recommend what Paul said:

> *"And having shod your feet with the preparation of the gospel of peace." – Ephesians 6:15*

For thirst, the water of the Word is recommended. The soul needs it. Not even the best athlete can run without water.

For inspiration, I recommend looking at those who have already finished the race. Do not get inspired by losers! Nor by those sitting in the stands. Get inspired by those who have reached the finish line with honors:

> *"Remember those who rule over you, who have spoken the word of God to you, whose faith follow, considering the outcome of their conduct." – Hebrews 13:7*

Draw inspiration from people who died in faith, not from those in whom faith died. From people who chose to die running rather than live sitting. They await us on the other side:

> *"After these things I looked, and behold, a great multitude which no one could number, of all nations, tribes, peoples, and tongues, standing before the throne and before the Lamb, clothed with white robes, with palm branches in their hands." – Revelation 7:9*

I conclude with the words of a great, world-renown marathon runner: "In every marathon, there is a crucial moment. A moment when you can stop, give up, or say, 'I will keep going no matter what.'"

Keep going!

You do not have to be so tough that you do not feel the pain. But you do have to be strong enough never to give up...

July 16

THE WORLD VS. THE CHURCH OF CHRIST

"I have given them Your word, and the world has hated them because they are not of the world, just as I am not of the world." – John 17:14

The purpose of the Church is to become less like the world and more like Jesus every day.

The world moves towards division; Jesus calls the Church to unity.

The world harbors hatred; the Church is called to love.

The world finds pleasure in sin; the Church lives in holiness.

The world points fingers and judges; the Church bends down and embraces.

The world emphasizes the external and what is visible; the Church invests in the internal, in the immortal soul.

The world thinks about Heaven but lives for hell; the Church thinks about Heaven and lives for Heaven.

The world heads towards judgment day, carrying its own sins; the Church heads towards the heavenly wedding, carrying its longing for the One who has forgiven its sins.

The world seeks comfort in material wealth; the Church finds peace in spiritual richness.

The world promotes self-reliance; the Church relies on God's providence and grace.

The world chases after fleeting moments of happiness; the Church abides in the eternal joy of the Lord.

Are you part of the world or part of the Church of Christ?

July 17

THE CHURCH NEEDS FRUIT-BEARING TREES, NOT ORNAMENTAL TREES...

"But the fruit of the Spirit is love, joy, peace, longsuffering, kindness, goodness, faithfulness, gentleness, self-control. Against such there is no law." – Galatians 5:22-23

The weary traveler will not stop to take a picture of an ornamental tree but will surely take a break for a delightful snack by a tree full of fruit.

How many people have tasted from your LOVE? In how many hearts have you sown PEACE? How many people have been 'contaminated" by your JOY? How many times have you REFRAINED from gossip? How many times have you exercised LONGSUFFERING without complaining? How many times have you given as much as you wished to receive (KINDNESS)?

How many times have you done GOOD without any hidden agenda? How many times have you been GENTLE when you had the chance to be angry?

Repentance without fruit is like a spring without water, like a barn without grain, like a rose without fragrance.

The Bible speaks of fruit, MUCH fruit, and MORE fruit. Never too much fruit. May our fruit endure! Because the apple can get spoiled just before it is harvested...

One day, the difference will not be made by the car, the house, or the bank account but by the FRUIT OF THE SPIRIT.

Today is a new day when you can place even greater value on fruit – on character, on the inner person, on things that are not visible but have a significant impact when brought to the surface through the deeds of faith.

July 18

SUCCESS

The greatest challenge in life is success.

Why? Because when you reach the top, if you look down and then at yourself, you will be tempted to be full of pride. If you look down and then up, you will feel gratitude pulsating in your heart.

Our lives are sprinkled with all kinds of achievements, some bigger, some smaller.

It is true that we sacrificed for them. We worked, sweated, started from scratch more than once, and arrived where we are today.

But let us not forget that we could not have done anything without God. Every heartbeat is proof that He is the One who sustains life. Every conceived thought and every accomplished plan testify to this: our brains were structured by a great Architect. Every step we take is a sign that Someone gives meaning and power to our bodies.

Therefore, when we reach the 'top' in life, let us not forget to look ahead with confidence and backward with gratitude.

Success *without* God breeds pride and arrogance. Success *with* God breeds humility and gratitude.

In moments of triumph, remember who guided you through the trials. In times of glory, acknowledge the One who never left your side.

True success is measured not by what we achieve, but by how closely we walk with God in every achievement.

You choose!

July 19

THE LESSON OF THE WHEAT GRAIN

"Most assuredly, I say to you, unless a grain of wheat falls into the ground and dies, it remains alone; but if it dies, it produces much grain." – John 12:24

When you are a child, you must listen to your parent!

When you are a student, you must listen to your teacher!

When you are an employee, you must listen to your employer!

When you are a Christian, you must listen to Christ!

This obedience involves the death of your own self in order to make room for the will of the One who teaches you. Such learning may humble or displease you for a moment, but in the future, it will greatly benefit you as it shapes a special character inside of you.

The wheat grain teaches us that only through death can there be life. Only through bending down is there fruit.

Only what is born out of suffering has value. Thorns do not go where the wheat grain goes; they do not go through the combine harvester, nor through the mill, nor through the oven. You cannot make bread from thorns either.

You have died to yourself when criticism does not bring you down, and praise does not make you proud.

True transformation and growth come from the willingness to let go of one's own desires and ego, allowing God's purpose to take root and flourish. This sacrificial act is not a sign of weakness but of profound strength and faith. It is through this self-denial that we can truly reflect the character of Christ and bear fruit in our spiritual journey.

Moreover, just as the grain of wheat must die to produce a bountiful harvest, so must we embrace the trials and tribulations of life, trusting that they will cultivate perseverance, faith, and resilience within us. The path of a Christian is marked by these moments of surrender and renewal, leading to a deeper, more meaningful relationship with God.

JULY 20

SHEEP IN THE MIDST OF WOLVES

"Behold, I send you out as sheep in the midst of wolves. Therefore, be wise as serpents and harmless as doves." – Matthew 10:16

One of the harsh laws of the United States military emphasizes the fact that any officer who sends his soldier into battle without weapons will be sent to the Court-Martial. When I read this law, my thoughts immediately went to the fact that Jesus has sent us into the midst of wolves, likening us to sheep. At first glance, this raises much confusion, many questions, and a desire to understand our Lord's allusion...

What are our chances against the wolves? What do the wolves that Jesus refers to look like? What are our weapons against them? Is it really wise for Jesus to send us so vulnerable against such fierce wolves? How do I know if I am likened to a sheep or to a wolf?

Of course, we will not be able to answer all these questions in a single devotional essay, but it is good to meditate on them. However, I would like to highlight several thoughts.

One of the major differences between sheep and wolves is behavior. Sheep always exhibit a gentle character, while the wolf is known for its violence.

Also, the sheep has nothing to hide. Its walk is always the same, its character is transparent, and it does not know to play at both ends. The wolf, however, is characterized by lurking, by the desire to attack without revealing its intention, and by hypocrisy.

The sheep comes out of its fold in the morning and spends its day grazing food and obeying its shepherd. Its decisions are not individual but subject to the authority of the one who coordinates and leads it to *green pastures*. Its trust is not in its own strength but entirely in the shepherd. On the other hand, the wolf loves the night and hates the light of day. Darkness gives it an extra assurance that it will not be discovered in time, and that it will be able to easily attack its prey without being spotted. When the sheep goes towards the fold for rest, the wolf prepares to start a new hunting adventure.

If a person`s life does not match his talk, that means he has the character of a wolf, not of a sheep.

If greed rules, the danger is so great that the wolf will tell the sheep what it WANTS to hear, not what it NEEDS to hear...

> *"Beware of false prophets, who come to you in sheep's clothing, but inwardly they are ravenous wolves." – Matthew 7:15*

If you are part of Jesus' flock and not the Devil's pack, do not forget that the Lord is your defender. Let gentleness and kindness never leave you. Stay close to the shepherd all the time because the wolf can only tear apart the sheep that stray from the flock.

If you love the light of day and the *green pastures* of God's Word, the One who sent you to work will also guard you from those who love darkness and who, with violence and greed, seek to destroy.

Jesus did not ask us to fight with the wolves. Jesus only asked us to always be "on guard". To take the necessary measures not to fall into the traps of so many wolves who come near us dressed in sheep's clothing. You should not be taken by surprise when you see so much hypocrisy at every corner. You should never expect 'agape' love from this world and from deceitful 'brethren.' The shepherd's love is sincere; the wolf's love is hypocritical. The shepherd will tell you the truth; the wolf will tell you lies.

Continuous vigilance should never leave us. We should put our complete trust only in the Lord so that, when the character of so many hypocrites is exposed, we will not be taken by surprise.

> *"Let every man beware of his neighbor, and do not trust any brother; for every brother will utterly supplant, and every neighbor will walk with slanderers." – Jeremiah 9:4*

The law I mentioned in the beginning punishes the officer who sends his soldiers into battle without weapons. Such an officer would send the soldiers to battle but never go with them himself. He is a boss, not a leader.

Our Officer, Jesus Christ, goes with us. Not only does He accompany us, but He goes before us. Our weapons are not fierce fangs or dynamite. Our weapons are forgiveness, love, and gentleness. We will suffer, be considered *fools*, ridiculed, attacked, hit, bitten, but never defeated.

We will have to endure and continue our journey through this earthly jungle, always paying attention to our every step until we reach the pasture of eternity. For the promised salvation in eternity, it is worth enduring anything:

> *"And you will be hated by all for My name's sake. But he who endures to the end will be saved." – Matthew 10:22*

There, in the plains of eternity, we will be able to look at each other with confidence, without fearing that the sheep next to us might be just a disguised wolf who changed its costume.

Be careful with pictures! Make sure you are not taking a selfie with a wolf.

Be careful with the text messages you receive! Behind many "hearts" prowl wolves who only love themselves and who desire only your body.

Be careful with your circle of friends! Evening walks with friends should not lead you to the forests where the eyes of many hungry wolves are lurking, and where their fangs eagerly await their next prey.

Be careful with marriage! Nothing is more destructive in this life for a lamb than having to spend 50 years with a wolf by his side at home... Be careful! Be careful! Be careful!

JULY 21

PRAISED BY GOD OR BY PEOPLE?

When we follow God, we must pay a price. He paid the price of salvation for us, and we must pay the price of ministry.

The world may appreciate the worldly person, but it will not tolerate the spiritual Christian.

We are in danger of giving up the standards required by the Bible in order to please people. Through actions or words, there is a tendency not to speak the whole truth, to sweeten up the Bible a bit, and to tell everyone that we will all end up in Heaven at the end of our lives.

Paul did see this danger and warned us about it:

> *"But as we have been approved by God to be entrusted with the gospel, even so we speak, not as pleasing men, but God who tests our hearts." – 1 Thessalonians 2:4*

Today might be a day when you have to suffer because you are a Christian. When you have to be ignored, persecuted, spoken ill of, or simply challenged by those around you at school or work.

Do not be afraid! Be worthy of the calling you have as a good Christian because, in the end, it is God's opinion that matters, not the opinion of men.

It is better to be praised by God and scorned by men than rejected by God and applauded by men!

Remember, the applause of people is temporary, but the approval of God is eternal. Strive to live in a way that honors Him above all else. True reward comes from faithfulness to God, not from seeking human approval. Keep your focus on the eternal prize, and let your actions reflect your commitment to Him.

July 22

ONLY IN STORMS OR ALSO IN GOOD TIMES?

Have you noticed people who call upon the Name of God only when they are in the hospital? People who turn to the church only when their child is sick? People who seek prayer support only until they pass their exams?

The three young men did not call upon God only in the fiery furnace. Neither did Daniel think of Heaven only when he descended into the lions' den. The distinctive quality of a true Christian is steadfastness. Their faith and devotion to God were unwavering, irrespective of their circumstances.

A true Christian does not cling to God only when the wave comes; he walks with God all the time. He does not call upon the help of the divinity only when human conditions are precarious; he has the good habit of listening to God and living according to His pleasure every day. This consistent relationship with God is what sustains them through both the calm and the storm.

To truly follow God means to obey Him in good times as well as in bad. It's about cultivating a daily relationship with Him, seeking His guidance and honoring Him in every aspect of life. When we make a habit of walking with God in the calm, our faith is strong and ready to face the storms.

Steadfastness in faith means trusting God and remaining obedient not just in desperation, but in our everyday lives. It's about recognizing His presence in the mundane and the miraculous, in joy and in sorrow. This continual devotion ensures that when trials come, we are already anchored in Him, confident in His faithfulness.

July 23

CONDITIONS AND PROMISES

One of the most beautiful chapters in the book of Joshua is the very first chapter. A new work, a new challenge, and a new calling for young Joshua. Here we find the **promise of conquest**, preceded by the **condition of action:**

"My servant Moses is dead. Now, therefore, arise, go over this Jordan, you and all this people, to the land which I am giving to them—the children of Israel. Every place that the sole of your foot will tread upon I have given you, as I said to Moses." – Joshua 1:2-3

I also noticed here the **promise of success**, but it is preceded by the **condition of steadfastness:**

"...do not turn from it to the right hand or to the left, that you may prosper wherever you go." – Joshua 1:7

With joy, we also notice the **promise of assistance**, which, again, does not come for free but is **conditioned on obeying God's command:**

"Have I not commanded you? Be strong and of good courage; do not be afraid, nor be dismayed, for the Lord your God is with you wherever you go." – Joshua 1:9

Last but not least, we should notice that the **promise of wisdom** depends on **our relationship with the Word of God:**

"This Book of the Law shall not depart from your mouth, but you shall meditate in it day and night, that you may observe to do according to all that is written in it. For then you will make your way prosperous, and then you will have good success." – Joshua 1:8

Very often, we remember God's promises, but quite rarely do we recall the conditions of these promises.

Let this be a significant warning for us not to remember only God's promises but also the conditions set for Him to fulfill those promises.

Let us pay attention to the conditions, and God will honor His promises.

July 24

DISCONTENT, PRIDE AND REBELLION

In Numbers 16, the Bible speaks of Korah, Dathan, Abiram, and another 250 people who rebelled against Moses. They were dissatisfied because, in their ministry, their position was too low, while Moses' and Aaron's positions were too high.

Moses tries to make them realize that the Lord chooses the place for each person in ministry, but they remained unconvinced.

> *"Moses said to Korah, 'Hear now, you sons of Levi: Is it a small thing to you that the God of Israel has separated you from the congregation of Israel, to bring you near to Himself, to do the work of the tabernacle of the Lord, and to stand before the congregation to serve them; and that He has brought you near to Himself, you and all your brethren, the sons of Levi, with you? And are you seeking the priesthood also?'" – Numbers 16:8-10*

The devil is so cunning; he keeps those who do not serve occupied with scorekeeping, gossip, non-involvement, and throwing stones at those who serve. However, those who serve are tempted by higher positions, dissatisfaction, and rebellion.

How can you easily tell when a person is attacked by this pack of demons? Simple: besides the fact that he starts speaking well of himself and ill of those above him, there is also an element of insubordination within him.

> *"Moses sent to call Dathan and Abiram, the sons of Eliab; but they said, 'We will not come!'" – Numbers 16:12*

The secret of your authority is staying under authority. Without the levels of authority established by God, the Church would be in chaos. The family would be in chaos. Society would be in chaos.

Pray sincerely to God today that you are able to control any thought you have that might be similar to that of Korah, Dathan, and Abiram, and make it obedient to Christ. Do not take such serious attitudes lightly. They do not appear overnight. The Devil patiently and slowly sows dissatisfaction, rebellion, and disobedience, and over the years, they sprout towards the ruin of those who accept them.

Let us be watchful. The first sin in the Universe was dissatisfaction, then pride and rebellion appeared in the heart of the Devil. Since then, he seeks to tempt others with these 'cookies' that produce spiritual diabetes.

God will not ask us at the end of our lives if we liked the place in which He put us but if we served with humility and sacrifice where He placed us.

Character is more important than comfort, and staying under authority is more important than the ministry itself.

JULY 25

SACRIFICE, NOT GLORY...

It is not wrong to want to be a leader. Be cautious, I said LEADER, not BOSS. The boss leads through threats, constraints, and harsh words. The leader leads by personal example, with gentleness and understanding.

The boss reaches the top through his connections.

The leader reaches the top through his competence.

The boss reaches the top because he wants a position from where he can be seen. The leader reaches the top because he wants a position from where he can lead the respective organization toward success.

The same applies in the spiritual realm. Jesus told us that the greatest must lead by example. He must be a servant to all. He must seek the interest of God's work, not personal interest.

An authentic leadership role involves sacrifice. Exactly what Jesus did: He is the Head of the Church because of the sacrifice at Calvary.

Division occurs when people want glory without sacrifice. Peace prevails where people desire sacrifice without glory.

Be a person of sacrifice. A person who pays the price. An Elisha who pours water on Elijah's hands.

And the day will come when you see that those who are humble are given grace. Those who have labored and who have been faithful in small things will be promoted and entrusted with greater responsibilities.

July 26

THE PITS OF HIDDEN TALENTS

"But he who had received one talent went and dug in the ground and hid his lord's money." – Matthew 25:18

For each of us, God has a well-established plan that we will figure out as we draw near to Him and follow the guidance of the Holy Spirit in our lives. However, this plan will be fulfilled not only through the guidance we receive but also through the talents we are offered. Talents represent exactly the blessings that God has given you, and you must use them for His glory.

Some are blessed with remarkable singing voices. Others with a unique charisma in speaking. Some with a powerful memory. There are people blessed with the gift of helping others. People who have the wisdom to organize certain things. The list of gifts that God has placed in us varies from person to person.

Today, I do not want to dwell on talents but on pits, because there is no use in receiving blessed gifts if you keep them hidden. What are the pits in which we hide our talents?

• The first pit is **comfort**. We understand the gift and the calling from God, but we do not want to step out of our comfort zone to do that work. Sandwiches cannot be sent through a text message; you need to get up from your couch, go shopping, come home, and prepare them. Then get up again and go distribute them where needed. The pit of comfort has buried many talents. It is a deep pit, and many people have fallen into it.

• Another pit is **apathy**. Although I see sick people around me, I do not care. I see the need for someone to lend a helping hand at church, but I think about the popular excuse, "It's none of my business." I see an empty seat in church, but I do not care to call that person and see why they no longer come to the church fellowship...

• Another pit is **mockery**. Anyone who buries their talent here will idle all day long and judge those who are serving. Such a person will find the mistakes of others who are working, forgetting that it is better to make mistakes while working than to make mistakes by doing nothing. Most of the people who judge and criticize those who work do it because they themselves are not busy doing anything.

The devil is not afraid of your talents as long as you keep them buried in the pit of judgment. On the contrary, he is very pleased that, through words of mockery, he keeps the one with the buried talent busy and, at the same time, inflicts wounds on those who work. Oh, how successful the devil is, unfortunately, through this pit...

Have you noticed that a busy person does not have time to analyze everything others do, nor to give grades or count the speech errors, nor to fulfill other such purposes?

• I will mention one last pit, although there are many more: **the pit of giving up**. I have met people who have given up working with the gift that God has placed in them precisely because they were hurt. They were told words that caused wounds so deep that they decided not to do anything anymore. I would like to remind these people that soccer players do not stop running when the people in the stands curse them or say harsh words about them. Soccer players have only one purpose: making the coach happy, not pleasing the fans. We want to please the One who enlisted us in His army (2 Timothy 2:4).

While writing these lines, I got a call from a fellow minister. He is working on renovating the church with the help of "a handful of people" and told me, "Brother Cristi, we are very few at work, and one of us has cancer, but even though he has throat cancer, he is here working by our side!"

After I hung up the phone, I wiped the tears from my eyes. Why? Because I realized that it is harder and harder to find people who are still available for God. Those who give everything often have the least. Those who are sicker seem to want to get more involved than the healthy.

A few minutes later, the mother of a sick girl called me. A girl who has been suffering for many years. A few days ago, her husband also became quite seriously ill. She called to... ask if I knew of a family in need because she wanted to donate something in the name of the Lord. Wouldn't such people have legitimate reasons to dig pits and bury their talents? What will we, the healthy ones, answer before the throne of God's judgment when He shows us such examples?

I do not know what kind of pit the Devil is trying to make you dig. What I do know is that we must listen to God, the One who has invested in us and blessed us so that we can also be a blessing – we should not listen to the Devil who tempts us to dig pits:

> *"I will make you a great nation; I will bless you and make your name great; and you shall be a blessing." – Genesis 12:2*

Do you know which were the fundamental qualities of those who did not bury their talents? Goodness and faithfulness:

"His lord said to him, 'Well done, good and faithful servant; you were faithful over a few things, I will make you ruler over many things. Enter into the joy of your lord.'" – Matthew 25:21

You cannot work for the Lord if you do not have goodness in your heart. But **long-term** goodness, not just one day a year. This means faithfulness. Goodness sees the need and intervenes, while faithfulness ensures that this action is repeated throughout all your life.

When you start digging pits, you cease to be faithful. When you bury what should be traded, cruelty will emerge instead of goodness. Instead of involvement, there will be indifference. Instead of sweating in the Lord's field, the "seat of the scornful" will appear (Psalm 1:1).

Remember: it is not enough to understand your calling from God! You must also identify the pit you are tempted to dig. Only a danger we are aware of is one we can avoid.

Lord, protect us from these pits!

July 27

VIRTUES THAT ACCOMPANY MEEKNESS

"Blessed are the meek, for they shall inherit the earth!" – Matthew 5:5

The Sermon on the Mount has its surprises. The principles of the Kingdom of God are opposite to those of the world's kingdom.

The world says that happy people are the strong ones, those who know how to assert themselves, who show their superiority, who demand their rights, and who do not let themselves be trampled upon. Yet, Jesus comes and says that the truly blessed people are the meek—those who are kind, peaceful, friendly, gentle, and express goodness.

Meekness does not come alone. It comes along with other virtues that the Bible emphasizes profoundly.

First, meekness is a characteristic of a **humble** person.

"Take My yoke upon you and learn from Me, for I am gentle and lowly in heart, and you will find rest for your souls." – Matthew 11:29

Someone once said that you cannot humiliate a humble person, just as you cannot take away the chair of someone who is standing.

John Bunyan reminds us that the one who kneels on his own cannot be brought down to his knees.

Only the humble person can spread meekness around him. The proud one can never do that.

Secondly, meekness is a characteristic of a **wise** person.

"But the wisdom that is from above is first pure, then peaceable, gentle, willing to yield, full of mercy and good fruits, without partiality and without hypocrisy." – James 3:17

The wisdom that comes from God expresses the kindness of God. David said:

"The king said, 'Is there not still someone of the house of Saul, to whom I may show the kindness of God?' And Ziba said to the king, 'There is still a son of Jonathan who is lame in his feet.'" – 2 Samuel 9:3

What a high level of wisdom! David could have sought revenge on Mephibosheth because Saul, his grandfather, had persecuted David for years. Yet, he did not. Because a gentle and wise person understands that you cannot counter darkness with darkness but only with light. You cannot remove the coldness from the enemy's heart by placing an Antarctic iceberg over it but only with the warmth of meekness.

Thirdly, let us not forget that meekness is a characteristic of a **peaceful** person. The one who seeks to avoid an argument or conflict at all costs:

"...to speak evil of no one, to be peaceable, gentle, showing all humility to all men." – Titus 3:2

"And a servant of the Lord must not quarrel but be gentle to all, able to teach, patient." – 2 Timothy 2:24

Today is a day when you can seek meekness. But to find it, you must first seek humility, wisdom, and peace.

The results will be evident. Your colleagues will notice your meekness. Neighbors and family will be astonished. Most of them will look at you strangely because you do not conform to the world's standards.

Do not be discouraged! Happiness is not defined by what people say about us but by what God says about us.

July 28

HOW DOES A GENTLE PERSON BEHAVE IN INFLAMATORY CIRCUMSTANCES?

Our character is tested every day. If yesterday you decided to be a gentle person, the day probably did not end before you faced challenges. You may have wondered, "How should I respond to mockery? To offence? To insults?"

Firstly, a gentle person pays attention to how they respond verbally.

We learn from the Lord Jesus that silence is also a response:

"He was oppressed and He was afflicted, yet He opened not His mouth; He was led as a lamb to the slaughter, and as a sheep before its shearers is silent, so He opened not His mouth." – Isaiah 53:7

It takes a lot of wisdom to know when to BE SILENT and when to SPEAK!

We do NOT need to respond to mockers because we cannot change them.

"When He was reviled, He did not revile in return; when He suffered, He did not threaten, but committed Himself to Him who judges righteously." – 1 Peter 2:23

However, there are sincere people who, in a moment of distraction, may speak inappropriately and provoke us. In such cases, we need to know how to respond:

"A soft answer turns away wrath, but a harsh word stirs up anger." – Proverbs 15:1

In Genesis 13, we find an example of a correct response to daily challenges. Abraham and Lot:

"An argument arose between the herdsmen of Abram's livestock and the herdsmen of Lot's livestock. The Canaanites and the Perizzites were then dwelling in the land. Abram said to Lot, 'Please, let there be no strife between you and me, and between my herdsmen and your herdsmen, for we are brethren.'" – Genesis 13:7-8

Abraham's answer prevented the dispute among the servants from escalating to their masters. In other words, Abraham said, "Take what you desire, and I will take what is left." Only a truly gentle and spiritually mature person can utter such words.

A gentle person does not seek to make justice for himself. He does not seek revenge. He knows he has a God who will not let him lose in the long run, even if he loses certain advantages in the short term.

Secondly, a gentle person seeks to resolve and smooth out the conflict through good deeds.

> *"A gift in secret pacifies anger." – Proverbs 21:14*

The apostle James said,

> *"Who is wise and understanding among you? Let him show by good conduct that his works are done in the meekness of wisdom." – James 3:13*

Give a gift to someone who does not really like you! Give a present that makes him ponder! Even if they do not respond positively, before God, you can show that you have done your part. Let us not forget that gentleness is the fruit of the Holy Spirit!

> *"The fruit of the Spirit is love, joy, peace, longsuffering, kindness, goodness, faithfulness, gentleness, self-control. Against such there is no law." – Galatians 5:22-23*

If you want to face daily challenges with success, you need to be filled with the Holy Spirit. You cannot have a little Spirit but a lot of gentleness.

Lastly, the Bible tells us that a gentle person seeks to restore those who have fallen. Such a person is ready to bend down, lift up, and help the weary people with love:

> *"Brethren, if a man is overtaken in any trespass, you who are spiritual restore such a one in a spirit of gentleness, considering yourself lest you also be tempted." – Galatians 6:1*

A police officer might harshly reprimand someone who caused an accident, but a doctor is not allowed to do this.

Be a doctor! We have enough police officers...

July 29

COMPETING IN THE RACE OF GENTLENESS

"Now the man Moses was very humble, more than all men who were on the face of the earth." – Numbers 12:3

It is very easy to prove that you have an exceptional character when you are applauded. It is easy to answer with a smile when you are appreciated. However, for Moses, the doctorate exam had come. He had been through many exams (when the people rebelled against him), but never such a colossal test:

"Then Miriam and Aaron spoke against Moses because of the Ethiopian woman whom he had married; for he had married an Ethiopian woman." – Numbers 12:1

Is it not true that nothing hurts more than when your own family offends you?

Miriam and Aaron began to envy Moses' ministry. They started nitpicking aspects of his life because that is what envious people do: they look for flaws in those they resent.

What did Moses do? He remained silent. Remember what we learned yesterday? When a gentle person is silent, God speaks:

"Suddenly the Lord said to Moses, Aaron, and Miriam, 'Come out, you three, to the tabernacle of meeting!' So the three came out." – Numbers 12:4

Is it not interesting that Moses, the man who smashed the tablets of the law, now acts like a lamb? That Moses, the courageous man who confronted Pharaoh, now does not confront his own sister?

Do you know why? Because in that instance, it was the work of the Lord and the name of Moses at stake, but now it was his personal reputation!

That is how we, as servants, should also be: zealous against sin but gentle when someone mocks us.

God confronts Miriam and Aaron, speaking words from which we have much to learn:

"...How is it you were not afraid to speak against My servant Moses?" – Numbers 12:8

Do you have the fear of speaking against the servants the Lord has raised up?

"The Lord's anger was aroused against them, and He departed." – Numbers 12:9

The most dreadful thing you can do in this life is to anger God!

"The cloud departed from above the tabernacle, and behold, Miriam became leprous, as white as snow. Then Aaron turned toward Miriam, and there she was, a leper." – Numbers 12:10

God withdraws when His servants are unjustly attacked and mocked out of envy! When the Holy Spirit comes, His arrival is heard, but when He leaves, He does so quietly... You know the continuation... Miriam is punished with leprosy. What does Moses do? Rejoice, right? No! The gentle person does not rejoice when God punishes his enemies but prays for them.

"Moses cried out to the Lord, saying, 'Please heal her, O God, I pray!'" – Numbers 12:13

The gentle person does not speak against the guilty but prays for the guilty. Forty years of "full time" education taught Moses the lesson of gentleness.

"And the Lord said to Moses, 'If her father had but spit in her face, would she not be shamed seven days? Let her be shut out of the camp seven days, and afterward she may be received again.'" – Numbers 12:14

When God wanted to compare Miriam's actions to something, He said: mocking God's people is as shameful as spitting in someone's face: "So, as Moses was mocked, let you be like that now..."

"Miriam was shut out of the camp seven days, and the people did not journey till Miriam was brought in again." – Numbers 12:15

Mockery isolates you from God and His people. Mockery halts the progress of an entire nation... Two million people were stationary for 7 days because one person was not watchful and was dissatisfied with the place in which God had put her...

Even though Miriam was punished and forgiven, she carried a tainted name for the rest of her life! Seven chapters later, Miriam dies... After the rebellion against Moses, there is no record that the Lord ever used her again...

Moses defended God in front of any man but did not defend himself in front of anyone.

This is true gentleness... I wish you a successful doctorate exam!

We do not reach Heaven until we pass through this exam as well...

July 30

"TO BE" IS MORE IMPORTANT THAN "TO HAVE"!

The first two verbs we memorize when we start to learn a foreign language are: *to be* and *to have*. They are the most used verbs in any language on this earth. Why? Because every person, when introducing themselves, needs them...

In the eyes of the world, the verb "to have" is very important. You are valuable by what you possess, the world says. You are valuable by what you own: lands, houses, cars, phones, etc.

In the eyes of God, however, what you *are* matters more. Your character more than your wealth.

Do you notice the difference? When you do not know God, all your goals boil down to one: to accumulate as much as possible HERE. When you know God, however, you understand that the true purpose is the transformation of your character to prepare it for meeting God.

Nowhere did Jesus Christ and the apostles of the Bible say: *trample over others to accumulate more.*

Compromise any principle just to have heaps of money. Work until exhaustion to show that you are valuable through what you own. No! Not because it is wrong to have, but because the Bible emphasizes character.

"Be!" Peter tells us "Be!" 17 times. James tells us the same thing 5 times! Paul, 43 times.

The school that children and young people attend can resemble life. The Bible is the curriculum, and the exams are the daily life tests we get. Therefore, if you want a solid character, you need to be close to the Word of God.

You cannot get high grades on exams if you skip classes! You cannot have a solid character with eternal perspectives if you do not follow the rules of the King from Heaven.

I met a man of God in Cimpa[20] who knows by heart over 60 chapters of the Bible. In the USA, I visited a friend whose mother, over 70 years old, has read the Bible 138 times.

---

[20] A village located in Romania.

In 2022, at the beginning of the year, in Hunedoara (Romania), I went to a man`s funeral. During the first 45 years of his life, he had read the Bible only twice. Then, having gone through a severe illness, when he recovered, he spent the next 25 years reading the Bible 157 times and serving in over 1,300 churches, most of them being simple congregations, as we say, from the countryside.

Jesus is preparing dwellings for us in Heaven, and here on earth, He is preparing us for Heaven. Now, in the eyes of the world, it matters how much land you have. However, in the afterlife, it will matter how much Heaven you have.

Be holy! Be forgiving! Be humble! Be people of your word! *To be* is more important than *to have*.

What you are gives you value, not what you have.

July 31

LONG-TERM VICTORIES

In life, there is the danger of believing that if one day we have a victory, this guarantees that on the following day we will also be successful. There is a danger of measuring victory short-term instead of long term...

I have met people glad that they did not watch pornography yesterday. That last week, they managed not to lie but only tell the truth. That they did not cheat on their spouse in the last month; examples like these can go on endlessly.

The challenge I present to you today is to think about long-term victories.

David defeated Goliath in a single day, but with Saul, he had to fight for over 10 years... And he triumphed!

Joseph was sold by his brothers in a single day, but with himself, with forgetting and forgiving, he had to fight for over 10 years.

Moses, in one day, was defeated by the desire to seek justice through killing, but then, for the next 80 years, he understood the sweetness of gentleness...

You cannot see an apple grow in a single day, but in a few weeks. You cannot see a planted seed take root in a few hours – it takes a few days. And then, several months more to see the fruit.

I do not know how you have measured your victories so far. I do not know if you have measured them in seconds or in months. What I do know for sure is that a life of true discipline and sacrifice, of triumph and self-control, is measured in the long term.

Be a person with a lifelong vision! Be a person who understands that eternity is determined in this life.

Those who run marathons in front of tens of thousands of supporters are training for years.

Those who lift weights at world competitions have many years of daily struggle behind them.

You cannot change what is in the past, but you can influence what will be in the future.

I really like Paul's vision, a vision not just for one Sunday a week, not just for Christmas and Easter, but for a victory throughout life and even beyond:

"Brethren, I do not count myself to have apprehended; but one thing I do, forgetting those things which are behind and reaching forward to those things which are ahead, I press toward the goal for the prize of the upward call of God in Christ Jesus." – Philippians 3:13-14

But he continues and says that this thought, this vision, this desire for long-term victory, is not just for him, but also for us:

"Therefore, let us, as many as are mature, have this mind..." – Philippians 3:15

May God help us in this endeavor!

AUGUST 1

THE CITADEL

"A city that is set on a hill cannot be hidden." – Matthew 5:14

We are called not to be "undercover Christians." We should not hide our true identity. We should be aware every day that many people look up at us and have certain expectations from us.

When you truly serve Jesus, Heaven, earth, and hell should know who you are.

"Then the evil spirit answered and said, 'Jesus I know, and Paul I know; but who are you?'" – Acts 19:15

The sons of Sceva were not known to the devil. They had never bothered his kingdom.

When asked about Job, the Devil did not shrug unknowingly. Not only did he know his name but also his address and his zip code.

Saints cannot hide. We are not called to be like the undercover police officers, dressed plainly in the crowd.

Today is just another day when you must be careful about your reputation.

You should not have to hide! People who live righteously have no reason to be ashamed!

Living in the light means our actions and words are always on display. Every deed, every word spoken in truth reflects the light of Christ. Hiding in the shadows not only dims this light but also hinders others from seeing the glory of God through us. We must let our lives be testimonies of His grace and love, openly and without fear.

Remember, the world is watching. In our workplaces, neighborhoods, and even within our families, our faith should be evident. Just as a city on a hill cannot be hidden, neither should our faith be concealed. Embrace your role as a beacon of hope and let your light shine brightly for all to see, illuminating the path to Christ.

August 2

TODAY'S DECISIONS, TOMORROW'S TESTIMONY

Every success in life is the result of small decisions. Every beautiful testimony we hear has a key point in its past when the respective person decided to do a specific thing. These pivotal moments shape our future and define the stories we will one day tell.

Joseph decided to forgive, turning betrayal into a story of redemption and reconciliation.

Esther decided to speak up, risking her life to save her people and becoming a symbol of courage and faith.

David decided not to harm Saul's cloak, choosing integrity over vengeance and demonstrating profound respect for God's anointed.

Ruth decided to go with Naomi, embracing loyalty and faithfulness, which led her to become part of the lineage of Jesus.

Peter decided to leave the fishing net and obey the call of Jesus, and thus turning from a fisherman into a foundational pillar of the early Church.

Matthew decided to give up the gains of his position as a tax collector in exchange for his position as an apostle, illustrating the power of prioritizing eternal values over earthly wealth.

Remember: the decisions you make today will influence your testimony tomorrow! Each choice, no matter how small, contributes to the tapestry of your life story.

You will not be able to tell your grandchildren a beautiful life story unless you make a worthy decision today. The legacy you leave is built one decision at a time. Choose wisely, live faithfully, and your testimony will be one that inspires future generations.

AUGUST 3

"I HAVE BEEN..."

"He said, 'I have been very zealous for the Lord God of hosts; because the children of Israel have forsaken Your covenant, torn down Your altars, and killed Your prophets with the sword. I alone am left; and they seek to take my life!'" – 1 Kings 19:10

Elijah's past sounded glorious with the miracles God did through and for him. He prayed for drought, and God listened to him. He prayed for rain, and it happened. He prayed for fire, and it came down. He prayed over the last meal of a widow, and his prayer was listened to. That last meal was never 'the last" one again. Ravens had delivered food for him in the past, and the brook Cherith provided him with water. These were years full of challenges but filled with beautiful miracles.

How about right now? He was in a cave. Hidden. A fugitive. From a courageous prophet, he became a fearful man. His fear of Jezebel took over...

Yesterday's success did not guarantee today's peace. Yesterday's victory did not provide tranquility for today.

When God asks him, "What are you doing here, Elijah?" he answers in the past tense. He wants to avoid the present. He wants to bring his past victories to face this challenging question in the present.

How about you? Have you been?

Have you been a burning candle? Salt that has taste? Fragrance that smells like Heaven? A spring that quenches the thirst of the thirsty? Have you been close to Heaven in prayer? Have you shed tears in worship? In special fellowship with fellow believers?

Why do we talk in the past tense? Why do we feel abandoned in the present? Why do we avoid the question that brings healing? Why would we believe that the coldness of the cave could help us in any way?

God does not ask in an accusing manner. He is not looking for you in order to abandon you. He is interested in the abandoned man. In the one that has fallen. In the one for whom the only comfort is the past...

"The Lord said, 'Go out, and stand on the mountain before the Lord.'" – 1 Kings 19:11

It is time to come out of hiding. Out of the place where you withdrew. Out of the cave of depression. It is time to stand in the presence of the Lord.

You have not finished the task entrusted to you. There are still some peaks to conquer. Still some thirsty travelers to whom you must give water. Still some intercessory prayers to be listened to. Still some roads that need to be illuminated by the light God has placed in you.

Stop saying, "I was."

Do not speak in the past.

The present with God ensures a better future than the past...

AUGUST 4

ILLNESSES WE SHOULD NOT BE HEALED OF

"Who is blind but My servant, or deaf as My messenger whom I send? Who is blind as he who is perfect, and blind as the Lord's servant?" – Isaiah 42:19

Most of us are blessed with healthy eyes and good hearing. We can look at a mountain spring and hear the chirping of a bird. We can look our children in the eyes and hear the beautiful words of those who are close to us. But why does the Bible say that the servant of the Lord should be blind and deaf?

If we only saw beautiful things, we would be blessed. If we saw only those in wheelchairs, only the orphaned children, and the cancer patients at "Marie Curie" hospital in Bucharest, oh, how blessed we would be! If we saw the worries of a mother with many children and if we rushed to lend a helping hand, what wonderful eyes we would have!

Unfortunately, we see what we should not see... We see that the neighbor's car is more expensive than ours, and envy creeps in. We see the vacation that our cousins took and that we could not afford; and on that day we lose the strength to pray. We see someone looking at us with disdain, and we get upset so quickly...

Hearing works the same way. If we heard the cry of aborted babies, how blessed we would be! If we heard the cry of missionaries in need of help, as Paul did, how useful we could be to ministry!

"In the night, Paul had a vision: a man of Macedonia stood and pleaded with him, saying, 'Come over to Macedonia and help us.'" – Acts 16:9

If we heard the cry of the widow's children and took action, how useful we would be! If we heard only good words, only the chirping of birds, and only beautiful songs, our soul would revive. If we heard the sighs of the lonely or the cries of the elderly taken to a nursing home by their children, how useful we could become...

Unfortunately, we also hear gossip about us. And the mocking that tries to stop our work. We hear the slanders. And the terrible news broadcast at 5 o'clock. And the newspaper headlines. Many times, we hear what we should not hear.

Do you want to be truly a servant of the Lord? You will have to be selective about what you look at and about the sounds you listen to. When Saul was anointed king, he pretended not to hear:

"However, certain worthless men said, 'How can this man save us?' So they despised him and brought him no presents. But he held his peace." – 1 Samuel 10:27

After a strong victory, people wanted to reveal to him who were those who had mocked him:

But the people said to Samuel, "Who is he who said, 'Shall Saul reign over us?' Bring the men, that we may put them to death." – 1 Samuel 11:12

Now Saul pretended not to see them.

"But Saul said, 'Not a man shall be put to death this day, for today the LORD has accomplished salvation in Israel.'" – 1 Samuel 11:13

Do you know that there are victories that defeat us and defeats that give us victory?

You would think that if you have seen someone near you making a mistake and you go to accuse them, you are bringing justice – justice that brings disturbance in your life for the next twenty years. A temporary victory with defeat. I have seen people go through courts for years because they *saw* some land they could get back. They got the land back, but they lost their health. Others, seeking revenge for a few words, obtained justice, but lost the joy of salvation.

However, I have also seen people who chose to lose. They pretended not to hear when someone spoke ill of them. They continued their service in the most beautiful kind of freedom: the slavery of Christ. They were defeated in the eyes of men, but victorious in the eyes of God.

I recently spoke with a pastor who reached the beautiful age of 85. On a festive occasion, someone insulted him in a despicable way and used the name of an animal in that insult. After a few days, the one who insulted him fell seriously ill. The pastor, instead of harboring that insult in his heart indefinitely, decided to hear the cry of the guilty one who needed medical attention. He took him to a nearby hospital as if nothing had happened, and thus, his life was saved. The pastor joyfully told me, 'This man became my best friend for the years to come'."

Moses was insulted by Miriam. He pretended not to hear.

Stephen was stoned. Instead of looking at those who were hitting him, he decided to look at Heaven.

Paul was left alone. Instead of writing letters to those who abandoned him and rebuke them, he decided to move on. And instead of looking at those who left him, he decided to look at the One who remained with Him:

> *"At my first defense, no one stood with me, but all forsook me. May it not be charged against them. But the Lord stood with me and strengthened me, so that the message might be preached fully through me, and that all the Gentiles might hear. And I was delivered out of the mouth of the lion." – 2 Timothy 4:16-17*

All of us who serve God should have **selective blindness and deafness.** We should hear what should be heard and know how to shut our ears to what is not beneficial. We should see the needs and get involved but close our eyes to the stones flying towards us.

Let us not look towards the earth anymore but towards Heaven. Let us not gaze at fleeting riches and do all we can to reach the top; instead, let us look at what Jesus looked, humbling ourselves and serving so that we can be exalted for eternity.

Let us not hear everything anymore. Let us not light a fire out of someone else's mistake. Let us not carry in our hearts words that were said several years ago, but rather carry in our hearts the joy of salvation.

Blessed are those who are deaf and blind in this way. They see what few see and hear what only God's people hear.

As Traian Dorz used to say, "Blessed are those who are deaf to the noise of the world but hear the sweet whisper of the Holy Spirit..."

August 5

TESTED THROUGH BLESSING: ACKNOWLEDGING THE SOURCE

"Then the Lord said to Moses, 'Behold, I will rain bread from heaven for you. And the people shall go out and gather a certain quota every day, that I may test them, whether they will walk in My law or not.'" – Exodus 16:4

Most of the time, when we talk about trials, we think of losses—loss of health, loss of a job, loss of a pregnancy, or other problems we may face in life.

However, the Bible reveals something extraordinary: we can be tested through blessings as well. Through what God blesses us with every day...

When Esau meets Jacob after years of separation, he says:

"Esau said, 'I have enough, my brother; keep what you have for yourself.'" – Genesis 33:9

But Jacob replies,

"Please, take my blessing that is brought to you, because God has dealt graciously with me, and because I have enough." So he urged him, and he took it.'" – Genesis 33:11

What a colossal difference... One presents his wealth by looking at his qualities, at what he has amassed and achieved, while the other acknowledges that God is the one who blesses.

Job said:

"Naked I came from my mother's womb, and naked shall I return there. The Lord gave, and the Lord has taken away; blessed be the name of the Lord!" – Job 1:21

Job states an exceptional truth here—namely, that the One who gives can also ask for it back. The God who gives health is the One who can take it away. The God who gives you a shelter is the One who can take it away. The God who gives you life is the One who can ask for it back whenever He desires.

If you acknowledge that all the things you have are from God, then you will not panic or resort to antidepressants when He asks them back. Instead, you will say, like Job: "Blessed be the name of the Lord."

Do we have the habit of praying for our daily bread? Do we have the habit of recognizing that even that bowl of soup is a gift from God?

> *"So you shall eat and be full, and you shall bless the Lord your God for the good land which He has given you." – Deuteronomy 8:10*

Those who do not acknowledge God in small things will not acknowledge Him in great things!

Wouldn't you like, from this day on, to start acknowledging that God has blessed you and that everything you have is from Him?

> *"Every good gift and every perfect gift is from above and comes down from the Father of lights, with whom there is no variation or shadow of turning." – James 1:17*

The wise man said it so well,

> *"In all your ways acknowledge Him, and He shall direct your paths." – Proverbs 3:6*

AUGUST 6

TESTED THROUGH MY HEART'S ATTITUDE TOWARDS THE BLESSINGS I RECEIVE

"When your herds and your flocks multiply, and your silver and your gold are multiplied, and all that you have is multiplied; when your heart is lifted up, and you forget the Lord your God who brought you out of the land of Egypt, from the house of bondage." – Deuteronomy 8:13-14

Being tested through blessings also means being tested through the attitude of the heart toward the blessings received from God.

The first pitfall our heart can fall into is pride. When you look at what you have, you can fall into the trap of superiority, pride, looking down on others...

Even Nebuchadnezzar fell into this trap. God waited twelve months for this king after sending him a warning through Daniel to humble himself. Look at what he said:

"The king spoke, saying, 'Is not this great Babylon, that I have built for a royal dwelling by my mighty power and for the honor of my majesty?'" – Daniel 4:30

What a tragedy to speak in the first person when you should speak in the third person.

The second pitfall we can fall into is clinging to blessings instead of clinging to the One who gives the blessing. That is what the prodigal son did: when he saw his father's wealth in his wallet, he left.

From here, we must learn a very important thing: everything God gives us becomes waste if we move away from Him, and everything God gives us remains a blessing if we stay close to Him!

The third pitfall we can fall into when we are tested through blessings is getting used to the blessings we have received. We wake up healthy in the morning and do not kneel next to our bed to thank God. Our salary is deposited into our bank account, and we do not give our tithe to God. Our heart beats 100,000 more times for the next 24 hours, yet this no longer moves us.

Instead of habit, God expects gratitude. Where there is gratitude, there is thanksgiving. Where there is thanksgiving, there is worship, and worship accompanied by thanksgiving brings huge gain.

Loaded with many riches, gold, and money, the Britannica ship was supposed to carry everything to America.

In its journey, it hit the coastal rocks of Brazil, and began to sink.

In an attempt to save the precious cargo, the sailors, in haste, hit the boxes to break them apart, and the money were scattered on the deck. The short time allowed them only to release the lifeboats and hurry to get into them.

The captain, who, according to naval orders, had to descend last, glanced for the last time to the deck to see if there were any passengers left there. Surprised, he saw a man sitting on one of the treasure boxes surrounded by money. “Man, what are you doing here?” the captain shouted. “Get in the boat; can’t you see the ship is sinking?” “Yes,” the man replied, “I see that it is sinking, but, captain, all my life I have been poor, and now look how much money and gold I have. I am rich! I have decided to die like this...”

Let us not forget that we are mere passersby in this world, and we are not in a race. We will pass the test with flying colors if, instead of allowing our hearts to cling onto material things, we let our hearts cling onto God.

August 7

TESTED THROUGH WHAT I DO WITH THE BLESSINGS I RECEIVE

"I will make you a great nation; I will bless you and make your name great, and you shall be a blessing." – Genesis 12:2

Two spouses traveling in Korea saw a father and his son working in the rice field. The old man guided the heavy plow while the boy pulled it.

"I suppose they are very poor," the man told the missionary who was accompanying them.

"Yes! They are part of the Chi Nevi family. When the church was built, they wanted to give something, but they had no money. So, they sold their ox and gave the money to the church. This spring, they will plow the field themselves."

"That was truly a sacrifice," the woman said after a long silence.

"They would not call it a sacrifice; they would just say they are glad they had an ox to sell," the missionary replied.

Since God has given us certain blessings, He has the right to ask us to give an account of how we have used them. Money, backyard land, air, time, health - all are gifts from Him. And the manner in which we have used them will influence our eternal reward.

Do what you can with what you have for as long as you still can! Do not wait until you lose your health to regret not helping the sick! Do not wait until you lose everything financially to regret not helping when you had the means! Do not wait until the end of your life to regret not appreciating it when you were in the middle of it.

When Job lost everything, he could say with joy:

"Because I delivered the poor who cried out, the fatherless and the one who had no helper. The blessing of a perishing man came upon me, and I caused the widow's heart to sing for joy. I put on righteousness, and it clothed me; my justice was like a robe and a turban. I was eyes to the blind, and I was feet to the lame. I was a father to the poor, and I searched out the case that I did not know." – Job 29:12-16

I ministered one Sunday evening in a small church. At the end of the service, a sister in a wheelchair waited for me with about $35 in her hand. She asked me to give it to a needy family. I was deeply moved by her gesture and told her that I could not take this money for others because she needed help herself, in her difficult situation. She replied, "Brother Cristi, I gave birth to 7 children just as you see me. My husband married me shortly after the train cut off my legs. I have many reasons to thank God. I want to serve Him all my life with as much as He has given me..."

How will we stand next to such people on the Day of Judgment? Next to people who sacrificed themselves entirely for God? Next to people who do not want shoes, only legs? Next to people who do not want the latest car model but only to be able to take one step on their own? And yet, they do not complain, but serve God, however they can, with the blessings they have received.

Do you have valid reasons to complain? Do you have valid reasons not to be a blessing to others?

Today I invite you to meditate on a few lines from the poem "Some and others" written by Licuța Pântia, a mother who has been raising a child with serious health problems for over 25 years... A mother who divides the world in two through her poems. On which side are you?

Some want wealth, fame, riches,
Others health for their children;
Some want their own sunrise,
Others just to forget what they loved...

Pilgrims through the world between no and yes,
Every soul has its wound!
Not everyone who laughs is happy,
Just as not for all who cry everything has ended!

Fight for yourself, ease your pain,
And if that is not possible, accept your destiny;
Be of good cheer and always believe:
When no one else comes, God does come!

AUGUST 8

IS IT WORTH WORRYING?

"Therefore I say to you, do not worry about your life, what you will eat or what you will drink; nor about your body, what you will put on. Is not life more than food and the body more than clothing?" – Matthew 6:25

We have all experienced worries: unknown circumstances on the horizon and worries that come with them. The first day of college. The first day at work. A visit to the doctor. Medical labs. Layoffs at work. Rent we cannot pay on time. Utility bills that have increased. And how many other reasons for worry don`t we have in life?

It is necessary to distinguish between taking care of our family and ourselves on the one side, and worrying about the situations we go through on the other. Taking care is necessary. Worrying is useless.

Worry paralyzes the heart, and all attention is given to fleeting things. It brings stress and anxiety, and later, illnesses that will not be easily overcome.

It is said that 85% of the things we worry about never happen. Also, worry is useless because it never changes anything; it only makes the situation worse. It is scientifically proven that a person under continuous stress and anxiety will act hastily, without reason, with the possibility of making mistakes that will affect his future in the long run.

Jesus wanted our attention and care not to be directed towards material things. The more you worry about earthly things, the less concerned you will be about Heaven. The more you stress about comfort, the less concerned you will be with character. When we run 24 hours a day only for our earthly life and worry about doing what the world does, we will lose sight of preparing for eternity.

"For after all these things the Gentiles seek. For your heavenly Father knows that you need all these things." – Matthew 6:32

When you worry, you lose sight of the fact that God is in control. You are like a child who cannot go to bed at night because he is worried and keeps asking, 'Do my parents have what is needed to feed me tomorrow?'

Worry takes God out of the equation of your life. It gives you the impression that you are responsible for everything, and by doing so, the Devil gains ground in your life. Worry changes your priorities, and a shift in priorities over decades will bring ruin to your life.

Our priority must be the Kingdom of Heaven. Holiness. The Word. Prayer. Fellowship. Investing in heavenly things:

"But seek first the kingdom of God and His righteousness, and all these things shall be added to you." – Matthew 6:33

When you are concerned with holy things, God will take care of the necessities of physical life. And if this body does not have everything it desires, but the inner man takes on the likeness of Jesus, what have you lost? And if you have everything the world has to offer and you anxiously strive to satisfy the desires of the flesh, but in the end, you do not enter the Kingdom because you did not prepare for it, what have you gained?

I have decided to cast all my worries into the arms of Jesus:

"Casting all your care upon Him, for He cares for you." – 1 Peter 5:7

You should do the same!

AUGUST 9

GREAT VICTORIES WITH FEW RESOURCES

"Elisha said to her, 'What shall I do for you? Tell me, what do you have in the house?' And she said, 'Your maidservant has nothing in the house but a jar of oil.'" – 2 Kings 4:2

The widow had only a jar of oil at home. David had only a sling with a few stones. Gideon had only 300 soldiers facing a vast Midianite army. She had only two coins. The boy from the multiplication of the loaves had only 5 loaves and 2 fish.

Often, we believe that God needs us to bring very large resources in order to achieve victory. That is not true! God wants us not to rely on ourselves but on Him. If Gideon had gone to war with the initial 32,000 soldiers, he would have said, "The sword of Gideon!" With 300, however, he said, "The sword of God and Gideon!"

A little makes you place God first. The widow of Zarephath had only two portions of food left at home. Do you know how she addresses Elijah?

"And she said, 'As the Lord your God lives, I do not have bread, only a handful of flour in a bin, and a little oil in a jar...'" – 1 Kings 17:12

When the Living God is put face to face with insufficient resources, He will multiply those resources. Sincere humility makes a person realize that he has no other option but God. And when all you have left is God, you will see that He is enough.

We look at our *fish* and our *loaves* and see that they are few. We look at the money in our wallet and realize that it is not enough. We look at our small faith and think that we cannot overcome the great mountain.

Reading the Bible, we notice that God did not need a multitude of resources to bring great victories. On the contrary! Most of the time, He wanted to show the mortal man that our resources are not important, but His presence and blessing are.

Saul had powerful armor, and yet, he dared not face Goliath. David stepped forward. Because when you have only a simple sling, you are 100% aware that without God, you do not stand a chance.

From time to time, God blows away the resources we usually rely on, and scatters them. And when we are left with little, we cling tightly to Him because we have nothing else left.

Faith grows when the rest of the resources in which we trusted are diminishing. Prayer flares up when friends no longer answer the phone. Problems that you thought could be solved with money remain unsolved because God wants you to fall to the ground in humility and trust in Him.

Come forward with the little you have. But put that little entirely at His disposal.

The miracles that can be explained are no longer miracles.

In a church in Romania, when its renovation began, the first money placed into the offering box was from a ten-year-old girl. She gave for the work of God a third of the money she had saved with much sacrifice. There are no explanations that can solve the dilemma of how the renovation work was eventually completed. Why? Because the little of a 'little' child moved the heart of God. And a blessed 'little' brings along blessings that cannot be measured by anyone.

God's interventions in your life will be true miracles when you realize that a sincere, humble heart, and strong faith do more than all the material resources others have accumulated.

All the money in this world offered to the Church by a proud person helps with absolutely nothing and is not blessed by God. However, two coins given by a widow have greater value in the eyes of God. God's blessing is not attracted by quantity but by the humility of the heart, by the 'little' we bring with fear and reverence.

Our 'only little' is enough for Him.

It is not easy at all to become so broken and crushed that you say, "I have only..."

However, do not forget that this is when the greatest victories are won.

August 10

HOW WILL THE OUTCOME BE?

"Remember those who rule over you, who have spoken the word of God to you, whose faith follow, considering the outcome of their conduct!" – *Hebrews 13:7*

Is it not true that Noah's story does not make you nervous anymore, since you already know how it ends?

It is so easy to read about Joseph's life in prison when you already know that he became the prime minister of Egypt.

You can reread about Job's losses without worrying because you know that, in the end, he was blessed twofold.

David's story advancing against Goliath with a sling in hand seems easier to go through when you already know how it ends...

It is much simpler to tell your children about Daniel in the lions' den when you already know that he was not eaten by the lions.

It is very beautiful to read about the three young men thrown into the fiery fire when you already know that God sent His Angel to adjust the oven's temperature.

Gethsemane and *Calvary* do not sound so sad when you know that the day of resurrection followed.

All these and many other heroes of God did not know the ending... They had an exceptionally strong faith in God and pressed forward, understanding that everything God does is good.

Can you move forward even if you do not know the ending? Without seeing, without knowing, without being able to visibly touch the finish line?

You cannot do it alone. You can only do it by faith.

It is worth going through anything when you know the ending will be beautiful.

The One who orchestrated the song of your life will ensure that the final notes will be the highlight of the concert.

The One who called you to climb the mountain by His side has surely prepared an amazing scenery for you to gaze upon for eternity without getting bored.

The One who led you through the valley of the shadow of death in this life will surely prepare an ending that contains no more tears in the life beyond.

August 11

SHAPING YOUR CHARACTER THROUGH MARRIAGE

"And as the church is subject to Christ, so let the wives be to their own husbands in everything. Husbands, love your wives, just as Christ also loved the church and gave Himself for her." – Ephesians 5:24-25

Nothing shapes our character more powerfully than marriage. That is where God forbids us to separate when something displeases us or becomes inconvenient, and instead, He asks us to forgive, not to hold grievances against our spouse, and to continue fighting for our marriage, with agape love.

When an angry person separates from his spouse, he thinks that the anger stays behind. That`s false. If an angry, selfish, and proud person separates from his spouse and enters into another relationship, he will carry those feelings with him and will encounter the same problems in the new relationship as well.

Therefore, the solution is not separation but reconciliation. The way out is not hatred but forgiveness. Not the court but unconditional love. Not changing the spouse but changing myself...

The key to marriage is nothing other than following the example of Jesus and the Church. Jesus "strips" Himself of His glory and comes to sacrifice Himself for His Church. The Church, in turn, comes with repentance, humility, and tears and enters into this holy matrimony not out of fear of eternal punishment but conquered by the depth of the Savior's sacrifice.

Jesus earned the respect and submission of the Church through sacrifice, not through words without deeds. What love conquers is never lost...

The culture we live in today strictly seeks personal happiness in marriage. Ignoring the Bible and its principles, the world thinks that a beautiful marriage requires many material things, much pride, much stubbornness, and satisfying all pleasures. Therefore, today, most marriages fail. Without following the "instruction manual" of the One who designed the family, no marriage can endure.

I do not know how your marriage is "going." What I do know is that on the wedding day, we made a covenant. We said that we would love unconditionally. That we would stay together for better and for worse.

Is it 'worse' now? Then you have a new challenge: to accept the crushing and do what Jesus did: to love even if it hurts! Take care of your spouse even if he does not deserve it.

Is it 'better' now? Be on guard, be vigilant, and have a strong relationship with God! Today's success does not guarantee tomorrow's victory.

Marriage is a continuous challenge, and it changes us if we accept it. It makes us more holy, more forgiving, more dependent on grace.

And when we leave our marriage by leaving this earth, we will have the image of Jesus in us, and the angels will look amazed and say: 'How well you resemble your Bridegroom!'

August 12

"I WILL BE WITH YOU!"

"The Lord Himself goes before you and will be with you; He will never leave you nor forsake you. Do not be afraid; do not be discouraged!" – Deuteronomy 31:8

Everett R. Storms spent a year and a half of his life categorizing the promises of the Bible. Eventually, he found 7,487 promises made by God to man, 991 promises made by one person to others, and 290 made by people to God.

The most common promise offered by God to man is: "I will be with you!"

"When you pass through the waters, I will be with you; and through the rivers, they shall not overflow you. When you walk through the fire, you shall not be burned, nor shall the flame scorch you." – Isaiah 43:2

This promise was made in various forms to Noah, Abraham, Jacob, Joseph, Moses, David, Amos, Mary, Paul, and many others...

I do not know how you feel today. Maybe you feel alone. Maybe abandoned. Perhaps disappointed. Probably tired of human promises. Perhaps saddened by those close to you.

Do not forget that there is Someone who remains faithful. Someone who does not leave when problems come. Someone who answers the call made on our knees even when friends no longer respond. Someone who stays by our side when the waves hit our boat, when our labs come back abnormal.

Hold on to one of these 7,487 promises. Understand today that God does not "speak in vain." He Himself has guaranteed the validity of His words:

"Heaven and earth will pass away, but My words will by no means pass away." – Matthew 24:35

All those to whom God has promised that He will be with them, because they have stayed close to Him, have had complete victory. They were not exempt from problems, valleys, or tears. But because God was with them, they could keep on fighting.

My fear is not that God will not be with me, but that I might drift away from Him. My fear is not that He will leave me first, but that I might leave Him.

"And Azariah went out to meet Asa, and said to him: 'Hear me, Asa, and all Judah and Benjamin. The Lord is with you while you are with Him. If you seek Him, He will be found by you; but if you forsake Him, He will forsake you.'" – 2 Chronicles 15:2

Let us think about this warning. Let us meditate on it. Let us live in such a way that the distance between us and God decreases every day.

"I will be with you!" Remember these words when you are down. When you are defeated. When you are hurt.

God, the Creator of the Universe, promises to be with you, a human being. A lump of clay. A vapor that passes quickly.

What an honor! What a joy!

And if God is with us, does anything else matter?

"So, what shall we say to these things? If God is for us, who can be against us?" – Romans 8:31

AUGUST 13

FORGIVENESS AND SCIENCE

"In Him, we have redemption through His blood, the forgiveness of sins, according to the riches of His grace." – Ephesians 1:7

"For me, Jesus is the greatest Teacher of all times. I do not believe in Jesus just because I was taught by my parents in this way. I am an intellectual who has been through schools, seeking to make sense of the world. But among all the great minds who have lived on Earth (Buddha, Confucius, Pythagoras, etc.), Jesus has the most perfect scientific coverage. Because absolutely all His words are perfectly superimposable on current sciences. Do you know what Jesus brings in addition to Buddha? Not only love but also forgiveness. It is extraordinary! What does forgiveness mean? Spiritually, it means peace and harmony. Scientifically, do you know what forgiveness means? It simply means changes at the DNA level, that is, at the foundation of our genetic makeup.

It means erasing the pathological program (the pathological model of disease). Through forgiveness, the negative pattern is simply erased at the DNA level, and good chemistry and energetic balance are installed in the body. It is fantastic; it is simply like restarting a computer. This can only be erased through forgiveness.

In simpler terms... do you want to heal a serious illness you have? Make peace with all those who hate you! This is exactly the message of the Savior given to those who came and sought healing. Jesus could have said, 'I healed you,' but He chose to say, 'Your faith has healed you.' When you believe, you mobilize all your healing mechanisms. But knowing that God exists is not everything. Only Christianity gives you the experience of the transformative emotion, that openness of the soul through which you truly live the relationship with God. Not only going to church is important, but also the power of prayer that you can utter wherever you are.

So, after 2,000 years, I have explained this fantastic exhortation of Jesus, forgiveness through genetics. Do you realize that what I am saying is true, that Jesus is the greatest Teacher of all times? I discuss about Jesus not from a theological point of view, because it is neither my competence nor my duty; I discuss about Jesus from the perspective of a scientist, of scientific knowledge.

The fact that today we can explain all of Jesus' words in terms of modern science seems extraordinarily important to me. After 400 years of disputes between science and religion, the new science comes to confirm religion, the existence of Divinity..."

These are the words of Professor Dumitru Constantin Dulcan[21]. He is a scientist of high caliber from Romania, who supports the existence of God and has written books showing the world that science proves the existence of a Creator and that life under the sun makes sense only when God is at the helm of the Universe.

The burdens we carry in our hearts weigh us down not only spiritually but also physically. Many illnesses come from stress, from the problems we choose to carry with us every day, the issues we go to bed with and wake up with. And from among these problems, conflicts are the ones that torment us the most.

We remember for years the people who have wronged us, and unknowingly, we do ourselves the greatest harm. We carry in our hearts as prisoners all those who have wronged us, and we wake up at night to "feed" the inmates of our hearts. We talk to these "prisoners" daily, bringing back to the present something that happened in the past. We exhaust almost all our resources and energy in these battles that are of no help to us.

Saint Augustine said, "Are you suffering from the injustice of an evil man? Forgive him so that you may not become the second evil man!"

Today, you have two extraordinary opportunities that I urge you not to miss.

First, take your sins to Jesus and ask Him for forgiveness, so that you can gradually feel the joy of deliverance.

Then, moved by the forgiveness you have received, take the keys of kindness and love, go to the prison of your heart, and release the prisoners you have in there.

And then, you will realize what Max Lucado meant when he said: "Forgiveness is unlocking the door to set someone free and realizing that you were the prisoner."

---

[21] Romanian neurologist, psychiatrist, and author of philosophical and metaphysical literature.

AUGUST 14

CHEN SI

"So which of these three do you think was neighbor to him who fell among the thieves? And he said, 'He who showed mercy on him.' Then Jesus said to him, 'Go and do likewise.'" – Luke 10:36-37

Chen Si is a simple Chinese man. In 2003, he was selling vegetables in a market in the city center. One weekend, he decided to take a walk on the 2-mile-long Nanjing Bridge, a bridge over the Yangtze River. There, he saw a 22-year-old woman crying and wanting to end her life by jumping off the 230-feet bridge. He approached her, talked to her, and convinced her to give up suicide.

Since then, 19 years have passed until today (2022). Chen Si has managed to save over 400 people from suicide so far. "I do not have a special gift," he said modestly. "I am simply moved by people's needs and try to understand their pain."

Chen Si has spent hundreds of thousands of yuan on the people he has saved. He bought food for most of them and gave them money to travel back home.

He spent his meager earnings and took money from his wife and child more than once to save the lives of those in depression.

"Saving people is hard and painful. But staying at home each weekend and doing nothing is even more painful..." Chen Si said.

Chen Si was abandoned by his mother when he was 7 years old. He was bullied by schoolmates for many years. He went through pain, and now he understands the pain of others. Instead of complaining all his life about the traumas he experienced in childhood, he chose the optimistic path: I take my pain, learn from it, and put myself in the shoes of those who are suffering.

I do not know what traumas you have been through. I do not know what your job is. I do not know what your financial situation is right now. What I do know, however, is that there are people around us who need our attention. A kind word. A shoulder to cry on. A hamburger. A sincere encouragement.

Christianity has this extraordinary essence: love for our fellow human beings. Sympathy for the one who has fallen. Spending from what you have for the one who was robbed by thieves. Helping the wounded. Sacrifice for the one with a sad stare and tears on his cheeks.

Look around you. There are people longing for a hug. For a word of encouragement. For a warm look and a sincere smile.

People will not be impressed by our speeches, but by our actions.

Jesus did not tell the teacher of the Law to memorize a few more psalms. He knew well what needed to be done. That is why Jesus told him, "Go and do likewise." May God help us do the same!

AUGUST 15

THE TABLES OF THE BIBLE

Mealtime is a special moment that creates a framework in which a certain group of people fulfills its daily physical needs in an atmosphere of fellowship, communion, or friendship.

However, the Bible warns us to be careful about whom we share a meal with. We cannot sit at the table of demons and also at the table of the Lord. We cannot have on our table a bottle of beer next to the communion`s fruit of the vine. We cannot sit with those who curse and blaspheme God from Monday to Saturday and then sit at the table of the Lord to partake communion on Sunday.

Throughout our lives, we will have meals even in the wilderness.

"Yes, they spoke against God: They said, 'Can God prepare a table in the wilderness?'" – Psalm 78:19

You may encounter the wilderness of your life in solitude, in disappointment, in heat, and in the dryness surrounding your heart.

Remember that in the wilderness, no matter how great the drought is, our God is greater! No matter how rare a water spring may be found, our God is the Source that never dries up. He can spread tables even in the wilderness, and we thank Him for it.

At other times in life, we may be forced to eat with enemies. David said:

"You prepare a table before me in the presence of my enemies; you anoint my head with oil; my cup overflows." – Psalm 23:5

If you are pure and innocent, you can dine with your greatest enemies. Even three course meals if necessary. They may not have an appetite, but you, who can love and forgive, will be able to cater to them and serve their plates personally. Joseph did this with his brothers:

"Joseph's brothers sat down before him, the firstborn according to his birthright and the youngest according to his youth; and the men looked in astonishment at one another." – Genesis 43:33

God prepared Joseph for this meal for years. And it was worth it. Do you know where their astonishment came from? They remembered that the last time they ate together, Joseph was in a pit, while they were eating from the food he had brought for them...

Joseph could have sought revenge, but he invited them to the table. What love! What character!

Another meal the Bible talks about is the meal of service.

"For who is the greater, one who reclines at table or one who serves? Is it not the one who reclines at table? But I am among you as the one who serves." – Luke 22:27

It is a special grace to dine at the table, but it is an even more extraordinary grace to serve there. He who descended from Heaven taught us what practical humility means. What a rare meal! The One who could order whatever He wanted at that meal stooped down and wiped the dust off the feet of His disciples...

I have found another blessed table in the Bible, namely the table of gratitude:

"Show kindness to the sons of Barzillai the Gileadite, and let them be among those who eat at your table, for so they came to me when I fled from Absalom your brother." – 1 Kings 2:7

David did not forget that, when others persecuted him, mocked him, and chased him away, Barzillai brought him provisions and laid out a blessed meal for him... And now the time for gratitude had come.

David understood what we must also understand today: when you rise in life, do not forget to be grateful to those who stood by you when you were down...

Finally, I mention the table in Heaven. The most blessed meal history will ever know!

"And they shall come from the east, and from the west, and from the north, and from the south, and shall sit down [at the table] in the kingdom of God." – Luke 13:29

In Eden, the Devil gave us a meal that tasted of death. In Heaven, God will give us a meal that will taste of eternity. Be there! Do not miss it!

AUGUST 16

CHOICES AND CONSEQUENCES

"See, I have set before you today life and good, death and evil... I call heaven and earth as witnesses today against you, that I have set before you life and death, blessing and cursing; therefore choose life, that both you and your descendants may live." – Deuteronomy 30:15,19

God created us with the freedom to choose. In this way, we enjoy three significant freedoms: the freedom of *thought*, the freedom of *speech*, and the freedom of *action*.

God did not make us robots. Love requires freedom to manifest itself. No one wants to love or be loved without being able to decide it voluntarily.

Due to this freedom, our lives are filled with choices. And the choices we make have consequences. These consequences ultimately determine not only how we live on this earth but also where we will spend eternity.

Do you think deeply about consequences when you make choices? Are you aware that those future consequences are the result of the present choices?

Eve chose to eat from the forbidden fruit. Cain chose to kill his brother. Dinah chose to look at the "daughters of the land." Samson chose to love women who did not know God.

The consequences did not delay appearing. Eve and Adam lost Eden. Cain lost God's blessing. Dinah lost her purity. Samson lost his eyes.

Abel chose to obey. Joseph chose to forgive. Ruth chose to go with Naomi. Esther chose to speak up. Daniel chose to pray.

Likewise, their consequences are blessed. Abel had an offering that was accepted by God. Ruth entered into the genealogy of Jesus. Esther remained in history as a woman willing to die as a hero rather than live like a coward. Daniel was delivered from the lions' den.

We will choose based on the principles we have. That is why ignorance of Scriptural principles and the desire to live without God lead to matching choices and disastrous consequences. On the other hand, obedience to the Word of God will influence the choices we make, and the consequences will be entirely different.

Today is a new day in which you need to weigh your choices. Be wise! Be mature! Children choose by taste, by momentary pleasure, by the toys at hand. However, a spiritually mature person chooses based on health, morality, and character. Children choose for the short term—momentary pleasure, satisfaction for a few minutes. A spiritually mature person chooses for the long term, seeking holiness first and then happiness.

Choose your circle of friends carefully. Choose your spouse with great responsibility. Choose carefully the role models you allow to influence you.

You will not be able to blame anyone else later. Our present is nothing more than the arithmetic average of the choices we made in the years gone by. Our future will be the same if we do not change something today.

Do you choose gambling? Do you choose betting? Do you choose alcohol that takes away your freedom to choose? Do you choose the company of Godless people? Do you choose immorality? Do you choose a spouse without principles? Do you choose sin? You have every right to choose all these things, but you will not be able to blame anyone else when negative consequences appear.

You will not be able to blame God if you make choices without Him! It is a dreadful deception to believe that you can reap what you did not sow!

> *"Do not be deceived, God is not mocked; for whatever a man sows, that he will also reap." – Galatians 6:7*

Do you choose fellowship with holy people? Do you choose prayer? Do you choose to remain pure in the midst of a dirty world? Do you choose a spouse who wants to go to heaven? Do you choose holiness? You also have every right to do this. In the short term, people will point fingers at you, colleagues will ignore you, and everyone around you will look at you strangely. When you go against the flow of the world, you take a risk. But do not be discouraged; the long-term horizon for such choices is a blessed one.

> *"Blessed is the man who endures temptation; for when he has been approved, he will receive the crown of life which the Lord has promised to those who love Him." – James 1:12*

Choose blessing instead of cursing!

Choose holiness instead of sin!

Choose love instead of hatred. Choose forgiveness instead of revenge!

Choose life instead of death!

Choose what God recommends so that you can be with Him for eternity and under His blessing.

August 17

LIZZIE ATWATER'S FINAL LETTER

"Precious in the sight of the Lord is the death of His saints." – Psalms 116:15

The Boxer Rebellion was a violent, xenophobic, and anti-Christian movement that took place in China at the end of the Qing Dynasty, between 1898 and 1900. In the summer of 1900, 188 foreign missionaries and over 32,000 Chinese Christians were massacred simply for serving Christ.

The most severe persecution occurred in the northern province of Shanxi, where the province governor, Yu Xian, was a prominent sympathizer of the Boxers. However, in Fenzhou, northern Shanxi, local officials seemed more amiable toward missionaries than in most other locations. A few missionaries gathered in Fenzhou at the invitation of the workers stationed there, thinking they would be safe until the trouble passed. However, shortly after their arrival, the governor appointed a new magistrate over Fenzhou, who promptly placed an armed guard around the foreigners.

The missionaries knew they had walked into a trap and contemplated the worst.

Lizzie Atwater, a young pregnant woman who had come to China as a missionary, wrote her final letter to her parents in the U.S. on August 3, 1900:

"Dear ones, I long for a sight of your dear faces, but I fear we shall not meet on earth. I am preparing for the end very quietly and calmly. The Lord is wonderfully near, and He will not fail me. I was very restless and excited while there seemed a chance of life, but God has taken away that feeling, and now I just pray for grace to meet the terrible end bravely. The pain will soon be over, and oh the sweetness of the welcome above! My little baby will go with me. [...] I cannot imagine the Savior's welcome. Oh, that will compensate for all these days of suspense.

Dear ones, live near to God and cling less closely to earth. There is no other way by which we can receive that peace from God which passeth understanding. I must keep calm and still these hours. I do not regret coming to China but am sorry I have done so little. My married life, two precious years, has been so very full of happiness. We will die together, my dear husband and I. [...] If we escape now it will be a miracle. I sent my love to you all, and the dear friends who remember me."

Twelve days after her letter was written, Lizzie Atwater, her unborn child, and six other missionaries were brutally killed by the swords of the guards, and their mutilated bodies were thrown into a pit.

This story provides just a glimpse into the events of 1900 in China. Thousands of other Christians endured persecution with extraordinary faith to the end. They loved God more than they loved their lives, and thus, they were ready to pay the price of their lives for that love.

What would you write to others if you were in a similar circumstance?

August 18

"HERE RESTS THE BONDSERVANT OF THE LORD..."

"Paul, a bondservant of Jesus Christ, called to be an apostle, separated to the gospel of God." – Romans 1:1

Imagine a slave market: Africans being auctioned off, bound in chains, and sold like animals. Separated from their spouse or their children. Forced to work for masters who most often had not even a bit of compassion for them. Frequently beaten and reviled, they had no chance of defense or success for their cause.

Extremely rare were the cases where certain masters bought slaves out of pity and wanted to set them free. However, surprisingly, in some of these cases, the slaves bought to be set free chose to remain willingly as servants to their redeemers.

This is also our story. Sin enslaved us, destroyed the lives of most of us, and left us without a future.

But Jesus came and paid for us with His blood, and following this redemption, we decided to willingly be His servants.

"We know that our old man was crucified with Him, that the body of sin might be done away with, that we should no longer be slaves of sin." – Romans 6:6

The first quality of a servant is his unconditional **obedience**. A servant does not do what he wants but what the master desires. If we were once slaves to sin, now we are slaves to righteousness.

"Do you not know that to whom you present yourselves slaves to obey, you are that one's slaves whom you obey, whether of sin leading to death, or of obedience leading to righteousness?" – Romans 6:16

A second quality of a servant is **availability**. No slave in ancient times could ever be permitted to say to the master that he does not have time when asked to do something. He could not complain about the weather or about his personal health. He was obligated to be available at any time to execute what the master wanted.

Isaiah not only heard God's call but was also available to fulfill it:

"I heard the voice of the Lord, saying: 'Whom shall I send, and who will go for Us?' Then I said, 'Here am I! Send me.'" – Isaia 6:8

It is painful to see Christians who listen with their ears but are not available with their deeds. They understand the Master's will, but it is only of second importance for them. In their lives, unfortunately, personal matters and material desires are the priority, and only somewhere at the end of the list are spiritual matters.

Another quality of a servant is **faithfulness**. He does not obey and is not available only one day a year. Nor just two Sundays a month. He is ready to give up his own will and do whatever the master wants at any time, continuously. He will not be stopped by the ridicule of people; he will not give up because of tiredness and will not find excuses to stop the work he was entrusted with.

Can you imagine how the churches would look like if every Christian were obedient, available, and faithful, and in addition to all these, he acted with a fourth quality in everything he does, namely **kindness**?

"Well done, good and faithful servant; you were faithful over a few things, I will make you ruler over many things. Enter into the joy of your lord." – Matthew 25:21

A father came to his wife's graveyard with his little boy. While cleaning his wife's grave, the child, who had just learned to read, began to spell out what was written on the crosses! "Here rests the servant of God X," "Here rests the servant of God Y," "Here rests the servant of God Z," etc. After a while, the young child came to his father and asked a surprising question: "Dad, were all the people in this cemetery servants of God?" "Yes, son!" came the prompt reply. "Then, Dad, where are the thieves buried? What about those who did only bad things? And in which graveyard are the criminals buried, Dad?" The father pondered for a moment. The child was absolutely right! Not all the dead in the cemetery had been servants of God!

My invitation for all of us for today is to live our lives in such a way that if our cross at the cemetery reads, "Here rests the servant of the Lord...", this epitaph will be a truth, not a lie.

The most beautiful freedom is to be a slave to Christ. But it does not have to be something written on a cross - rather, something etched in the hearts of each one of us.

August 19

MUDDY PITS

"So they took Jeremiah and cast him into the dungeon of Malchiah the king's son, which was in the court of the prison, and they let Jeremiah down with ropes. And in the dungeon, there was no water, but mire. So Jeremiah sank in the mire." – Jeremiah 38:6

Jeremiah had repeatedly spoken the truth from God to the people. He urged the people and their leaders to change their ways and follow God in obedience, turning away from idolatry. He tried to make them realize that God's judgment upon them and the Babylonian captivity were not mere happenstance.

However, neither the prophet nor his prophecies were well-received. They isolated him, threw him into prison, and later into a pit with mud, hoping he would stop proclaiming the truth.

When we cannot bear someone's message, we are tempted to inflict wounds on that person. When we run out of arguments, we are tempted to resort to personal attacks.

When we dislike someone, the easiest thing is to sling mud at them.

How many servants are not believed because they have been unjustly slandered? Splashed with mud and smeared, thrown into the pits of defamation, and gossiped about worse than thieves and criminals.

I do not know if you have ever thrown mud at someone. I do not know if, when you did not like the message, you chose the path of stones and gossip. What I can tell you on behalf of God is that His people need prayer.

"Praying always with all prayer and supplication in the Spirit, being watchful to this end with all perseverance and supplication for all the saints— and for me, that utterance may be given to me, that I may open my mouth boldly to make known the mystery of the gospel." – Ephesians 6:18-19

Alexander the coppersmith is remembered in history as someone who struck Paul when he could have been remembered in God's records as a fellow believer:

"Alexander the coppersmith did me much harm. May the Lord repay him according to his works." – 2 Timothy 4:14

Those who serve with sincerity and dedication will have a rich reward. However, those who drag others into pits will also be rewarded, but in a different way...

Life is so transient. For eternity, we will reap what we have sown.

He who sows mercy will reap mercy

He who deals with mud will remain with dirty hands...

The following words written by Magda Isanoș[22] are so true:

And it seems so strange that one can still find
So much time for hatred,
When life is barely a drop
Between this minute that ticks

And the next one – and it seems incomprehensible
And sad that we do not look to Heaven more often,
That we do not pick flowers and do not smile,
We, who die so quickly.

[22] Romanian lawyer, poet, and writer, born in Iași.

August 20

JESUS, THE BREAD OF LIFE

"And Jesus said to them, 'I am the bread of life. He who comes to Me shall never hunger, and he who believes in Me shall never thirst.'" – John 6:35

Just as our body needs physical food, our soul needs spiritual food. Just as today, in those times bread was the most used food.

Jesus Christ draws a comparison between the most commonly used food for the body and Himself, who is our daily spiritual need. He wants to demonstrate that if you cannot live without the most important physical food, you will not be able to live without the most important spiritual "food" either.

Jesus, the Bread of Life, can fulfill all your spiritual needs. After you "taste" from Him, you will no longer need to go anywhere else to seek resources for your soul. That is why the psalmist says:

"Oh, taste and see that the Lord is good; blessed is the man who trusts in Him!" – Psalms 34:8

Instead of the taste of sin, the Bible asks us to taste holiness. Instead of transient things, let us taste from the eternal things. Instead of the stale and moldy bread of the Devil, let us taste from the fresh Bread of Heaven.

Refusing to feed yourself physically will lead to exhaustion in a matter of days. First, you will lose your strength to work, then, step by step, your body will weaken more and more, and after several dozens of days without food, the body will die.

If you want to be spiritually strong, you need spiritual food. If you want to work in the Lord's field, you need the "calories" given by the Bread of Life. If you want to resist the Devil in daily battles, you need to eat every day from the spiritual food of the Word.

Have you fed yourself today from the Bread of Life?

August 21

JESUS, THE WATER OF LIFE

Jesus answered and said to her, "If you knew the gift of God and who it is who says to you, 'Give Me a drink,' you would have asked Him, and He would have given you living water." – John 4:10

At Jacob's well, Jesus encountered a Samaritan woman. The sixth Jewish hour corresponds to noon in our time. Most people came to the well in the morning or evening to avoid the fatigue of carrying water when it was exceptionally hot. The Samaritan woman chose the noon hour to avoid meeting other people from the village of whom she was ashamed because, as she herself confessed, she had lived with five different men up until that day...

Sometimes, Jesus arranges a meeting with us when we no longer desire to meet anyone. When ashamed of our deeds, we want to avoid additional questions and the curiosity of those around us.

While she draws water from the well, Jesus tells her about a much better Water. About Living Water.

About an Oasis for the soul that is devastated by sin. About a Spring that never runs dry. About our fundamental need: Jesus.

She knew about Jesus in theory:

"The woman said to Him, 'I know that Messiah is coming' (who is called Christ). 'When He comes, He will tell us all things.'" – John 4:25

but she did not know about the surprise at that moment:

"Jesus said to her, 'I who speak to you am He.'" – John 4:26

Have you had the opportunity to meet Jesus, the Water of Life?

When this meeting takes place, all other things become secondary:

"The woman then left her waterpot, went her way into the city, and said to the men..." – John 4:28

Jesus transforms a woman with a dubious past into a trustworthy woman. Jesus changes those to whom people point in a negative way, transforming them to be later held up as examples of changed lives.

When you authentically meet Jesus, the Water of Life, you receive Water that will benefit others too:

"He who believes in Me, as the Scripture has said, out of his heart will flow rivers of living water." – John 7:38

Do not forget to drink daily from the Water of Life, and then be ready to give to drink to others who are thirsty all around you...

August 22

JESUS, THE LIGHT OF THE WORLD

"Then Jesus spoke to them again, saying, 'I am the light of the world. He who follows Me shall not walk in darkness but have the light of life.'" – John 8:12

From a spiritual perspective, sin brings darkness. On the ID card of many Jews, next to the address, it read, "the land of the shadow of death." Not only did they live in darkness, but they also walked in darkness 24 hours a day:

"The people who walked in darkness have seen a great light; those who dwelt in the land of the shadow of death, upon them a light has shined." – Isaiah 9:2

When Isaiah announced the birth of Jesus, he spoke about darkness, but he also spoke about light. And where light comes, joy comes too:

"You have multiplied the nation and increased its joy; they rejoice before You according to the joy of harvest, as men rejoice when they divide the spoil." – Isaiah 9:3

Someone who stays in the dark will always make uncertain choices. Arbitrarily. Like rolling the dice... Based on carnal instincts and without any fear of God. When a person stays in the dark, he lives in a chaotic life, without priorities and without goals.

In a house where it is dark, losses occur. The coin was lost in the house because of darkness.

"Or what woman, having ten silver coins, if she loses one coin, does not light a lamp, sweep the house, and search carefully until she finds it?" – Luke 15:8

Some light the lamp before they lose their health, the years of their life, their children, etc. These are the few... The majority, however, realize the need for light just like the woman above: after suffering considerable losses...

Where the Light of the world is present, there is transparency. There are no hidden things between children and parents, nor between husband and wife. Phone passwords are not meant to hide the cobwebs of sin. Honesty and truth come only where darkness disappears.

Plato said, "We can easily forgive a child who is afraid of the dark; the real tragedy of life is when men are afraid of the light."

The Devil and those who follow him do not desire the Light.

"And this is the condemnation, that the light has come into the world, and men loved darkness rather than light because their deeds were evil." – John 3:19

Do you love the Light? Have you allowed Jesus to kindle it in your life? Do not forget that "windows not facing the sun have little value."

August 23

JESUS, THE DOOR OF THE SHEEP

"Then Jesus said to them again, 'Most assuredly, I say to you, I am the door of the sheep. I am the door. If anyone enters by Me, he will be saved, and will go in and out and find pasture.'" – John 10:7, 9

Usually, a door serves to separate one room from another or to distinguish the outside from the inside. It allows only certain people to enter a particular room.

From a spiritual perspective, Jesus is the only Door to enter the Kingdom of Heaven. He paid the price for our sins, and only through Him do we have access to God the Father.

Just a few moments before saying the above words, Jesus had healed a blind man. However, the Pharisees found various reasons not to believe in that healing. It was not the first time they denied Jesus' actions and identity. They had become so legalistic that they rejected anyone and anything that did not come through them and with their approval.

In this context, Jesus comes and says, "I am the Door, not you. I have the first and last word, not you."

There are people to whom no one gives a chance anymore. They are pointed at and ignored, not allowed to enter the Kingdom by the religious leaders of the time:

"Woe to you, scribes and Pharisees, hypocrites! For you shut up the kingdom of heaven against men; for you neither go in yourselves, nor do you allow those who are entering to go in." – Matthew 23:13

Or if they are allowed, all sorts of conditions are imposed that have no biblical basis.

Jesus comes and reminds us: "I am the Door." We do not enter the Kingdom through certain saints, nor through worshiping certain paintings, or through certain canons. Only through the sacrifice of Jesus and through repentance.

The night of the hell`s eternity is getting closer and in it, those who remain on the outside will weep forever.

Have you entered the "sheepfold" of the Kingdom of Heaven through Jesus Christ, so that you may find eternal rest?

August 24

JESUS: THE WAY, THE TRUTH, AND THE LIFE

"Jesus said to him, 'I am the way, the truth, and the life. No one comes to the Father except through Me.'" – John 14:6

Jesus defined together the three elements necessary for each person to have a blessed future. If these three are not exactly as defined by Jesus, they make no sense.

Who would want a way without having, in the end, eternal life?

Who would want life without truth?

Who would want to know about the truth, hear about eternal life, but not know the way to them?

In a world where there are many ways:

"There is a way that seems right to a man, but its end is the way of death." – Proverbs 14:12

Jesus showed us only one Way that matters in the end.

In a world where there are many lies, Jesus showed us who the Truth is:

"Sanctify them by Your truth. Your word is truth." – John 17:17

In a world where each one of us will die a physical death, Jesus told us that the first death is not dangerous, but the eternal one is:

"And do not fear those who kill the body but cannot kill the soul. But rather fear Him who is able to destroy both soul and body in hell." – Matthew 10:28

Have you found the true Way? Have you found the Truth? Have you met the only One who can give eternal life?

Is it not better for the Bible to rebuke you through the truth and show you the way to eternal life than to make you feel comfortable in a lie and, in the end, live eternity away from God?

Many teachers throughout the centuries believed that they knew the truth and could speak about the truth, but only Jesus could say, "I am the Truth!"

Stay on the Way, stay in the Truth, and, in the end, you will rejoice in eternity with Him.

August 25

JESUS, THE TRUE VINE

"I am the true vine, and My Father is the vinedresser." – John 15:1

God is the Vinedresser. The branches of the vine that are to bear grapes are the saved people. The Vine (the main vine stem) is symbolized by Jesus Christ.

The greatest thing we can do, if we do it without Him, it is nothing:

"...apart from Me, you can do nothing." – John 15:5

The branch cannot be anchored in the air, nor directly in the ground. It needs the vine stem to draw the sap necessary to bear tasty grapes.

Only those who bear fruit are true believers. When it comes to branches, the design, size, or other things that catch the eye do not matter. When the vinedresser takes control, the only thing that matters is the fruit. And producing fruit is conditioned by the branches` remaining in the vine.

"Abide in Me, and I in you. As the branch cannot bear fruit of itself unless it abides in the vine, neither can you unless you abide in Me." – John 15:4

John 15 talks about bearing fruit, much fruit, and more fruit. However, it does not say anything about too much fruit. Too much patience, too much love, or too much kindness is nonsense.

Today is a new opportunity to check if we are bearing fruit. If we are, we should expect pruning, suffering, and molding. If we were patient last year, God will take us through trials this year to make us even more patient.

If we do not bear fruit, let us not forget that at any moment we are threatened with being cut off.

"If anyone does not abide in Me, he is cast out as a branch and is withered, and they gather them and throw them into the fire, and they are burned." – John 15:6

Remaining in Jesus is the guarantee of bearing fruit. Stay in Him, depend on Him. Hold on to God every day, and you will have a blessed harvest!

August 26

JESUS, THE GOOD SHEPHERD

"I am the good shepherd. The good shepherd gives His life for the sheep." – John 10:11

The supreme sacrifice is not made up of *likes,* piles of promises, or sweet words. The supreme sacrifice is presented through an offering. And the greatest sacrifice is to give what is most precious to you, namely, your life.

This is what Jesus did for us. That is why it is worth trusting Him. That is why it is worth following Him. Confucius did not die for anyone. Neither did Buddha. Nor Allah. The only One who came to seek the lost sheep and bring them into the flock at the cost of His life is Jesus.

The Great Shepherd protects us from fierce wolves. He guides us to blessed pastures. He honors us with His voice and challenges us to listen to it and distinguish it from other voices:

> *"And when he brings out his own sheep, he goes before them; and the sheep follow him, for they know his voice. Yet they will by no means follow a stranger, but will flee from him, for they do not know the voice of strangers." – John 10:4-5*

The guarantee of our salvation is not the denomination to which we belong. There are 4,300 religions in this world. There are many strangers who call themselves "religious leaders." Many false shepherds. Many voices calling you.

Jesus has only one flock. One faith. One baptism. One way.

Be careful about the woods around you. Be careful of the bushes that the Devil puts in your way. Keep an eye out for anyone who says they are Jesus but lacks His character and sacrifice.

The sheep do not have to fight the wolves, just stay close to the Shepherd.

August 27

LEARN FROM THE BEE

"Son, eat honey because it is good, and the honeycomb is sweet to your taste!" – Proverbs 24:13

For two pounds of honey, 1,200 bees cover over 25,000 miles and collect nectar from two million flowers.

A lifespan of 6 weeks. Work. Exhaustion. Running around. Daily effort. And for what? Just to produce honey. The bee teaches us that what you do with your life is more important than life itself. It is not important how long you live but what you do while you live. I have met people who lived for 80 years and left only garbage behind: quarrels, scandals, and a life unworthy of following.

What are you leaving behind?

The fly goes through the garbage. The bee flies among flowers. You cannot walk all day through the world's dumpsters and produce acacia honey. Your environment will define the purpose for which you live. The bee does not seek advice from spiders, nor does it gossip with flies.

Another thing: when the bee stings, it dies. Its role is to make honey, not to sting. When it changes its role, it dies.

Beware of stings. Let others deal with them. You have a noble purpose. Do not ruin your life in court. Nor in quarrels and replies to scoffers. They will ruin the noble purpose for which you were created by God.

May God help you leave something sweet in the heart of every person you meet in this life.

August 28

LEARN FROM THE ANT

"Go to the ant, you sluggard! Consider her ways and be wise!" – Proverbs 6:6

Have you ever seen an ant begging? Or sitting on a bench, counting the cars that pass by? Have you seen an ant wearing sunglasses and taking selfies all day, showcasing its wealth or the beach where it relaxes?

Every time I have seen an ant, it was in motion. At work. Carrying something on its back. It was in a group with other ants working.

Diligence is one of the treasures that every person should have. Diligence does not linger on dreams but moves to action. As someone once said, "The pessimist says, 'It cannot be done.' The optimist says, 'It can be done.' The diligent one says, 'I have done it.'"

Each ant has two stomachs: one for accumulating food for itself and another for the colony. And we have two hands.

With one, we should accumulate, and with the other, we should give. We work for ourselves to be able to help others. Not the lazy ones but the sick, the orphans, the widows, or the poor who work but cannot overcome their needs on their own.

> *"He who steals must steal no longer, but rather he must labor, performing with his own hands what is good so that he will have something to share with one who has need." – Ephesians 4:28*

Marin Preda[23] said something interesting: "An ant cannot overturn a mountain, but it can move it from its place slowly, piece by piece." At a wedding, while counting the money, the bride and groom saw an envelope more transparent than the others, with a note inside. They thought it was a check for a car or a ticket for a vacation. They carefully opened it. They found the following words on the note: *Start working, dear ones!*

Let's be diligent! So diligent as if we were to live for a long time... So attached to material things as if we were to die tomorrow!

I conclude with what John Wesley said: "Be honest, holy, diligent, frugal, economical, gain all you can, then give, and thus you will never go astray. Earn as much as you can, save as much as you can, give as much as you can."

---

[23] Romanian novelist, born on August 5, 1922, and known for his significant contributions to literature.

AUGUST 29

STAND UP FOR JESUS!

"But there are some Jews whom you have set over the affairs of the province of Babylon—Shadrach, Meshach, and Abed-Nego—these men, O king, have not paid due regard to you. They do not serve your gods or worship the gold image which you have set up!" – Daniel 3:12

The golden image in the Plain of Dura was 90 feet high. Its consecration was imminent. With its consecration, everyone present had to worship this image.

The instruments started the parade. People threw themselves face down one by one. However, three young men "ruined" the celebration. They remained standing because the only One worthy of our worship is God!

They agreed to be thrown into the fiery furnace and pay the price of obedience. There, in the fire, God sent His Angel to adjust the temperature of the furnace.

We need people who will stand for God. More and more people have this fear: *Will I lose my job? Will my friends abandon me? Will God abandon me?*

Fear often paralyzes us, and the shame of not being different and then being ridiculed tempts us to worship. But the persecution we may endure from those around us is a blessing if we look through the eyes of faith:

"Blessed are those who are persecuted for righteousness' sake, for theirs is the kingdom of heaven!" – Matthew 5:10

Contemporary Christianity desperately needs people with a backbone. People ready to face any fear and any ridicule and stand in the gap for the Truth! People who say: *Regardless of what I lose, what matters most is not losing my faith...* We should fear God, not people. We should listen to Him, not to colleagues or friends.

"But Peter and the other apostles answered and said: 'We ought to obey God rather than men!'" – Acts 5:29

Do not be afraid to stand!

Those who stand in the Plain of Dura will be blessed with the presence of God in the fiery furnace!

AUGUST 30

THE FALL OF AN EMPIRE

"And what I say to you, I say to all: 'Watch!'" – Mark 13:37

Edward Gibbon was an English historian and member of the British Parliament. His most important achievement is "The History of the Decline and Fall of the Roman Empire", a work published in 6 volumes, which involved enormous work in studying primary historical sources.

According to Edward Gibbon, the 5 major causes of the fall of the Roman Empire are the following:

1. The rapid increase of divorce, with the undermining of the sanctity of the home, which is the basis of society.
2. Higher and higher taxes; and the spending of public money on bread and circuses.
3. The mad craze for pleasure, sports becoming every year more exciting and more brutal.
4. The building of gigantic armies to fight external enemies, when the most deadly enemy, the decadence of the people, lay within.
5. The decay of religion; faith fading into mere form, losing touch with life, and becoming impotent to guide it.

Any nation that falls seems to follow the same path. Any empire or union of countries that accepts compromise in the family (which is the fundamental cell of society) will have the same end: entering into the anonymity of history. Any people who no longer values the fear of God and does not allow divine principles to govern them will, sooner or later, end up in the dustbin of history.

The family must remain family. Christianity must affirm its values at all costs. The pursuit of pleasure and sin must be replaced by the pursuit of righteousness. God must remain first in every individual's life, and then all other things will be in order.

Pubs should close and more churches should open. Dancing clubs and festivals should be replaced by public religious gatherings to ask God's forgiveness and preach the gospel.

Abortion clinics should go bankrupt, and parents should turn to their greatest wealth, namely children. Not only to receive them, but to invest in them.

Family should be valued more than career. We should place higher value on children's education than on work.

As C.S. Lewis said, "Children are not a distraction from the more important work. They are the most important work."

Beautiful dreams, right?

Unfortunately, the world continues to walk down a steep slope to perdition. What are we, the Christians, doing during this time?

> *"Do not love the world or the things in the world. If anyone loves the world, the love of the Father is not in him. For all that is in the world—the lust of the flesh, the lust of the eyes, and the pride of life—is not of the Father but is of the world. And the world is passing away, and the lust of it; but he who does the will of God abides forever." – 1 John 2:15–17*

Stay on God`s side so He can stay by your side as well. Honor Him by living in obedience to His Word and you will not suffer the fate of the Roman Empire.

August 31

SAND IN THE SANDALS

"But now you yourselves are to put off all these: anger, wrath, malice, blasphemy, filthy language out of your mouth." – Colossians 3:8

The **"Coast to Coast Walk"** is the name given to the walking route from one coast to another in Northern England. It is 180 miles long, passes through three national parks, and can be completed in about 15 days of regular walking.

One person who completed this journey was asked, "What did you find most challenging? A specific mountain, a deeper valley, a lonelier path?" The answer was surprising: "The most challenging was the sand in the sandals..."

On our way to Heaven, most often, it's not the big sins that are the heaviest burden. Many times, we successfully give up alcohol, smoking, immorality, stealing, etc. Yet, there are a few smaller things we encounter daily.

If you make a list of the arguments you have had with someone in a year, you will notice that in 99% of the cases, you argued about small things. Trivial matters.

Some people progress very slowly towards their destination not because of a mountain but because of the sand grains in their sandals. The tiny grains of envy, dishonorable jokes, murmuring, moments of discontent. A little malice here and there, an untruthful word spoken about someone, or a half-truth.

Let us pause from time to time and shake off the sand from our sandals, and the next steps will be much easier...

September 1

A MOMENT OF ASTRONOMY

"Can you bind the cluster of the Pleiades, or loose the belt of Orion?" – Job 38:31

The speed of light is 186,000 miles per second. If we could travel at this speed, we would orbit the Earth 7 times in one second. In 2 seconds, we would reach the Moon. In 4 minutes, we would be on Mars, and in 5 hours, we would reach the farthest planet in the solar system, namely Pluto.

In 4 years, at the speed of light, we could reach the nearest star, Proxima Centauri. Going beyond our galaxy, the distance to the nearest galactic neighbor (the Andromeda galaxy) is about two million light-years. It is good to know, however, that there are billions of galaxies...

Isn't it true that just thinking about a fraction of these things leaves us in awe? Thus, we can say as the psalmist:

> *"When I consider Your heavens, the work of Your fingers, the moon and the stars, which You have ordained, What is man that You are mindful of him, and the son of man that You visit him?" – Psalm 8:3-4*

On the fourth day of Creation, God created a hundred billion galaxies, each with hundreds of billions of stars. Think about this: when we look with the naked eye at a clear sky, we can see a few thousand stars (up to 10,000 in ideal conditions). And the Milky Way, which includes the Solar System, has several hundred billion stars.

With great conviction, the psalmist declared:

> *"The heavens declare the glory of God, and the firmament shows His handiwork." – Psalm 19:1*

Such a magnificent God thinks more about you and me than about the stars. The complexity of creation and the mystery of salvation, as well as God's concern for humanity, are unimaginable.

September 2

THE SCOTSMAN'S OARS

"For as the body without the spirit is dead, so faith without works is dead also." – *James 2:26*

It is said that a wise Scottish boatman had a boat for transporting passengers. On one oar, he carved the word "faith," and on the other, the word "works." The moral he wanted to convey to all passengers was that using only one of the two oars would make the boat go in circles. Using neither would keep the boat stationary. Using both ensured a safe journey to the destination, with visible progress.

Likewise is our life. People say, "I believe." Yet, for most, the lack of works worthy of their faith causes them to go in circles. They are under the impression that they are progressing, that they are living a good life, and that declaring themselves Christians on a census form is enough.

Many have this mentality, thinking that a creed at the level of consciousness is sufficient and that you can do anything you want. However, the Bible contradicts this type of thinking:

*"I know **your works**, love, service, **faith**, and your patience; and as for your works, the last are more than the first."* – *Revelation 2:19*

When God looks at the faith in our hearts, He also looks at our outward actions. When He analyzes our thoughts, He also analyzes our steps. God is not satisfied that we know the creed by heart on Sundays. He desires us to be able to "recite" it through actions "worthy of our faith" throughout the entire week.

Richard Wurmbrand stated a profound truth: "If faith is not followed by deeds, either the faith is not true, or you do not believe in it."

Today, I pray that you, dear reader, may have strong faith. Authentic faith. Faith based on Scriptural truths. But at the same time, I pray that your actions may be the evidence of your faith.

Faith is invisible. Its actions, however, are remarkably visible.

September 3

"I HAVE NO ONE TO FORGIVE ME!"

"Then He said to her, 'Your sins are forgiven!'" – Luke 7:48

Marghanita Laski was a well-known writer who publicly admitted to being an atheist and lived her life away from God. Not long before her death in 1988, she said on television, "What I envy most about you, Christians, is forgiveness; I have nobody to forgive me..."

The burden of our sins weighs heavily on our conscience. Because we are created with several compartments (physical, emotional, familial, spiritual, etc.), this spiritual weight cannot be resolved by a solution from the other areas of life. I have seen people burdened by the sin and guilt of living without God, people who have attempted to solve this problem through material, educational, or emotional means, but who, of course, have not succeeded to do that.

The only one who can offer forgiveness to the sinner is Jesus Christ, if we sincerely repent:

> *"If we confess our sins, He is faithful and just to forgive us our sins and to cleanse us from all unrighteousness." – 1 John 1:9*

Then, as a response to the forgiveness he received, the forgiven person will be ready to forgive those who wrong him:

> *"Bearing with one another, and forgiving one another, if anyone has a complaint against another; even as Christ forgave you, so you also must do." – Colossians 3:13*

Have your sins been forgiven? Do not wait until your deathbed to address this issue. Come to God now with tears, humility, and repentance, and He will forgive you. Then, go and do the same with those around you.

SEPTEMBER 4

"I STAND WITH THE GOD OF MY MOTHER!"

Robert Ingersoll was known not only as a lawyer and writer but also as a great agnostic speaker. After one of his lectures, two students were talking on their way home:

"I think he dismantled the foundations of Christianity quite well, don't you?" one of the students said.

"No, not at all. Ingersoll could not explain my mother's life. And until he can explain her lifestyle and her walking with God, I stand with the God of my mother!" the other replied.

There are many speeches. Opinions and ideas abound from various people who wish to dismantle Christianity. Atheism is gaining more ground, and the abandonment of faith is continuously increasing. The display of human wisdom has reached a high threshold without realizing that beyond that threshold lies sheer madness:

"Professing to be wise, they became fools." – Romans 1:22

What atheism can never dismantle is a simple and faithful believer`s walk with God. History has testimonies of many people who trusted in God and were willing to die at the stake for Him. Therefore, when the Bible speaks of role models, it urges us to carefully consider not the people in whom faith died but those who died in faith:

"Remember those who rule over you, who have spoken the word of God to you, whose faith follow, considering the outcome of their conduct." – Hebrews 13:7

A young man from a family with 17 children, visibly marked by the example and sacrifice of his mother over her 47 years of marriage, once told me, "Brother Cristi, if my mother does not make it to Heaven, I do not know who else will..."

Testimonies around us influence us. The life with God of someone we have personally known will surely make us ponder. Philosophers come and go. Agnostics will continue with their questions to which they themselves are not sure they have answers. What truly matters, however, is not rhetoric but lifestyle. Not the advertisement but the product. Not the talk but the deed...

The steadfast faith of simple believers acts as a beacon of truth, unshaken by the changing tides of intellectual trends. These lives, deeply rooted in the practice of their faith, challenge the core of atheistic arguments not through debate, but through the undeniable evidence of a life transformed by God. In the end, it is the authenticity of a lived faith that speaks louder than any philosophical discourse.

I do not know any atheist willing to be burned at the stake for his ideas. The ultimate testimony is not in eloquent arguments, but in the willingness to lay down one's life for the truth. Such commitment and sacrifice underscore the profound difference between mere belief and living faith, drawing a stark contrast that no skeptic's speech can erase.

September 5

"I DID NOT KNOW HOW TO LIVE!"

"I have been crucified with Christ; it is no longer I who live, but Christ lives in me; and the life which I now live in the flesh I live by faith in the Son of God, who loved me and gave Himself for me." – Galatians 2:20

In a hospital in the U.S., suffering from cancer and connected to an oxygen tube, an orthodox Jew was living his final moments. He struggled to breathe, and there was no relative or friend by his side to comfort him in the intense suffering he was going through. When Ming He, a fourth-year medical student, entered the Jew's room, he looked at her and said, "Now, on the verge of death, I realize that I did not know how to live." Ming He later admitted that she did not know what to say to the Jew.

Life without God is lived without purpose. It is lived only for pleasures and entertainment. For the here and now.

As an advertisement once said, "Live in the moment!" When you think that everything ends at the grave, your only purpose will be to live each moment to the fullest. You will use any opportunity of sin to satisfy your personal pleasures and your ego. You will do absolutely everything you desire, whether it is moral or not, because you think that you do not have to give an account to anyone after death. But Ecclesiastes says otherwise,

"Rejoice, o young man, in your youth, and let your heart cheer you in the days of your youth; walk in the ways of your heart, and in the sight of your eyes; but know that for all these God will bring you into judgment." – Ecclesiastes 11:9

Life with God is different from the life pagans live.

"Now this I say, and testify in the Lord, that you should no longer walk as the rest of the Gentiles walk, in the futility of their mind, having their understanding darkened, being alienated from the life of God, because of the ignorance that is in them, because of the blindness of their heart." – Ephesians 4:17-18

A life that leaves no regrets on the deathbed is one lived according to the principles of Scripture and in obedience to God. It is a life lived with the purpose of being helpful to those around you and spreading the fragrance of Christ in the hearts of those you meet.

Have you learned how to live?

September 6

"BE STRONG, RIDLEY!"

"Therefore whoever confesses Me before men, him I will also confess before My Father who is in heaven. But whoever denies Me before men, him I will also deny before My Father who is in heaven." – Matthew 10:32-33

Hugh Latimer lived in the 16th century. Shortly after being ordained as a Catholic priest, he began to embrace the ideas of the Reformation and to biblically expose the heresies of the church in which he ministered.

He started publicly preaching about the need to translate the Bible into English, even though not long before, William Tyndale's translation of the New Testament had been banned.

Once, he was invited to preach before the King of England, Henry VIII. Latimer declared, "I heard two voices. One told me, 'Preach in such a way as to please the King of England.' And the other told me, 'Preach in such a way as to please the King of kings.'"

He chose to preach only what the King of kings had asked him to say. He fell out of favor with Henry, and not long after, he was sentenced to death by burning at the stake.

When he learned of the death sentence, he said, "I thank God most heartily that He hath prolonged my life to this end, that I may in this case glorify God by this kind of death."

On the day of execution, he walked toward the stake along with another close friend who shared the same convictions. It is said that the last words he said to Ridley were, "Play the man, Master Ridley! We shall this day light such a candle, by God`s grace, in England, as I trust shall never be put out!"

Oh what men of God they were! What a price these heroes paid for the proclamation of the Bible!

They were not ashamed of anyone but were able to preach before the King. Are you able to preach before your neighbors and colleagues without being ashamed of God?

September 7

WHAT DO YOU DO IN THE YEARS OF PEACE?

"They had been three years without war between Syria and Israel." – 1 Kings 22:1

In our lives, we have moments of peace and tranquility, but we also have moments of suffering. We have years when we are healthy, but we also have years when we suffer. There are periods when, financially, everything is fine, but we also go through times when we have to depend on extremely limited resources. We have days when we are appreciated, but we also have days when we are unjustly slandered.

Have you considered that the years of peace are years when we can prepare for turbulent periods?

There is a huge risk that when everything is going well, we become lazy, forgetting that dark clouds are on the horizon, and celebrating victory before the war is over.

The challenge I have for you today, reader, is this: in the area where things are going well for you, start preparing for the day when it will not be the same.

If you are doing well financially, prepare for the moments when you will be on the edge. Such moments will surely come. Joseph asked the Egyptians to do this, and it turned out to be a miraculous salvation for the later times.

If you are doing well in terms of health, invest this time in helping the sick. When the wheel turns, you will enjoy the visits of the healthy.

If you have plenty of free time, invest those hours wisely. Other years will come when you will be extremely busy, and you will rejoice knowing that when you had free time, you did not waste it.

The years of peace are years of opportunities. Daniel prepared for the lions` den years in advance, when he was not threatened by anyone or anything.

The young men in the fiery furnace prepared for the Plain of Dura by daily worshiping the One who deserves all worship. David prepared for the battle against Goliath while tending the sheep. Let us value the times of peace.

They are so short...

SEPTEMBER 8

"EMPTY-HANDED..."

She said, "He gave me these six measures of barley; for he said to me, 'Do not go empty-handed to your mother-in-law.'" – Ruth 3:17

Whenever we visit my parents or my wife's parents, they have this desire, like any other parents who sacrifice for their children: "Do not leave empty-handed." A jar of pickles. A box of tomatoes. Something offered with love, from the heart, by parents who have been generous throughout their entire lives. Parents who have sacrificed so much for their children. Parents who have given up a lot for themselves in order to be able to offer to the next generation from whatever little they had.

They always rushed to bring something else while we were on our way to the car. A jar of apricot jam, because "this one is so good, and you do not have any." A jar of canned fruit from the pantry. And with that jar, they brought their hearts as well. But we did not understand this until we became parents ourselves...

What does the Bible ask us to do in return for the sacrifices of our parents?

"If any widow has children or grandchildren, let them first learn to show piety at home and to repay their parents; for this is good and acceptable before God." – 1 Timothy 5:4

To repay. To honor. To put gratitude to work.

Your mother's wrinkles and your father's calloused palms deserve your full appreciation. They do not expect big gifts. But a nice gesture from a child to a parent is always welcome.

Flowers should not be given at the grave but while the person is still alive. Wreaths on the day of the funeral have the "too late" fragrance. Words of thanks and gestures of appreciation should be done while our parents are still alive.

Brad Meltzer said, "No matter how far we come, our parents are always in us."

If they had not given us life, where would we be today? If they had not raised us, where would we have ended up? They always looked at us, and all they wanted was for us to become what they could not be. To reach higher in life. To earn money with less effort. To carry a suitcase in our hands, because they had carried the hoe long enough...

Never go to visit them emptyhanded.

Empty hands hide a poor heart. A heart without affection, without gratitude, without appreciation. And no matter how much money you have, what position you hold, or what car you drive, when your heart is empty, you will not enjoy anything...

Never turn your face towards them with empty hands...

Fill a bag with goodies for them.

And the heart with words of appreciation.

And when you cannot visit them face to face, dial their number.

As long as mom or dad answers at the other end, you are rich...

SEPTEMBER 9

THE LEVEL OF THE GOSPEL

"Hold fast the pattern of sound words which you have heard from me, in faith and love which are in Christ Jesus." – 2 Timothy 1:13

When a bricklayer lays brick upon brick, from time to time, he needs to check with a level if that row of bricks is perfectly straight horizontally. When a craftsman installs tiles or ceramics, he is required, likewise, to use a level to ensure the quality of his work.

The eye deceives, but the level does not. The wall may appear to have been plastered straight, but only the level will prove it...

Our lives will never be beautiful without the level of sound teachings. "It seems like this...", "You might be right...", "I think it does not work this way..." – these are versions that do not help you reach the target. What provides security in a world of personal opinions is the Word of God.

What remains as a ruler that draws perfect lines is the Bible.

Perhaps you left a trail of steps behind you and are not sure about it. Use the "level" and see what needs correction.

Maybe you left a few words in the hearts of others, and you wonder if all those words were good. Use the "level," and the next conversations will be closer to what God wants you to speak.

Use the "ruler of the Gospel." Use the level that others have used and safely reached the finish line.

Do not make decisions without the Scripture. Do not take a step without opening the Holy Book that provides guidance when there are moments of uncertainty. The closer the level is to the craftsman, the better the work will turn out:

"This Book of the Law shall not depart from your mouth, but you shall meditate on it day and night, that you may observe to do according to all that is written in it. For then you will make your way prosperous, and then you will have good success." – Joshua 1:8

Now, we are building in our lives. Now, we are preparing our souls for the meeting with their Creator. Now, we need strong principles in the family. Now, while we are still working, let us confidently use the level...

When the house is finished, it is no longer needed.

September 10

WHY DO YOU CRY TO ME?

"Then the Lord said to Moses, 'Why do you cry to Me? Tell the children of Israel to go forward.'" – Exodus 14:15

The sight was truly terrifying. The Egyptians behind them, the Red Sea ahead of them. The dust raised by the Egyptian chariots was getting larger, and horror gripped the Israelites. The clamors began. The cries of the Jews grew louder. The panic and fear that had set in could not be appeased by anything.

"Now when Pharaoh drew near, the children of Israel lifted their eyes, and behold, the Egyptians marched after them. So they were very afraid, and the children of Israel cried out to the Lord." – Exodus 14:10

They began to cry out to Moses and demand an explanation for leaving Egypt. Regrets started. Unfounded accusations. Complaints. People who had recently been at the highest level of excitement were now ready to forget all the good that God had done for them and all the miracles of the past few weeks.

What did God tell them and what does He tell us as well? Stop talking so much and start moving forward. Stop being terrified by what is behind you and be ready to step forward in faith. Standing still and complaining did not help anyone reach Canaan. Accusations against leaders and regrets about leaving Egypt were of no use.

When you start moving at the prompting of God`s Word, His Angel goes between you and the problem that follows you from behind and tries to catch up with you:

"The Angel of God, who went before the camp of Israel, moved and went behind them; and the pillar of cloud went from before them and stood behind them." – Exodus 14:19

When you step forward and you take God at His word, darkness comes over your problem, and light comes over you.

"He took off their chariot wheels, so that they drove them with difficulty; and the Egyptians said, 'Let us flee from the face of Israel, for the Lord fights for them against the Egyptians.'" – Exodus 14:25

For you, God opens up new paths, and for the problem behind you, He closes up the Sea.

Step forward in faith.

No problem has yet been invented that could kill the faith in God in the heart of a child.

Excuses and lamentations do not produce miracles. Only stepping forward in faith does...

SEPTEMBER 11

TOO LATE...

Immediately after the first plane hit the Twin Towers on September 11, 2001, over 1000 calls were made by victims in just a 10-minute span. Some spoke directly to their loved ones, while others left desperate messages, a few of which were the following:

"Mom, I love you a lot, I'm sorry..." a girl said to her mother.

"Dad, I love you! Please call Sean (the newlywed husband) and tell him where I am and that I love him!"

"There are a few of us young people stuck here on the upper floors, and we are NOT ready to die! Oh, Lord!" one victim screamed at the 911 phone line.

I learn from this not to wait until the last day of my life to ask for forgiveness from those I have wronged. Nor to tell my loved ones that I love them!

I also learn that relationships matter more than wealth. That "being" is more important than "having".

And most importantly, I learn to prepare to die. After all, it does not matter how long I live but how I live.

For a believer, death is just the door to true life: a life without pain, without curses, without tears.

Do not wait for your last day indifferently!

SEPTEMBER 12

HAVE YOU DONE WHAT YOU COULD?

"She has done what she could. She has come beforehand to anoint My body for burial." – Mark 14:8

You have just read one of the most remarkable commendations made by Jesus during His earthly life to a particular person.

The woman in question came with an alabaster jar, which was only manufactured in a certain region from China and was very expensive. It contained a special perfume. That jar with precious perfume could be unsealed only once. And she chose to pour this precious perfume on Jesus' head.

The murmurs started. Judgments from others. Do you know why? Because if you do nothing, you are judged. And if you do something, you are also ridiculed by those who do nothing. The envy and hatred of those who stand on the sidelines became so great that Jesus had to intervene.

"But Jesus said, 'Let her alone. Why do you trouble her? She has done a good work for Me.'" – Mark 14:6

Jesus will always take the side of those who sacrifice, those who do everything they can with what they have, those who give Him their most precious possessions...

How relieved the woman must have felt in those moments! To have Jesus on your side, defending you - what could be more beautiful than that?

Have you done something beautiful for Jesus? Have you done something for which He can appreciate you?

Have you managed to overcome the ridicule of those around you and give Him the most precious things in your life?

You may not have an alabaster jar, but you have the "vessel of your body." You may not have expensive perfume, but you have the sincere desire of your heart to serve Him with tears and fervor all your life.

Let's not fall into the trap of those who point fingers, of those who want to do good deeds with what others have, not with what they have, of those who push others to sacrifice and then boast that they did it.

I have decided to do what I can with what I have. With my time. With my health. With my family. What things could be more precious than these?

I have decided that if my vessel must be broken, it shall not be shattered in the grandstands of the world but at His feet.

If we are going to use up our resources, let us do it for Jesus, not for the pleasures of sin.

And at the end, Jesus will do for us what He did for that woman: He will give us the most beautiful 'like' we have ever received. It is the only 'like' in the universe that cancels the ridicule of others and brings with it an eternal reward...

SEPTEMBER 13

THE INVISIBLE BONE CANCER

"A sound heart is life to the body, but envy is rottenness to the bones." – Proverbs 14:30

Cain envied Abel. Joseph's brothers envied Joseph. Miriam spoke harshly against Moses out of envy. Saul could not stand to hear that David had become more loved by the people than he was.

Herod was filled with rage when he heard that the magi were seeking a recently born King. The priests and scribes handed Jesus over to Pilate out of envy...

Envy makes the one who accepts it to speak unthoughtful words and make disturbing gestures. Envy halts growth in any field. Being envious of someone else's success will actually cut off your own chance for success.

Have people who have progressed in any field ever been envious? They were too busy with their own work to envy others.

If they had wasted their lives hitting others with envy, they would not have used their own abilities to fulfill their calling.

Be glad for the honest and well-deserved progress of others. By avoiding envy, you will be able to look clearly at the methods and skills of those people and thus gain wisdom by learning from their dedication.

Peter wrote less than Paul, and yet God used him at the level of his own calling. Can you imagine what Peter would have looked like as an apostle envious of Paul? Can you imagine the divisions and party strife he would have caused in the early Church if, instead of words of appreciation, he had used words of envy!

> *"Consider that the longsuffering of our Lord is salvation—as also our beloved brother Paul, according to the wisdom given to him, has written to you, as also in all his epistles, speaking in them of these things, in which are some things hard to understand, which untaught and unstable people twist to their own destruction, as they do also the rest of the Scriptures." – 2 Peter 3:15-16*

Only by appreciating the beautiful work of your neighbor will you grow and become more useful in the work you also have to do.

The man of God does not seek to climb higher by hitting others with envy but by learning from others. What use is it for me to conquer the Everest peak if, during my journey, full of envy, I push into the deep abyss those who are also climbing with great effort? Do I have any honor if I reach the top by doing such a thing?

Flee from envy!

It is a terrible sin that comes from hearts that are frustrated and unfulfilled, but full of bitterness because of the success of others...

It may seem sweet, but instead, it is nothing more than well-disguised poison...

SEPTEMBER 14

HOW DO WE RESPOND TO INSULTS?

"When He was reviled, He did not revile in return; when He suffered, He did not threaten, but committed Himself to Him who judges righteously." – 1 Peter 2:23

Throughout life, we will encounter people who will insult us. Whether at work, in the marketplace, in church, or in another setting, life will bring us face to face with individuals who, through lack of respect and hostile attitude, will try to mock and humiliate us in one way or another.

The first temptation when such circumstances happen to you is to respond in kind. To believe that that person has something personal against you and to give them a reply in the same tone and with similar language.

I want you to understand today that mockers do not have something personal against you; they have something against themselves. They have accumulated frustration, envy, unfulfillment in various areas of their lives, and you just happened to be the person they unleash it upon.

If you respond in kind, you will only open the floodgate for all the ammunition they have at hand and that they will pour out against you from the "dumpster" of their hearts. They will ruin not only your day but also your emotional health (and not infrequently even your physical health when the conflict extends for a longer period of time), and thus they will engage you in a battle that you will never win.

I have not found one instance in the Bible where Jesus responded to mockers with the same tone or with the same words as theirs. He did not waste His time trying to defend Himself in front of those who mocked Him; He clearly understood that the problem was theirs, not His.

You should look at mockers with pity. With compassion. With pain in your heart. Pray for the day when they will understand their behavior and become aware that hurting someone else while they themselves are sunk in mud up to their neck is not at all the solution to salvation.

Be careful with your attitude. With your reactions. With your challenges.

"Silence is the answer of the wise given to fools," someone said.

The next mocker is waiting for you soon enough...

Respond to him with your silence.

SEPTEMBER 15

DANGEROUS CHAIRS

The Bible speaks of a few chairs on which we should not sit. They may seem tempting and inviting for a moment of rest, but they are extremely dangerous. Those who have sat on them paid a high price later.

The first chair on which we should not sit is **the mocker's chair**.

"Blessed is the man who walks not in the counsel of the ungodly, nor stands in the path of sinners, nor sits in the seat of the scornful." – Psalm 1:1

The path towards this chair starts with accepting an invitation to join the gathering of the wicked. Then, seeing the prospect and the team of sinners, you are tempted to linger there for a while. To like the company of people who love iniquity. And eventually, to become friends with them. "Part of the gang," as they say. Familiar. And this familiarity makes you sit on their seat and be "one of them."

The mocker's chair is the seat of those who insult others. Who offend and are rude. Who humiliate and laugh at those around them. This chair seems stable and gives a feeling of superiority to the one sitting on it, but the day will come when God will judge those who have loved such seats.

Do not be one of them!

Another chair we should avoid is **the chair of pride**:

"After these things King Ahasuerus promoted Haman, the son of Hammedatha the Agagite, and advanced him and set his seat above all the princes who were with him." – Esther 3:1

All his life, Haman desired this seat just as many people long for it today... When he got to sit on it, he began to look down on others. To desire honor from the people. To ask for their appreciation at any cost. From there, from this chair, he became filled with anger when he saw that Mordecai did not bow down to him. It was also from this seat that he planned the killing of the Jews. But God was watching and He brought him down from this chair, punishing him severely for his pride.

Last but not least, I would mention another dangerous chair, namely Eli's chair:

"As soon as he mentioned the ark of God, Eli fell backward off his chair by the side of the gate, and his neck was broken and he died, for he was old and heavy. He had judged Israel forty years." – 1 Samuel 4:18

Eli's story is a disturbing one. It is a story in which a father covers the sin of his children who served in the Temple. His sitting on the chair of tolerance was not just for a year, but for decades. He was warned by prophets to correct his behavior and take necessary measures against those who allowed sin to enter the Temple, but it was in vain.

Compromise was present then, and unfortunately, it is present today as well. People who serve but are completely dominated by greed. People who have the name of God on their lips and Mammon in their hearts.

Holiness leads the church into the world. Sin leads the world into the church. Therefore, it is extremely important, based on the authority God has given us, to love all people but not tolerate sin. This chair serves as a warning especially to all leaders called by God not to allow those living in sin to perform any service in the Church of Christ.

Watch out for these chairs! The Bible speaks to us through the examples of others so that we are warned not to fall like they did.

It is better to sit down at the feet of Jesus, like Mary, than on the dangerous and enticing chairs of the Devil:

"Now she had a sister called Mary, who also sat at Jesus' feet and heard His word." – Luke 10:39

Those who sit at the feet of the Lord shall never fall...

SEPTEMBER 16

BLESSED CHAIRS

The Bible speaks of several blessed chairs. People who sit on them are a blessing to those around them. Their altruism comes not from mere presence but from active involvement. Being a blessing to those around us through community involvement brings eternal rewards.

When David passed the baton to his son Solomon, he entrusted to him the plan for the Temple he was to build. One of the items in the blueprint was the **mercy seat.**

"David gave his son Solomon the plans for the porch, its houses, its treasuries, its upper chambers, its inner chambers, and the place of the mercy seat." – 1 Chronicles 28:11

David understood what we should also understand today: that we need to judge every case around us with compassion. Justice has its place, but only mercy can overcome judgment.

Do you have such a chair among your prized possessions? Do you occasionally sit on it, speaking uplifting words to those around you?

Whoever sits on this chair will act with empathy and compassion for the fallen. The Good Samaritan had a whole collection of such mercy seats...

Another chair I noticed in the Bible, metaphorically speaking, of course, is **the chair of receiving guests.** The woman from Shunem had such a chair, and her hospitality sparked a special desire in her heart to do something for the man of God, Elisha.

"Let us make a small upper room on the wall; and let us put a bed for him there, a table, a chair, and a lampstand; so it will be, whenever he comes to us, he can turn in there." – 2 Kings 4:10

When you offer hospitality, you need to make expenses. To ensure they have a pleasant stay, an abundant meal, and exceptional rest, someone must be ready to make sacrifices.

Let us be people who offer hospitality! This chair is becoming rarer because it requires much effort. It demands a fervent love because only this kind of love goes from 'likes' to deeds.

"Above all, love each other deeply, because love covers over a multitude of sins. Offer hospitality to one another without grumbling." – 1 Peter 4:8-9

The last chair I will mention is **the birth stool.** Pharaoh spoke of it negatively:

"And he said, 'When you do the duties of a midwife for the Hebrew women, and see them on the birthstools, if it is a son, then you shall kill him, but if it is a daughter, then she shall live.'" – Exodus 1:16

But we know that each of our mothers sat on it. This chair requires the greatest sacrifices. Recently, I ministered in Spain, where I heard a story about a family that has nine dogs. I thought of my parents. If they wanted an easy life, they would not have raised nine children. But because they feared God, they chose children over dogs, and today, in turn, we, their children, can enjoy blessed lives and families.

God bless all the mothers who sacrificed immensely for their children. The birthing stool is rewarded very little here, by the state, but in eternity, God will reward with the crown of righteousness all the effort you made.

SEPTEMBER 17

DOGS AND CHILDREN

Internet headlines: "Foal rescued from a well." "Curly-haired puppy narrowly avoids being hit by a car." "Ducks managing to cross the street in heavy traffic, miraculously surviving."

What about news about aborted children? What about abandoned children in need of help? What about children with disabilities? What about children achieving excellence at Competitions?

Or, perhaps, animals are already more important than humans? Some people from the Diaspora told me, "If you have 5 children, the chances of finding an apartment to rent are minimal." "But if you have 5 cats or 6 dogs, you are welcomed anywhere..."

Soon, we will be kindly invited to shed tears for stray cats. But who sheds tears for the 9,000 children who are abandoned every year? "Shelters are full of stray dogs," the NGOs complain. Fine, but how about the orphanages that have been full for so long?

How is it that an animal can be adopted more easily than a poor child? If, due to carelessness, a car hits a dog, the whole country must know about it. But does anyone care about the fact that an INTENTIONAL abortion is performed every 5 minutes?

Oh yes, I know I will probably be accused of verbal harassment against animals. I am amazed at God's patience with our world that has changed its values into non-values.

We have 5,000 parents waiting in line to adopt one of the 40,000 abandoned children. However, the law does not consider the child's interest... We have the highest number of orphans in Europe. And yet we are more concerned about whether or not a cat crosses the road safely...

If we continue like this, baby formula will be on the verge of disappearance, and pet food will be displayed at the entrance of every store, on special discount... Then we will build slides for puppies and swings for cats. And selfies with puppies. And having children will become a rarity...

I met children who do not know what Colgate means. Children who washed their clothes while taking a shower for the first time in their lives. We have children for whom a hug would be worth more than a visit to the Eiffel Tower.

We have children who have never been on a camp or field trip in their entire lives. Children who think that the end of the world is at the exit of their village... This is something worth investing in, not dog leashes and muzzles.

Wake up, Romania! Investment in pets only lasts for a few years. Investment in children is for eternity. The home designed by God is not in a dog's cage but around a table where children say "The Lord`s Prayer," and parents smile happily holding their little ones' hands.

SEPTEMBER 18

CONTENT WITH LITTLE

"All the days of the afflicted are evil, but he who is of a merry heart has a continual feast." – Proverbs 15:15

People are different from each other. So different that when they look at a half-full glass, some see the empty half, while others see the full half.

Discontent arises from pessimism. From complaining all day that you cannot do this or that, or that you do not have what someone else has.

It is extremely harmful to the family, colleagues, and the church to be a grumpy person; someone who always sees only what is lacking, what the boss did not offer, or what life has not provided enough of.

We are called to be optimistic and grateful. Called to look at what we have while others do not, and not at what others have and we do not.

You cannot enjoy a vase full of flowers if you have not learned to appreciate a single flower.

There is so much peace in a home where both spouses are joyful people. Content with little just as they are with much. Joyful on sunny days, but also on cloudy days.

I was recently told about a wife who, when her husband gave her a gift worth several thousand dollars, she criticized him for getting a too cheap gift. How sad! How much pain! What a tragedy it must be in a family where one spouse had to constantly increase the price tag in order to please the other.

There is so much happiness is a home where you can enjoy the little things, such as a new day of life, an apple on the table, a slice of bread, or a glass of water...

Rejoice even with little because it will never be lacking!

What we are is more important than what we have...

September 19

WHAT DO STUDIES SAY ABOUT HAPPINESS?

"For all the law is fulfilled in one word, even in this: 'You shall love your neighbor as yourself.'" – Galatians 5:14

In 1938, a decades-long study began at Harvard with 268 students to investigate their physical and mental health, specifically to discover the secret of joy in life. Of the students initially included, only 19 are still alive.

To broaden the study, both the children and grandchildren of these initial participants, numbering over 1,300, were included. Some became lawyers or doctors, while others became schizophrenic or alcoholics. Some kept their families together, while others divorced multiple times.

What the study discovered was surprising: the quality of our relationships and the joy derived from them strongly influence our happiness but also our physical health. More than money or fame, what brings joy and health to our mind and our body is the quality of our relationships, both within the family and within the community (close friends). Those involved in conflicts, divorces, lawsuits, or disputes suffered greatly, while those who loved, sought peace in relationships, and acted altruistically gained on both fronts (both physically and mentally).

Do you think the Bible asks us in vain to love one another and seek peace? God created us in such a way that we cannot be fulfilled when we seek revenge, when we answer evil with evil, or when we act selfishly.

Take care of the relationships you have! Avoid the toxic ones. Love and forgive. Leave revenge in God's hands.

Look for things that build up, that bring people closer. Look for bridges, not fences. Be an outstretched hand, not a striking hand. Be a lighthouse for others, a path to light for those around you.

Do your part, and God will do His.

"And the peace of God, which surpasses all understanding, will guard your hearts and minds through Christ Jesus." – Philippians 4:7

SEPTEMBER 20

HOLD YOUR CHILD'S HAND!

"Arise, lift up the lad, and hold him with your hand, for I will make him a great nation." – Genesis 21:18

The most challenging day of Hagar's life had come. The bread and the water-skin received from Abraham when she was cast out together with her son Ishmael had run out. She threw her child under a shrub and distanced herself a few feet, not wanting to witness the dehydration and death of her beloved lad.

Tears began to flow like rivers. She reached the limits of existence. She wept, and her child wept.

Suddenly, a miracle happened. An angel from heaven called out to her, saying that God had heard the voice of the child. Then the angel asked her to take her lad by the hand.

Hagar obeyed, saw a well of water, and things gradually returned to normal.

As parents, we are called by the same heavenly voice to take our children by the hand. Heaven desires to see us, parents, close to our children. The desert of this world, like the desert Hagar went through, is full of dangers. Water sources are scarce, and the shrubs of the world invite our children to detach themselves from us.

When the distance between parents and children increases, the gap between children and their school peers decreases. When parents become estranged from their children, strangers become their friends. When we spend little time with them, technology will fill the remaining time and take them away.

We are responsible before God to take our children by the hand. To take them by the hand and lead them to the place of worship. To take them by the hand and invite them to the daily altar of home prayer. To take them by the hand and read the Bible with them. To take them by the hand and tell them about our return to God and the wonderful experiences of walking with Him.

Let us take our children by the hand!

It is not enough to just give them clothes, notebooks and books. Food and comfort. They need us the most.

We do so much for them, but we do so few things with them...

Let us take our children by the hand!

Let us keep them close!

And if we, as parents, keep our children close, God commits to stay close to them as well.

"So God was with the lad, and he grew and dwelt in the wilderness and became an archer." – Genesis 21:20

September 21

SHALOM

"I hope to see you shortly, and we shall speak face to face. Peace to you. Our friends greet you. Greet the friends by name. Amen." – 3 John 1:14

September 21st is the International Day of Peace, a day that encourages deep reflection. Over the years, divorce rates in Romania have seen a significant increase. What was once a less common occurrence has now become more prevalent, affecting one in every two Romanian families.

How do these families celebrate today`s holiday? The traumas of such family issues will haunt those involved throughout their entire lives...

At the same time, it's a day that invites us to contemplate, especially as Putin has recently called for the mobilization of 300,000 Russians.

Jesus Himself said:

"Peace I leave with you, My peace I give to you; not as the world gives do I give to you. Let not your heart be troubled, neither let it be afraid." – John 14:27

How do the parents of those who died in the war in Ukraine celebrate this day? When your child dies on the front line, what could still comfort you?

Why else is the International Day of Peace so strange? Because Isaac the Syrian said, "If you are in dispute with your brothers, you are in peace with demons." Lawyers and judges barely have time to take a break. The pending cases are most often related to... the lack of peace.

More than a greeting is needed. Polish people say "Pokuj." Romanians say "Pace." Jews say "Shalom." Arabs say "Salaam."

A person without God has no peace:

"'There is no peace,' says the Lord, 'for the wicked.'" – Isaiah 48:22

And you cannot offer what you do not have! There is no peace without the elimination of sin, just as there can be no pleasant smell without getting rid of the filth.

Do you have a spouse with a clean heart? Then you will have peace in the family. Do you have a congregation that seeks to please the Lord? Then there will be peace there. Do you have a nation that desires to distance itself from sin? Then you will have peace within it.

Man's problem is that he wants the pleasures of sin at the same time with the peace of God... This is impossible! You cannot live next to the filth of dumpsters and enjoy the smell of roses!

The entire media promotes violence, negative news, and yet we wonder why we lack peace. When was the last time you saw an article about someone reconciling two brothers who had not talked to each other in 20 years? Or two families that could not visit each other? Or two neighbors who did not greet each other? When?

God desires peace for us, but do we desire it too?

> *"'For I know the thoughts that I think toward you,' says the Lord, 'thoughts of peace and not of evil, to give you a future and a hope.'" – Jeremiah 29:11*

I remember reading the story of a couple who argued and threatened with divorce. Their four-year-old son had teary eyes watching the arguments. At one point, he took his father's hand, then his mother's hand, and continued to pull until he clasped the two hands together. He became a peacemaker.

This child understood what we also need to understand: that we need peacemakers. They are the ones with a special status:

> *"Blessed are the peacemakers, for they shall be called sons of God." – Matthew 5:9*

One of the young people who started attending our church a few weeks ago told me, "I feel a special peace whenever I come here, and this peace continues to accompany me even when I leave..."

Only in the presence of God there is peace. And He does not promise it to us just once a year but every day.

Shalom Aleichem!

September 22

WEAKNESSES

"For we do not have a High Priest who cannot sympathize with our weaknesses, but was in all points tempted as we are, yet without sin." – Hebrews 4:15

Each of us has certain weaknesses, specific areas where we are more vulnerable to the Devil's temptations.

Cain was vulnerable to envy. Esau, to food. Samson, to his eyes. Judas, to silver. Demas, to the voice of the world.

The Devil knows our weaknesses and attacks us there. That is why it is crucial for us to recognize them. After discovering them, we should take them to God before the Devil brings them to us.

Elijah also had weaknesses, but he came in prayer before God and gained victory:

"Elijah was a man with a nature like ours, and he prayed earnestly that it would not rain, and it did not rain on the land for three years and six months." – James 5:17

The Devil knows your "hunger." He knows your "thirst." He knows your desires. If these have not been fulfilled by the presence of God and His Word, he will come with his own offers. Are you thirsty for the world's attention? He will offer it, but not for free. Are you hungry for success without God? For dishonestly gained wealth? For vain glory? He will offer them but will take your soul in exchange.

"And what does it profit a man if he gains the whole world and loses his own soul?" – Luke 9:25

Do not hide your weaknesses. A soldier who relies on strengths and neglects vulnerable spots will be struck exactly where he least expects it.

I have met people who walked for years with their chests puffed up with pride. They claimed to be strong and perfect, posing as heroes who never shed tears in prayer. They believed that crying, humbling oneself, and acknowledging that they are mere dust is outdated... Unfortunately, in the end, they were powerfully struck by the Devil. Exactly where they struck others, they themselves were defeated.

Do not think of yourself as strong. Do not see yourself as a hero before the war is over. Do not boast about medals until you have the shield of faith and the breastplate of righteousness.

Do not envision yourself on the podium until you have managed to overcome yourself...

Let us remain vigilant, humble, and in prayer. The Devil is watching us all the time:

> *"Be sober, be vigilant; because your adversary the devil walks about like a roaring lion, seeking whom he may devour." – 1 Peter 5:8*

Come before God with your weaknesses! He gives grace to the humble. He lifts up those who acknowledge their sins. He stretches out a helping hand to those who admit they are weak.

God will not point fingers at you, laugh at you, or reject you. On the contrary, He will give you strength, victory, and help to be more vigilant in the areas where you are most vulnerable.

SEPTEMBER 23

YOUTH WITHOUT OLD AGE

The desire of mankind from the most ancient times is to find even the slightest possibility to postpone old age and evade death.

However, no mortal has succeeded in this endeavor, no matter how much they have tried.

Nevertheless, the Bible presents us a way, only one, in which physical death can be faced with dignity, peace, and assurance in the heart. To explain this, we first need to talk about birth.

The Bible speaks of two births: the physical birth (of the body) and the spiritual birth (being born again):

"Jesus answered and said to him, 'Most assuredly, I say to you, unless one is born again, he cannot see the kingdom of God.'" – John 3:3

The first death, which is of the body, cannot be avoided by anyone.

But those who are born again through the spiritual birth can bypass the second death:

"But the cowardly, unbelieving, abominable, murderers, sexually immoral, sorcerers, idolaters, and all liars shall have their part in the lake which burns with fire and brimstone, which is the second death." – Revelation 21:8

To be born again means nothing else but to have a personal encounter with the water (the Word of God) and with the Holy Spirit:

"Jesus answered, 'Most assuredly, I say to you, unless one is born of water and the Spirit, he cannot enter the kingdom of God.'" – John 3:5

Following this personal experience, a person's spirit, assisted by the Bible and the Holy Spirit, will transform the soul of that individual (the mind, reason, and will) and make him like that of Jesus Christ.

The new birth is an event, while the transformation of the old self is nothing but the process of sanctification.

What is the good news? The good news is that whoever has the spiritual birth does not die anymore (spiritually speaking) and does not go through the last judgment!

"Most assuredly, I say to you, he who hears My word and believes in Him who sent Me has everlasting life, and shall not come into judgment, but has passed from death into life." – John 5:24

Don't you want to have youth without old age? Without the fear of physical death? An eternally young spirit?

"Therefore we do not lose heart. Even though our outward man is perishing, yet the inward man is being renewed day by day." – 2 Corinthians 4:16

Physical death will not be a problem if the spirit within us has risen and taken control of our body and soul, transforming them according to the will of God!

SEPTEMBER 24

TAKE RESPONSIBILITY!

When it comes to success, it is so easy to want to claim it, even if we played only a small part in that victory. However, when it comes to failure, disaster, or sin, it becomes extremely difficult for us to take responsibility, and we often seek excuses and other people to blame for our own failure.

Who do we usually blame when things go wrong?

Sometimes we blame our spouse. When God asked Adam why he did not obey, he pointed to Eve:

"The man said, 'The woman whom You gave to be with me, she gave me of the tree, and I ate.'" – Genesis 3:12

Many family failures remain unresolved because the two spouses blame each other back and forth. These problems will never be solved as long as you can still hear words like "It's your fault!", "We're in this mess because of your parents!", "You wanted us to take that loan!"

These phrases should be replaced with words that demonstrate responsibility and accountability: "My dear, it is my fault!", "I apologize for making this decision..." and so on.

At other times, we blame God for our failures. Adam also said, "The woman whom You gave me." Oh, how many people look in the mirror when things go well and blame God when things go wrong, cursing and swearing at Him!

I have also noticed that sometimes we blame our siblings. Cain's sacrifice was not accepted by God, while Abel's was. However, the Bible emphasizes that God first looks at the person offering the sacrifice and only then at the sacrifice itself:

"...the Lord respected Abel and his offering." – Genesis 4:4

I understand from this that Cain's choice to look at Abel with anger and malice was one of non-accountability. And when you do not acknowledge that you have serious behavioral problems and you upset God, you will strike Abel instead of changing yourself.

There is also a tendency to blame the community or the church for our failures. Saul was questioned by Samuel:

"Samuel said, 'What then is this bleating of the sheep in my ears, and the lowing of the oxen which I hear?'" – 1 Samuel 15:14

Saul spoke in the third person plural, pointing the finger at the people:

"Saul said, 'They have brought them from the Amalekites; for the people spared the best of the sheep and the oxen, to sacrifice to the Lord your God; and the rest we have utterly destroyed.'" – 1 Samuel 15:15

However, the Bible clearly states that Saul initiated the disobedience, and the people did only what he commanded as king:

"But Saul and the people spared Agag and the best of the sheep, the oxen, the fatlings, the lambs, and all that was good, and were unwilling to utterly destroy them. But everything despised and worthless, that they utterly destroyed." – 1 Samuel 15:9

Many people blame the ministers of God for their sins and failures, just as Ahab did with Elijah:

"So it was, when Ahab saw Elijah, that Ahab said to him, 'Is that you, O troubler of Israel?'" – 1 Kings 18:17

Elijah was the prophet who lived in full obedience to God. Ahab was one of the worst kings, and instead of changing, he constantly sought to kill Elijah. Examples can go on endlessly, but the conclusion is simple: if you are in the mud, it will be of absolutely no help to you to blame the person who walks on the sidewalk and avoids potholes.

If you are a slave to gambling, immorality, lies, or any other sin that will destroy your life here and in eternity, take responsibility for it! God forgives sins, not excuses!

David provides an extraordinary example:

"Have mercy upon me, O God, according to Your lovingkindness; according to the multitude of Your tender mercies, blot out my transgressions. Wash me thoroughly from my iniquity, and cleanse me from my sin. For I acknowledge my transgressions, and my sin is always before me." – Psalm 51:1-3

No student will progress as long as they blame the teacher for getting a failing grade. No young man will have a blessed marriage as long as he blames God for the immorality in which he indulges.

No family person will see his family as a heavenly place as long as he blames his spouse for the chaos at home.

Be like David! Take responsibility for your fall! Admit your failure! Confess your mistake! Taking responsibility is the first step toward restoration.

SEPTEMBER 25

SACRIFICE, DISCIPLINE AND CONTINUOUS PREPARATION

"The Lord will make you the head and not the tail; you shall be above only, and not be beneath, if you heed the commandments of the Lord your God, which I command you today, and are careful to observe them." – Deuteronomy 28:13

It is very important to have a goal to pursue, both spiritually and in terms of family, material, or social aspects.

However, having a goal is not enough. THREE other things are needed to reach it: sacrifice, discipline, and preparation.

If I want to become an Olympic athlete in mathematics, I need to sacrifice playtime for practice. Also, I must make this action a daily discipline. These two, along with thorough preparation, meaning a desire for continuous learning, will help me achieve my dream.

The same applies to all other areas. Do you prefer mediocrity? Then you do not have to do anything. It is enough to go "play ball" in the back yard while others are preparing for the Olympics.

Do you want excellence? Aim high. If you have a goal, then you will know the steps to take in order to get there.

Success is not a straight path; it is filled with twists and turns that require unwavering commitment. Sacrifice means giving up short-term pleasures for long-term gains. Discipline involves setting a routine and sticking to it, even when it's hard. Preparation means being ready for opportunities when they come, by continually improving and expanding your skills. These elements combined forge a path to true excellence.

Remember, the journey to achieving your goals is as important as the destination. Each step, each challenge faced with courage and perseverance shape you into a person capable of not only reaching your goals but also sustaining that success. Embrace the process, and let the values of sacrifice, discipline, and continuous preparation guide you towards a fulfilling and impactful life.

September 26

THE RED SEA

"And Moses stretched out his hand over the sea; and the Lord caused the sea to go back by a strong east wind all that night, and made the sea into dry land, and the waters were divided." – Exodus 14:21

God did not erase the Red Sea for the people of Israel, but He parted it with a strong wind so that the people could pass through.

What can we learn from this?

That sometimes God does not eliminate the problem you are going through, but He makes a way through it.

For the three young men in Babylon, God did not extinguish the fire, but He was with them in the fire.

For Daniel, God did not kill the lions, but He sent His Angel who shut their mouths.

For the widow in Zarephath, God did not send a truck of flour or oil, but He made sure the last portion would never be the last...

God did not get Joseph out of prison, but He was with him there.

Trust in God and accept the path He has set for you! Most of the time, His solution is not the elimination of problems but rather His presence in the midst of our problems.

The trials you go through show you the limits of human existence. And these limits bring you to your knees. From there, from your knees, you can speak openly to the One who has solutions to every problem.

Even if it does not work the way you want, do not forget that He... is working!

September 27

TOO MUCH TIME ON TECHNOLOGY?

"All things are lawful for me, but not all things are helpful; all things are lawful for me, but I will not be brought under the power of any." – 1 Corinthians 6:12

A recent survey in Germany, with responses from 43,500 children, shows that German 9th graders spend around 7.5 hours a day in the digital environment. Many of them sleep less than they spend on the Internet.

Technology is a miracle for adults but a danger for children. Their brains are still developing, and any activity leaves deep traces there.

According to studies, London taxi drivers navigate much better than an average person because they do not use GPS. Why? Because people who exercise their minds intensely can lift heavier mental weights.

Economists Joshua Angrist and Victor Lavy have shown that after the introduction of computers in Israeli schools, there was a decrease in math performance among 4th grade students and there were negative effects on other subjects for students in higher grades.

Marcus Aurelius said that, in the long run, your soul takes on the colors of your thoughts. And our thoughts are strongly influenced especially by the information that comes through what we look at.

When the frontal lobe is not functioning well (when you are tired), self-control does not work as it should. For this reason, those who spend too much time on technology have problems with both fatigue and self-control. The generation that is prioritizing phones and the Internet in life is the generation that wants everything instantly and therefore finds it hard to wait for results for a long time.

Also, virtual socialization has replaced real socialization. Those who talk a lot through text, audio, or video messages have major difficulties in having a conversation in the real world with a person on a specific topic.

Continuous consumption of visual information seriously affects our creativity. Our current dependence on technology has long-term negative effects.

May God help us to be balanced individuals in this area as well. May we use technology rather than allow it to use us. May we have the strength to turn off the phone whenever we want to, not when it "dictates" to us.

SEPTEMBER 28

SUBMISSION, THE SECRET OF VICTORY

"Then He went down with them and came to Nazareth, and was subject to them." – Luke 2:51

I was amazed today when I read the verse above during the daily devotion time. Jesus, the Son of God, was submitted to His biological parents?! The Creator of the Universe did not talk back and did not slam the door in annoyance when asked to do a chore? Could the Son of God humble Himself so deeply as *to obey*?

What a magnificent example! What a high state of humility we see in Jesus! What exceptional modesty and obedience!

Jesus could have impressed His parents by naming the stars. He could have shocked them by reciting the entire history of the people of Israel. He could have proven to His parents that He knew more than them and had no reason to obey, but rather do whatever He wanted.

But He chose to submit to the order established by God the Father. He chose to sweep the workshop if Joseph asked Him to. He chose to bring the water jug whenever Mary commanded Him to do so. He chose to sleep at the time His earthly parents asked Him to.

Jesus understood that true wisdom does not avoid obedience but is perfected through it. Our knowledge should make us more obedient, not more proud. Our wealth does not exclude our submission. Jesus had the entire Universe in His hands, and yet He learned to listen:

"Though He was a Son, yet He learned obedience by the things which He suffered." – Hebrews 5:8

Dietrich Bonhoeffer said, "One act of obedience is better than one hundred sermons." If you are a child, the next time your parents ask you to do something and you do not like it, or when you feel like talking back or making a comment, remember Jesus!

If you are a wife and you feel like not respecting your husband and not submitting to his requests, remember Jesus' submission!

If you are a husband and you are not submitting to Christ and not loving your wife as Jesus loved the Church, remember Jesus!

If you are a member of any congregation and find it difficult to submit to the pastor, remember Jesus!

Our blessing comes from staying under authority. Of course, not the authority of sin but of holiness. Not blind submission but submission in love and within the limits of Scripture.

If Jesus submitted and obeyed, we are called to do the same.

I want to add what someone said, “The cost of obedience may seem great, but it is nothing compared to the cost of disobedience.”

September 29

"WHAT HAVE THEY SEEN IN YOUR HOUSE?"

"Isaiah asked, 'What have they seen in your house?' Hezekiah replied, 'They have seen all that is in my house; there is nothing among my treasures that I have not shown them.'" – 2 Kings 20:15

The miraculous healing performed by God in Hezekiah's life reached the ears of Berodach-Baladan, the king of Babylon. Astonished, he sent envoys with a gift to Hezekiah, likely with the desire to see firsthand what had happened and hear about the miracle of healing directly from the formerly sick king.

When the envoys arrived, the topic of the miracle was quickly exhausted. From prophets, healings, and miracles, Hezekiah shifted to material possessions. He proudly displayed silver and gold, spices, armory, lands, and granaries to the Babylonian envoys.

After the envoys left, Prophet Isaiah returned with a piercing question: "What have they seen in your house?" This question haunts me and makes me ponder... The prophet did not ask this question just for the sake of asking. It came directly from God and carried within it the pain of forgetfulness. The pain of a healed person who turns back to material things. The pain of someone who can talk about what the Lord has done for barely 5 minutes but can talk for hours about their own achievements.

What do guests see in your house?

What do neighbors hear in your yard?

What are the things you display? The scar from the accident God miraculously saved you from, or the triple-layered flooring? The child who returned home after God saved him from drugs, or your 300-horsepower car?

What do you speak about with the most passion? Is it the exam you passed triumphantly because God gave you wisdom, or is it your social status? Is it the wonders of the Lord, or is it your finances? Is it your experiences of walking with God, or your own achievements?

What do our children see in our homes? After Hezekiah came Manasseh. In that same home where healings took place, where prophets walked, and where the Word of the Lord was present, a boy was born three years after the healing.

Manasseh is a materialistic child. An idolatrous child. A child who rebuilds the idols that had been demolished by his father. He is the child who seeks diviners and witches (2 Kings 21:6). A child raised by others because his father, in the 15 years of life granted to him by God, was caught up with business. With building ponds and water channels.

Hezekiah believed what many parents believe today: that our children need material things, not spiritual ones. Tablets and the latest phones, not the Bible. We think they will respect us more if, at 18, we gift them a car. "Let them have what we did not have..." is the excuse we use to be absent from home for another month just to earn some more money. This is the excuse we use to wash our hands of the responsibilities that God has assigned to us as parents...

Excessive concern for material things and the desire to display what we possess is a trap that looms over all of us. It is the trap that causes pain to God. The trap into which our children fall if we do not repent.

What have those who visited your home seen so far?

When he was sick, Isaiah told Hezekiah to set his house in order. To place the Bible open on the table. Evening prayer with the family should not be absent, and neither should singing in the Temple while holding your children`s hand. Discipline and obedience should be honored. Respect and the fear of God should be diligently instilled by parents into their children.

Hezekiah was healed. And along with healing, the tears of prayer disappeared as well. God's requirement was quickly forgotten. The pursuit of material things easily erases from our memory what God asks of us...

When Isaiah finished the question, he also delivered the verdict: *"Servitude awaits your children... Material loss awaits you, Hezekiah!"*

"No problem," said Hezekiah. *"If it happens after my death and not now, it's fine..."*

Hezekiah was physically healed, but spiritually he became very sick... He had beautiful houses but lost his home. He gained much money but lost his children. He had a collection of weapons, but he was defeated by the arrow of pride that entered his heart... What do people see in your house?

SEPTEMBER 30

THE LIFE OF A BEE

"Precious in the sight of the Lord is the death of His saints." – Psalm 116:15

I met Filimon Neag in 2013, shortly after moving to Deva. It is about 15 miles from my home to his. I visited him more than once, and he welcomed me with much love. Whenever we left his home, he always wanted to give us something. "Don't leave empty-handed from my home," he would say...

On the morning of September 26, 2022, at the age of 69, Filimon did not wake up anymore. His heart gave in, and the Master's call was heard for him.

At his funeral, I spoke about the life of a bee. Filimon had been taking care of bees for many years, and I found 3 similarities between him and these creatures, similarities from which we can all learn.

Firstly, **a bee "travels" a lot.** It covers about 500 miles in a lifetime. In a single journey, it visits 50 to 100 flowers.

Filimon traveled a lot. By train, on foot, by car, with whatever means he could find. He visited many "flowers" (churches). He worked hard for himself, for his family, but he also worked hard for God. Filimon knew what the psalmist meant when he said that our steps (our wanderings) are counted by the Master we serve:

> *"You number my wanderings; put my tears into Your bottle; are they not in Your book?" – Psalm 56:8*

Secondly, **a bee "carries" a lot.** It has a stomach pouch with which it carries 60 loads for 1 gram (0.035 ounces) of nectar.

Brother Filimon carried a lot. He took the poems received from the Lord to many churches, and from there, he brought the nectar of fellowship to the hive of his family.

Thirdly, **a bee leaves something sweet behind.** Brother Filimon called me a few years ago to ask about the steps needed to print a book. "I want to leave something behind me," brother Filimon said with much satisfaction.

He printed 3 volumes of poems. Besides these, he has many others handwritten in notebooks. He did not have much education, but through the Holy Spirit, he managed to express profound truths in simple lines. He learned a lot at the feet of Jesus, living a costly repentance...

Did you know that honey is the only food that contains all the elements necessary for life and that it never expires? It has enzymes, vitamins, minerals, and water. No wonder the psalmist compares the Word of God to honey...

Brother Filimon had the gift of writing poems. He intertwined his gift with the Gospel, and in this way, he touched many hearts. It is not enough to have a gift; you must know what to do with it. Many people know how to compose or sing, but without intertwining this gift with the spiritual calling, they can only use it for the world and its perishable things...

Did you know that a bee colony produces three times more honey than it needs? The people of God are called to do the same. Not everything just for myself. Not everything just for my home. But also for others - both spiritually and materially, so that we can help those in need...

The causes of bee deaths can be many, but their natural death is due to exhaustion. They deplete themselves, but they do it for a good cause... They exhaust themselves not to gather rubbish but to produce honey...

Deacon Filimon's heart, like the hearts of many servants throughout history, gave in. In their hearts, they carry the family, the church, and the work of God's Gospel... Many widows, poor, and orphans ate from the physical honey produced by brother Filimon's bees. All of us who listened to him reciting have partaken from his spiritual honey, beautifully arranged in poem verses...

There are many hearts that give in because of legal issues in court, because of drinking or using drugs, but there are also hearts that give in because they have been consumed for a good cause...

I remember the moments when we served together, and I heard him crying in church. A cry of longing for God. Tears in prayer and tears of longing for an encounter with Him. Haven't such cries become rare in our congregations?

I told my wife today that I regret not inviting him to Deva more often. I do not know how to explain this, but only after a valuable person among us leaves, our regrets arise. Our remorse. Our desire to have spent more time together and in the House of God...

Honey is expensive... And those who produce it are becoming rarer - this is true both physically and especially spiritually...

Be a diligent bee too! Carry useful things and leave something sweet behind you!

In memory of the one who was a husband, father, grandfather, servant, and poet: Filimon Neag.

OCTOBER 1

FILLED WITH THE SPIRIT...

"Then Jesus, being filled with the Holy Spirit, returned from the Jordan and was led by the Spirit into the wilderness..." – Luke 4:1

Jordan is the place of celebration. Baptism, white clothes, taking pictures and giving flowers. Emotions and congratulations. But Jordan lasts only one day. The covenant is an event. The wilderness, however, is long. You can only overcome its tests through the fullness of the Holy Spirit.

Jesus did not leave the Jordan until He was filled with the Holy Spirit. He knew that before He began the actual ministry, He had to go through the trials of the wilderness. Because He left full of the Spirit and full of Scripture, He had victory over the devil.

How much do we desire the filling of the Holy Spirit through prayer? When the Holy Spirit comes, He brings His **fruit**, His **armor**, and His **gifts** – the complete equipment for a humanly invisible war.

The empty water bottle makes noise if you squeeze it in your hand.

Under squeezing, under hitting, under pressure, the empty man cannot withstand. But the man who is full will be at peace. Fullness with the fruits of the Spirit brings victory over any challenge.

You will meet around you people who would like to be full. Full of money, full of fame, full of the satisfaction of a high position. The world offers its own fullness. And a man without God, after becoming full of any of these things, realizes that he is emptier than ever.

Someone said, "I was up there. I was on the high places of success. There is nothing valuable there!"

True fullness is on your knees. At Jesus' feet, with tears of gratitude for the joy of salvation. In the fullness that only He can offer.

What did you set out to be full of today?

"...be filled with the Spirit." – Ephesians 5:18

October 2

JOB'S SPIRITUAL WEALTH

Job was a rich man. Very rich indeed. And the wealth he had is presented by the Bible in a particularly important order.

First, the Bible describes Job`s **spiritual wealth.**

"There was a man in the land of Uz, whose name was Job; and that man was blameless and upright, and one who feared God and shunned evil." – Job 1:1

Second, it lists his **family wealth:**

"And seven sons and three daughters were born to him." – Job 1:2

Third, the Bible shows us the 11,500 animals that Job owned, that is, his **material wealth:**

"Also, his possessions were seven thousand sheep, three thousand camels, five hundred yoke of oxen, five hundred female donkeys, and a very large household..." – Job 1:3a

At the same time, we note **the richness of social status:**

"...so that this man was the greatest of all the people of the East." – Job 1:3b

If you do not have the spiritual foundation and wealth, when the Devil strikes you in the other three types of wealth, you will fail the test and abandon God. But if you do have the foundation, even if all three other types of wealth are taken away from you, you remain with God.

Why do people commit suicide? Why do some leave God when their paycheck stops coming? Why do some people curse Him in His face when their child becomes sick or dies? Because they are anchored in temporary riches and not in the wealth of a noble soul that takes you into eternity.

When the Devil took away Job's health, wealth, and children, he thought he had taken everything from him. But he understood later that God was, in fact, Job`s everything!

Job loved God for who He was, not for what He offered! Job loved God's face, not His pocket.

Invest in your spiritual wealth! It's the only one which matters in the end...

OCTOBER 3

SORROWFUL AFTER MEETING JESUS

"But when the young man heard that saying, he went away sorrowful, for he had great possessions." – Matthew 19:22

All the people who came to Jesus sincerely left with their problem solved. Jesus never said: *I cannot help you.* He never rejected anyone. He always had the solution at hand for those willing to be changed and obey His will.

And yet, there were some people like the rich young man. At first glance, he was eager for heaven. Keen of Jesus' presence for eternity. Thirsty for eternal life. However, he left Jesus full of sorrow and with his problem unresolved...

Why couldn't the Creator of the universe help him? Why did Jesus, who raised some people from the dead, let the rich young man go away sorrowful and without the guarantee of eternity?

Because there are some things that *Jesus* does, and there are some other things that *we* must do. The doctor writes the prescription but does not swallow the medication instead of the patient. The doctor is not interested in whether you like the taste of medicine or not. He will not give you what you like, but what you need...

Jesus knows the things that enslave us or bind us with strong chains. Jesus did not ask of anyone else in the Bible what He asked of the rich young man. Some are tied to their fortunes. Others have riches but are not tied to them. Some have phones and are enslaved by them. Others have them but are not enslaved. Some cannot even give up one meal. Others eat anything and do it so that they can live; they do not live so that they can eat.

"...for by whom a person is overcome, by him also he is brought into bondage." – 2 Peter 2:19

Jesus' requirements are according to your shackles. If you are bound by lying, accept to tell the truth from today on! If you are bound by pornography, fight at all costs to be freed of it! Are you tied to money? Put them in another place, not in the first place of your life! Are you enslaved by work and have no time for anything spiritual? Balance the scales! Do not mistake greed for diligence!

Are you tied to a vicious group of friends? Tied to friends who push you toward sin? Detach yourself from them and cling to Jesus, the true Friend.

That which overcomes you, will master you. And when anything except Jesus rules over you, you cannot inherit the eternal life.

I would like you to leave the meeting with Jesus full of joy. Do what He asks of you even though you may not like it.

Jesus' solution is always the perfect solution to your shackles.

October 4

WARS THAT DO NOT CONCERN US

"After all this, when Josiah had prepared the temple, Necho king of Egypt came up to fight against Carchemish by the Euphrates; and Josiah went out against him." – 2 Chronicles 35:20

Josiah was an extraordinary king. A reformer. A man who turned to God with all his heart and challenged the people of Judah to do the same. He fixed the House of God. He found the book of the Law and went back to the original. He renewed his covenant with God. He celebrated Passover like no one else since Samuel had celebrated it.

After he finished with the renovations, however, he made a big mistake. He noticed that Necho had gone to war against Carchemish. Josiah thought it was a good opportunity to go to war too, although Necho warns him,

"But he sent messengers to him, saying, 'What have I to do with you, king of Judah? I have not come against you this day, but against the house with which I have war; for God commanded me to make haste. Refrain from meddling with God, who is with me, lest He destroy you.'" – 2 Chronicles 35:21

Josiah, however, disobeyed and was wounded fatally.

"Nevertheless Josiah would not turn his face from him, but disguised himself so that he might fight with him, and did not heed the words of Necho from the mouth of God. So he came to fight in the Valley of Megiddo. And the archers shot King Josiah; and the king said to his servants, 'Take me away, for I am severely wounded.' His servants therefore took him out of that chariot and put him in the second chariot that he had, and they brought him to Jerusalem. So he died, and was buried in one of the tombs of his fathers. And all Judah and Jerusalem mourned for Josiah." – 2 Chronicles 35:22-24

Do you know what I am learning from this? Not to meddle in conflicts that do not concern me and that I cannot win. The Bible says so clearly:

"He who passes by and meddles in a quarrel not his own is like one who takes a dog by the ears." – Proverbs 26:17

Has God called me to carry words from one person to another? Has God called you to destroy your health with the immense stress caused by meddling into arguments between other families? Has He called you to make phone calls all day long and consume yourself when it is not even your battle?

Do you know that there are conflicts that we ignite with our own hands because, instead of staying on the sideline in silence, we meddle, believing that our words will make a difference and actually the opposite happens?

"Whoever guards his mouth and tongue keeps his soul from troubles." – Proverbs 21:23

Be a wise man! If you are not asked for your opinion, stay out of it! And if you are asked, pay attention to the words you use! A word spoken without consideration will just add gas to the fire instead of water, and all the firefighters in your area will not be able to extinguish that burning flame.

Your regrets cannot extinguish the fire after you light the match. Just water, lots of water!

But it is better to prevent than to treat...

October 5

A POWERFUL MAN DOES NOT HAVE AN EASY PAST

When we look at God's heroes in the Bible, but also throughout Christian history, we notice some common traits: all those who have been used by God have been put through many spiritual battles by Him.

Have you heard of David without knowing about Goliath? Could you have admired a Joseph without having heard of his brothers and the prison? Would you have recognized Moses as a titan if he had not gone with the people on the 40 year-journey through the wilderness?

What would an Elijah look like without the brook Cherith, without the lodging at the widow of Zarephath, and without the cave? What about a John the Baptist without wild honey, locusts, and a Herod? What about a Paul who says at one point, "*They have all forsaken me*"? How about Stephen who sees heaven open up while being stoned?

Have you heard of a George Müller without the orphans? How about a Jim Elliot without the cannibals of the Auca tribe?

Of a Hudson Taylor without the death of his wife and 9-year-old daughter on the mission field? Would you admire a David Livingstone sitting in an armchair or one going to Africa to carry the Gospel to the darkest places and dying at 4 a.m. on his knees, exhausted from so much running?

Why are there no books printed about people who did nothing? Why do lazy people not end up on podiums, and why do mockers not receive golden trophies at ceremonies?

If mankind's history does not record the idlers of the world, how do you imagine that God's history would record those who give up and turn back?

"But we are not of those who draw back to perdition, but of those who believe to the saving of the soul." – Hebrews 10:39

In the life of a soldier there is the period of conscription, the period of training, the period of war and the period of getting medals. Just like in the life of an athlete. You cannot skip the middle stages!

There is no podium without sweat. There are no medals without crushing. There is no Heaven without the Cross. Nor Resurrection without death.

There are no heroes without deep battles. Nor watchmen without watch towers. No victories without defeats. No crowns without scars.

Bowed knees are our training for battle day. The sorrows here are the laurels on the crown we will receive in Heaven. Our tears are the preparation for the podium. The deep valleys of sorrow are our narrow aisle towards the awarding ceremony in Heaven.

Crushing makes us stronger. Humility, more loving. Trouble, more patient. The betrayal of our friends makes us cling harder to God, and storms take us closer to port.

> *"This is a faithful saying: for if we died with Him, we shall also live with Him. If we endure, we shall also reign with Him." – 2 Timothy 2:11-12*

There are many people starting the race. However, only the victors arrive at the finish line...

Be among the strong!

October 6

AT THE BAPTISM WITH FIRE

"I indeed baptize you with water unto repentance, but He who is coming after me is mightier than I, whose sandals I am not worthy to carry. He will baptize you with the Holy Spirit and fire." – Matthew 3:11

At the baptism with fire, we do not receive flowers. Instead, we receive mockery, reproach, trials, pains and... grades. Walking with God is often sprinkled with life lessons. And then, from time to time, just like in school, between a few recesses from class, the tests are taken.

True faith is faith that is tried. Saying you hold on to God with mere words is one thing. Proving it by deed is another.

"Who shall separate us from the love of Christ? Shall tribulation, or distress, or persecution, or famine, or nakedness, or peril, or sword?" – Romans 8:35

The marriage that falls apart when money runs out was a marriage based only on interest. The marriage that breaks down when you move out from a mansion to a rented home was never based on agape love. The spouse who leaves when the other one gets sick is a spouse who did not understand anything about true love.

In faith it is the same. Many beautiful words are uttered when everything goes well:

"Now in my prosperity I said, 'I shall never be moved!'" – Psalm 30:6

But what do we do when the fire comes? When the fridge is empty!? When cancer appears!? When our friends leave!? What do we do when the boss starts firing his employees? When are we hit by the stones of gossip and slander?

Stay when others leave! Keep on fighting when others give up! Get involved when others back down! Keep sweating when others do nothing but keep the score!

Kneel down when others give a standing ovation! Be persistent when others say, "I cannot do it anymore"!

At the baptism with fire, we do not receive flowers, but grades. But at the final award ceremony, we, the overcomers, will receive Heaven...

October 7

THINGS THAT ARE PRECIOUS TO GOD

The world has its valuable things, but God also has His own precious things. For those of us who live on earth with our thoughts set on heaven, it is a great challenge not to confuse fleeting values with eternal ones.

Am I interested in finding out what is precious in God's sight? What is valuable in His eyes? What would I gain if, in the end, I realized that I considered valuable what He considered cheap?

The first thing that is of great value in God's sight is **faith.**

"...that the genuineness of your faith, being much more precious than gold that perishes, though it is tested by fire, may be found to praise, honor, and glory at the revelation of Jesus Christ." – 1 Peter 1:7

In a world where everything is by sight, faith is firm confidence in what is not seen. The faith of such a man makes him live according to God's will and not seek worldly fashions and pleasures.

Do you possess this, since it is more expensive than gold? Are you keeping your faith in a good conscience, as Paul said?

Another thing of great value in God's sight is **gentleness.**

"Rather let it be the hidden person of the heart, with the incorruptible beauty of a gentle and quiet spirit, which is very precious in the sight of God." – 1 Peter 3:4

The tranquility of the man who cannot be troubled by anything. That state of high spiritual value that understands that everything is under God's control and that remains at peace even when everyone around him becomes disturbed and maybe even speaks ill of him. The value of a cliff in the sea is not seen when the sea is calm, but when it is rough. It remains quiet and firm regardless of the waves hitting around it and even in it.

Last but not least, **a believer's departure into eternity** is another precious thing before God.

"Precious in the sight of the Lord is the death of His saints." – Psalm 116:15

How can the entrance into glory not be a thing of value? How could walking through the "gates of heavenly splendor" not be, for the sacrificial Lamb, an immense joy? The joy of receiving a man who was harassed by the Devil all his life, and yet managed to love and forgive through God's help.

I want to stay among the precious things of Heaven. To continue to believe with all my heart, to desire a gentle and quiet spirit and to live in such a way that leaving here will make Jesus stand up, as He did at Stephen`s death.

What are the precious things for you?

October 8

"I CANNOT DO IT ANYMORE!"

You have said something like this yourself, and not once, haven't you? Did you feel the burden weighing you down and wanted to let go of it? You thought that if you take the cry of your heart that you had been carrying inside you for months, and let it become a loud sigh, it will make the pain easier, haven't you?

"I cannot do it anymore!" – we say in **distress**. In the years of illness, when we have pain in our bones. When we spend our money on doctors. On endless lab tests and expensive prescriptions.

Let us take courage as we remember Job. With a shard in hand and on a pile of ashes. Instead of saying, "I cannot do it anymore," he accepted the suffering. The Devil wanted to hear him grumble, murmur, or complain, but Job chose to accept the pain and not sin:

"...In all this Job did not sin with his lips." – Job 2:10b

"I cannot do it anymore!" we say in **temptation**.

"I couldn't endure it any longer, brother, and I took revenge, that's how much I was tempted!" someone said to me. And yet, the Bible encourages us:

"No temptation has overtaken you except such as is common to man; but God is faithful, who will not allow you to be tempted beyond what you are able, but with the temptation will also make the way of escape, that you may be able to bear it." – 1 Corinthians 10:13

Joseph, in front of Potiphar's wife, did not say, "I cannot help it!" He remained firm and God-fearing, and thus refused sin. Although he ended up in prison, he remained free from sin.

Samson, in front of Delilah, said, "I cannot help it!" He opened his heart to her, and he ended up without eyes. Sin takes away your most precious possession. Therefore, I plead with you today: do not give in to temptation!

"I cannot do it anymore!" we say in **ministry**. These are the words of an exhausted mother. These are the words of the father exhausted by the disobedience of one of his sons. These are the words of a pastor overwhelmed by the problems in the congregation. And here the Bible has great encouragement for us:

"I can do all things through Christ who strengthens me." – Philippians 4:13

You can do it! Not by your own strength. Not through your repeated attempts, but through the Creator who blesses you with His presence every day!

"But you, be strong and do not let your hands be weak, for your work shall be rewarded." – 2 Chronicles 15:7

Put them all in His hands, and then you will see His hands in them all!

October 9

A NOBLE HEART

"These were more fair-minded than those in Thessalonica, in that they received the word with all readiness, and searched the Scriptures daily to find out whether these things were so." – Acts 17:11

At Berea, Paul met a category of believers different from other Christians. Not with more education necessarily nor with more wealth. Not with fewer trials or an easier life. But he met a category of people who had a more noble heart, who were more fair-minded.

"A nobler character," says another version. More open to hearing the Word. More enthusiastic about holy things. More eager to deepen God's character revealed in Scripture.

Shallowness is the flu that plagues most Christians these days. People ready to scroll on their phones until late at night, but who will become very irritated if you happen to go past 12 noon on Sunday with the church service.

Such people are superficial in their relationship with God and in their relationship with the Scripture. Most of them want heaven with a verse from the Bible read once a week. They would like George Müller's rewards, but they have never visited an orphan. They wish they had the fruit of over 50,000 converts like Adoniram Judson, but they have not told anyone about Jesus yet.

What kind of heart do you have? What kind of character? If Dr. Luke could do another heart test today, would he define you in the same terms as those from Berea?

A man of noble character (or fair-minded) is not satisfied with little from a spiritual point of view. He will not say, "They can do it without me" when referring to the weekly prayer service. The noble character does not boast about what others do for God, as if those accomplishments belonged to him. A noble heart seeks peace. Seeks unity. Seeks fellowship. It is ready to spend itself with sacrificial love, just to gain Christ.

The noble heart has passion for the unsaved. For the prodigal son who ran away from home and who left his parents heartbroken by grief. A noble character is ready to come to the rescue. To intervene with fasting and prayer. To stretch out a helping hand when others throw mud. To lift up the one whom others pushed down.

In a town in Europe, a grief-stricken mother had to go with her daughter, who had been suffering for years, to several checkups each week. During that time, she needed someone to watch her husband who had been bedridden for more than 2 years due to a stroke. A plea was made on the church group for this unpaid and unseen service.

Do you know who offered to help?

A woman who was sick with cancer. She was physically ill, but had a noble heart... People ignored by us, but who have a noble character in the sight of God...

It is not enough to have hearts.

We must have noble... fair-minded hearts.

So that it may be written on our cross in the cemetery: *"Here rests a noble heart!"*

It seems to sound better than, *"Here rests the servant of the Lord!"*, right?

OCTOBER 10

WHAT HAVE I LEARNED AFTER A FEW YEARS OF MARRIAGE?

I have learned that the most valuable diamond you can have in your family is peace. That is why Proverbs 17:1 tells us it is the best "butter" you can put on your slice of bread every day. What is in your heart is more important than what is on the table.

Psalm 34 exhorts us to run after it. Because it keeps on trying to escape us. And if you let it out of your house, many years may pass before you can catch it again.

I have learned that the greatest blessing is a hardworking, God-fearing wife. My words are too poor to describe how grateful I am for Crina.

I have learned that most of the time, our children do what they see us do, not what we tell them to do.

I have learned that family is a great value. This is why the Devil fights against Christian families; a thief wants to break into a place where there is something valuable to steal. I am so thankful in my heart that the Angel of the Lord has protected us even if most of the times we did not deserve the Lord`s protection and shelter.

I have learned that ministry comes at a price. And most of the time, the price is paid by the spouse who "stays" at home, not by the one who travels....

I have learned that time passes quickly. The most important thing is time. Money you can make anytime, but time... you cannot. So those who are dearest to us deserve the most of our time...

I have learned that the storms of life have nothing to do with the tiles in the house, but with its foundation.

I have learned that the world around us needs our involvement more than our advice.

I thank those who carry us in fasting and prayers. The Lord will reward the intercessors who support our family and without whom we would not have come this far.

October 11

SHORT HISTORY OF TECHNOLOGY

Do we use technology to change the world, or does the world use technology to change us?

That is the question that makes us ponder... Technology has evolved. Bows and arrows. Wheels and axles. Then iron tools and weapons. Printers and clocks. Steam engines. Railways. Cars and planes. Computers and mobile phones.

Each invention opened the way for man to new goals and dreams. But at the same time, it changed the way in which people interact with each other and with God.

The first watches were invented in the 15th century and were used strictly by sailors to determine longitude. Wristwatches began to be worn only in the 19th century.

The invention of the telephone brought in one place the calendar, the weather, the email, pictures, writing, reading, etc. On average, we check our phone 81,500 times a year, that is, once every 6 minutes.

We switch between the virtual and the real every 6 minutes.

God calls us to stop and consider what are the things in the world that catch our attention, what are the consequences of these distractions, and how to fight to guard our hearts.

"Above all else, guard your heart, for everything you do flows from it!" – Proverbs 4:23

What are the dangers of the mobile phone? Do we need to be on guard when using it? Can it affect us in any way?

We will find out in the devotionals that follow. Stay tuned!

October 12

FELLOWSHIP OR SOCIALIZING?

"I have much to write to you, but I do not want to use paper and ink. Instead, I hope to visit you and talk with you face to face, so that our joy may be complete." – *2 John 1:12*

John used the technology of that time (writing down) for communication, but he understood that being face to face with the person you want to communicate with means true fellowship.

Paul had the same desire for Timothy:

"Recalling your tears, I long to see you, so that I may be filled with joy." – *2 Timothy 1:4*

We must understand that socializing is not the same as fellowship. Many Christians are ready to socialize, but they are not ready to fellowship with each other. Socialization focuses on my needs, on entertainment, on personal interests, while fellowship focuses on physical encounter for spiritual edification.

The phone has its place. But why does it sometimes happen that, although we are next to our spouse or our parents, we want to constantly check the phone? Why can we socialize for hours so many times, but when it comes to communicating with the person face-to-face, we get bored in a few minutes? Haven't we replaced what is less valuable with what is truly valuable?

Why do more and more teenagers talk for hours with each other and very little with their parents? Why do many couples drift away when it comes to verbal communication, but when chatting online with their friends, they are very open and communicative?

Paul said to Timothy:

"Recalling your tears, I long to see you, so that I may be filled with joy." – *2 Timothy 1:4*

And only then he told him about the books.

Technology should not rob us of physical presence and face-to-face relationships. Your physical presence at your church's services should not be replaced by your online presence except in special circumstances.

October 13

WHO IS ON THE FIRST PLACE?

"Love the Lord your God with all your heart and with all your soul and with all your mind and with all your strength." – Mark 12:30

Of the 8,000 Christians surveyed, 5,840 admitted to checking their phones in the morning, before praying or reading the Bible.

Our life is composed of urgent things and important things. It is urgent to see what your teacher emailed you, but it is more important first to see what God wants to tell you for the day from His Word. It is quite urgent to see if the people at work have sent you a message asking for help, but it is more important to get down on your knees first and talk to the One who gave you another day to live.

Douglas Groothuis said, "It is difficult to serve God with our heart, soul, strength and mind when we are diverted and distracted and multitasking everything."

The more distracted we are by the digital world, the more we lose ground in the spiritual world. Why? Because we will increasingly look for the things that can be done easier. Is it not easier to look at a friend's Facebook pictures than to pray? Is it not easier to check the news than to study the Bible? It is easier, but it is not more beneficial.

Let us be wary of this danger too! Let us not change priorities. When the phone comes first in our lives, it becomes an idol. The word *idol* appears over 200 times in Scripture, and always as something hated by God because, when accepted and embraced, it takes God's place.

The danger of valuing your relationship with your phone more than your relationship with God is constant.

Let us be watchful!

October 14

SO WHAT IF I DO NOT KNOW THEM?

Access to the virtual world opens the way to reach so-called friends whose public life you can observe (through images and videos carefully selected by them), but whose private lives you cannot truly know.

There is this danger of being fooled by people we do not know. Do you remember Absalom who was winning the hearts of the people of Israel with sweet words while in his heart he thought about vengeance against his father?

It is painful to see children for whom friends on Instagram or TikTok are more important than their parents at home. It is tragic to see teenagers who find more joy in the anonymous people on the Internet than in the honest people in their church...

Why do you open up so easily to someone you do not even know, while ignoring and avoiding those near you, whose beautiful lives you know so well?

> *"You, however, know all about my teaching, my way of life, my purpose, faith, patience, love, endurance."* – 2 Timothy 3:10

Paul reminds Timothy to persevere in the seven character qualities he learned from him. Why?

> *"But as for you, continue in what you have learned and have become convinced of, because you know those from whom you learned it."* – 2 Timothy 3:14

It is extremely important not to let ourselves be fooled by all the nonsense circulating on the Internet. Someone said to me, "I have followed this person so much on TikTok that now, when I close my eyes, I see him and, in my mind, I hear only his voice." Unfortunately, he was not referring to a positive person, but to a negative one.

Let us also be alert when it comes to this danger. Let us not give up on those we know up close as good life examples in exchange for those we do not even know.

The voice of wolves dressed in sheepskin can be heard with almost every click.

And the voice of the Shepherd seems to be fainter and weaker, for most...

Let us hold on to the voices we know and trust!

October 15

IMAGE OR CHARACTER?

"Do not love the world or anything in the world. If anyone loves the world, love for the Father is not in them. For everything in the world—the lust of the flesh, the lust of the eyes, and the pride of life—comes not from the Father but from the world." – 1 John 2:15-16

On social media, people will always show the things that bring appreciation (*likes*) and praise comments.

Have you noticed, for example, that a picture of painted nails brings much more likes than nails soiled by the soil in the vegetable green house?

Have you noticed that the boy who posts a photo of himself walking towards church with a Bible in his hand is ridiculed, while the guy with the latest type of BMW and a girlfriend in his arms gets thousands of likes?

Have you noticed that the phone is the means by which people display much of what they have and little of what they are?

For many young people, revealing their body has become more valuable than the principle of purity and modesty. For many people, vulgar language and tight clothes are more appreciated than the language of Scripture and decent clothing.

In people's eyes, the number of views matters. In God's eyes, however, the hidden man of the heart is what truly matters. Samuel almost got deceived by the looks of David's older brother and he almost clicked *like* based on what he saw:

"When they arrived, Samuel saw Eliab and thought, 'Surely the Lord's anointed stands here before the Lord.' But the Lord said to Samuel, 'Do not consider his appearance or his height, for I have rejected him. The Lord does not look at the things people look at. People look at the outward appearance, but the Lord looks at the heart.'" – 1 Samuel 16:6-7

In this case, Eliab had a gorgeous body, but in his heart, he had pride. David was simple on the outside and did not catch the eye, but he had sincerity in his heart. And a pure and sincere heart is more valuable in God's eyes than any body displayed on social media platforms...

Jasmine, a 20-year-old young woman, said on Instagram, “I have ended up doing everything I do just for likes, for image, for fame. I buy expensive clothes with my credit card just so I do not take pictures wearing the same clothes... I eat at expensive restaurants just so I have menus to take pictures of, so that my friends can praise me... I have ended up desperate and unhappy.”

True character, shaped according to the Scriptures, does not need tattoos to get likes. Nor fake lashes or botox. It will not succumb to worldly demands, nor will it lower its standards just to get more views.

Appreciate the natural! Appreciate the truth! If you are following someone, follow the modest man. The one with a humble heart. The one you can learn from.

Do not be fascinated by the image! Do not let yourself be flattered by what strikes the eye!

The looks pass.

The character remains...

October 16

CELEBRITIES OR HEROES?

Viorica Agarici[24] is remembered by history for her courageous gesture of laying down in front of train cars transporting deported Jews. On July 3, 1941, one of the "death trains" passed through a station, filled with children, women, and men, all Jews, who had been locked in those train cars for days without food and water.

Upon the arrival of the convoy, Viorica Agarici and her sisters were on the platform and asked the German soldiers to immediately open the cars so they could provide first aid to the imprisoned Jews and remove the bodies of those who had died during the transport. Initially ignored, she then risked her life by standing in front of the train and thus forcing the soldiers to open the doors of the wagons. She thus managed to fulfill her mission as a representative of the Red Cross, by offering first aid to those struggling between life and death.

Her heroic gesture of high-class humanism saved many of those who would have died of asphyxiation and dehydration during the ordeal of the long journey that lasted seven days in the heart of that summer.

I posted what you read above one day on my Facebook page. Do you know how many *likes* my post got? 28.

During the same period, a star posted a picture in which she had an interesting sock pulled on one leg. It got 25,000 *likes*.

A photo post by the *Fragrance of Heaven Association,* which showed some poor children receiving jars of honey, gathered 252 likes. The picture of a superstar in our country petting his dog has 41,200 likes.

You do understand what I mean, don't you? Do you understand that heroes are formed based on character, while celebrities and superstars are formed based on *image?*

What do you appreciate with your phone? Sin or holiness? Pride or modesty? Courage or guts? Shooting super-stars or heroes?

[24] Known for her brave act of blocking a train transporting deported Jews from Iași to Călărași during World War II, where she stood against the inhumane treatment of Jewish passengers.

October 17

DOES ANYONE SEE ME?

Your phone gives you the advantage of staying anonymous on the Internet. If you physically go to stores, you are being filmed, you cannot hide, but on the Internet you can remain anonymous.

Immoral sins in the media find great value in this: "My husband, my wife, my parents cannot see me!" That is true. But do not forget that God sees you:

> *"Nothing in all creation is hidden from God's sight. Everything is uncovered and laid bare before the eyes of him to whom we must give account." – Hebrews 4:13*

Even from the Garden of Eden we see in man this desire to hide. To be able to do whatever he wants, without facing God.

Snapchat has an option to automatically delete the conversation between two people when they leave the chat. You can chat about anything, about anyone and in any way, because there is no evidence left that you ever wrote anything about it.

But can you really erase these conversations from the book of deeds in which God writes everything?

> *"But I tell you that everyone will have to give account on the day of judgment for every empty word they have spoken. For by your words you will be acquitted, and by your words you will be condemned." – Matthew 12:36-37*

A.M. is a site for married people who want to find partners for extramarital affairs.

Based on your email address and for a small fee, you could enter into the database and plan secret dates with other people on the site. Over the years, tens of millions of people registered on this site. One day, the database was hacked, and everything became public. Many wives were able to check if their husbands had an account there and were devastated for life when they found out that they had cheated on them.

Do you know what the sinful and filthy slogan of this aforementioned site is?

"Life is short. Schedule an extramarital affair!"

Oh yes. Life is short. But the sequel should add something else: "Eternity is long!"

Many sinful things are done in the darkness – we will mention only what Paul said:

"It is shameful even to mention what the disobedient do in secret." – Ephesians 5:12

Anonymity is sin's favorite place, but at the same time, it is the biggest lie of the virtual world...

Do not hide in the virtual world, hide in God! That is the place where the Devil can never find you!

"For you died, and your life is now hidden with Christ in God." – Colossians 3:3

October 18

SO WHAT IF I AM WASTING MY TIME?

The platform on which young people and teenagers waste the most time today is TikTok. It is amazing how quickly this platform managed to gain popularity, considering that it was invented recently, in 2017. In 2019 it surpassed Facebook, and after another year it surpassed Instagram.

Of course, there are thousands of ways we can waste time through technology.

Used for entertainment and fun, technology will ruin your life by robbing you of what is most valuable: your time.

When we are born, we are framed in time, matter, and space. When we die, we leave behind these three dimensions. There is no other reincarnation, no other period in eternity when we can make better choices with our time.

Time is your life. It is the most important thing. You can make more money anytime, but time... you cannot.

Do not forget that your phone's last danger is wasting time. Videos of dogs and cats. Of jokes and memes. Of all sorts of comics that take your life in exchange...

Do not forget what Paul says:

"Walk in wisdom toward those who are outside, redeeming the time." – *Colossians 4:5*

Many people shout at doctors on their deathbeds, asking them to do everything they can to extend their lives.

But my question is: what did they do with their lives until then?

Your phone can take away the time you could invest usefully, and waste it on trivialities.

Make time for valuable things! Technology can help you tremendously to learn new things, to be better professionally, to listen to spiritually uplifting materials, but at the same time, it can be a great waste of time.

You decide!

Filter all the offers that come to you on the phone and do not forget about what is really worth your time!

OCTOBER 19

AN UNUSUAL MARRIAGE PROPOSAL

Ann Judson is remembered as a special and dedicated missionary in the history of the Christian church. She is considered the most influential missionary woman in American history. Her decision to marry Adoniram Judson made her and her husband be among the first missionary couples sent by America to other parts of the world.

Here is the letter Adoniram wrote to her father asking for his consent to their marriage:

"I have now to ask, whether you can consent to part with your daughter early next Spring, to see her no more in this world; whether you can consent to her departure, and her subjection to the hardships and sufferings of missionary life; whether you can consent to her exposure to the dangers of the ocean; to the fatal influence of the climate of India; to every kind of want and distress; to degradation, insult, persecution, and perhaps a violent death.

Can you consent to all this, for the sake of him who left his heavenly home and died for her and for you; for the sake of perishing immortal souls; for the sake of Zion, and the glory of God?

Can you consent to all this, in hope of soon meeting your daughter in the world of glory, with a crown of righteousness brightened by the acclamations of praise which shall resound to her Saviour from heathens saved, through her means, from eternal woe and despair?"

Her father consented. They left for India in 1812. Because they were forbidden to work in India, the Judsons sailed to Burma, Myanmar. Ann did evangelistic work, adopting orphan girls and educating children.

In 1824, war broke out between the British and the Burmese, and Adoniram Judson was arrested along with other foreigners. Ann saved his life by lobbying government officials, bringing him food to prison, and pushing for his freedom for the next two years.

After the British victory and the release of Adoniram, she died exhausted by persecution and the family and missionary responsibilities that overwhelmed her during his imprisonment.

Her last words were in Burmese, the language she learned so that she could serve the people there with love and passion. Their daughter also died 6 months after her mother's death...

Can you compare that kind of Christianity to what we live today?

OCTOBER 20

ARE YOU EXCHANGING SOMETHING FOR NOTHING?

"Yet indeed I also count all things loss for the excellence of the knowledge of Christ Jesus my Lord, for whom I have suffered the loss of all things, and count them as rubbish, that I may gain Christ." – Philippians 3:8

One of the missionaries of AREA Foundation[25] chose to serve in Dobrogea[26], following God's personal call for him. When he moved from Wales, someone asked him:

"Are you moving from having something to having nothing?"

The missionary replied, "I move from nothing to something!" What a formidable response!

For some, the house, the wealth, the money, the job, they all mean *something.* And they do everything they can for it, so that they climb the ladder as high as possible. For fewer, however, God's call means something, and what the world can offer means *nothing.*

What do you struggle for every day? For what the world calls "something" or for what God calls "something"?

We make use of fleeting things, but they are not our goal.

Our goal is Heaven, and the way there passes though God's will for each of us. By understanding His calling, we can serve Him with all our resources.

And one day, we will leave this earth and take flight to Heaven.

Then it will be the ultimate moment when we will go from nothing to something – forever...

---

[25] Aims to establish Pentecostal churches in every Romanian city, focusing on cities without existing evangelical churches and municipalities with over 10,000 residents.

[26] A region in southeastern Romania.

October 21

WHAT IS IT FOR YOU TO KNOW?

"And He said to them, 'It is not for you to know times or seasons which the Father has put in His own authority.'" – Acts 1:7

Is it not true that we often deal with the things about which Jesus said, *"It is not for you to know"?*

We are very focused on the future. On dates. On times. And, not infrequently, we forget that we live in the present and have a purpose to fulfill here and now. We have a commission from God:

"But you shall receive power when the Holy Spirit has come upon you; and you shall be witnesses to Me in Jerusalem, and in all Judea and Samaria, and to the end of the earth." – Acts 1:8

In God's eyes, being filled with the Holy Spirit and being His witness is truly a task entrusted to us, and it is far more important than God's mysteries *("which the Father has put in His own authority").*

It is a good opportunity today to reflect again on our commission. On the ministry that God has entrusted to us. In the present tense, not in the future. To reflect on humans, not on calendar dates. On evangelistic activities, not on times and due dates.

Time passes anyway. The future we do not know will be revealed to us when it becomes present to us. But today we have the chance to carry with us, as a fulfilled goal, the deeds of the present and the mission entrusted by God to us.

Let us prepare for the future by accomplishing in the present what we have been entrusted with.

Only in this way will we have the full satisfaction of a job well done, when we stand face to face with Him who holds time in His Hand...

October 22

22.000 BREATHS

Yes. That is about the number of breaths a man takes, on average, per day.

Breathing is a complex process in which the nose, mouth, trachea, and lungs are involved. A process that is essential for our lives. A common thing that we often do involuntarily and automatically.

Do you know that every breath is a gift from God?

"O Lord, by these things men live; and in all these things is the life of my spirit; so You will restore me and make me live." – Isaiah 38:16

Today I ask you to think about one breath. About the Creator who has blessed you with the grace to take one more breath. About all the oxygen that comes from the lungs and reaches the blood, thus keeping you alive.

Do you know that there are people who depend on oxygen masks? People who struggle with oxygen insufficiency? People who would value each second of life differently if they could turn back time?

If they could return to those moments when everything was normal and flowed forwards with ease...

About one minute has passed since you started reading this article. Do you know that during this time, 107 people around the globe stopped breathing?

Perhaps I have never thanked God for the 22,000 breaths I take each day.

We can do it from today forward!

October 23

SPIRITUAL BURDENS AND PHYSICAL ILLNESSES

"Beloved, I pray that you may prosper in all things and be in health, just as your soul prospers." – 3 John 1:2

Japanese researchers have conducted several studies that provide broader insight into the causes of many diseases. Below I list some of these diseases and the smaller or greater connection between them and soul issues.

1. **Acidity:** it is not only caused by diet issues, but more often it is caused by stress.

2. **Hypertension:** it is not only the result of eating too much salty food, but above all it is caused by the mistakes we make in managing our emotions.

3. **Cholesterol:** it is not only caused by fatty foods, but also by excessive laziness or a sedentary lifestyle.

4. **Asthma:** not only due to disruption of oxygen supply to the lungs, but often sad feelings make the lungs unstable.

5. **Diabetes:** caused not only by too much glucose intake, but also by a selfish and stubborn attitude which can disrupt the function of the pancreas.

6. **Kidney stones:** not only because of calcium oxalate deposits, but rather because of hatred...

7. **Spondylitis:** not only in L4-L5 or cervical pain, but it can also be caused by burdens or too many worries regarding the future...

I conclude with Paul's verse that mentions physical health, but also its connection with the relationships between us that must be maintained through bonds of peace.

"Greet all the brethren with a holy kiss." – 1 Thessalonians 5:26

I wish you good health!

October 24

DOES THE DEVIL HAVE SOMETHING IN YOU?

"I will no longer talk much with you, for the ruler of this world is coming, and he has nothing in Me." – John 14:30

Jesus knew the battle that was going to come. Gethsemane. Calvary. Suffering. The disciples fleeing. The priests mocking. Jesus considered all these the devil`s methods of intimidation to make Him give up. Back down. Not follow through with the plan.

Jesus says something special here: *He has nothing in Me. That means, he does not have anything against Me. He cannot defeat Me because I do the will of the Father, not the will of the Devil. In this way, victory is assured. The battle has been won!*

Any sin in which we live consciously and continuously is a sin through which the devil has an open door to us. Therefore, we need spiritual cleansing on a daily basis.

The closer we get to Him, the more the Devil will draw near to us to intimidate us, harm us, and stop our desire for daily sanctification. But when he does, we should remember John's words:

"You are of God, little children, and have overcome them, because He who is in you is greater than he who is in the world." – 1 John 4:4

Do not let the devil have something in you. If you have done something wrong, bend down on your knees and ask the Lord for forgiveness and strength to be a conqueror from now on.

Do not play with sin! Do not joke around about preparing for the battle day! Do not put your trust in your own strength!

Remove any dirt that the Devil has given you! Cast out any word that is not sprinkled with grace and salt! Stop any action that is not biblical! Let Jesus overwhelm your whole life with His presence!

Only abiding in Jesus can give us victory. Only through Him can we emerge victorious when the ruler of the world comes against us.

October 25

THE LAST MEAL

"And Elijah said to her, 'Do not fear; go and do as you have said, but make me a small cake from it first, and bring it to me; and afterward make some for yourself and your son.'" – 1 Kings 17:13

The death of her husband had pierced her heart deeply. Left without the "pillar" of the house and without any help from outside, she lived her life from one day to the next with her dear son. For the past several months, food had been scarce, and today they had reached their last meal. A handful of flour and a few drops of oil were all they had left...

She went outside to collect some sticks for the last hearth fire. She knew she had no other chance. The bitterness of their last meal and the thoughts running through her mind made the two logs in her arms seem heavier than they really were. She could not look her child in the eye because of the pain she felt deep in her heart...

On the horizon she saw a stranger approaching. It was Elijah. The prophet. And his cry reached her ears:

"Please bring me a little water in a cup, that I may drink." – 1 Kings 17:10

The widow returned to get water. But the prophet's voice continued, "Bring me a piece of bread as well..."

That is when she gave in. She felt that she might collapse. She was overwhelmed by dark thoughts. How can a prophet demand the last portion of food from a widow and her child? How can God be so merciless as to...

"It's the last portion!" she cried through tears...

"Do not be afraid," said Elijah. "Give it to me first!"

How did she make the last fire? From where did she find the strength to knead the last cake? Was what the prophet said true? What will the child who has endured hunger until now say when he sees that the entire cake goes to Elijah?

Will God really provide? Can I, through tears, see the miracles that faith brings? Could it be that, behind the prophet who asks me to give him first, is God who tests me?

A pastor told me a few years ago about the hard times of his childhood. A home full of children. A family living from farming. Parents with calloused hands, but with great faith. He told me that one summer they had only 10 bags of wheat for the whole winter ahead of them!

He went to put them in the barn. The father took 2 bags and said, "These are for widows and orphans."

"But Dad, even now, when we already have so little? How are we going to live with the other 8 bags for an entire winter?" asked the future minister, as a child, looking at his father who was materially poor, but full of faith.

"The Lord will provide!" said the father, turning his eyes away, in tears...

And the Lord did provide. They put the 8 bags of wheat in the barn and took out 12 when, at the beginning of the frosty winter, they had to take the wheat to the mill.

"The Lord your God lives!" said the widow to Elijah. Perhaps her statement was more like an oath than a great faith. Maybe it was more of a justification, so that she is taken at her word, so that Elijah will not ask for himself first anymore...

Today, Zarephath is the most excavated and studied Phoenician locality. Its ruins are divided into two distinct parts: the old port to the north and a series of columns, coffins, and graves to the south.

The fortress collapsed. Historians look for whatever they can still find of value.

We found in Zarephath something more precious than the pieces of carved ivory and ceramic vessels discovered by historians.

We found a widow and her son. And Elijah who stayed with them for a long time.

And we were surprised that from the last two portions of food at least three people kept on eating for a long time...

And we have learned that when you give from your little to God first, it will always be enough...

October 26

AFRICA AND LACK OF WATER

Did you know that more than 800 children under the age of five die every day in Africa due to lack of water or due to contaminated water?

Imagine for a moment the life of Meliyio Tompoi, a 35-year-old mother of six who lives in the Narok district, in southwest Kenya. Most of the water spots in the area are dry, and she has to walk over 15 miles on foot to collect water. This takes six hours every day. Although her household requires about 10 gallons of water per day, Meliyio can only carry 4 to 5 gallons by herself. So sometimes her family may eat only once a day due to lack of water. Unfortunately, there are millions of women like Meliyio worldwide.

While nearly one billion people worldwide live without access to clean water, the crisis disproportionately affects women and girls. As caregivers and housekeepers, women bear the overwhelming responsibility of finding and collecting water for their families.

If you are among the 7 out of 10 people on the planet who have clean water available at home, consider yourself blessed. Hundreds of millions of people are not so blessed, and their families pay the daily price.

Water-related diseases destroy their energy. Carrying buckets of dirty water for hours prevents mothers from earning money and children from going to school. They do not have the water they need to irrigate crops or give to their animals. And at the end of the day, it is hard to rest knowing that the next day will be the same.

While we choose what brand of still or mineral water to drink (not to mention juice), there are children who die every day because of these vital shortages...

I would like to invite you to think about them for a moment when you drink the next glass of water...

I would like you to think about them the next time you cook food in clean tap water...

Then think about yourself and your family... When was the last time you thanked God for the water?

OCTOBER 27

CALIFORNIA GOLD RUSH

The California Gold Rush began in January 1848, when gold was discovered on Sutter's farm in Coloma. The news spread rapidly, attracting more than 300,000 people from the rest of America and abroad.

These early gold seekers traveled to California by ship and in wagons across the continent, often facing great hardships along the way. At first, they extracted gold from riverbeds and streams by simple methods such as straining, but later more sophisticated extraction methods were developed, which were then adopted around the world. Gold worth billions of US dollars was mined, bringing considerable fortunes for some people; however, many other people returned home not much richer than they had come.

Those people died, and none of them took along an ounce of gold with them.

"For we brought nothing into this world, and it is certain we can carry nothing out." – 1 Timothy 6:7

And yet people's search continues. They keep running from morning until nighttime for that *nothing* that will remain here. Wouldn't you want us to run after what actually matters?

One of the quests that the Bible recommends is the search for God:

"Seek the LORD while He may be found, call upon Him while He is near." – Isaiah 55:6

Another worthy quest is the search for the Kingdom and for holiness:

"But seek first the kingdom of God and His righteousness, and all these things shall be added to you." – Matthew 6:33

Last but not least, we must seek to read the Word of Scripture and fulfill it.

"This Book of the Law shall not depart from your mouth, but you shall meditate in it day and night, that you may observe to do according to all that is written in it. For then you will make your way prosperous, and then you will have good success." – Joshua 1:8

I wholeheartedly wish you success in such blessed pursuits!

OCTOBER 28

THE PANDEMIC AND SOCIAL DISTANCING

When Covid appeared, it brought many rules and norms regarding our behavior in open or closed spaces. One of the rules imposed was social distancing: the requirement to keep a certain distance from others in order not to contaminate them or be contaminated by them.

Do you know that the Bible also has distancing requirements? It warns us that there are certain things or people that can harm us, and we should take all necessary measures to stay away from them.

First, the Bible tells us to keep our distance from the youthful lusts.

"Flee also youthful lusts; but pursue righteousness, faith, love, peace with those who call on the Lord out of a pure heart." – 2 Timothy 2:22

Another translation of the same verse goes like this:

"Stay away from the bad things that young people your age are used to doing."

If you increase the distance from sin, you will automatically decrease the distance from holiness.

Second, the Bible asks us to keep our distance from people who hate God and love sin. Paul writes a list of people we meet at every turn, but with whom we should neither associate nor make friends:

"But know this, that in the last days perilous times will come: For men will be lovers of themselves, lovers of money, boasters, proud, blasphemers, disobedient to parents, unthankful, unholy, unloving, unforgiving, slanderers, without self-control, brutal, despisers of good, traitors, headstrong, haughty, lovers of pleasure rather than lovers of God, having a form of godliness but denying its power. And from such people turn away." – 2 Timothy 3:1-5

Friendship with such people will alter your character and destroy your life. Their sins will also come upon you, and their immoral habits will affect you.

Last but not least, God's Word asks us to distance ourselves from divisive people.

> *"Now I urge you, brethren, note those who cause divisions and offenses, contrary to the doctrine which you learned, and avoid them." – Romans 16:17*

Staying close to divisive individuals can erode our spiritual well-being and unity within the community. Their influence can sow discord, create conflicts, and distract us from our purpose. The negativity and strife they bring can lead us away from the path of righteousness, causing unnecessary turmoil in our lives. By distancing ourselves from such influences, we protect our hearts and minds, allowing ourselves to focus on positive, God-honoring relationships that build up rather than tear down. This separation is essential for maintaining a healthy, harmonious, and spiritually fulfilling life.

A child of God should leave peace behind, not destruction.

The pandemic is over; so are social distancing rules. The requirements of the Bible, however, remain valid, and we need to pay close attention to them.

So help us God!

October 29

WHAT IS YOUR MOTHER`S NAME?

Naomi and Elimelech, along with their two boys, left for Moab because of the financial and material crisis that came over Israel. The circumstances were such that Naomi ends up losing her husband and two sons there, and when she returns to Israel, something also else happens, beside the change of residence.

Naomi is a special name and translates to *pleasant, delightful.* But Naomi demands that her name be changed when she meets her old acquaintances in Israel. She prefers to be called Mara which means *bitterness, sadness.*

We have particularly pleasant mothers among us. Mothers who, with many sacrifices, have raised children who today are teenagers and young adults. And yet, something has changed. From the smiling mother holding her baby, an initially unseen transformation occurred inside her, as the years passed. Tears, sadness, endless questions.

Was it worth it? Why does the child I gave life to do this to me? Why is this happening to me? But I have told him so many times, why did he not listen to me?

Maybe you are a young man reading these lines. Let me ask you: what is your mother's name? Did you change her pleasant name into a bitter one?

Listen to me, child... You cannot inflict pain on your godly mother and expect God's blessing! If a mother has been shedding tears for years because of you, how do you think God can give you happiness?

I would like you to ponder on this question... Wouldn't you like to make her life pleasant again? Wouldn't you like to see the smile appearing on her face again, like a sunrise, after having lost it years ago?

Mara is surrounded by storms. By clouds. By pain. By betrayals.

Naomi, however, is full of life. A life not fulfilled by material things, but by her children's walk with God. By the fact that you listen to her, and you love the God with whom she talks much in prayer about you...

What's your mother's name?

October 30

THE DAY WHEN GOD TURNS BACK THE CLOCK

"And what's the sign?" Hezekiah asked timidly the greatest prophet at that time, hoping for a Word from God.

Isaiah answered with a distinct firmness in his voice, *"God will turn back the clock for you today, Hezekiah!"*

First, **the day God turns back the clock is the day He listens to your tears and prayers.** This was Hezekiah's luggage when death waited for him at the door, but it soon left when it saw its weight.

Keep collecting countless tears and prayers! Those that fall into handkerchiefs or napkins are not thrown into the trash can but gathered by God in His bottle. And the day He answers your prayers, you will see that time will stand still and moments of joy will flood you.

Second, **the day God turns back the clock is the day He makes you healthy.**

God not only hears our prayers, but He also fulfills those prayers that are according to His will. What is tragic is that we always desire physical health while God emphasizes spiritual health. There is no disease worse than sin, and He can heal you of it too. You will feel as if you are flying, as if all you still need to climb to the place of the saints are some angel wings.

Also, **the day God turns back the clock is the day He adds years to your life.** He gave Hezekiah 15 more years of life so that he could tell everyone about the miracle of healing and of an extended life. How sad it was that he wasted these years flaunting his wealth to those who had hoped to hear about something else from him.

We may not get 15 more years, but I assure you that when God stopped time at Calvary, when those seconds were measured in hours of agony for the One who created time – that`s when we received eternity. Ever since then, we have been able to say like the poet:

We will live eternities of love,
Thousands of years, tens of thousands, thousands of thousands;
/:If a moment with Him is an amazement
How will it be in eternity?:/

People turn back the clock and their first thought is, "I will sleep more tonight!"

But when God turns back the clock, He does it so that every tick will ring in our ears the sound of grace, goodness, and mercy. This will not last long, however, because the Bridegroom has already started the countdown to the HEAVENLY wedding, the celebration when no one will look at the clock anymore.

Until then, let us adjust our clocks according to that of the Great Watchmaker. And the day will seem short to us because of how much work there is in the field of the Gospel... and the night will seem too long.

But dawn is coming, and from then on, no one will turn back their clocks anymore.

October 31

WHAT WILL YOU BUY ON HALLOWEEN?

"And all who sat in the council, looking steadfastly at Stephen, saw his face as the face of an angel." – Acts 6:15

An American decorated his house and yard for Halloween in such a way that neighbors called the police. Several dolls resembling people being murdered in barbaric manner were placed around the courtyard and six gallons of fake blood were splashed everywhere. The officers congratulated him on his ingenuity. The moral degradation of the world has reached such an extent that you are now congratulated for stupidity.

If you have never committed a murder, Halloween gives you the opportunity to simulate a scene like this without getting fined. If you like spiders, werewolves and you really like devils all year round, Halloween is a day when you can take a selfie with them. If you wear masks all your life, Halloween is a unique occasion when you can shout your madness to the whole world.

I do not know if it was October 31st when the demons inside the people screamed at Stephen for preaching the truth to them. Demons cannot stand the Bible nor the person who preaches and lives it.

Stephen had the face of an angel when he preached. It was the Holy Spirit who accompanied him and gave him boldness in front of those with stones in their hands.

When they could not stand the sermon anymore, they took him outside. And they started throwing stones at him. That was what they knew how to do best. To throw stones...

We should resemble angels, not demons. Demons wear masks to scare you. Aren't you scared when he tells you he loves you and then he cheats on you? When he flatters you in the face and then gossips about you behind your back? When is promises to tell the truth while lying? You are frightened not by his deed, but especially by the duplicitous character you have discovered.

There used to be a saying: "I caught him lying about it." Today, the truth is so seldom told that soon we will be hearing something else: "I caught him telling the truth about it."

Demons do not need wings. You do not need to fly towards hell. Lucifer did not fly from heaven – he fell from there. He was knocked down, thrown away, removed (Isaiah 14:12).

Angels have wings. Those who look like them quickly get to where a good deed is needed. They immediately send an encouragement thousands of miles away. They are ready to protect you with their "wings".

They are ready to defend you in front of gossipers, to fight for you in fasting and prayer.

When Lazarus died, the angels were waiting for him.

"So it was that the beggar died, and was carried by the angels to Abraham's bosom. The rich man also died and was buried." – Luke 16:22

We read nothing about the stingy rich man. When the angels are not waiting for you, it goes without saying who it is that receives you. Every sin in a man`s life has a demon behind it. If you have been listening to the demons' advice all your life, it is clear that it will be them waiting for you to "congratulate" you at the end.

Perhaps it is time to throw away the masks. Instead of hypocrisy, let us take the wings of sincerity.

Heaven is full of wings – for those ready for sacrifice and missions that come directly from God. For those who want to run faster because there is no time to lose.

Get them now – holiness, sincerity, truth, goodness... and many others like them. You will need them soon.

"And He will send His angels with a great sound of a trumpet, and they will gather together His elect from the four winds, from one end of heaven to the other." – Matthew 24:31

What do I buy for Halloween?
Some... wings.
You should do the same!

NOVEMBER 1

Biblical financial education: WHAT DO I DO ABOUT THE DEBTS?

The Bible never speaks positively about debt. On the contrary, it describes it as a weight that adds a great burden on the person who has it and even on his family (see the example of the widow in 2 Kings 4).

The Bible makes it clear that the borrower is the servant of the lender:

"The rich rules over the poor, and the borrower is servant to the lender." – Proverbs 22:7

A life of bondage is a life under constant pressure. It is a life without freedom, without peace and without security.

There are cases when we must go into debt for something urgent (unless we have an emergency fund set aside, which is extremely necessary). But more often than not, people get into credit card debt for things that are not vital and then there is stress and conflict when those payments can no longer be made on time.

Avoiding debt involves a few steps. They are not easy at all, but easy roads in life usually lead nowhere...

First of all, make a budget every month, according to your salary. Do not exceed that budget except in an emergency.

Then try to buy everything you need with the money down. Yes, it is hard to raise money for a car for three years, but this discipline will educate you a lot and help you avoid being a slave to any bank or person. It is hard not to get the suit you want this month, because you have exceeded your clothing budget. It is hard indeed, but it gives you peace and freedom that you have not added another debt to your credit card balance.

When you raise money for a certain expense you have in the future, you learn patience. In a world of speed, a world that wants everything instantly, that always wants to have the latest model of whatever appears on the market, you will patiently go against the flow. When others have immense stress and problems caused by debt, you will have patience and peace. The state of your heart is more important than anything else.

To get out of debt, the secret is to first want it with all your heart.

Keep praying and asking God for help. And start with the smallest debt! Every debt you get rid of will motivate you on your journey to financial freedom.

Elisha did not tell the widow in 2 Kings 4, "Go on vacation first!" Nor did he say, "Do not worry about it, the lender has enough money. Forget about him!" Elisha told her that the first thing she should do when she got the oil income was to pay off her debt.

"Then she came and told the man of God. And he said, 'Go, sell the oil and pay your debt; and you and your sons live on the rest.'" – 2 Kings 4:7

I conclude with Paul's exhortation, an advice of great benefit to all of us:

"Owe no one anything except to love one another, for he who loves another has fulfilled the law." – Romans 13:8

NOVEMBER 2

Biblical financial education: SHOULD I SAVE MONEY?

"He who gathers in summer is a wise son; he who sleeps in harvest is a son who causes shame." – Proverbs 10:5

Remember that every product at the mall or in the ad *shouts* at you, "Buy me!" A simple hasty click on an ad transfers money from your pocket into someone else's.

A piece of cake cannot be eaten now and also saved for tomorrow. While for most people today's joy means tomorrow's failure, your sacrifice today determines tomorrow's joy!

The common person (95% of the people) works so that he can spend. The other 5% of the people work so that they can save and then invest.

Think deeply about this: if I continue to spend money at the same pace as I have been spending so far, I will have the same results as before.

If I want different results, I need to change whatever I was doing in the past!

I cannot have another person's good savings while also spending like a man who goes bankrupt gambling!

The wise man differs from the foolish man even by the savings he makes. Through the money he sets aside for difficult times:

"There is desirable treasure, and oil in the dwelling of the wise, but a foolish man squanders it." – Proverbs 21:20

The wise man is content with things that do not strike the eye because he is in the process of saving. While the unwise man buys all that is newest and most fashionable, the wise man sets aside now so that he can enjoy what he saved later.

The wise man has an emergency fund. When the car breaks down, when it is necessary to pay for an unforeseen event in the child's health, he does not need to borrow and enter the cycle of endless debts again.

The wise man also has a safety fund equal to several months` wages. His way of thinking is this: "If I lose my job today, what do I do until I find a new one?

I know what I will do: I will use my safety fund!" And this helps him enormously not to borrow, but to take his time to find a new job.

The wise man knows that he does not live forever on this earth and that one day he will depart from it. And when it comes to his savings, he thinks about his children and does everything he can to help the next generation.

"A good man leaves an inheritance to his children's children, but the wealth of the sinner is stored up for the righteous." – Proverbs 13:22

I have known unwise people who got the latest phone model and who ended up not being able to pay for their winter firewood. People who had a sick child in bed and yet they were ordering food delivery. Many people lack wisdom, not money! That is why financial education is extremely important from the biblical perspective.

Be a frugal man! Be prudent, just like the ant. No matter how much they abound in fruits, summer and autumn will eventually end...

NOVEMBER 3

Biblical financial education: HOW MUCH SHOULD I SPEND?

When spending money, we need to ask ourselves several essential questions:

"Do I really need that item? If I have an iPhone 12 and 15 just came out, do I really need the 15?"

"How does that help me? Do I earn anything with it? Will it just waste my money or generate more?"

"How much does it cost to maintain it?"

"What is the motivation for buying it? So that I can show off to my friends?!"

If you spend on image, *likes* or cheesy appreciations, you will have to continue spending more and more in order to be more satisfied! Narcissism is a bottomless pit! Feeding your ego and wanting to be appreciated strictly for what you wear or own is the sure path to total ruin!

I cannot understand this: Why would someone be ready to pay $1,500 for the latest phone model while his salary is $500 a month? But if you tell him about a valuable book that costs $15, he laughs in your face...

The desire of many people to look rich, even though they are not, has caused them to remain poor all their lives.

When we spend, we need to differentiate between NEED and PLEASURE. Housing, shelter, utilities, food, and transportation are *needs*. That expensive purse, those eye-catching shoes that cost a lot of money, the exotic vacation, going out every night or that expensive watch – all are just *pleasures*. If you keep spending money on pleasures, you will soon have to borrow for your needs!

Write down all your expenses! You will be shocked to notice, after a month, how much money goes on things that are not useful to you!

Watch out for ads! 12 hours a day of browsing on the web will bombard you with dozens of ads. Will Rogers said, "Advertising is the art of convincing people to spend money they don't have for something they don't need!"

Do you notice that money is a mentality issue? Money does what you tell it to do. Money is a good servant if you are well informed and have strong

Scriptural principles. But at the same time, money is a bad master, and it will ruin your life if you do not know how to spend it...

When you spend everything that you earn in a month, you are like a wheat sower throwing the seed to the trash can.

That is what most people do! Instead of saving and then investing so that the seed produces more wheat, they spend everything they earn! Instead of planting a peach tree with the pit inside and then enjoying the fruit of a peach tree in a few years, they throw away the pit!

Last on the list of fruits of the Holy Spirit is self-control. This extremely valuable characteristic applies here too! Know when to say "YES" and when to say "NO"! Know when to stop and when to move forward. Do not throw the hard-earned money out the "window" of so many useless products!

Avoiding debt, using cash for shopping, communicating with your spouse about finances, and having a set budget are the surest ways to spend money wisely.

NOVEMBER 4

Biblical financial education: HOW CAN I GET A RAISE?

One of the easiest ways to increase your income is to increase your current salary. But this does not happen by chance. It takes a few steps to convince your boss that you deserve that raise.

One of the surest ways to prepare yourself for a raise is to become more skillful at work.

Communication, knowledge, and **quality of work** are the most important factors when it comes to a promotion.

If you want to **earn** a salary that is higher than most of your colleagues, you need to **become** better than most of your colleagues.

Most people use their TIME and MONEY for entertainment, instead of using it to enrich their knowledge!

No one will give you a higher salary just because you laugh more heartily. No raises are offered for TikTok entertainment, jokes, or computer games.

The raise will come as compensation for your knowledge!

Those who want to reach their true potential will avoid taking part in activities that do not bring any progress.

Instead of focusing on games, movies, and matches, such a person will read books, attend seminars, listen to podcasts, and be interested in any material that can contribute to his development.

Most people stop learning when they finish school. Therefore, they will keep on making, for years, the minimum wage and will always use phrases such as, "One more month, one more paycheck!" Meanwhile, they look at those who have more than them and, with audacity and arrogance, say, "They must be doing something shady. They surely make money from illegal business!"

At the opposite pole are the few – those who reach the top in any field because they have continued to learn all their lives. They own up to their mistakes and become more responsible. They learn from their own failures and do not point fingers at others.

The people in the first category spend between 4 and 7 hours a day on their phone or watching TV, thus wasting much time. They look forward with great joy to the moment when they can leave work so that they can use the rest of their time for entertainment and fun.

The people in the second category use the extra time they have left in a day to enrich their knowledge. There are not too many such people around. That is why, wherever we turn, we see people who have been stuck in the same place for decades. They have wasted their time on fleeting pleasures and indulged in mediocrity.

We should admire and, especially, follow the example of those who, day by day, have made efforts for personal and professional development!

NOVEMBER 5

Biblical financial education: IS IT WORTH INVESTING?

"Wealth gained by dishonesty will be diminished, but he who gathers by labor will increase." – Proverbs 13:11

The big difference between the common man and the man who wants more in life (we do not refer here to a greedy person, but to a person who wants to have time later for more important things than his daily job) is that the first one works for money, while the second puts money to work for him. The first one offers time for money, while the second one offers money for time.

It is not how much money you can make that's the most important, but what you do with that money! A person who earns $1,500 a month and knows how to use this money properly will be richer than the one who makes $6,500 a month but wastes it all!

One of the big changes is to understand that if you spend money on something that will continue to waste more of your money but produce nothing, you will remain poor all your life.

For example, with $1,500 you can buy the latest phone model which will not bring you any income, or you can buy a few shares in a company that offers you dividends.

Do not invest with the desire to earn overnight! Do not be greedy! What comes quickly is also risky, but what grows slowly is blessed!

First of all, invest in yourself! In your knowledge. In your training.

Continue investing in your family. In the education of your children. In their future.

Then think about investing in something that brings you a small, steady income. You need to ask for guidance and wisdom from God about this, but at the same time, you need to become informed.

Do not invest in something you do not understand how it works! Do not put all your hard-earned money in a single basket. The collapse of a company can wipe out all your capital...

Do not invest until you have saved for an emergency fund! Do not invest until you have paid off your debts! If you put your money into something that brings a return of 4% per year, but you have a loan for which you pay 9% interest per year, you have earned nothing. Quite the opposite...

Also, do not forget: the higher the investment return, the greater the risk.

Often it is better to move forward slowly but surely than in a hurry and end up in bankruptcy.

> *"The plans of the diligent lead surely to plenty, but those of everyone who is hasty, surely to poverty." – Proverbs 21:5*

NOVEMBER 6

Biblical financial education: HOW DO I FIGHT FINANCIAL TEMPTATIONS?

There is a paradox I have noticed in many people's lives: they are physically free, but they are spiritually enslaved. Do you know that there are people who are enslaved by immorality? By food? By gambling!? By daily love affairs in which they waste all their income and destroy both their life and their family!? The Bible tells a particularly valuable truth:

"The labor of the righteous leads to life, the wages of the wicked to sin." – Proverbs 10:16

You managed to get out of debt. To save. To put some money aside. Do you think everything is okay now?

There is this trap that plagues us all, a trap into which many people fall as soon as they become financially successful: using your wealth for sin.

Drinking. Smoking. Drugs. Gambling. Sports betting. Going out with friends who take advantage of you and, like a sponge, want to take everything you have.

Money is neutral. It does whatever you ask it to do. That is why what you accept in your heart plays an important role. It is from there that the orders go to your pocket or wallet.

When the prodigal son left his home, he said, "Father, give me." When he returned, he said, "Father, make me!"

He understood firsthand that without a father, money is used for debauchery and eventually leads to bankruptcy on all levels. It was not the money he received from his father that was the problem, but his character. Therefore, when he returns, he asks for help to change on the inside. He understood that it was not how much you have in your pocket that was most important, but who you really love in your heart is what truly matters. When your love for the Father is greater than the passion for the material things, the temptations will no longer bring you to your knees. You will be able to stand tall in front of them and say 'NO!'.

I would like to shout this out so that I am heard well: all the people who valued money and fled from God's presence eventually failed!

All those who sought God's pocket more than His face have fallen into vices from which most of them have never recovered...

Why does the wise man say that the fear of the Lord is the beginning of wisdom?

Because when I live daily in obedience to God and respect for His will, I will use material things for life, not death, so as to be useful to my family and to those around me by being a blessing for them.

NOVEMBER 7

Biblical financial education: DO I REALLY HAVE TO BE GENEROUS?

"The generous soul will be made rich, and he who waters will also be watered himself." – Proverbs 11:25

It is not a problem if you got rich honestly. It would be a problem if you became stingy and started to love that money and were unwilling to help those in need.

The normal cycle God has designed for each of us is this: work, earn, use for your needs, and give for the needs of others.

When David noticed that the cup of blessings had already overflowed, he called Mephibosheth to his table. A lame man at the King`s table. David was first a shepherd and then he became King, but the strong relationship he had with God guided him to be a blessing to those around him.

We work for ourselves and for our family first and foremost but let us not forget that the income from this work contains our share, but also the share of others.

"As for every man to whom God has given riches and wealth, and given him power to eat of it, to receive his heritage and rejoice in his labor—this is the gift of God." – Ecclesiastes 5:19

There, in the affluence God has given you, there is a part that belongs to the widow and the orphan, to the poor and the sick. Listen, I did not say 'the lazy.' You must carefully analyze those you plan on helping, so that your help will truly be a blessing for that person!

In the Old Testament, tithing was mandatory. In the New Testament we most often encounter the terms 'giving' and 'almsgiving.' That is because Jesus came willingly to die for us. And His desire is for us to serve Him not out of obligation, but joyfully.

"So let each one give as he purposes in his heart, not grudgingly or of necessity; for God loves a cheerful giver'." – 2 Corinthians 9:7

When we identify ourselves with those who need our blessings and then we joyfully help them, we are actually identifying with Jesus:

> *"And the King will answer and say to them, 'Assuredly, I say to you, inasmuch as you did it to one of the least of these My brethren, you did it to Me.'" – Matthew 25:40*

The law gives out of obligation. With a sigh in the heart. With judgment on the lips. With great care lest it exceeds 10%. However, love is not about percentages or calculations, but about the heart. Love understands that 10% is the minimum, and the maximum does not exist...

Giving reminds me at least 12 times a year that God owns everything I have, and I am just the steward.

You are blessed in order to become a blessing! Discipline yourself in this area too! The first money that must leave your home when any kind of income comes to you is for the "Lord's share." The 10% you give at the beginning gives you the assurance that the remaining 90% is blessed by the Lord!

When you give the Lord`s share, you become less stingy and less selfish. You become a better husband and a better wife. And during your life, these small gestures build in you an extraordinary character of giving, sacrifice, and offering. Thus, Jesus takes form in you, and also, these gestures help you enormously not to cling to fleeting things!

At the end, you will notice something special: that we are happiest when we give, not when we keep for ourselves. This is how we were created by the One who gave Himself so that He could have us with Him in eternity...

NOVEMBER 8

WHAT ARE ANGELS?

The world we live in has its own perspective on angels: *books, movies, babies with wings, T-shirts with inscriptions...* But let us take a look at angels from a biblical perspective.

Angels are *beings created by God* before the creation of the heavens and earth:

"You alone are the Lord; You have made heaven, the heaven of heavens, with all their host, the earth and everything on it, the seas and all that is in them, and You preserve them all. The host of heaven worships You." – Nehemiah 9:6

They **have no material body,** so they are not subject to earthly physical laws such as gravity.

"And Elisha prayed, and said, 'Lord, I pray, open his eyes that he may see.' Then the Lord opened the eyes of the young man, and he saw. And behold, the mountain was full of horses and chariots of fire all around Elisha." – 2 Kings 6:17

Also, Jesus Christ says that angels **do not marry or die** because they are outside of matter, time and space.

"...nor can they die anymore, for they are equal to the angels and are sons of God, being sons of the resurrection." – Luke 20:36

Angels are more powerful than humans, but not almighty:

"Bless the Lord, you His angels, who excel in strength, who do His word, heeding the voice of His word!" – Psalm 103:20

At the same time, angels know more than humans do, but **they are neither omniscient nor omnipresent,** as God is:

"But of that day and hour no one knows, not even the angels of heaven, but My Father only." – Matthew 24:36

Today we briefly saw what angels are, and tomorrow we will find out what angels do.

Until then, do not forget that one day we will be like them...

NOVEMBER 9

WHAT DO ANGELS DO?

Angels have different missions entrusted to them by God. It is very interesting to notice in Scripture their obedience and the way they carry out these missions, which we will briefly mention.

First, angels **bring answers to people's prayers**. They do not formulate the answer but receive it from God and deliver it.

> *"Then an angel of the Lord appeared to him, standing on the right side of the altar of incense. But the angel said to him, 'Do not be afraid, Zacharias, for your prayer is heard; and your wife Elizabeth will bear you a son, and you shall call his name John.'" – Luke 1:11,13*

A Romanian brother from America was once going through a great financial crisis: he was on the verge of losing his house to the bank because he had been laid off. While he was praying, his little girl entered the room and said, "Daddy, the Mister said he sees you!"

The father did not understand the little girl's words, so she repeated. The third time, she said, "Mister, make my father see you too!"

Then he saw an angel who said to him, "You have been heard, you will be granted victory!"

In the evening, someone called him and offered him a job, and the bank contacted him shortly after to tell him that they had a new meeting and decided to extend the due date of his payment.

Second, angels can have **missions of protection and defense.** Protection does not come from angels but can come through angels when God delegates them for it.

> *"For He shall give His angels charge over you, to keep you in all your ways." – Psalm 91:11*

A young woman who was a believer was returning home from work one evening in an infamous New York neighborhood. She saw a man lurking stealthily near a building and became scared. She began to pray silently as she walked on. She saw that the man started to follow her, but he did not do anything to her. A few minutes after arriving home, she heard police sirens. A neighbor told her the next day that someone had been raped at the exact time she was coming home from work...

She went to the police, identified the prisoner and realized he was the very man she had seen the night before. Astonished, she asked the police officer, "What made this man not attack me?" The policeman asked the prisoner, and the prisoner remembered seeing her that night. He said, "I could not get closer to her because to her left and to her right were two men accompanying her..." Then the young woman understood that they were the angels of the Lord!

Third, angels can carry out certain **sentences from God.**

> *"And it came to pass on a certain night that the angel of the LORD went out, and killed in the camp of the Assyrians one hundred and eighty-five thousand; and when people arose early in the morning, there were the corpses—all dead." – 2 Kings 19:35*

We would like to emphasize the fact that we recognize the ministry of angels, but we do not bring glory or worship to them – only to God:

> *"And I fell at his feet to worship him. But he said to me, "See that you do not do that! I am your fellow servant, and of your brethren who have the testimony of Jesus. Worship God! For the testimony of Jesus is the spirit of prophecy." – Revelation 19:10*

Let me add one more thing: the angels worship God in heaven continually.

> *"Then I looked, and I heard the voice of many angels around the throne, the living creatures, and the elders; and the number of them was ten thousand times ten thousand, and thousands of thousands, saying with a loud voice: 'Worthy is the Lamb who was slain to receive power and riches and wisdom, and strength and honor and glory and blessing!'" – Revelation 5:11-12*

Interestingly, they do not get bored during the time of worship. They do not get tired of praising Him. If you get bored in God's presence, there is a great chance that you have not yet met the true God...

In conclusion, **we understand that the ministry of angels will always be consistent with God's work and His Holy Word:** no one can claim that an angel spoke to him a message that contradicts the Holy Scripture!

May God be praised for all the ways in which He works for our benefit if we remain obedient to Him.

NOVEMBER 10

THE IMPORTANCE OF THE ROOT

"But the ones on the rock are those who, when they hear, receive the word with joy; and these have no root, who believe for a while and in time of temptation fall away." – Luke 8:13

Enthusiasm for sermons. *Likes* for testimonies. Comments on YouTube. Christians who are full of joy because of another big event. Another successful service. Is this truly the essence of Christianity?

In the verse above, Jesus tells us that joy is a beautiful state, a positive response to hearing the Gospel, but in the day of temptation, it is not joy that gives you victory, but the root.

Did you know that a large oak tree has roots stretching for dozens, even hundreds of feet around? Why is the root so important?

First, the root **feeds the plant**, supplying water and minerals.

The growth of *what is visible* depends on the existence and value of what *is not visible*. A Christian without fasting, prayer, humility, sanctification, and the Word will be a withered Christian who does not have, in a disciplined and daily way, a real relationship with Jesus Christ.

"But when the sun was up it was scorched, and because it had no root it withered away." – Mark 4:6

It is very important, when times of drought or hardship come, that the root exists and continues to feed the plant. It is exactly the same spiritually! We live in times of such religious confusion that only a real relationship with God can provide us with the necessary sap in these times of desolation.

Secondly, another purpose of the root is **to hold up the plant**. When a storm comes over an oak tree, its trunk and crown will stay in place if that oak tree has strong roots.

The same happens in the life of a Christian. Temptation wants to dishearten him because of his positive answer to sin. The Devil wants to knock him to the ground, to shake his faith. What makes a difference in such times? The root.

It is important to note that the root does not grow over night, as many Christians imagine when they say, "I will read the Bible when the day of trouble comes!"

I will go to church when I am in need! I will pray when I am sick!'

This is the need we feel today in almost every church! There is excitement, events, sermons, songs, concerts, etc. But these are not paramount. Do not be fooled by image! By what you can see! Look for the root! This is the most important thing in a community, in a church, in a family, and in your personal life.

The rootless Christian is like a skyscraper built on a 5-inch foundation.

On the day of the storm, the proud will be slammed to the ground, while the humble will stand. On the day of temptation, it is not the lights on stage that will help, but the fasting and prayer that have been done in private. On the day of persecution we will be amazed at how many Christians, who are now bragging to be strong, will fall so easily because they have no root:

> *"Yet he has no root in himself, but endures only for a while. For when tribulation or persecution arises because of the word, immediately he stumbles." – Matthew 13:21*

The storm makes the difference! The drought brings out true value! Trouble, not comfort, will bring out our true character...

You really are just as strong as your root is.

November 11

"BE QUIET! BE QUIET! I AM TOO BUSY!"

Who can forget April 15, 1912? The events of that fateful evening were recapped almost minute by minute, and the details provided by the survivors brought to light the scale of the disaster and the painful truth of ignoring warnings...

1. California ship, around 7 p.m., radioed a message to the Titanic, warning them of an iceberg that California had nearly collided with.

2. Captain Stanley Lord decided to stop his ship during the night, concluding that it was too dangerous to continue the voyage. As he left his shift, he saw the lights of the Titanic on the horizon, about 5 miles away.

3. California ship sent another message to the Titanic, warning that they had stopped and were surrounded by ice. The radio signal was so strong that it interrupted the usual communication of the Titanic, and the response of the radio operator on the Titanic was **"Shut up! Shut up! I'm busy."**

California turned off its radiotelegraph station at 11:30 p.m., and the Titanic hit the iceberg ten minutes later.

At 2:20 a.m., almost 3 hours after impact, the Titanic would sink. Of the 2,224 passengers and crew on board, more than 1,500 lost their lives in that tragedy.

Doesn't it seem to you that today's world behaves similarly from a spiritual point of view? Busy with everything related to material and fleeting things, most of the people are heading towards the abyss of eternity, and when you want to warn them, they reply, "Shut up!"

We hand out evangelistic flyers, we call people to salvation, we use social media to stop people from running madly to hell, and they reply, "Shut up! We are busy!"

God, the Creator, comes and knocks at the door of man's heart. He did it through His Son 2,000 years ago at Calvary, and people said "shut up" then and they say the same thing today. Ever since then, through health, through the air, through the heartbeat and through every breath He gives us as a gift, God calls us to salvation, and people reply, "Shut up! I'm too busy! I do not have time!"

The sigh in God's heart is a long one with a rhetorical question:

"What more could have been done to My vineyard that I have not done in it? Why then, when I expected it to bring forth good grapes, did it bring forth wild grapes?" – Isaiah 5:4

I pray today that you will not reject God's call. The warnings He sends through His messengers can change your life. The eternal Word of Scripture can save you from eternal death.

Instead of being occupied, may God help you become preoccupied.

Preoccupied and concerned about your salvation and the salvation of your family. Concerned about your ship, which is on the brink of shipwreck, but which could be saved by God's warnings and the sacrifice of His Son.

Let us reply to God's calls like Samuel, "Speak, Lord, for Your servant is listening."

NOVEMBER 12

THINGS THAT JESUS DID NOT PROMISE TO US

During His earthly life, Jesus made us more than 90 unique promises in the four Gospels. They are part of many areas, such as forgiveness, salvation, eternal life, and so on!

However, there are some promises that Jesus never made, and below I will list three of them.

First, **Jesus never promised that there would be many of us who would follow Him.** On the contrary, He says:

> *"Because narrow is the gate and difficult is the way which leads to life, and there are few who find it." – Matthew 7:14*

Ask yourself serious questions when you are on the side of the majority – when you are on the side of the many who declare themselves Christians but do not have an authentic life.

Take time to withdraw from the crowd from time to time. Go aside and pray. Read a book. Turn off your phone. Do what few people do.

At Bethel, Jacob was alone. No family, no friends, no horizontal relationships. There, in solitude, he met God. He received special promises from Him and, in turn, made wonderful promises to God.

Second, **Jesus did not promise that the world would love us.** Jesus showed us the reality directly:

> *"Remember the word that I said to you, 'A servant is not greater than his master.' If they persecuted Me, they will also persecute you. If they kept My word, they will keep yours also." – John 15:20*

The price paid by those who follow Him does not consist in the applause of the world, nor in the *likes* he gets, but on the contrary, in blame, mockery, defamation and slander. A sister from church said to me not long ago, "I have been criticized in my family for the past 30 years, because I chose to serve Him!"

One of the surest confirmations that you belong to Jesus is that the world is your adversary. That those who serve the Devil reject you. That Jesus' adversaries are also your adversaries.

You cannot make everyone love you, but you have to love everyone.

Third, **Jesus did not promise to give us the success the world pursues.** He did not promise that we would do well, that we would all reach enviable positions, that we would have immeasurable fortunes or that we would be healthy happily ever after.

The world values fun, entertainment, and laughter. Jesus promised us tears, trials, molding, tribulations and tests here, and true happiness beyond.

"These things I have spoken to you, that in Me you may have peace. In the world you will have tribulation; but be of good cheer, I have overcome the world." – John 16:33

In the eyes of the world, success means high positions and material wealth. Jesus calls us to pick up the towel, be humble and serve unconditionally, focusing on the eternal reward.

When you remember Jesus' promises, also remember what Jesus *did* not promise to us...

I wish that the lyrics of the following hymn will remain deeply imprinted in your mind, so that in your days of trouble they may give you the hope and edification you need...

God hath not promised skies always blue,
Flower-strewn pathways all our lives through;
God hath not promised sun without rain,
Joy without sorrow, peace without pain.

But God hath promised strength for the day,
Rest for the labor, light for the way,
Grace for the trials, help from above,
Unfailing sympathy, undying love.

God hath not promised we shall not know
Toil and temptation, trouble and woe;
He hath not told us we shall not bear
Many a burden, many a care.

God hath not promised smooth roads and wide,
Swift, easy travel, needing no guide;
Never a mountain, rocky and steep,
Never a river, turbid and deep.

Authors: Annie J. Flint & Alfred B. Smith[27]

---

[27] https://www.hymnal.net/en/hymn/nt/720

NOVEMBER 13

THREE CATEGORIES OF PEOPLE

"Understanding is a wellspring of life to him who has it. But the correction of fools is folly." – Proverbs 16:22

Our life is a continuous process of learning. We learn at school, we learn at work, we learn from personal experiences or from the experiences of others. Sometimes we learn by smiling, and other times by crying. The courses that life teaches you always come with matching tests.

The first category of people I have met is **the happy people.** They learn from the mistakes of others and, with enthusiasm and much wisdom, try to overcome life's obstacles by paying attention to other people`s failures. They see how a family can end up destroyed, and do exactly the opposite so that they do not end up in the same place. They pay attention to what it means to have a youth that has failed, has been godless and full of lust and vice, and they choose to go against the flow.

They study deeply God's Word, which is the ultimate source of wisdom, and take note of the principles that lead to life and the missteps that lead to eternal death.

The second category of people I have met is **the sad people.** They learn from their own mistakes. It hurts, but they still get up and, with the lesson learned, move on, trying not to repeat the same mistake. The fall cost them and caused them a lot of headaches, but they are trying to get out of it by learning from their own experience.

The third category of people is **the people who never learn.** The Bible calls them fools. Not because they are mentally impaired, but because they deliberately avoid any form of wisdom.

The major difference between a fool man and a wise man is that the wise man always has doubts, while the fool is always self-confident. The humble and wise man admits that he always has more to learn, while the fool is especially pleased that he knows everything...

Be a wise man! Be ready to learn as little as possible from your own mistakes and as much as possible from those of others.

NOVEMBER 14

WHO DO YOU CONSIDER THE GREATEST?

"When Saul and all Israel heard these words of the Philistine, they were dismayed and greatly afraid." – 1 Samuel 17:11

There is a valuable secret in the story of David and Goliath. And this hidden thing has 3 important perspectives.

The first image I want to underline is the **way the people of Israel looked at Goliath.** They looked at the giant's height, his armor, and his attitude. Israel saw Goliath in the foreground and God in the background.

The second image in this text is **the way Goliath looked at David.** He saw him as a simple child with a slingshot that represented no threat against his armor. Goliath heard David's words about God, but he could not take them seriously because he was focused on what he saw in the little shepherd coming from his sheep.

In the eyes of people without God, what is seen is always more important than what is not seen.

A third perspective in this battle is provided by **the way David looked at Goliath.** For David, the armor or height of the enemy was not frightening. He clearly knew that a man without God, even if he is heavily armed, would lose the battle! David saw God as bigger than the problem called Goliath, while Israel saw the problem as bigger than God...

Who do you see bigger? The crisis you are going through or God? Your failure or His power? The lab results you got from the doctor or your faith in His Name?

David said clearly what we also should say:

"Then all this assembly shall know that the Lord does not save with sword and spear; for the battle is the Lord's, and He will give you into our hands." – 1 Samuel 17:47

Go forward in the name of the Lord! Advance towards Goliath by the power of God! The secret is not the sword or the slingshot, but His presence. Fix your eyes on Jesus, not on Goliath!

When He is with us, no Goliath can defeat us.

NOVEMBER 15

8 BILLION

On November 15, 2022, the world's population reached 8 billion. Of these, 1.45 billion live in China and 1.41 billion in India. The U.S. is in 3rd place with 335 million people.

Four babies are born every second, while two other people die every second.

From a religious point of view, the situation is as follows:

- 2.1 billion declare themselves **Christians** (31%);
- 1.6 billion are **Muslims** (23%);
- 1.12 billion are **atheists**, agnostics or non-religious – for example, in the US, one in five people are in this category (16%);
- 1 billion are **Hindus** (15%);
- 487 million are **Buddhists** (7%);
- 455 million are of **other religions** (7%).

O. Smith said it so well, *"We talk of the Second Coming; half the world has never heard of the first..."*

As we read these painful statistics, let us remind ourselves of the mission that each of us who professes to be a Christian has:

> *"And He said to them, 'Go into all the world and preach the gospel to every creature. He who believes and is baptized will be saved; but he who does not believe will be condemned.'" – Mark 16:15-16*

Have you fulfilled your mission?

At the end of your life, God will not ask you if you did what you liked to do, but if you did what He asked you to do...

November 16

ISAAC NEWTON, THE SAND AND THE IRON

"...in a moment, in the twinkling of an eye, at the last trumpet. For the trumpet will sound, and the dead will be raised incorruptible, and we shall be changed." – 1 Corinthians 15:52

Once some students asked Isaac Newton how he, such a learned man, could believe in the resurrection of the dead at the Last Judgment. Newton took a handful of sand, placed it on the table of his laboratory, mixed the sand with some iron filings, and then asked the students to separate the iron from the sand. "That is impossible!" they said.

Newton smiled, took a magnet and with it, in a few seconds, he extracted the iron particles from the sand.

"If I can do such a thing, then He, who made the world and the people, must also have a magnet with which to gather at the end of time all the particles of our body and resurrect it!"

This is the greatest event we have been waiting for! But we are not waiting for it idly, but in continuous preparation. Paul said,

"...that I may know Him and the power of His resurrection, and the fellowship of His sufferings, being conformed to His death, if, by any means, I may attain to the resurrection from the dead." – Philippians 3:10,11

We cannot understand how this will happen, but we have faith that the One who planned it organized everything in the smallest detail.

We cannot understand how the instant exit from space, time and matter will occur. But we are not called to understand it. Our Creator holds these mysteries in His hand as well and will coordinate them according to His pleasure.

What can we do as we prepare for that moment?

"Therefore gird up the loins of your mind, be sober, and rest your hope fully upon the grace that is to be brought to you at the revelation of Jesus Christ." – 1 Peter 1:13

NOVEMBER 17

10 DIFFERENCES BETWEEN A GIRL AND A WOMAN

A woman`s path to maturity goes through several stages in life. In the past, a woman who became wise, mature, and devoted in marriage was most likely first brought up as a little girl who faced the challenges of her age and managed to overcome them successfully. Some girls, however, have remained little girls for many years and they are a real challenge for many boys.

1. Girls attract with their body, while women attract with their character.

Boys (I did not write *men* so as to differentiate between the worldly, immature, pleasure-seeking man and the God-fearing, mature man who truly lives by biblical principles) are attracted to the girls` exterior – makeup, extravagance, tight clothes and revealing clothing – and the girls know this all too well and use it to the fullest.

The wise woman, however, knows that the outside attracts the eye, while the character attracts the heart.

That is why she will not be offended if the guys passing by do not give her attention. The wise woman will not seek the appreciation of adventure-seekers but will try to please God and value inner standards.

2. Girls want adventures, while women want a family.

Girls want to be surrounded by boys. They love clubs, affairs, and one-time dates. They are aware that boys use them, but because they do not have higher values, they cannot expect more and do not fight to change anything.

The real woman, however, wants a blessed family. She is aware that such a family cannot be built with a *ne`er-do-well,* but with a responsible man who loves God, is respectful and dedicates his life to noble goals.

3. Girls want attention, while women want love.

Girls are desperate for praise. For *likes.* For any boy who can give them a cheesy comment. They find out later, with shock, that in fact all these praises were made by boys who were interested only in their bodies. Many of them fall into depression, saying that "true love does not exist."

On the other hand, the balanced woman understands that life is not only about what you receive but is based mostly on what you give. And the phrase "everyone gives what he has" makes the remarkable woman accumulate possessions more important than material ones. Therefore, she knows that true love is not about heart emojis sent on WhatsApp, but is about offering patience, sacrifice, dedication and whatever is needed emotionally, materially, or spiritually for a lasting relationship. But these qualities are based on agape love, a diamond so rare that only the truly precious woman can find it...

4. Girls are sassy, while women are respectful.

If a girl does not respect her father, she will not respect her husband either. Girls maintain their childish behavior: getting what you want by displaying anger or throwing a tantrum. And if you do not get it, being impertinent is your backup plan.

The girl who matures will become a polite and respectful woman.

She understands that relationships are maintained through forbearance, patience, and understanding. And these things can only be asked of someone who has grown up and has left her childhood behind.

5. Girls do not know what they want, while women have a well-defined purpose in life.

Girls go with the flow. With the majority of the class. They do not want to step outside of the typical life for fear they will be called nerds. If everyone skips school today, they will also skip it. For these girls, it does not matter what teachers or parents say, but what the clique says. The responsible woman knows that life is unique and is a gift from God. She knows that today's decisions will determine tomorrow`s reputation. She will take the seed of today's effort and plant it with certainty and confidence, understanding that that seed will bear fruit over the years and reward each effort.

6. Girls want entertainment, while women want education.

Social media is, for the most part, used for fun. For laughter, for dog and cat videos, and for lots of idle chat. That is why when girls surf the internet, they only do it for the things mentioned above, and the years will pass by fast, not giving them a chance to grow up.

At the same time, the internet offers the chance for much deeper learning than in school. It is a chance for those who want more.

That is why mature women will use the internet to learn a recipe, to get inspiration from an interior designer for a new idea in their room, or to get some training.

7. Girls expose themselves, while women hide.

A girl cannot wait to update her social status on Instagram, share news or gossip on TikTok, broadcast a live stream, or take a group selfie to demonstrate how popular she is.

The woman sees value not in chatting with a randomly chosen name from the internet, but in a face-to-face conversation. While the girl chats to 10 teenagers at once, the real woman hides herself and creates an atmosphere of mystery around her. She will not share all her feelings in the marketplace because she understands the value of intimacy. The valuable woman is not interested in what the world has to say, nor will she seek to meddle into the lives of others with all kinds of stories and gossip.

8. Girls take advantage, while women offer.

Have you seen girls hanging out with guys who are decades older than them? Have you seen girls open up to the first boy who comes in a fancy car and are ready to follow that guy anywhere? They use their bodies as bargaining chips. For them, beauty is just something they can use to control and manipulate. Girls take advantage to the maximum. Since they have made no effort in life to learn, to look for a stable job or to earn their bread by themselves, they will need someone to do these things for them. That is why girls are extremely dangerous. They love out of interest, while their partners believe they are loved wholeheartedly.

There is nothing more painful in life than finding out that someone loved you out of interest. That he texted you hearts in exchange for thousands of dollars that you spent out of sincere love. Sadly, I have encountered so many such cases! Alas, how many men`s lives were destroyed forever because of a Dalila who took advantage of them!

The hardworking and God-fearing woman cannot take advantage of anyone. Through her diligence she knows what it means to earn money with honest work. That is why she will not be easily enthralled when someone drives in circles to impress her. She is impressed neither by muscular abs nor by dandiness, but by balance, diligence, and seriousness.

9. Girls envy, while women appreciate.

A girl's frustration is immediately apparent when a friend of hers shows up with a more expensive purse or a phone that is newer than hers.

Girls cannot stand anyone to be better than them in any field. If certain people somehow succeeded in life more than they have, the girls will say that *they surely made compromises, shady deals, and who one knows what kind of connections they have somewhere up the social ladder...*

Women do not look at life this way. They are aware that if someone achieves something with honest work, they deserve appreciation and respect. A woman knows how to appreciate another person's work, and if a person is better than her, instead of envying that person, she will feel challenged to think and develop more.

10. Girls give birth to children, while women raise children.

Billions of people were born throughout history. But history also shows that many mothers just gave birth. When it came to upbringing and education, many of them could not offer something precious to their children because they themselves lacked certain qualities.

The woman who has a high goal in life and who has divine values deeply imprinted inside of her knows that every child is an inheritance from God. Children are like arrows that will be shot towards a target. In this sense, the wise woman will do everything in her power so that, as a result of her personal relationship with God, she can cultivate in the hearts of her children everything they need to reach the *target* for which they were created.

I conclude by appreciatively and respectfully reminding all the girls that God has a special plan for them. Becoming mature is not optional, but it is necessary. And for an efficient maturity we need a source of solid life principles (the Bible), a healthy group of friends and the daily discipline to go against the flow that is promoted by this ever-decomposing world.

It is good to take some time to meditate after reading these lines. To get to know yourself better. To know your sensitive spots, as well as your weaknesses. To hold fast onto God, who can guide your steps and bless your future. He can provide timely answers to all your questions, but your purpose in life is to love Him.

By helping you become mature, God is actually working on your character to make you a gift for someone.

> *"Houses and riches are an inheritance from fathers, but a prudent wife is from the Lord." – Proverbs 19:14*

Let His hand mold you so that this gift will bring complete joy to the one who receives it. Be a unique gift that will only open to the person God has prepared you for!

November 18

BEWARE OF FOXES!

"And He said to them, "Go, tell that fox, 'Behold, I cast out demons and perform cures today and tomorrow, and the third day I shall be perfected.'" – Luke 13:32

Why did Jesus call Herod a fox? Did he have red hair? Did he have small pet-foxes at home? Not at all!

Herod Antipas was the son of Herod the Great (who died when Jesus and his parents fled to Egypt). It was Herod who killed John and to whom Jesus was sent for judgment by Pilate (Luke 23:6).

Have you ever wondered why Jesus calls him a *fox*? Herod Antipas was the man who loved how John preached.

"...for Herod feared John, knowing that he was a just and holy man, and he protected him. And when he heard him, he did many things, and heard him gladly." – Mark 6:20

But do you know that when John confronted Herod for the sin he was living in with his sister-in-law, Herod changed his attitude toward him and put him in prison, and eventually beheaded him?

These fox-style people are very treacherous people. Hypocrisy is the garment they wear every day!

"What a beautiful solo you sang today!" he tells you to your face, and then he goes home and says to his daughter, **"They should have put you sing, not that hoarse-voiced man!"**

"Oh, what a beautiful car you got! You really deserved it, after having worked so hard over the past few years!" he says with false feelings of admiration, and then he goes to his best friend and accuses you of defrauding and becoming rich in an unjust manner...

"Alas, brother, you really told them what they needed to hear today, with your sermon!" And if you ask the one who just praised you why he does not come to the Tuesday prayer services, he gets all fired up immediately... Because he is ready to appreciate you when you preach to others, like Herod appreciated John, but don`t you dare touch him...

Fox-type people are unscrupulous people. People who are ready to shed a tear when listening to a YouTube sermon but who are not ready to repent.

They write great comments on how God touched them, how God spoke to them, but after 10 years you find them in the same sins. They love to hear, but they do not want to change.

They want to see miracles and signs like Herod, but they do not want to repent:

> *"Now when Herod saw Jesus, he was exceedingly glad; for he had desired for a long time to see Him, because he had heard many things about Him, and he hoped to see some miracle done by Him." – Luke 23:8*

Beware of foxes! Stay away from people like Herod! All their life, they listen to sermons, but they never take them for themselves – always for others. They are ready to flatter, appreciate, and applaud you for being honest until you are honest with them. There are people who praise you in your face and stab you in the back. They appreciate you to the fullest for being upright and telling the truth, until you start telling them the truth. Then you become their worst enemy and they will not forget about it until they die!

Beware of foxes! They have multiplied lately like "mushrooms after rain!"

And we, the honest ones, fall most easily into their trap.

Why? Because the honest person thinks that everyone else is also honest...

Have you ever seen a tamed fox?

Me neither!

NOVEMBER 19

BEWARE OF DOGS!

"Beware of dogs, beware of evil workers, beware of the mutilation!" – Philippians 3:2

When Paul wrote to the Philippians to beware of dogs, he was not referring to animals, but to people with dog-like behavior. There were such people back then, and unfortunately there still are such people today.

Dogs bark. They make noise. They are ready to cause a commotion for anything they find suspicious. They are characterized by mockery and conflict. That is why we recommend avoiding the conflict that such people cause – at all costs. If you respond to them with noise, you only stir them up even more. That is why it is better to stay away from them.

Dogs also bite. They cause injury. They like to sink their fangs deep into other people's souls. They destroy families with their bites.

Pity is not one of their characteristics at all, so they will act without any feelings of mercy. They are greedy for money and for other people's possessions and will do anything to get something. They can be easily bribed and are ready to go from biting to tail wagging if they get the desired piece of the pie.

Beware of such people! Let them make noise! They will stop when someone throws them a bone. They will be quiet when they also get a small piece.

Do not hang around dogs! Do not click *like* for their barking! Do not clap when you see them biting someone! They will also turn against you one day if they sniff you around.

Do not try to grab them by the ears! Do not get into the conflicts that those dogs have with others...

"He who passes by and meddles in a quarrel not his own is like one who takes a dog by the ears." – Proverbs 26:17

Instead, like David, pray that God will protect you from them:

"Deliver Me from the sword, my precious life from the power of the dog!" – Psalm 22:20

NOVEMBER 20

THE KING IS WITH US!

"But the boat was now in the middle of the sea, tossed by the waves, for the wind was contrary." – Matthew 14:24

A beautiful ship was leaving South Africa for Holland. Suddenly there was a strong storm. The waves rose dreadfully, and panic set in among the sailors. Some were looking for ways out, while others were doing everything they could to keep the ship afloat.

At one point the door of a booth opened, and an elegantly dressed gentleman said:

"Folks, calm down!"

"What do you mean, sir?" they replied with the same fear in their hearts. "Don't you see that we are sinking?"

"Folks, calm down! I am the master of the ship! The ship was built according to my orders and has weathered storms stronger than this! Why are you fussing?"

The passengers and sailors continued to be terrified and anxious. But the gentleman continued:

"I am the King of Holland! Today you are traveling with the King! Before long we will reach the shore and in peace and quiet we will head to our homes!"

The same story happens with those who journey towards heaven. We are aboard the ship of salvation, and storms do not elude us. The waves hit hard, and the clouds rarely seem to disperse. But do not forget something very important: **the King is with us!**

He never promised us an easy journey, but He did promised to take us safely to the heavenly shore. From time to time, however, we need to hear His voice to assure us once again that He is with us. That He is at the helm. That no storm will stop His Church from reaching the shore.

Would you rather have an easy journey with an unhappy ending or a hard journey that will anchor in the harbor of eternal happiness?

November 21

YOU CANNOT...

You cannot take winter out of the calendar, but you can prepare for it.

You cannot stop the storm, but you can buy an umbrella.

You cannot fight against all the water in the ocean, but you can make sure it does not get into your boat.

You cannot feed all the orphan children in this world, but you can feed one.

You cannot change everyone around you, but you can change yourself.

You cannot prolong your life, but you can live it in a meaningful way.

You cannot eliminate all the darkness in the world, but you can light a single candle.

You cannot solve all the world's problems, but you can make a difference in your corner of it.

You cannot control every circumstance, but you can control your response.

You cannot predict the future, but you can live faithfully in the present.

In a world full of things beyond our control, remember that your small actions have great significance. Each step you take, no matter how small, contributes to a greater good. Focus on what you can do, and do it with all your heart.

NOVEMBER 22

EXCUSES OR SOLUTIONS?

"But they all with one accord began to make excuses. The first said to him, 'I have bought a piece of ground, and I must go and see it. I ask you to have me excused.'" – Luke 14:18

"I do not have time to come to church!" "I am too busy to pray!" "The wife is to blame!" "My children do not listen to me!" "I am too young to convert!" "I am too poor to get involved!" "I will not succeed!"

Have you heard such excuses? You may have even used some of them. When it was necessary to defend or exonerate ourselves, we resorted easily to such phrases. We eased our own conscience or at least made the other person understand us.

How did you act the last time you needed to help someone? What excuse did you use when it came to your personal involvement in a particular activity? What obstacles have you had that stopped you from being more responsible with your children? What are the grievances and excuses you used, as a teenager, in your relationship with your parents?

Do you see the problem? That is why you have been stuck in the same state for years. Therefore, your journey forward is not in accordance with the Scripture:

"Meditate on these things; give yourself entirely to them, that your progress may be evident to all." – 1 Timothy 4:15

95% of the people in a community find excuses, while only 5% take responsibility and look for solutions. They do not say: "It cannot be done!", but rather: "Let us see what we can do about it!" They say like Paul:

"I can do all things through Christ who strengthens me." – Philippians 4:13

Be the person who looks for solutions! Be different than those who always find excuses and be the man of initiative! The man who gets involved! The man who always, through Christ's guidance, comes up with solutions. The man who wants more! Who helps more!

There is no reward for those who make excuses, only for those who have found solutions.

November 23

CIGHID: THE EXTERMINATION CAMP OF THE CHILDREN OF ROMANIA

On October 12, 2022, IICCMER[28] revealed that 15,000 children died between 1967 and 1990 in hospital homes in Romania where children considered irrecoverable (with severe disabilities) were sent.

One of these "concentration camps" was the dormitory in Cighid[29]. Between 1987 and 1990, 160 children of the 183 who were hospitalized there, died.

"There were about 25 children sleeping in 3 beds. They could not lie down. They would sit down hugging their knees and that is how they would sleep through the night. In the cold. There was no stove, there was no light. The rats worked hard and really ate them alive. They were sentenced to death at Cighid" – this is the testimony of Elena Toth, former nurse at Cighid.

The truth was revealed only 3 months after the fall of the communist regime, when reporters from Spiegel TV entered that horrendous camp, filmed it and made public those images in a documentary.

Those images were bone-chilling: children left to lie in their own feces, screams and the obsessive squeak of rusty beds hitting cold walls. In winter, the children crowded into each other so they would not freeze to death, and in the morning the nurses found them covered in frost.

Among the first people to hug the children of Cighid was the German pastor Karl Heinz Pelican. "He came with the truck, with medicine. And he also made the crosses in the cemetery and wrote on them the names of the children and the age at which they died," says Sîrmanca Fechete, one of the survivors.

Romania has the highest number of children in state care in the EU: almost 50,000. Only 5,000 of them have complete files and can be currently adopted. But even for them there are not enough people who can adopt, because only

---

[28] Institute for the Investigation of Communist Crimes and Memory of the Romanian Exile – The organization responsible for revealing that between 1967 and 1990, 15,000 children died in hospital homes in Romania, where children with severe disabilities were sent.

[29] A notorious institution in Romania described as a "concentration camp" where between 1987 and 1990, 160 out of 183 hospitalized children died under severe conditions.

3,000 Romanians are certified for adoption. Even worse is the fact that, in the last three years, only 3,530 children were adopted in Romania.

There is, unfortunately, also the category of "hard-to-adopt children." In their case, at least 9 months have passed since it was established that they can be adopted, but those responsible have not found suitable families, or they have certain health problems, are already too old, or have obvious features of a certain ethnicity. There are few happy cases in which these children find parents.

Did you find this article long? Think about how long their suffering is, and let us each ask ourselves personally: what can we do for them?

God is ready to help these orphans.

"But You have seen, for You observe trouble and grief, to repay it by Your hand. The helpless commits himself to You; You are the helper of the fatherless." – Psalm 10:14

But He wants to do it through us. If we have open ears. And outstretched hands.

Why did Pastor Heinz Pelican have to come from Germany with the medicine truck?

Why should Guido Flori, a Swiss entrepreneur raised in the Swiss protection system, get involved instead of us?

Is it because we sleep in the slumber of carelessness?

Poor Fechete also said: "The hardest thing for me is darkness. When I see darkness, I scream. Now I always sleep with the lamp on. At night the most horrible things were happening to us..."

Let us turn on the light for them too. The light of love. The light of involvement. The light of kindness.

I cried when I read about these horrors. But I do not want to just stick to tears. Not just words.

I want to do more. You should do the same...

NOVEMBER 24

BRIDGES, NOT FENCES

"But also for this very reason, giving all diligence, add to your faith virtue, to virtue knowledge, to knowledge self-control, to self-control perseverance, to perseverance godliness, to godliness brotherly kindness, and to brotherly kindness love." – 2 Peter 1:5-7

The longest walking route in the world is from Cape Town (South Africa) to Magadan (Russia). There is no need for planes or boats because there are bridges. It is 13.910 miles long and takes 4,492 hours to journey on foot. That is about 187 days of walking without stopping or 561 days of walking 8 hours a day. Along the route you pass through 17 countries, six time zones and all seasons of the year.

Do you know why such a road is possible? Such a long journey!? Such a challenging route!?

Thanks to bridges. They provide a crossing in places where normally there was no chance of crossing on foot.

They add extra steps for the traveler who has a strong desire to continue this journey.

The road of life is probably similar. We would need more bridges. More hands of peace reaching out to us. More meals with enemies, so that we can win them over. More bridges between the healthy and the sick. Between the rich and the poor. Between the person that no one notices and the one in high rank.

I invite you to build bridges, not fences. We have enough fences. We made them tall so that no one could look over, into our yard. We isolated ourselves more and more from others, believing that it would do us good. And then, many of us end up on depression medication and with tears in our eyes because no one knocks at our door anymore...

Gossip also builds a fence. Betrayal makes it even taller. Hypocrisy paints it beautifully. Hate decorates it. Today one, tomorrow another. And finally, you wonder why you are in a pillbox. No heat. No light. Isolated from everyone...

Build bridges! With humility and love. With appreciation and respect. With a good deed. With a kind word.

Shouldn`t we start tearing down fences and building bridges? Let us start with:

Forgive me!

It is my fault!

Oh, that was not a problem.

Whenever you need it.

I only texted to check how you are... I have been thinking about you... I love you...

November 25

WAR PRISONERS

"Bring back our captivity, O Lord, as the streams in the South!" – Psalm 126:4

Have you ever thought about the traumas experienced by the war prisoners? There, disarmed, without any possibility of contact with their loved ones, these human beings are dehumanized and deprived of many of the rights that we, the free, enjoy every day.

They no longer drink whatever they want or whenever they want. They do not get *orange juice,* nor *sugar-free coke.* If they get water, even that is a big deal. If they can drink as much as they want, that is even bigger. Also, the food they receive is not 5-star restaurant food. Food is rationed and is rarely in a state worthy of being called *food.* Also, their shelter is not an enviable one. The concentration camps showed the filthy conditions in which many prisoners of war died. They do not rest whenever they want. They are traumatized by the guards` conduct and few of them survive.

The experiences of the World War II prisoners confirm that many of them were too hungry or too weak to attempt any escape, and those who managed to break through the barbed wire fence were shot on the spot.

Do you find the conditions described above painful? Do you find them exaggerated?

You should know that the spiritual condition is similar to the physical one. Imprisonment in the grip of the Devil is similar to it. Such a man is deprived of the Water and the Bread of Life. He is trapped in the camp of sins and vices and cannot escape from there by himself. Most people under these spiritual conditions will die since they no longer have any spiritual strength in them and are trapped by sin and enslaved by lust until the last moment of their life.

But God sent His Son to deliver us from the bondage of the Devil. To offer us a new garment. To offer nutrition of the highest quality. To offer the status of a free man in Christ. To offer a life without barbed wire and without spiritual dysentery.

I was released from there. I recognized the need for salvation and the filth in which I was and this changed my life forever.

What are you waiting for?

NOVEMBER 26

WHO GIVES YOU ADVICE?

"But Amnon had a friend whose name was Jonadab the son of Shimeah, David's brother. Now Jonadab was a very crafty man." – 2 Samuel 13:3

Our life is surrounded by people who, to a greater or lesser extent, have influence on us. Their actions or advice challenge us, directly or indirectly, to make certain decisions that in the long run turn out to be a blessing or a curse.

Amnon was influenced by Jonadab with advice that ultimately led to his death. Rehoboam was influenced by the young people in his entourage with advice to make the nation's life harder. Ahaziah listened to his mother's counsel which was sinful counsel:

"He also walked in the ways of the house of Ahab, for his mother advised him to do wickedly." – 2 Chronicles 22:3

Timothy was counseled by Paul on several occasions toward a life closer to God. The sons of the Rechabites were counseled so well by their father that, through the prophet Jeremiah, God in heaven praised their obedience and principles to all the people.

When we receive advice, it is very important to see the **character of the people** who give it to us. No bitter water comes out of a freshwater spring. People will always give advice to others according to the principles by which they guide their own lives.

Jonadab was a crafty man. A shrewd man. A person with a *fox character*. Why did Amnon not realize that a fox could not give you advice that would benefit you spiritually?

At the same time, when we receive counsel, we need **to check that counsel against the Scripture**. If that advice does not have biblical support, it will surely ruin us.

Also, when we receive advice, if it is wise advice, we would better heed it and **implement it**. We may not like it, it may not be sweet, but it can bring us salvation.

"Therefore, O king, let my advice be acceptable to you; break off your sins by being righteous, and your iniquities by showing mercy to the poor. Perhaps there may be a lengthening of your prosperity!" – Daniel 4:27

Daniel gave advice that was unpleasant to hear, but of great benefit to Nebuchadnezzar if he listened to it.

What is the use of having your doctor's advice written on the prescription if you do not heed it?

God wants to advise us if we allow ourselves to be taught. He wants to correct us with His advice, and if we obey it, we will reach eternity safely:

"You will guide me with Your counsel, and afterward receive me to glory." – Psalm 73:24

NOVEMBER 27

THE CHAIR OF THE EARLY CHURCH

"And they continued steadfastly in the apostles' doctrine and fellowship, in the breaking of bread, and in prayers." – Acts 2:42

The classic chair has four legs that are of equal length to provide balance and safety. If one leg is missing, the chair will be unstable and when a person uses such a chair, he may easily injure himself.

The early church had four basic things on which it was founded: teaching, fellowship, communion, and prayer. They are vitally important both in the life of the Church as an organization and in the life of each person.

Recently someone said to me, "I know the Bible very well, but I do not need to go to church." How sad! To think that you can sit on a chair that has at least one leg missing! Paul says so clearly:

"...not forsaking the assembling of ourselves together, as is the manner of some, but exhorting one another, and so much the more as you see the Day approaching." – Hebrews 10:25

It is worth asking ourselves today: do we have the 4 components in our daily spiritual life? Do we give our souls time for both teaching and prayer? Are we physically present both at Communion and at the other church services? Are we in fellowship with those in the community? Do we know their troubles and needs? Do we act as members of the Body of Christ?

The Devil will seek to take one of our 4 legs. So that we do not have time to go deeper into Scripture. So that we pray hurriedly. So that we go to church only when we feel good and when we feel like it...

NOVEMBER 28

THE SUGAR ON THE DEVIL'S TRAY

Excess sugar is the cause of many problems, such as: obesity, fatty liver, diabetes, high blood pressure, cardiovascular disease and so on. Its taste is extremely pleasant, and sugary foods are consumed with great pleasure. In the short term, it provides an increase in the dopamine level in the brain, but in the long term, the sweetness turns into the 'bitterness' of diseases that torment our lives.

It is not this sugar I want to talk about today, but the sweet jelly on the Devil's tray. Sins that offer short-term pleasure but destroy your life in return and, if you do not repent of them, they even destroy your eternity.

Bread contains quite a lot of sugar nowadays. The Bible also mentions that the bread **of lies** is similar:

"Bread gained by deceit is sweet to a man, but afterward his mouth will be filled with gravel." – Proverbs 20:17

In the short term, it gives you satisfaction. You can move on easily. You feel like you played a trick this time, too. But let us not forget the place of liars is in hell:

"But outside are dogs and sorcerers and sexually immoral and murderers and idolaters, and whoever loves and practices a lie!" – Revelation 22:15

Cakes also contain a lot of sugar. And about these the Bible also warns us, metaphorically, to be very careful:

"The words of a talebearer are like tasty trifles, and they go down into the inmost body." – Proverbs 18:8

It is sweet to hear about the foolish things that someone else has done. To get another message with **gossip.** To have up-to-date information. To increase the dopamine of curiosity by digging through the garbage of others. It is sweet indeed, but it is also harmful. Let us not forget what a Spanish proverb said: "Anyone who shares gossip *with* you is always ready to gossip *about* you."

At the same time, let us be wary of **flatterers**. Of people with sweet words on their lips, but with bad thoughts in their hearts. Of the hypocrite who tells you what you like to hear, and then stabs you in the back.

> *"The words of his mouth were smoother than butter, but war was in his heart; His words were softer than oil, yet they were drawn swords."* Psalm 55:21

Let us be careful with sweets. Insulin does not smell like strawberries, and cardiovascular diseases cannot be treated with cakes.

Likewise, let us beware of the added sugar of the Devil.

It brings a lot of bitterness later on... Pleasure... is costly!

NOVEMBER 29

DO NOT CLOSE THE BLINDS!

"So let each one give as he purposes in his heart, not grudgingly or of necessity; for God loves a cheerful giver." – 2 Corinthians 9:7

In a restaurant in Haiti, a pastor sat down at the table, famished. He ordered a delicious meal at the end of a long day of ministry in which he wished he had a few moments of respite. The table was by one of the restaurant windows, so the pastor could enjoy watching what was happening outside while waiting for his food to arrive.

When the waiter appeared with the plate in his hand, the pastor grabbed the knife and the fork and got ready to start eating. But suddenly, his gaze stopped somewhere to the right. There, with their noses pressed against the window glass, staring at his food, were four small street children, ragged and starving.

With their faces glued to the window, they stared at the food on the pastor's plate.

The waiter, noticing the delicate situation, with a quick movement closed the blinds so that the pastor could no longer see the faces of the hungry children.

Do not worry! Enjoy your food in peace, the waiter said.

The pastor, however, could not continue the meal. His heart, moved by that image, began to beat differently... He knew that eating quietly, with the blinds closed, was the exact opposite of what he was preaching...

When was the last time you closed the blinds in front of such an image?

The rich man in Luke 16 was gobbling up hearty and delicious menus while poor Lazarus kept his nose glued to the window. But the blinds did their job well. The story of Jesus confirms that Lazarus was never invited to the warm side of the blinds. He was never called upon to taste the rich man's delicious dishes...

Shouldn't we ask God to help us open the blinds and see who we are called to serve with love and sacrifice?

Today a mother of 12 children called me and said she wanted to do something for the poor.

Stunned by her request, I negotiated a lot to make her understand that someone else, with a better financial situation, with a more luxurious car, with fewer children should have made such calls. I did not succeed...

Stop closing the blinds when God shows you the need of the person next to you, the one sitting outside in the cold and wishing for a hot meal! Stop closing the blinds when you see someone with tears in their eyes, someone who needs financial help and who may not even dare to ask for it! Because most of the time, those who really deserve to be helped hide their needs inside their hearts and do not complain out loud, hoping that we, those around them, have clean eyes and open blinds so that we can see these needs...

Closed blinds can create, in the short term, an atmosphere of tranquility, safety, and answers like: "It is none of my business." But in the long run, the blinds on the windows of your soul will only harden your heart even more. They will make you colder, more insensitive, and more distant.

The heart of the Christian in which Jesus lives no longer has the blinds closed.

NOVEMBER 30

EMOJIS FROM PRISON

Today most prisons have good conditions. Toilets, regular food, clean clothes, and the possibility of taking walks in the yard and interacting with other inmates. Visits, packages, and even training courses are also allowed.

But Paul was in a 12-feet deep prison, which historians describe as disgusting, grimy, filthy, and dark. Many of the prisoners died of starvation or by hanging.

That is where Paul was when he wrote the epistle to the Philippians, a book considered by many theologians to be the most joyful of the Bible.

In it, Paul writes, first of all, about **gratitude**:

"I thank my God upon every remembrance of you." – Philippians 1:3

Second, Paul writes about **hope**:

"... according to my earnest expectation and hope that in nothing I shall be ashamed, but with all boldness, as always, so now also Christ will be magnified in my body, whether by life or by death." – Philippians 1:20

Third, he writes about **trusting God**:

"For I know that this will turn out for my deliverance through your prayer and the supply of the Spirit of Jesus Christ." – Philippians 1:19

Paul also writes about joy more than 15 times in this book.

I do not know what kind of prison you are in today. Maybe you lost a job, or a loved one died, maybe you are lonely, in debt, depressed or have certain vices. What I can tell you is that our prisons can become the happiest chapters of our life if we manage them through and with Christ.

"I can do all things through Christ who strengthens me." – Philippians 4:13

All the water in an ocean cannot sink a boat unless water enters that boat.

All the problems you go through cannot sink you as long as you do not let them get inside you.

Rejoice in the Lord! Be optimistic. There, in prison, remember what Paul said:

"Rejoice in the Lord always. Again I will say, rejoice!" – Philippians 4:4

Be happy! Keep hoping! Trust God! Pray! Look at how many good things have happened to you so far!

Smile!

Even if you go through the prisons of life...

Even if you go through the prisons of life remember that God has a purpose for every trial. Each challenge we face is an opportunity to grow stronger in our faith and closer to God. Paul found joy in his imprisonment because he saw it as a chance to spread the Gospel and demonstrate the power of Christ in his life. We, too, can find meaning and purpose in our struggles by trusting in God's plan and relying on His strength.

Moreover, consider the testimony your joy can bring to others. When people see you maintaining a joyful spirit despite your circumstances, it can be a powerful witness to the transformative power of faith. Your attitude and resilience can inspire others to seek the same peace and strength in Christ. So, let your joy be a beacon of hope, showing that with God, even the darkest prison can become a place of light and transformation.

December 1

THE ROMANIAN WITHOUT GOD

The following sentences are addressed to our Romanian people in order to awake them and tell them that it's not enough to have a flag, a union day and a country. We need GOD more than anything else.

The Romanian without God[30], even with a full pantry, remains hungry. Even with plenty of cases of sparkling water next to him, he remains thirsty.

Even if his wallet is full, the Romanian without God is still poor. Even with good medical labs, he is still sick. Because the most severe illness is not hepatitis C or cancer, but sin.

Even if he has the best bed in his bedroom, the Romanian without God will still not find rest. Even with the heater turned up to the maximum, in the middle of winter, he will still shiver with cold because the greatest blizzard is in the heart that has not yet known the warmth of God's love.

Even if he is dressed in the finest clothes, the Romanian without God will still feel naked. Even if he is wearing the best perfumes, he will still smell of sin. Lies, theft, and corruption are not removed by expensive perfumes.

Even if surrounded by many friends, the Romanian without God will still feel alone.

Loneliness cries out in hospital wards, in nursing homes, and in the hearts of mothers who have abandoned their children, but few hear her voice.

Only humility, prayer, and turning away from sin towards holiness can change Romania. Some want us to live well, others want us to live better, but truly well live only those who have encountered the supreme Good.

"...if My people who are called by My name will humble themselves, and pray and seek My face, and turn from their wicked ways, then I will hear from heaven, and will forgive their sin and heal their land." – 2 Chronicles 7:14

The tricolor flag is beautiful, but the flag about which Ioanid said "God is my flag" is the one that can lead any nation to its greatest victory.

It is beautiful to be a patriot! I thank the Lord for the country where I was born, but I have set out for a more beautiful country. A place where angels

---

[30] December 1st is Great Union Day (Romanian: *Ziua Marii Uniri*, also called *Unification Day or National Day)*, a national holiday in Romania.

sing, where the white of snow is not mixed with the gray of duplicity. Where songs are not sung for the glory of men, but for the glory of God. Where there are no abortion clinics and no prisons.

I dream of a Romania with full churches and empty clubs. With parents who spend money on new sneakers for their children instead of cigarettes. With hospitals without bribing envelopes and nurses who do not have coat pockets.

With children who say “The Lord`s Prayer” before classes begin at school. With formula milk for babies being sold better than cat food. With families that start their day with a song and end it with a prayer.

We began the revolution with “The Lord`s Prayer” and with „We live the end times.” We began believing that all Romanians need God when things go wrong. But now, when things are going well for us, who still needs Him?

Awaken Thee, Romanian! The slumber of death is the slumber of sin. The tyrants are the demons who have pushed you into the mud. Now or never, carve out another destiny for yourself. An eternal fate. A destiny in the arms of God. He is the only one who can heal Romania...

DECEMBER 2

WHAT DOES THE SPIRITUAL WINTER BRING IN THE BELIEVER'S LIFE? (I)

"And it happened, when Jehudi had read three or four columns, that the king cut it with the scribe's knife and cast it into the fire that was on the hearth, until all the scroll was consumed in the fire that was on the hearth." – Jeremiah 36:23

Children's favorite season is winter. Sledding, snowmen, snowball fights, ice skating, and skiing are special attractions for them.

However, I noticed that the Devil also loves this season. I noticed that he likes "trees" without leaves and without fruit.

Jeremiah had dictated to Baruch the prophetic word received from God. Baruch told some leaders about this message, and the leaders ran to the emperor thinking that he would pay attention to it. The emperor, however, although he probably kept 73°F inside his house, had coldness inside his heart.

The words of God proclaimed through Jeremiah could have brought him the warmth he needed from a spiritual standpoint, but he refused them.

When the relationship between man and God cools down, distancing from the Bible also occurs. Paul threw thorns and thistles in the fire, but the emperor threw the Word of God in the fire...

When the relationship between man and God cools down, there is a distancing between man and his fellow human beings. Why? Because of sin:

"And because lawlessness will abound, the love of many will grow cold." – Matthew 24:12

The "freezer" type of love. Beautiful words, but no action to back them up. Love is not measured by the quantity of words, but by the quality of deeds. But what deeds can you expect from cold love?

First of all, coldness freezes the heart, which is the headquarters of our feelings.

"And they told him, saying, "Joseph is still alive, and he is governor over all the land of Egypt." And Jacob's heart stood still, because he did not believe them." – Genesis 45:26

Lies produce icebergs in the heart of the person who is being lied to. And cold hearts are devoid of joy, comfort, and solace.

What do you cause in the hearts of your parents?

Secondly, coldness can also affect the body. Peter's mother-in-law was in bed, suffering from chills:

"But Simon's wife's mother lay sick with a fever, and they told Him about her at once." – Mark 1:30

That is why the person will be absent from the Sunday morning fellowship. Because they are in bed, suffering from chills. A sick person cannot heal another. Also, coldness can affect the family too. Thus, relationships between parents and between siblings can also become cold.

"But when his brothers saw that their father loved him more than all his brothers, they hated him and could not speak peaceably to him." – Genesis 37:4

Envy produces coldness. It causes distance.

It kills slowly.

Death by freezing is the easiest death. When the body`s temperature reaches 95°F, the body enters in a state of hibernation. The peripheral circulation stops and the respiratory rate and heart rate slow down. At 70°F, the body enters a state of immovable "preservation". Although still alive, the person appears to be dead.

"...that you have a name that you are alive, but you are dead." – Revelation 3:1

Jesus stretched out His hand to Peter's mother-in-law. Hot tea warms the body, and a warm hand invigorates the soul. Some shake your hand and pull you down. Jesus stretched our His hand and lifted her up. Then He began to serve them. Do you know why? Because movement prevents frostbite.

Do not stop moving! Do not stop serving! Do not stop running!

Let the warmth of the Bible warm you up and then, go ahead and warm those around you as well, using the love you have received from God.

"Since you have purified your souls in obeying the truth through the Spirit in sincere love of the brethren, love one another fervently with a pure heart." – 1 Peter 1:22

December 3

WHAT DOES THE SPIRITUAL WINTER BRING IN THE BELIEVER'S LIFE? (II)

Children have so much fun in winter, when they can play on ice. But I have never seen an elderly person sledding down the hill while shouting for joy...

When you are a kid, slipping on ice is so much fun. But when you are mature, you know slipping can be dangerous.

It is similar from a spiritual point of view. Winter in the life of a Christian also brings ice. Slipping. Uncertainty. The spiritual toboggan.

We slip and slide away when we no longer remain in the Lord's arms. Delilah taught Samson to ski spiritually. And at the bottom of the slope, she waited for him with her scissors ready.

We slip when we do not strengthen our calling:

> *"Therefore, brethren, be even more diligent to make your call and election sure, for if you do these things you will never stumble." – 2 Peter 1:10*

Because they do not want to change and get close to Him, the Lord allows the wicked in slippery places:

> *"Surely You set them in slippery places; You cast them down to destruction." – Psalm 73:18*

But what happens to those who are sincere and seek to do His will?

> *"You enlarged my path under me, so my feet did not slip." – Psalm 18:36*

If you hold on to God, you will not slip on the ice of sin. The bruises caused by such slips, even if you miraculously manage to recover, will become life-long scars. It is better to prevent than to treat.

The psalmist Asaph found the most appropriate solution.

> *"Nevertheless I am continually with You; You hold me by my right hand. You will guide me with Your counsel, and afterward receive me to glory." – Psalm 73:23-24*

Let us hold onto God with both hands! And He will not leave us until He has delivered us from the threats of winter definitively and until we are in the glory of heaven.

December 4

WHAT DOES THE SPIRITUAL WINTER BRING IN THE BELIEVER'S LIFE? (III)

We find one more element of winter in the Bible, namely, the smoke coming out of the chimney.

It is so nice to see smoke rising above the homes in wintertime. The Bible, however, does not stop at this beautiful scenery, but goes deeper into the essence. God wants fire, not smoke:

> *"Therefore they shall be like the morning cloud and like the early dew that passes away, like chaff blown off from a threshing floor and like smoke from a chimney." – Hosea 13:3*

People who sin constantly (Hosea 13:2) and who do not heed God's warnings are likened to smoke. With something quickly fleeting. With excitement during an evening of carols. With one hand raised high at the altar call, but with a life that remains unchanged.

When the Holy Spirit descended in Acts 2, tongues of fire were seen, not icicles of ice.

That is a huge difference. It is what God wants from us: to burn for Him.

There is one danger that plagues each of us: amazement without change:

> *"As for you, son of man, the children of your people are talking about you beside the walls and in the doors of the houses; and they speak to one another, everyone saying to his brother, 'Please come and hear what the word is that comes from the Lord.' So they come to you as people do, they sit before you as My people, and they hear your words, but they do not do them; for with their mouth they show much love, but their hearts pursue their own gain. Indeed, you are to them as a very lovely song of one who has a pleasant voice and can play well on an instrument; for they hear your words, but they do not do them" – Ezekiel 33:30–32*

Smoke means nothing more than *"Wow, what a beautiful sermon!"*

But have you made new decisions? Have you started to change your life? Or did you just settle for pictures of saints without pursuing a holy personal life?

The man who is satisfied with just *hearing* but does not also *listen* is similar to the one who hears the alarm, but presses "snooze." With the one who goes to the doctor, gets the prescription, but never takes his medicine. With the one who hears the phone ringing but does not pick up.

Do you want to be fire and not smoke? Then you must take into consideration the way in which a person may be called 'blessed' by God:

"If you know these things, blessed are you if you do them." – John 13:17

Let us be the flames of God!

Let us fight the cold not with cold to the power of two, but with heat. Let us fight hate with love, lies with truth, and ice with salt.

Oh, Lord, bring spring into the souls that have freezing icicles inside! Let Your love melt the frost in our hearts. Then buds will appear in the trees planted near the springs of water, and Your sun will warm us in summer, so that we may have good crops in the autumn of the harvest.

December 5

WHERE DOES YOUR GREAT STRENGTH LIE?

"So Delilah said to Samson, 'Please tell me where your great strength lies, and with what you may be bound to afflict you.'" – Judges 16:6

There is strength that is visible in the eyes of the world. Some are strong through the connections they have. Others are powerful through the money they possess. Other people are strong through the information they have accumulated and through an enviable general knowledge. Or they are strong because of the authority they hold granted to them by their important social position.

Samson was a strong man. Dedicated to God from an early age, he was endowed with special strength. He caught 300 foxes in one day. He carried an 800 lbs. gate over a distance of about 50 miles. He killed a lion without a weapon. He knocked down 1,000 Philistines with a donkey's jaw.

His locks were the sign of his strength, not the seat of his power.

His strength came from having been dedicated to God. Seven locks of hair had Samson. He did not lose them when Delilah cut them off with the help of a Philistine, but some time before.

His strength came from the fact that he was dedicated to God. From the descent of the Spirit upon him. From abiding within the boundaries drawn by the Lord.

Where does your strength come from? Are you known as a man of visible power in the eyes of the world or as a man of special power in prayer? Are you known as a successful bodybuilder or as a man who bows down on his knees and has tears in his eyes as he worships God?

We are told that we are strong if we take revenge, but the man who forgives is the one who is truly strong.

We are told that we are strong if we have the last word. If we pound our fist on the table. If we know how to control and seek justice. But from God's perspective, the man who is strong is the one who seeks peace. The one who knows how to keep his mouth closed when challenged. The one who knows how to control himself.

We are told that we are strong if we accumulate earthly things at a fast pace. If we have something to quickly impress people with. If people stop to give us their attention... From a spiritual point of view, it matters to have patience. It matters to value kindness and courtesy.

Where does your strength come from? From the applause of the world or from its mockery?

From the earthly or the spiritual things? From your horizontal or your vertical relationships?

Be a strong person!

Like David who overcame through modesty, not like Goliath who was defeated through pride.

Like Rebekah who impressed with her diligence, not like Delilah who betrayed through her body.

Like Timothy who stayed by Paul's side, not like Demas who left him.

Like Paul who did much good, not like Alexander the Coppersmith who did much evil...

Like Daniel among lions, not like Nebuchadnezzar on the roof...

Be strong by God's standards, not by the world's standards...

DECEMBER 6

EMPTY HAND

"You open Your hand and satisfy the desire of every living thing." – Psalm 145:16

When we were little, our parents played with us an interesting game that you will surely remember. It was that game of hiding something in one of their hands and we, the children, had to guess in which one it was hidden. The parents were greatly satisfied when we would point to the hand in which that object was hidden, and they would open it and smile at us, congratulating us for the right guess.

Do you know what I would like to remind you of today? That God never showed us an empty hand. Every morning when we woke up, we found a hand full of blessings: health, air, water, food, clothing, shelter over our heads, a family near us, and so on.

And each time He opened His palm to give us His goodness, God wanted nothing in return except to acknowledge that all those blessings come from Him. Let us bow our knees down and thank Him. Let us walk humbly and grateful every day. Let us seek His face, not just His hand...

The devil's palm was always empty. It seemed to be full of dreams, of illusions, of "I do whatever I want with my life, brother pastor!" But in fact, it was an empty hand. Empty of love, understanding, and affection. Empty of promises that have disappeared and hopes that have crumbled. And yet, most people choose him...

For 8 billion people on the planet, God opens His hand daily, and it is never empty.

Are you among the few who thank Him?

December 7

HAVE YOU DUG TODAY?

"He is like a man building a house, who dug deep and laid the foundation on the rock. And when the flood arose, the stream beat vehemently against that house, and could not shake it, for it was founded on the rock." – Luke 6:48

Have you ever tried digging into solid rock? Sweating tirelessly after every blow of the sledgehammer or chisel? Is it not true that it is not that easy?

People think that to repent means just raising your hand up. Just going through the water baptism. Just becoming a member in a church registry.

But Jesus says otherwise.

"Whoever comes to Me, and hears My sayings and does them, I will show you whom he is like." – Luke 6:47

The man who comes to Him, who hears and does what He says, is compared to a man who digs **deep**. A man who does not settle for little. For shallow things.

For spiritual puffs. No! The man who lives every day with Jesus is the man who goes deep. The man who looks for more. The man who kneels more often. The man who strives harder. Whose cheeks are wet with tears... Whose Bible is underlined and worn...

Such a man knows that a solid foundation is needed for a pure youth. So he digs deep.

He knows that a strong foundation is needed for a blessed marriage. So he digs deep.

He knows that a foundation on solid rock is needed for authentic ministry. So he digs deep.

People see the building floors, but God sees the foundation.

When the storm comes, it will not test the couch, nor the drywall of your home. It will test the foundation.

Have you dug deep today?

December 8

THE THIEF AND THE SILENT GOD

For three and a half years, Judas was by Jesus' side with the other 11 apostles. He was the treasurer of the group, and the Bible says of him that he spoke beautifully, but lived dishonorably:

"But one of His disciples, Judas Iscariot, Simon's son, who would betray Him, said, 'Why was this fragrant oil not sold for three hundred denarii and given to the poor?' This he said, not that he cared for the poor, but because he was a thief, and had the money box; and he used to take what was put in it." – John 12:4-6

Jesus never embarrassed him in front of the other disciples. He never said, *"You thief, you crook!"* or other nicknames of that kind. Even on the night of His betrayal, He said, *"Friend..."*

Not even on the evening of the Last Supper did the disciples realize who the traitor was, which is why they were wondering:

"Is it I?" – Mark 14:19

Do you know what I make of this sad account? That Jesus waited in silence and love for Judas to change. He washed his feet on the evening of the Last Supper as a last gesture of amazing love, an act that should have shattered Judas's heart of stone but did not.

Judas believed what many still believe today: that if God does not strike them with a "lightning bolt", that means He agrees with them. Someone said to me:

"Did you see, pastor, that I cursed at Him and He did not strike me?"

"Do you think," I replied, "that if He did not strike you, that means that He agrees with you? Or do you think God is so easily annoyed that a swear word of yours causes Him to jump off the throne?"

God is silent not because He approves of what sinners do, but because He is still longsuffering:

"The Lord is not slack concerning His promise, as some count slackness, but is longsuffering toward us, not willing that any should perish but that all should come to repentance." – 2 Peter 3:9

Take advantage of His silence! Do not wait until He speaks! Do not wait until He says:

"But Jesus said to him, 'Judas, are you betraying the Son of Man with a kiss?'" – Luke 22:48

If He is silent, it does not mean that He agrees with sin. It does not mean you can go on forever in that state. On the contrary, His silence should wake you up. If He did not punish you and continued to give you health, air, life and everything you need, it means that He urges you to change.

Start it now!

DECEMBER 9

THE GENERAL HELPED BY A LITTLE GIRL

We do not know what that little girl's name was. There are only three verses in the Bible describing her. Taken prisoner by the Syrians, she became a servant in General Naaman's household.

We know nothing about her parents. We do not know how she was captured nor for how long she served as a slave in the general's house. We only know that one day the general got sick. Leprosy is not impressed by positions and titles.

The girl's reaction, however, is astounding. The law allowed her to rejoice in the trouble that came upon her master. She could have said, *"God is just. An eye for an eye, a tooth for a tooth. He hurt me, my family, and my people, and now God gives him what he deserves..."*

And yet, she did not act that way. She was saddened to see her master's illness. She began to sigh, and one day he said a few words that reached the general's ear:

> *"Then she said to her mistress, 'If only my master were with the prophet who is in Samaria! For he would heal him of his leprosy!'" – 2 Kings 5:3*

What strong faith this little girl had! What a character! What beautiful memories from her home country...

Believing her word, Naaman went to the king of Syria. Then to Israel. Then to Elisha. Then to the Jordan...

Then he came back home healed...

Sometimes God shows generals that a little girl can provide solutions for the ear that is ready to humble itself and listen.

God shows us that the circumstances of our lives should not destroy our faith. And those who have mistreated us do not deserve our vengeance, but our help.

The general, helped by a little girl, remained in the history of the Bible because a little girl allowed herself to be used by God...

December 10

THE TASTE OF AIRPLANE FOOD...

Statistics say that when we eat on the plane, our taste buds lose their strength. In other words, we feel about 30% less taste, which is why food does not seem as appetizing as it does on the ground.

I think that this is also a spiritual truth. The closer a man of God is to heaven, the more his taste for earthly things decreases. The desire for material things should decrease and the thirst for eternal values should increase.

Paul described very well the purpose for which he lived:

"Yet indeed I also count all things loss for the excellence of the knowledge of Christ Jesus my Lord, for whom I have suffered the loss of all things, and count them as rubbish, that I may gain Christ and be found in Him, not having my own righteousness, which is from the law, but that which is through faith in Christ, the righteousness which is from God by faith." – Philippians 3:8-9

When you fail to get to the prayer service at church because of material matters, can you say that you are really closer to heaven?

When you are more and more eager to gather as much as you can and accumulate as much as possible, have you lost your taste for material things or for spiritual things?

Do you know that if you get closer and closer to heaven, the earth becomes smaller? From an airplane, it does not matter if your neighbor has a BMW, and you could barely afford a cheap Logan car, because you do not even see them from 30,000 feet altitude anyway.

From there, from above, it does not matter that the boss has a swimming pool in his backyard, while I did not even manage to finish my basement... From above, the material things appear tinier and tinier...

"Set your mind on things above, not on things on the earth." – Colossians 3:2

Let us detach ourselves more and more from the fleeting things and prepare ourselves for the moment when we will leave everything we have gathered here and find what we have sent beyond...

Do not be scared if you have lost your taste for material things...

It means you are in the right place...

December 11

THE PENCIL WITH TWO ERASERS

Generally, a pencil has an eraser intended for erasure and a sharp tip intended for writing. It would be quite unusual for a pencil to have an eraser at each of the ends, thus providing a distinct appearance from other pencils and eliminating its main purpose: writing.

I have seen simple people in this life who do not impress with anything special, but who have understood their purpose for living and, with the gift God has given them, they reach the final goal.

At the same time, I have met people who wanted to be more different than others, more special, more "cool," but who do not have a purpose in life. They are willing to do anything to be applauded by their peers, by the clique where they feel appreciated; they are ready to pose with anything that catches the eye, but if you ask them about the meaning of their lives, they will have no answer.

I have seen people who are successful in many areas. People who have diplomas, houses, money, special social positions.

They have become more special in different things, but many of them have lost the purpose for which they were created.

Today is a new day when we are called by God to analyze our lives. Mark Twain said, "The two most important days in your life are the day you are born and the day you find out why!"

We are called not just to be born. Not just to appear in a city hall registry. Not just to have an ID card in the wallet. Not just to breathe.

We are called to something higher. We are blessed to be different and to be able to help one another, so that together we may *"be to the praise of His glory."* (Ephesians 1:12)

At the end of our lives, we may realize that we accomplished significant things that made us stand out, that fulfilled us in certain areas, but did we accomplish what God intended us to accomplish? Were we more special than others or were we more useful?

Were we only members of a church or were we members of the Body of Christ?

Were we nominal Christians registered in a census or were we also every-day-disciples?

Have we just passed through life or have we lived our lives according to His plan?

The dual-eraser pencil may catch the eye for its unique design, but it fails in its fundamental purpose of writing. Similarly, our lives can be filled with impressive achievements and accolades, yet miss the core purpose that God has intended for us. We must strive not just to stand out, but to fulfill the role He has designed for us, using the gifts and opportunities He provides.

Pray that you may understand God's plan for your life, and keep this in mind: the dual-eraser pencil may be more special, but not more useful. Let us seek to be tools in God's hands, not for our own glory, but to fulfill His will and to be a blessing to others.

DECEMBER 12

4,094 ANCESTORS

An interesting calculation that appeared in social media caught my attention today, namely: in order for us to be alive today, there had to have existed 4,094 ancestors who made up at least 11 generations in the last 300 years. If we calculate the number of people, each generation represents:

2 parents;
4 grandparents;
8 great-grandparents;
16 great, great-grandparents;
32 great, great, great-grandparents;
64 great, great, great, great-grandparents;
128 great, great, great, great, great-grandparents;
256 great, great, great, great, great, great-grandparents;
512 great, great, great, great, great, great, great-grandparents;
1,024 great, great, great, great, great, great, great, great-grandparents;
2,048 great, great, great, great, great, great, great, great, great-grandparents.

Have you ever thought about the fact that God created you and organized everything perfectly so that through these generations you could be born at the right time? The people who lived in the past 30 years have endured much suffering.

Unfulfillment and hopes that were shattered too soon. Diseases from which they could never be healed.

Think about the fact that all these ancestors of yours did not have the technology you have today. Nor the physical conditions you enjoy. Nor the easy life that you have now. Fridge. Freezer. Ironing machine. Underfloor heating. Microwave. Photos on WhatsApp. Video chats. Heated car seats. Vacuum cleaner. Vehicles. Sandwich maker.

I wish you would not take everything for granted. I wish you were grateful to God, but at the same time, also think that your ancestors worked for decades for the progress that you enjoy today. Your ancestors did not even dream of what you have today. Your ancestors fought, sweated, sacrificed, and wished constantly for a better life, but most of them did not get it... Do you understand how much responsibility you have today? Do you understand that you are called to give meaning to your life?

December 13

THE DOOR THAT OPENED "BY ITSELF"

The town of Stei[31]. Before 1989. Behind the Old Post Office, sister Juliana was taken to the Secret Service Headquarters[32]. After an interrogation lasting several hours, she was told, "You cannot go back home anymore!"

She was taken to the end of a long hallway, locked up in a dark cell, and the guard pulled the latch loudly when closing the door.

Half an hour later, in that darkness, sister Juliana heard a voice.

"Press the doorknob, open the door, and go to Lenin Street. When you get home, your phone will ring and you will be asked, 'Where are you?' Tell them you are home."

When she heard the voice, she hesitated and wondered if it was fear that caused her to hear that voice...

The message, however, was repeated. Sister Juliana, with fear in her heart, put her hand on the doorknob. The door opened. She passed by the security guards who were having coffee and cigarettes in the hallway.

"I could see them stepping aside to the right and the left, making room for me to pass through, but none of them saw me," sister Juliana later confessed.

She exited the building. She walked down Lenin Street and got home. She bent down on her knees to thank the Lord, and the phone rang exactly as the voice said.

"Woman, we are all dumbfounded - how did you manage to exit? I locked the latch after you, so who opened it for you?" shouted an angry security guard at the end of the line.

"God," replied sister Juliana in a gentle voice.

"Why did you leave the premises?"

"I wanted to go home."

"This is the last time we warn you. From today on you must stop because you are no longer allowed to have fellowship with your brethren."

"I will not listen to this warning," replied sister Juliana.

---

[31] A town in Romania, located in Bihor County.

[32] Secret Service Headquarters: Refers to the local or national offices of a country's intelligence or security agency, typically involved in covert operations, surveillance, and national security matters.

The phone suddenly hung up.

Sister Juliana was a blessing in Stei, where God placed her. Through her, many people were encouraged, counseled and comforted.

On November 28, 2022, I preached at her funeral. At 91 years of age, she finished her race and entered into the wedding room. The sound of her deeds spread everywhere, and she was truly acknowledged as a servant of God.

I felt so small next to such a great servant of God... I do not have as many years of life as she had of daily repentance and walking with God (54 years out of 91).

She was once asked why she was not renovating her apartment, which really needed urgent restoration. And she replied, "With this money I can help some families who have greater needs than mine!"

I left thinking that God was the same—yesterday, today, and forever. He keeps His testimony and works with signs and wonders even today, just as He did in the past. He will never run out of people who serve Him and who are so passionate about it that, if need be, they are ready to be imprisoned for their faith.

See you soon, sister Iuliana!

Please wait for us in the realms of heaven.

We will be coming there whenever the Lord decides it is our time to go...

December 14

HAVE YOU SEEN EVERYTHING?

You have seen the mountains I climbed... But have you also seen the valleys through which I passed?

You have seen me smiling... But are you sure you have also seen the moments when I cried, hiding my soul in my palms, shaken by the chills of the carelessness around me?

You have seen me surrounded by friends... But have you also noticed the scars left by those who betrayed and abandoned me?

You have seen me holding the victory cup in my hands... But are you sure you have also seen the days when I was sweating and struggling while training?

You have seen me lifting my hands to heaven... But have you also managed to see me when I was slammed to the ground, with my head touching the dust of helplessness?

You have seen the light in my eyes... But have you seen the shadows that sometimes cloud them?

You have witnessed my moments of triumph... But have you truly understood the depths of my trials?

You have seen my strength... But have you acknowledged the battles that forged it?

You have seen... But have you seen everything?

December 15

389%

The percentage by which sex change surgeries in children have increased in 2018-2023 is 389%! It is astonishingly large, and legislation is increasingly lax with these matters.

Did you know that in the U.S. 1 in 5 teenagers identifies as transgender?

Did you know that there are over 1.6 million people over the age of 13 in the U.S. who admit to being "trans"?

Did you know that parental authority is diminishing, while the state is gaining more and more ground over our children?

King David, through the Holy Spirit, said:

> *"For You formed my inward parts; You covered me in my mother's womb. I will praise You, for I am fearfully and wonderfully made; marvelous are Your works, and that my soul knows very well. My frame was not hidden from You, when I was made in secret, and skillfully wrought in the lowest parts of the earth." – Psalm 139:13-15*

People's dissatisfaction with their identity and with how they were created comes directly from the Devil. Do you remember that the Devil was also dissatisfied with the place given to him by God and wanted another position?

Could God have been wrong? Is it not the Devil who comes to pervert the human mind? Through all kinds of spirits entering families through certain sins, he manages to convince a girl that it is better to be a boy, and vice versa.

Sex change surgery is an attack on God's sovereignty!

In a world that takes God out of schools, out of families, out of the state, it seems that the Devil's power is growing, and his demonic influence is attacking more and more young people...

We are at war, folks... And we do not realize clearly enough that the Devil, the usurper of this world, knows that he has little time left and attacks the family and the church more and more violently. He is not content with just tempting people but wants to defile all that is sacred as well.

We must fight in fasting and prayer, and thus return to the principles of Scripture and to living a holy life so that the Devil does not have access to our families!

December 16

DO YOU KNOW WHERE YOU ARE HEADED?

"I press toward the goal for the prize of the upward call of God in Christ Jesus." – Philippians 3:14

The story goes that during a train journey, when the inspector showed up to check the tickets, Einstein was forced to admit that, despite looking for it desperately, he could not find his ticket.

The inspector recognized Einstein and told him that it`s not a problem, he believed him that he had a ticket because he knew who he was. Einstein replied, "Young man, I know who I am too. What I do not know is where I'm headed!"

We all know our own identity. We all recognize that we are living beings. We all know our name and our home address. But the real question is: do we know where we are headed?

We might have special degrees. Lots of luggage. Perfumed outfits. Shiny shoes. Perfect calculation formulas like Einstein. And yet, we may not know our destination...

We may live only for the present. Only for what we can quickly sightsee through the train window...

If someone asked to check our ticket today, could we answer, "I know who I am and I know where I'm headed!"?

Sometimes illness asks to check our ticket... Other times, the betrayal of friends. Some other times, our children ask us, "Daddy, where are we going?"

What do you answer when trouble knocks on your door? Are you still sure about your last stop? Can you envision the station platform at the end of the life`s train line?

Paul knew where he was going. Einstein did not.

Do you know?

December 17

HOW DO YOU SEE YOURSELF?

Thomas Hooker was a great Puritan preacher. Before he died, a close friend told him: "Soon you will receive your reward for all you have worked for God." Humbly, Thomas replied: "Soon I will receive His mercy..."

One of the paradoxes of walking with God is this: the closer you draw to Him, the more you see yourself unworthy, humble, and dependent on His grace and mercy. The farther you stay from Him, the more you see yourself better and more worthy of all He has to offer.

It is like moving closer to a mountain: if you stay farther away from it, you will see yourself bigger, and the mountain smaller. But the closer you get, the mountain gets bigger, and you shrink as you compare yourself to it.

It is like a mirror: the farther you stand from it, you think you are clean, but the closer you get to it, you start seeing every stain or lint on your clothing.

It is like approaching a light source: the farther away you go, the more everything seems to be fine, but the closer you get, the more you see every detail because the light reveals it to you.

The Pharisees and scribes were holding the Scripture in their hands, and yet they were so far away from Jesus! The righteousness they displayed before the people and the spiritual pride in which they lived made them see themselves as good, but Jesus said to them:

> *"But go and learn what this means: 'I desire mercy and not sacrifice.' For I did not come to call the righteous, but sinners, to repentance." – Matthew 9:13*

You should know that we can easily assess the spiritual value of a person. The smaller and humbler he sees himself, the closer he is to God.

Whenever you hear someone saying, "I am fine, I am okay, I am healthy," you should know that they are actually far from God, and their spiritual state requires immediate change.

Paul said:

> *"For I am the least of the apostles, who am not worthy to be called an apostle, because I persecuted the church of God." – 1 Corinthians 15:9*

Do you know why? Because spiritually speaking, he was extremely close to God and walked with Him daily, with a passion almost unparalleled in Christian history. And his words confirm his closeness to God...

His unworthiness brings out the greatness of Jesus. Paul's humility shows his need for grace and his love for the Most High.

How do you see yourself?

December 18

WHAT DID YOUR PARENTS TELL YOU?

"Which we have heard and known, and our fathers have told us." – Psalm 78:3

Fairy tales like "Cinderella," "Jack and the Beanstalk," "Snow White," and "Hansel and Gretel" from various cultures have been enchanting children for generations, taking them to magical realms. A world with enchanted castles and mythical creatures. With brave heroes and magical objects. With fairy godmothers and evil witches. And when they grow up, they realize that all these stories were little lies...

Perhaps a better alternative would be to tell our children about the real experiences of our lives. About the lives of some missionaries. Some stories from the Bible.

Children ask questions, and God instructed Jewish parents to be prepared with appropriate answers:

"So it shall be, when your son asks you in time to come, saying, 'What is this?' that you shall say to him, 'By strength of hand the Lord brought us out of Egypt, out of the house of bondage.'" – Exodus 13:14

Every story you tell your child is a seed sown in the field of his heart. If you have sown, God guarantees that He is in charge of the increase:

"So then neither he who plants is anything, nor he who waters, but God who gives the increase." – 1 Corinthians 3:7

But what will grow and increase if we sow nothing? Weeds and thistles. Thorns and brambles.

What do you tell your children?

In a busy world, always on the run, in pursuit of more material wealth, do you still make time for an authentic and edifying story with your child?

December 19

WHAT IS THAT TO YOU?

"Jesus said to him, 'If I will that he remain till I come, what is that to you? You follow Me!'" – John 21:22

Jesus asks Peter 3 times:

"He said to him the third time, 'Simon, son of Jonah, do you love Me?'" – John 21:17

And after each question he gives him a mission: to take care of lambs, ewes, and sheep, which symbolize exactly the people in the Church of Christ, people who can be divided according to their maturity.

Jesus gives Peter a clear mission. A noble purpose for living his life: "Be of service to those in your Church! Take care of their nutrition! Take care of my flock, Peter!"

But instead of Peter focusing on his mission and even asking Jesus for details according to his needs, he chooses to take an interest in his colleague John:

"Peter, seeing him, said to Jesus, 'But Lord, what about this man?'" – John 21:21

Jesus answers:

"Jesus said to him, 'If I will that he remain till I come, what is that to you? You follow Me!'" – John 21:22

The danger Peter found himself in also prowls around us today – being interested in others. In their ministry. In watching them instead of looking at Jesus and at what He asked us to do.

Jesus says so clearly, "What is that to you?" (NKJV) or "What is your concern?" (Romanian translation).

I pray today that God will guard us from this danger. Let us focus only on what Jesus asked us to do, not on what He told others.

When you look at others, you will be disappointed. You will get carried away. You will start judging and comparing yourself to them, and you will waste your time measuring someone else's progress instead of measuring your own.

Today, Jesus tells you the same thing that He told Peter: “Follow Me! Look at Me! Be concerned only with the work I have entrusted to *you*!”

Why?

Because Jesus will not ask us about the tasks He entrusted others with, but about what He entrusted us to do.

As for Jesus' question, "Peter, do you love Me?", let us not forget that our service is always measured by the strength of our love. You can never serve more than you are able to love.

If we love Jesus, we will also love those with whom Jesus identifies. If we love Him, we roll up our sleeves and get to work… The work He asked us to do.

December 20

ARE YOU READY TO FORGIVE?

"And be kind to one another, tenderhearted, forgiving one another, even as God in Christ forgave you." – Ephesians 4:32

One of my friends recently testified about a strange experience he had. About 3 years ago, someone deeply offended him in public. Not long ago, however, that person called him and apologized, sincerely regretting that the gesture he had made against my friend had been influenced by the gossip of malicious people that ultimately proved unfounded.

"Can you please forgive me?" asked the guilty man.

"I have forgiven you long ago!" replied my friend. "How could I have served God and be happy in the midst of my family and community if I had waited 3 years until you asked for my forgiveness?"

What deep thinking! What logic and wisdom in this answer!

Some forgive only when expressly asked. They wait for years for the culprit to come forward and admit his mistake. And if he never comes, they prefer to keep him locked in the prison of their heart, gathering resentment and hatred towards that person. In this way, whenever they hear about that person, they experience a state of deep hostility, and because forgiveness has not occurred, hatred grows, and distress reaches its purpose.

Others, however, forgive immediately. They understand that forgiveness sets you free. Forgiveness keeps you from dragging the boulder of revenge with you for years on every road you take. They understand that if you do not forgive, you do not harm the person who wronged you, but you harm yourself.

Hahhah Moore said it so well, "Forgiveness is the economy of the heart... Forgiveness saves the expense of anger, the costs of hatred, the waste of spirits."

Are you ready to forgive?

DECEMBER 21

DREAM AND REALITY

I will write below, in a few lines, the testimony of a Christian worker, a testimony that calls us to check our ministry, but also the motivation behind it. The quality and the purpose for which we serve. Our investment in eternity and how God calculates rewards...

One day, after working hard for God`s kingdom, this Christian minister sat down on his couch and while meditating, he fell asleep. He was satisfied with the work he had done, because the fruits were already visible: many souls turning to Christ and receiving salvation.

Suddenly, a stranger entered his room. He had in his hands a scale with weights, a bag of instruments and a small device. His appearance was stern, and his eyes were fiery and full of energy but also kindness. Although he had not been invited there by the minister, the stranger, with grave silence, asked him earnestly, "How is your zeal doing?"

After a few moments of silence, the Christian man began to present his zeal with many words, but as he was speaking, a lump of soil formed up at his feet, growing steadily as he was describing his ministry.

Finally, the stranger pointed at the lump and said, "This is the work done with your zeal!"

Being asked to give his opinion, the stranger put the lump of soil on the scale and said, "It weighs 200 lbs.!"

The minister`s face radiated with joy, but only briefly.

Using the instruments he had brought with him, the stranger started analyzing the lump, which was now broken into pieces. After weighing each piece, he handed the Christian man a sheet of paper and left.

Stunned, the Christian read:

"Analysis of the zeal of minister X, contender for the crown of glory in the eternal kingdom.

Total weight – 200 lbs., of which:

7 parts material interests;

16 parts personal ambitions (the work of the ego);

15 parts religious pride;

11 parts love to lead;

10 parts sectarian struggle;
18 parts desire to be praised;
13 parts love of his gifts.
TOTAL: 180 lbs. of wood, hay, stubble.
3 parts love of God;
4 parts love of brothers;
3 parts pure zeal for evangelism;
TOTAL: 20 lbs. of gold, silver, and precious stones."

From all this analysis, 90% of the parts were things that would burn in the fire, and only 10% were clean as gold, silver, and precious stones - representing the real ministry.

Sorrow had made its way into the heart of the Christian man, which was now being touched by God.

Overwhelmed and on his knees, the minister understood the stranger's analysis, and realizing that the analysis was perfect and justly weighed, he cried out so loudly to God to rid him of himself that he woke up.

Since then, the Christian man has had no peace until he rid himself of the ego. At the same time, he did not know rest until he became convinced that the religious interest and pride were replaced by the light and humility of the Lord Jesus' love.

The words of the Christian minister that still resonate today are these:

"If you pray to God, pray that He will deliver you from yourself, from the pride that possesses you, from the disregard for His glory that is found in the lives of all Christians today. First, he who turns to God stops from the path of perdition and no longer steps toward sin. Secondly, by acknowledging who the Lord Jesus is, the believer is drawn to Him, separating himself from everything that does not please the Lord. Thus, with his face towards the Lord Jesus, he turns his back on the world and sin. Third, he starts on the pure path of obedience to God."

December 22

TEA BAGS

"If the spirit of the ruler rises against you, do not leave your post; for conciliation pacifies great offenses." – Ecclesiastes 10:4

Someone once said, "You can only really see what flavor is in tea bags after the water in the pot is boiling..." We encounter boiling circumstances in life not infrequently. Conflict. The fiery anger of those around us who, with certain words or gestures, provoke us to have a wrong attitude. They act in a certain way and then wait to see our reaction. And our reaction must always be not a response to their action, but a reflection of our character. So we must focus not on changing them, but on changing ourselves! In such 'boiling' situations, the Bible says that we can fall into one of the following categories:

"A fool vents all his feelings, but a wise man holds them back." – Proverbs 29:11

We need to ask God for a lot of wisdom. We need to be able to develop a state of self-control through the fullness of the Holy Spirit. When we get fired up quickly, we say words that we later regret:

"He who is slow to wrath has great understanding, but he who is impulsive exalts folly." – Proverbs 14:29

And the interlocutor will remember not what you said when you were calm, but what you said when you were angry. What is the use of being able to conquer cities if you have not conquered yourself?

"He who is slow to anger is better than the mighty, and he who rules his spirit than he who takes a city." – Proverbs 16:32

The true brave men are the people who have peace in the middle of the storm. Those who remain calm even when everything is scorching around. And the fragrance that such rare people spread is the perfume of peace with a taste of reconciliation.

Help us all, Lord, to be like this!

DECEMBER 23

THE OLD MAN, THE BAG AND THE CARRIAGE

Richard Wurmbrand told the story of an old man who was traveling with a heavy bag on his back. On the way, he met a coachman who invited him into his carriage, and the old man gladly accepted. At one point, the coachman noticed that the old man, although he was in the carriage, was still holding the bag on his back.

"Put down the bag next to you, old man," said the coachman.

"You were nice enough to take me in your carriage, so why should I add to your burden by putting the bag down as well?"

When God forgave and saved us, He did it for all our worries and sorrows as well. For all the daily burdens and problems we go through. But many times, we act like that old man: we carry these burdens ourselves instead of doing what the apostle Peter said:

"...casting all your care upon Him, for He cares for you." – 1 Peter 5:7

The burdens we carry by ourselves, even though we say we are in the Lord's arms, will cause us to look downwards more and more. They will cause us heartache and heavy thoughts will rush upon us. We will reach the crossroads of life and we will be disoriented, believing that the hard road is never ending. We will start sleeping less and less at night, and we will feel the dust of the ground getting closer and closer to us as we limp under the weight of our burdens.

Don't you think it is time to accept today the fact that everything that comes upon your life is controlled by the Lord? Don't you understand that nothing happens by chance?

Has God forgotten about your needs? Has the One who went to Calvary in your place stopped thinking about you now?

"Therefore do not worry, saying, 'What shall we eat?' or 'What shall we drink?' or 'What shall we wear?'" – Matthew 6:31

Our goal must be heaven. The end. The target. The prize for our race.

"But seek first the kingdom of God and His righteousness, and all these things shall be added to you." – Matthew 6:33

Not the bag of burdens. Not the sins of the past. Not the burdens of the harsh words you have received from others.

Throw the bag of your emotional burdens into His arms today and you will feel relieved.

Replace your fear with faith and worry with hope.

It is worth it.

December 24

THE PARADOXES OF THE SAVIOR'S BIRTH

Herod was troubled, while the shepherds rejoiced. The wise men traveled almost 1,000 miles to see Jesus, while the priests did not want to walk 4 miles from Jerusalem to Bethlehem to see if the prophecy of Micah, which they knew by heart, had been fulfilled.

The people of Jerusalem were near Bethlehem and yet so far from the newborn Child. It is not the lack of highways that keeps people away from church, but the pothole roads inside their hearts.

It was announced that the malls would stay open during the Christmas holidays. For some people, a perfume on sale is more attractive than the Manger Child.

Many wish to hear a choir of angels, but they are not willing to leave their daily work to go see the Child about whom the choir sings...

It smells like oranges in hospitals during the month of December, but from January to November it only smells like diluted disinfectant.

I personally think that many people are unfortunately just partying and only few are really celebrating. Some rejoice because of their business profit, others because of the new couch they got but very few rejoice in the Gift from heaven. Let us be among the few...

Many adorn their homes in December, but how many adorn their hearts all year round with the Light that came from above?

Children believe the lies about Santa Claus, and grown-ups do not believe the truths about the Child who grew up, lived a holy life, and died for us.

It is cold outside. Blessed are the hearts in which the encounter with Jesus brings warmth for the rest of their life...

December 25

WHICH STAR GUIDES YOU?

"...saying, 'Where is He who has been born King of the Jews? For we have seen His star in the East and have come to worship Him.'" – Matthew 2:2

They left the East guided by a star. A long journey, with many expenses. Exhaustion. Poor travel conditions. But they told themselves it was worth every effort to get to where the star would stop.

It stopped where the Child was. Because the real stars you have to follow in life are the ones that lead you to Jesus. Not to sin, not to Herod, not to the sword, but to the Lord of lords and King of kings.

We all have our stars. The things we secretly admire. Some better, some worse. Some that are shooting stars and others that are uplifting stars. Does what you follow point you to Jesus?

After meeting Jesus, the star disappeared. Because in the presence of the Sun all other stars fade away. No more signs when you meet Jesus. No more pointers. When you meet Jesus, you no longer need to ask Herod any questions. Nor those who know the Bible but do not live it, such as the scribes and Pharisees.

If you have not met Jesus yet, check to see what kind of star God uses to try to speak to you... Maybe it is the health you do not deserve. Perhaps it is the blessings from God that point you in the right direction. Maybe it is your grandmother who used to take you by the hand to church when you were little. Maybe there is a book you read some time ago, a book that spoke about Jesus.

Obey the star sent by God into your life.

It will lead you to an encounter with Jesus.

DECEMBER 26

THE MOST IMPORTANT STEP

It was 1969. The first man reached the moon successfully, but also very nervously, because he was only 25 seconds away from running out of fuel. Immediately after came the words heard by 600 million people watching the landing live: "That`s one small step for man. One giant leap for mankind."

We recognize the immense work of the 800 people who worked to make the Apollo 11 mission a success. We are glad that man has reached the only natural satellite of the earth.

What I want to emphasize, however, is the fact that the greatest event was not when man stepped on the moon, but when God came to Earth. When Jesus Christ stripped Himself of the heavenly glory and took the image of clay. When instead of shining in the sky He arrived in a dirty stable. When He first felt the chill of rejection.

At that time there were 2.5 million Jews in Palestine, of which about 600,000 were in Jerusalem alone... And yet, only a handful of people came to see the great step heaven took towards us...

Do you know that even the atheist counts the years in the same way - starting with the birth of Jesus? We all have a place on our ID where we reference the date of our birth in direct connection with the time of His birth. We all count our years in the same way, yet not all of us worship Jesus.

Just like then it is today. People are interested in the holidays, but not in the One who is celebrated. They are interested in lights, fireworks, but not in the Manger. They install the Christmas tree with great pomposity in the city hall building, but no one is interested in a Jesus who came to save us.

The manger does not get many *likes.* Straws are not attractive to the eye. Humility is always considered old-fashioned, and the newborn King can only be looked at with Herod's suspicion by those who hold onto their seats and positions with both hands.

Thank You, Lord, for thinking of me. For descending from Your light into our dust. For not coming down just for a stroll, but to pay the greatest price. The price for us to step into Your heaven.

Thank You for every step You took into our world.

For me at least it was worth it...

DECEMBER 27

"WONDERFUL IS THE HOLY NIGHT!"

In the winter of 1960, Nicolae Moldoveanu and Traian Dorz were imprisoned in the same barracks because of their love for the Word of God.

On a shard of glass greased with soap they wrote together a poem about the celebration of the Savior`s birth. Another prisoner betrayed them, so the two were taken to the commander's office. Walking around with the shard in his hand, he threatened them with a new case in court - but the accusations were soon dropped because the lyrics on the soap-greased shard faded away.

However, punishment was not long in coming. Thus, the two believers were isolated for 5 days in a damp room where they received food only once every 3 days.

In the harsh conditions of that tiny room, hungry, cold and tired, scratching the ground with a stick, the two men composed yet another song that they managed to learn by heart this time:

Wonderful is the holy night,
Wonderful!
Holy peace clothes
The whole world.
The heavenly joys fill
Human hearts.
Holy night, you tie in brotherhood
The whole world.

Uplifting is the holy night,
Uplifting!
Shepherds come, angels sing,
The manger is sunny.
The star burns brightly,
The Magi exalt Christ.
The Baby is sunshine, heaven is on earth,
The manger is sunny.

Joy in the holy night,
Joy!
Hell falls, death is broken
Forever.
The prophecy has been fulfilled,
Salvation has come to us!
Holy Messiah, be glorified,
Forever!

Mercy is the holy night,
Mercy!
Heaven blesses us
The grace is great.
Prepare your hearts
To receive the Messiah,
So He can make you happy,
The grace is great.

Nicolae Moldoveanu – "Wonderful is the holy night"

DECEMBER 28

THE BOX OF MARRIAGE

"Wives, submit to your own husbands, as is fitting in the Lord. Husbands, love your wives and do not be bitter toward them." – Colossians 3:18-19

Someone said some extraordinary truths about marriage:

"Most people get married believing a myth that marriage is a beautiful box full of all the things they have longed for: companionship, intimacy, friendship, respect, appreciation, kind words, etc. The truth is that a marriage at the start is an empty box. You must put something in before you can take anything out. There is no love in marriage, love is in people. People must put love in marriage. There is no romance in marriage; you have to infuse it into your marriage. A couple must learn the art and form the habit of giving, loving, serving, praising, and keeping the box full. If you take more than you put in, the box will be empty..."

Have you thought deeply about this aspect? Have you thought that when you get married, you come from your initial home with a baggage of knowledge, skills, but also behavioral attitudes?

Therefore, what we learn in the family follows us our entire lives. Our habits, our customs, our character traits, our worldview and our perspective on eternity will influence us not only in choosing our spouse, but also in what we put in the marriage box. You must know that you have to put something in there not just once, but many times during the decades of your life...

The adage "each one gives what he has" is especially relevant for marriage and not only. You will put forgiveness in the box of marriage if you knew how to forgive before getting married. You will put selflessness if you have not been a selfish person. You will put mercy if you have been a person filled with kindness. Similarly, you will also put revenge if you like resentment and negative memories from the past.

You will put dirty words and swear words in marriage if you had such language habits before the wedding. I hope we are all aware of the fact that the wedding church service does not change a person's language, aren`t we?

You will put appreciation, flowers, smiles, sacrifices, diligence in that box if you have developed these valuable traits before getting married. They do not come over you at the pastor's prayer, nor when the civil status registrar hands you the marriage certificate...

The mistake of young people and teenagers is that they focus on the box instead of focusing on what they need to develop inside of them in order to put valuable things in that box.

Most people see the box of marriage as something fabulous, like a forever pleasant vacation where everything comes naturally, without any effort. And when dreams end and they wake up to reality, they realize that, in fact, the box is empty (because if you have just been taking out but stopped putting in, one day it runs out). So, frustrated and angry, the spouses break up and run to the next person, believing that the problem is with their former spouse... But in fact, all they do is carry the emptiness of their own character into the next relationship.

Finally, allow me to ask you two very important questions:

If you are still single: how are you working at shaping your own character so that you are able to put special values into the box of marriage?

If you are married: what did you put in this box today?

DECEMBER 29

GIFTS AND THEIR PRICE TAG

"Let all that you do be done with love!" – 1 Corinthians 16:14

I think we all enjoy it when we have the opportunity to give a gift to a loved one. We pay attention to details and take into account the wishes and needs of that person. However, when it comes to giving gifts, we may notice three aspects not only about the gifts themselves, but also about the price we paid for them.

The first category of gifts includes **gifts from which we rip off the price tag because they are too cheap.** We would like the recipient to think they are valuable in content, but we do not want it to be known that we found them on sale. We would like no one to know that they did not cost us too much.

The second category includes **gifts from which we do not rip off the price tag, because we would like the recipient to see how much they cost us.**

To see how much we spent. To see that we have offered something of value.

A third category includes **gifts from which we rip off the price tag because love is not measured in money**. Because we simply give selflessly, without expecting the recipient to give us something just as valuable in return.

What do you do with the gifts for Jesus? Do you leave the price tag attached to them? What is the motivation behind your ministry?

Someone said, "I was so glad that they announced me by name in the church when it came to the money I gave for the renovation."

I remind you that it is worth giving everything to the Lord out of love. His sacrifice cannot be measured. We could have never paid the payment for our sins. And the heaven that awaits us is the greatest gift in the Universe that does not have the price tag displayed on it. In eternity, Jesus will never point out to us and brag about what He has done for us.

"And whatever you do, do it heartily, as to the Lord and not to men." – Colossians 3:23

The price of a whole heart offered to God cannot be displayed on the cashier screen at the checkout. Nor typed at the cash register.

The widow gave the last two coins.

Mary gave the jar of myrrh.

Nicodemus offered 25 gallons of myrrh and aloe.

They all gave out of love. Without showing the receipt. Without expecting anything in return.

What gifts are you giving to the One who came down from heaven for you?

Reflect on the depth of your love and devotion to God. Are your offerings marked by true sacrifice, or are they given out of abundance and convenience? The measure of our giving should not be based on its material value, but on the sincerity and love behind it. Just as the widow's mite was worth more in the eyes of Jesus than the large donations of the wealthy, our humble, heartfelt offerings are precious to God.

Consider the time and talents you have been blessed with. Are you using them for God's glory? Serving others, sharing your faith, and dedicating your skills to further His kingdom are profound gifts that go beyond monetary value. Our daily actions and the way we live our lives can be the most meaningful offerings we give to our Savior. Remember, true giving is not about the size of the gift, but the size of the heart that gives it.

December 30

THE YEARS LIKE THE SOUND OF A SIGH

"...we finish our years like a sigh." – Psalm 90:9

We are approaching the end of the year... We look back and ask ourselves: how did time pass so quickly? It was like a dream, like it was a vapor, it passed like a sigh...

What could we learn from the sound of a sigh?

First, **sound has duration.** The music note can be whole or just an eighth. A life can last for only a few months or for 80 years...

No matter how many there are, musical notes start fading away as soon as the sound has begun. Why? Because a sound is short just like our lives, just like David says in Psalm 39:5 when he compares his days with a mere handbreadth.

We always say we have time, but we forget that our life can break as easily as a thread...

No matter how long you live, when you look back you realize that everything passed so fast. That is why the Bible asks us to value the day we have today...

"Therefore, as the Holy Spirit says: 'Today, if you will hear His voice...'" – Hebrews 3:7

Secondly, **the sound is heard**. Our life does not remain hidden, our deeds have a reverberation, an echo. Everything is recorded...

"But I say to you that for every idle word men may speak, they will give account of it in the day of judgment." – Matthew 12:36

You cannot cover up the sound. You cannot cover up your actions, your words, your glances, or your gestures...

"And there is no creature hidden from His sight, but all things are naked and open to the eyes of Him to whom we must give account." – Hebrews 4:13

What an amazing grace it is not to blush when there are rumors about your life. When those who hear the sound of your actions do not have to cover their ears...

And if someone speaks ill of you unjustly, you have the opportunity to prove by your actions that what has been heard is not true.

Tabitha's deeds were known. It was also known about what the sinful woman did with the precious myrrh she had. And then Jesus said that the sound of her actions would always be heard as a memorial to her:

"Assuredly, I say to you, wherever this gospel is preached in the whole world, what this woman has done will also be told as a memorial to her." – Matthew 26:13

What is heard about you?

Also, **sound sends a message**. The trumpet in the Bible always conveyed a message. When the phone rings, it sends a message. The sound of an incoming text message informs you that someone has texted you something. Every sound has a message.

Did the sound of my life create a clear sound or a confusing one?

"For if the trumpet makes an uncertain sound, who will prepare for battle?" – 1 Corinthians 14:8

At many funerals you become confused... Did the deceased person walk with God all his life or was he just a name in the church register? Did he really love his spouse, or did they stay together just because of the kids? Is the fact that his cross says that he was the Lord's servant a complete truth or only half-truth?

We can leave a clear message behind us. On God's pentagram we can be a note that He can use to send a special message to those who will hear the sound of our lives, so they may be encouraged, motivated, and ready to move forward!

"At the blast of the trumpet he says, 'Forward!'" – Job 39:25

December 31

WHAT SHOULD WE WISH FOR THE COMING YEAR?

1. A pure heart

In a dirty house, you cannot enjoy rest, or food, or the company of loved ones until you clean up. Only "the pure in heart will see God."

2. Teary eyes

When you look at people you will complain, but when you look at Jesus you will weep...

You need to have tears of gratitude for every day when you crossed the street and Someone watched over you, tears of joy for the salvation you received freely and tears of compassion for those on the 3rd floor of the hospital`s ICU...

3. Calloused hands

Not from the keyboard, not from the phone games. But calloused from carrying bags of food to the poor. From the trowel with which Nehemiah was building the wall. If we have our hands calloused as a result of such activities, we will be able to say like him: "Remember me, my God, for good..."

In 2023, you must do at least one thing that will move God so much, that He will "pick up the pen" and write it down in the book of Chronicles...

4. Beautiful feet

Like the feet of those who bring good news. Of those who run for the Gospel. Of those who do not care about how much gas is left in the tank, nor about the weather outside. Do not forget that the feet of those who do not move end up stiffening and causing pain. And those who are in pain must be helped themselves, thus not being able to help others.

5. Bending knees

The heaviest burdens in life are carried on your knees, not on your arms. He who fights in prayer in the little room has great victories when he comes out of there...

6. Ears, but without any headphones on

Ears that hear the cry of the orphan and the widow. That hear the groans of the wounded on the front line. That hear the sermon and fulfill it. That hear the thousands of children who are abandoned every year and extend a helping hand...

7. Strong fists

Not to fight with the brethren, but to fight with myself. To box with the human flesh. To struggle hard with envy and discontent.

Sometimes you need to slap your ego so you do not end up in Delilah's arms...

8. New people in a new year

A new vision. A new ministry. Maybe for a time like this we have been placed where we are now. To put in a good word for God's people, like Esther. To give, to sacrifice while we still have good lab results...

9. Happy New Year

Only saints have happiness. Only those who flee from sin can rest at night, regardless of the quality of the mattress...

10. Many blessings

Through the lions' den, through fire or wilderness, on the mountain or in the rich plain, the journey we make is under the Lord`s watch!

Contents